Critical Essays on
EDNA ST. VINCENT MILLAY

CRITICAL ESSAYS
ON
AMERICAN LITERATURE

James Nagel, General Editor
University of Georgia, Athens

Critical Essays on

EDNA ST. VINCENT MILLAY

edited by

WILLIAM B. THESING

G. K. Hall & Co. / New York
Maxwell Macmillan Canada / Toronto
Maxwell Macmillan International / New York Oxford Singapore Sydney

Appearing in Sandra M. Gilbert's essay "Female Female Impersonator: Millay and the Theatre of Personality," 6 lines from "To Military Progress," and excerpts of under 1/4 from "To Statecraft Embalmed," "Marriage," and "Too Much" ("The Jerboa"—Part 1) reprinted with permission of Macmillan Publishing Company from COLLECTED POEMS OF MARIANNE MOORE. Copyright 1935 by Marianne Moore, renewed 1963 by Marianne Moore and T. S. Eliot. Excerpts of under 1/4 from "Virginia Britannia," "He 'Digesteth Harde Yron' " and "The Paper Nautilus" reprinted with permission of Macmillan Publishing Company from COLLECTED POEMS OF MARIANNE MOORE. Copyright 1941, and renewed 1969, by Marianne Moore. 2 lines from "His Shield" reprinted with permission of Macmillan Publishing Company from COLLECTED POEMS OF MARIANNE MOORE. Copyright 1951 by Marianne Moore, renewed 1979 by Lawrence F. Brinn and Louise Crane. World rights of the above lines granted by Faber & Faber, Ltd.

Special gratitude is extended to Elizabeth Barnett, Millay's literary executor.

G. K. Hall & Company
Macmillan Publishing Company
866 Third Avenue
New York, New York 10022

Maxwell Macmillan Canada, Inc.
1200 Eglinton Avenue East
Suite 200
Don Mills, Ontario M3C 3N1

Library of Congress Cataloging-in-Publication Data

Critical essays on Edna St. Vincent Millay / edited by William B.
Thesing.
    p.   cm. — (Critical essays on American literature)
    Includes bibliographical references and index.
    ISBN 0-8161-7310-9
    1. Millay, Edna St. Vincent, 1892–1950—Criticism and
interpretation. I. Thesing, William B. II. Series.
PS3525.I495Z634   1993
811'.52—dc20
                                                    92-38698
                                                    CIP

The paper used in this publication meets the minimum requirements of American National Standard for Information Sciences—Permanence of Paper for Printed Library Materials. ANSI Z3948-1984. ∞™

10   9   8   7   6   5   4   3   2   1

Printed in the United States of America

For Joanne Veatch Pulley and
the students of South Carolina College,
the Honors College of the University of South Carolina:

"The delightful interplay of minds and spirits"
—William A. Mould

Contents

General Editor's Note

◆

This series seeks to anthologize the most important criticism on a wide variety of topics and writers in American literature. Our readers will find in various volumes not only a generous selection of reprinted articles and reviews but original essays, bibliographies, manuscript sections, and other materials brought to public attention for the first time. This volume, *Critical Essays on Edna St. Vincent Millay*, is the most comprehensive collection of essays ever published on one of the most important modern writers in the United States. It contains both a sizable gathering of early reviews and a broad selection of more modern scholarship as well. Among the authors of reprinted articles and reviews are Harriet Monroe, Louis Untermeyer, Mark Van Doren, Allen Tate, Louise Bogan, Edmund Wilson, Suzanne Clark, and Jane Stanbrough. In addition to a substantial introduction by William B. Thesing, there are four original essays commissioned specifically for publication in this volume, new studies by Gilbert Allen, Joanne Veatch Pulley, Robert Wiltenburg, and Sandra M. Gilbert. There is also an important fictional interview of Millay by Arthur Davison Ficke published for the first time in this volume. We are confident that this book will make a permanent and significant contribution to the study of American literature.

JAMES NAGEL
University of Georgia, Athens

Publisher's Note

◆

Producing a volume that contains both newly commissioned and reprinted material presents the publisher with the challenge of balancing the desire to achieve stylistic consistency with the need to preserve the integrity of works first published elsewhere. In the Critical Essays series, essays commissioned especially for a particular volume are edited to be consistent with G. K. Hall's house style; reprinted essays appear in the style in which they were first published, with only typographical errors corrected. Consequently, shifts in style from one essay to another are the result of our efforts to be faithful to each text as it was originally published.

Introduction

William B. Thesing

One hundred years after Edna St. Vincent Millay's birth and forty years after her death, critical discussions of her work are rather somber and searching meditations. The talk at conferences and the tone of essay revaluations focus on what went "wrong," on the possible reasons for the decline and fall of a literary reputation or legend. Too often critics neglect to ask positive questions, for example, What went "right" to make Millay so endearingly success-ful—both by popular and critical standards—during the early decades of the twentieth century? In a review of a Millay conference held at Skidmore College in 1986, Ellen Bryant Voigt reported on some of the questions that had been posed regarding Millay's choices and reputation: "Could it be that the talent was major but the work was not?—that too much of it relied on a rigid and inauthentic persona, diction already archaic in the 1920s, and sentimentality?" To what extent was Millay a poet trapped in a persona? Was Millay one of several talented poets—E. A. Robinson and Robinson Jeffers also come to mind—who, in the words of Voigt, were victims of the early twentieth-century modernist movement, turning them into "poets swept out by the modernist broom"? Voigt concludes that "The failure may be as interesting as the success."[1] In a provocative and entertaining essay entitled "The Case of the Missing T-Shirt," Robert Erwin poses some further questions of a disturbing nature: "Edna Millay was an exceptionally talented and attractive person. Given this knowledge and given current concern with the status of women, wouldn't you expect to find her name on the roster of culture heroines? . . . Why," he asks, "are there no Edna Millay T-shirts?" Erwin is particularly critical of this generation's feminists, especially "today's women literary scholars," for turning their backs on Millay, for failing to acknowledge her as a model of the independent, self-determined woman artist.[2]

Millay's triumphs peaked in the mid-1920s. In 1923, she became the first woman to win the Pulitzer Prize for poetry. She served as a symbol for

1

individual freedom and women's liberation: her life demonstrated that women had an equal right to love, work, and write in urban centers. Clearly, she relished the attention and the feeling of accomplishment. In 1920 she wrote to Arthur Davison Ficke: "I am earning a creditable living by writing short stories under an assumed name. Just sold one for four hundred dollars. Now I am negotiating with a moving picture company concerning it.— Incredible!"[3] Later the same year she reported her good fortunes to Witter Bynner: "I am becoming very famous. The current Vanity Fair has a whole page of my poems. . . . Besides, I just got a prize of a hundred dollars in Poetry, for the Beanstalk. And I'm spending it all on clothes."[4] The glory and reputation lingered throughout the 1930s. A *New York Times* article reported on a 1931 survey by John Haynes Holmes in which Millay was named as one of the ten greatest living women; it called her "the chief glory of contemporary American literature."[5] Toward the end of her life, however, the cheering and popular acclaim had definitely subsided. In her last year, living alone after her husband Eugen's death in the isolation of the Steepletop farm, she wrote to her friend, Mrs. Mary V. Herron, the local Austerlitz postmistress and her devoted comforter: "He will not be coming down the hill to fetch the mail, this lovely autumn day. He never comes up the hill, either, any more."[6]

BIOGRAPHY

Millay's arrival in the circle of literary success in the 1920s was achieved after hardship and family struggle in her formative years. Her parents were divorced in 1900 when she was only eight years old. The ingenuity and hard work of her mother, Cora Millay, kept the family of three daughters together, and she encouraged their creative endeavors at every turn. Although Millay was very fortunate to secure publication at age nineteen of her famous poem, "Renascence," the treatment that she received from the editors who judged the literary contest in which she had entered the poem was somewhat deplorable. At her mother's urging, she had submitted her long poem in a competition that would select pieces for an anthology called *The Lyric Year*. One of the judges, Ferdinand Earle, prematurely notified "E. Vincent Millay" (as she had submitted her entry) that he expected the "Renascence" entry to win first prize. The other judges could not agree; the poem was, embarrassingly, ranked fourth in the final outcome. Nevertheless, publication won almost immediate critical attention for Millay, including admiring letters from two gentlemen who were to become important lifelong friends—Witter Bynner and Arthur Davison Ficke.

Supported by the generous patronage of Caroline B. Dow, who had been impressed by Millay's talents at a reading of "Renascence" in a Maine country inn, Millay went through the adventure of four years of college at Vassar as the guns of warfare roared over European skies. She was in her early twenties when she entered Vassar College in 1913; as a mature undergraduate, Millay often had a difficult time accepting the rigid regulations of the campus.

Millay was not allowed to attend graduation ceremonies in 1917 because of a series of campus rules infractions. She was confined to campus during spring term 1917 because she returned from spring break two days late. In May she went for a ride with some women friends. The sunny day passed, and the group found it necessary to spend the night at the home of one of the girls' parents. Officials became aware of her absence from campus through a chance discovery of Millay's hastily scrawled signature in a guest book where the group simply stopped for lunch. Disciplinary action was taken the next week.

Millay's time in Greenwich Village (1917–1921) fostered her reputation for enjoying breezy and numerous affairs with men, nurtured her interest in theater and musical productions, and secured her entrance into the best New York publishing houses. The Village milieu offered intellectual and cultural opportunities and fostered her unique independence of spirit. As she once said in a newspaper interview: "I am intensely an individualist."[7] This self-sufficiency is further demonstrated by her extensive—and for the most part lonely—travels abroad during the years 1921–1923. (It should be pointed out, however, that her mother was her constant travelling companion for about a year in Europe.) She lived in hotels and cottages in France, England, Italy, Austria, Albania, and Hungary. However, she experienced ill health during much of this time and very likely also had an abortion.[8]

Two significant events—one public and one private—took place in these postwar years. In 1923 she became the first woman in the United States to win a Pulitzer Prize for poetry. On 18 July 1923, her personal life changed dramatically and forever: she married a supportive and loving husband named Eugen Boissevain who gave her financial security and time to write. After an extensive world tour including various stops in the Orient and Europe, she decided to leave what she had described in a youthful letter as "a heartless metropolis."[9] In another letter she complained that "New York life is getting too congested for me,—too many people; I get no time to work."[10] She moved to a 700-acre farm named Steepletop in the isolated but beautiful hills of the Berkshires. This retreat near Austerlitz, New York, became the couple's home for the rest of their lives.

Nevertheless Millay's concern for human justice and equality continued to widen and found public expression in her participation in a controversial social protest in 1927. She marched with other protestors in Boston in defense of the convicted murderers, Nicola Sacco and Bartolomeo Vanzetti, who were soon to be executed. The sign carried by Millay read: "Free Them and

Save Massachusetts! American Honor Dies with Sacco and Vanzetti!" The excitement of the day led not only to her arrest but also to a personal interview with the governor of Massachusetts as she desperately pleaded mercy on their behalf at the eleventh hour. Of the protest, she later reflected: "I went to Boston fully expecting to be arrested—arrested by a polizia created by a government that my ancestors rebelled to establish. Some of us have been thinking and talking too long without doing anything. Poems are perfect; picketing, sometimes, is better."[11]

In 1936, two severe mishaps befell Millay. As a result of being accidentally thrown out of the passenger side of a car, she suffered a back injury that was to cause her pain for many years. Her work on the manuscript for *Conversation at Midnight* was delayed due to one of the most unfortunate setbacks in the annals of literary disasters—akin to Thomas Carlyle's loss of a portion of his manuscript for *The French Revolution* at the hands of John Stuart Mill's housemaid. Along with several other valuable possessions, Millay's draft manuscript for her work burned in a hotel fire as Millay looked on hopelessly from the Florida beach where she was vacationing. In an interview with Michel Mok, Millay recalled the painful loss: "Every scrap of my manuscript was burned, and the drafts of many other things besides. I had worked over the book like a ditch-digger for two years. It took the better part of another year of slaving to rewrite it."[12]

With the advances of Hitler's armies across Europe in the late 1930s and early 1940s, Millay deliberately turned her poetic lines into propagandistic ploughshares. It was a valiant, but controversial, tactic. In a Christmas letter to Witter Bynner, she wrote: "I *am* well enough to check the copies—well enough to check a whole Nazi motorized division simply by butting at it with my forehead! . . . I am so very busy,—yes of course, writing more verses for my poor, foolish, bewildered, beloved country. . . . A great part of the work on these poems (for I really think they are poems) was done long before the attack on Oahu."[13] She joined the war effort not only by collecting pounds of scrap iron from around her farm and by giving public speeches with such titles as "Nothing . . . If Not Enough" but, more importantly, by writing a series of poetry volumes on the many faces of war.

With her husband's sudden death in August 1949 from complications in an operation, Millay found it difficult to live alone at Steepletop. However, on good days, she was able to work on planning a new collection of poetry. She died while alone at her Steepletop home. Beekman W. Cottrell's description of her final exit captures the quiet drama, tenderness, and irony of her demise: "So it was that on October 19, 1950, the body of Edna St. Vincent Millay, clad in nightgown and slippers, was found seated at the foot of her staircase. She had come from the living room with a bottle of wine and a glass half-filled. As she started up the stairs she felt a warning. She put the glass and the bottle on the step beside her, sat down, leaned over, and died."[14]

Book-Review Responses, 1918–1956

The reviewers' comments on Millay's first three volumes of poetry—*Renascence and Other Poems* (1917), *A Few Figs from Thistles* (1920), and *Second April* (1921)—were the most favorable that she received during the three decades of her writing career. Praise for these early works appeared in a range of prestigious journals. To critics, "Renascence" was an impressive achievement in its youthful freshness and its strong emotional impact. Harriet Monroe in *Poetry* called it an exceptional achievement and hailed its ability to capture the "emotion of youth at encountering inexplicable infinities." Further, she remarked that "It requires a rare spiritual integrity to keep one's sense of infinity against the persistent daily intrusions of the world."[15] Louis Untermeyer declared that the pages of the volume "vibrate with an untutored sincerity, a direct and often dramatic power that few of our most expert craftsmen can equal."[16] Jesse B. Rittenhouse praised Millay's first volume as a demonstration that the poet had "imagination," "vitality," "simplicity and magic."[17]

Millay's second volume of poetry, *A Few Figs from Thistles*, was published in 1920. An anonymous reviewer in the *Dial* detected a "sauciness," a charm "scattered like salt on her verses" and compared Millay's gifts and achievement to those of Emily Dickinson.[18] In the *Measure*, Frank Ernest Hill explained the important interchange between the lyric and the dramatic: "These lyrics are, in fact, dramatic monologues in which the author is spying upon herself."[19]

Her next published collection, *Second April*, appeared in 1921. Although Padraic Colum objected to the classical allusions and poetic imagery in "Ode to Silence," calling the poem "nothing more than a literary exercise,"[20] other critics praised the power and maturity of her lines. Maxwell Anderson found several sonnets to be "powerful, humanly moving, perfectly touched, said as only a first-class artist could say them."[21] The response in Great Britain was more ambivalent, however. An anonymous reviewer for the *Times Literary Supplement* felt that Millay offered a "sensitive, receptive reading of life" and was "a writer to be reckoned with"; however, this reviewer found the collection uneven and marred by prosaic lines, sentimentality, and repetitious diction.[22]

Other volumes of poetry appeared in the 1920s and 1930s. *The Harp-Weaver and Other Poems* was published in 1923 by Harper and Brothers, the publishing firm that henceforth became Millay's sole business representative. John Gould Fletcher dismissed the title poem as "the unforgettable rhythm of Mother Goose, the verbal utterance of a primer—all used to deal out an idea which is wishy-washy to the point of intellectual feebleness."[23] A curious review in a British publication attempted to place her outlook in a line of British predecessors: "She excites interest and admiration by an individuality which is at once pointed and elusive, and which owes allegiance to no school, but combines with curious felicity the whimsicality of a Mary Coleridge and the *desiderium* of a Housman." In the shorter lyrics of *The Harp-Weaver* collection the reviewer for the *Times Literary Supplement* found "an ascetic hardness . . . which creates the illusion of moving in a world of pure idea."[24] In her long review of the book, Genevieve Taggard also sought to place Millay in the tradition of English sonnet writers. More significantly, Taggard is one of the first of a line of feminist critics to complain about the chauvinistic abuse that is often heaped on Millay by "gentlemen critics." Thus, she writes: "When Miss Millay is too sincere and simple for our age, she is called infantile; when she is brave and ironically wise, she is called flippant. The critics, usually dismayed gentlemen who are completely incapable of coping with both qualities, have said a good deal under each of these heads, while the world, meanwhile, rises with a roar to receive its poet."[25]

Millay's 1928 collection, *The Buck in the Snow and Other Poems*, was the first to include some poems deliberately for social protest. Especially controversial were the poems "Justice Denied in Massachusetts" and "Hangman's Oak." Mankind's penchant for waste and the infliction of pain and death on other creatures is criticized, sometimes bitterly, by Millay in this volume. It was a new turn and a new voice in her poetry. Predictably, there was a range of critical reaction. Two reviewers—Babette Deutsch and Louis Untermeyer—argued that the volume was a continuation of Millay's reflections upon the theme of death.[26] While Untermeyer was not pleased with the collection's somber tone, he appreciated the new technical experimentation in several of the poems.[27] Comparison of Millay's verse to great practitioners in English literature—including Sir Thomas Browne, Thomas Hardy, A. E. Housman, and A. C. Swinburne—was the approach taken by Percy Hutchison in the *New York Times Book Review*.[28] Max Eastman saw a new maturity and resonance in the lyrics in this volume: "There is more passion and less wit in these larger and freer rhythms," he wrote. "There are more thoughts."[29] Frederick E. Pierce's estimate of the volume was that the familiar themes of pain and death were expressed with "a compelling intensity of passion" and "a gloomy splendor of impression."[30] Harriet Monroe's continuing interest in Millay was expressed in her review in *Poetry*: "The theme of many of these poems is rebellion against death. . . . And the theme is emphasized by a group of poems wrung out by the Sacco-Vanzetti tragedy."[31] Social issues aside, Edd Winfield Parks in the *Sewanee Review* welcomed the emergence of a new philosophy behind the volume's lyric intensity.[32]

Fatal Interview (1931) was the next poetry collection by Millay to be published (with the exception of the compilation for young readers—*Edna St. Vincent Millay's Poems Selected for Young People*, published in 1929). In fifty-two sonnets, Millay recounts the story of a love affair (with George Dillon, according to recent scholarly reports). Millay dedicated the volume to Elinor Wylie, a fellow poet who stood for freedom and equality for American women before her early death in 1925. Allen Tate complained that in the volume Millay had failed to make full poetic use of the symbols that she had introduced. To Tate, she was "not an intellect but a sensibility." However, he singled out the final sonnet in the book ("Oh, sleep forever in the Latmian cave") as the best poem that she had written to date.[33] Other reviewers praised the technical competence and mature poetic diction of the volume. Katherine Bregy in the *Catholic World* called the artistry of the whole series of poems "always distinguished and often dazzling."[34] A reviewer for a British periodical, the *Morning Post* (London), predicted that the sonnets with their "pagan frankness and unreserve" would have shocked Christina Rossetti.[35]

Amid the Great Depression, Millay's *Wine from These Grapes* appeared in 1934. She deeply felt the loss of her mother who died unexpectedly in 1931, and she viewed the political turmoil that again beset Europe and the Orient with alarm. A tone of controlled anger permeates this new volume. The most famous poem in the book is "Epitaph for the Race of Man," which bemusingly contemplates both man's capacity for greatness and for self-destruction. The volume received serious attention from reviewers. Percy Hutchison analyzed the gravity of these new lyrics and called "Epitaph for the Race of Man" Millay's best work in sonnet form.[36] Louise Bogan compared Millay's "self-sufficing" accomplishment in this volume to W. B. Yeats's "conversion," his continual stages of demonstrating "maturing creation."[37] The opening lines of Philip Blair Rice's review in the *Nation* hailed "a growth not only toward intellectual maturity but also toward poetic integrity." Rice also made an interesting analysis of Millay's larger place in the American poetic tradition, viewing her as "the only poet of exceptional gifts to carry on the high romantic tradition with gusto."[38] Chauncey B. Tinker in the *Yale Review* called the lyrics "intensely introspective." Curiously, Tinker was surprised by Millay's new role as a Sibyl in "Epitaph for the Race of Man," and he was not pleased with the sentiment of "sheer defeatism" that she expressed in this poem. He called for a return to "the delicious impudence of Miss Millay's early verse."[39]

One of Millay's most experimental works, *Conversation at Midnight*, appeared in 1937. Various guests discourse in an after-dinner session in New York; here again Millay introduces contemporary and controversial social issues. In one caustic political epigram, Hitler is called "a pale, mustachioed soda-fountain Siegfried." Basil Davenport and Peter Monro Jack welcomed the work as a distinctive break from her usual style and were appreciative of its reflection on issues in a turbulent historical period.[40] John Peale Bishop, John Gilland Brunini, and William Plomer were all offended by the unpoetic mixture of forms and intolerant of the indeterminacy of the argument.[41] The *Newark Evening News* reviewer detected a "colloquial and anti-feminist approach to topics" in the dialogues.[42] Her close friend Edmund Wilson was somewhat disappointed with the volume's lack of "dramatic imagination," and he stated that he missed "her old imperial line." He could not see any "revelation [concerning] the confusion of cross-currents of the time. . . . The discussion doesn't seem to come to much."[43] Robert Hillyer in the *Atlantic* called it "a 122-page work which, to speak frankly, is unutterably dull—as dull as a dictaphone record."[44] Groverman Blake in the *Cincinnati Times-Star* appreciated the volume's atmosphere—"one of intellectual sophistication and disorderly opulence."[45] Although John Holmes in the *Boston Evening Transcript* was intrigued by a woman poet's decision to risk "the contemporary scene as subject matter" for poetry, he feared that "her admirers . . . will be right in feeling disappointed" and "bewildered."[46] Interestingly enough, in answer to the question "What books of 1937 do you nominate for this year's Pulitzer Prize awards?" posed by a poll in the *Saturday Review of Literature*, fourteen critics and literary editors—a vote total far ahead of any other title in the poetry field—chose Millay's *Conversation at Midnight*[47] This result is a clear demonstration of the professional and critical esteem that Millay held to the very end of the 1930s in the United States. Burton Rascoe further attested to her status in *Newsweek* in 1939: "Edna St. Vincent Millay is the most touted, the most publicized, and the most successful poet in America."[48] These assessments are difficult to reconcile with opinions of the 1940s that offer rock-bottom assessments of her critical reputation after the appearance of her so-called propaganda verse during the wartime years.

The final collection of Millay's poems to appear before the outbreak of World War II was *Huntsman, What Quarry?* (1939). Millay had been working on these poems for several years, and the collection was delayed because of her automobile accident in 1936. Robert Francis praised the various and successful dramatic voices in the work, with "the poet appearing in one part after another, effective in each." The price, however, was the lack of a unified poetic vision, a conflict between the Romantic and modern outlooks.[49] Burton Rascoe in *Newsweek* found many of the volume's verses to be "vituperative," "a series of versifying editorials on international problems which reach a new low in intellectual virginity."[50] Part IV of *Huntsman, What Quarry?* was written to Elinor Wylie, and John Holmes in the *Boston Evening Transcript* found this section to carry "conviction," and he found the "sonnets at the end as fine as any she has ever made."[51] Paul Rosenfeld's review in *Poetry* was in many ways a prophetic commentary. Although he found no lessening of Millay's poetic powers, he was critical of her political poems in the volume. He valued the poems that expressed personal emotion: "The majority of the lyrics in *Huntsman, What Quarry?* communicate feeling with all her former fancy, piquancy, verve, but also in instances with a powerful style and a plangent music not without sublimity." However, Rosenfeld was harshly critical of the poems that display "her entanglements in international politics." Thus, the imagery of "Say That We Saw Spain Die" is "sheerly decorative"; and the poetic attempt in the sonnet sequence "From a Town in a State of Siege" is "singularly fruitless."[52]

The wartime poetic volumes include: *"There Are No Islands Any More"* (1940, soon included in *Make Bright the Arrows*), *Make Bright the Arrows; 1940 Notebook* (1940), and *The Murder of Lidice* (1942). There is no doubt that Millay realized that these poems did not represent her best work, but she hoped that they would make a useful contribution to the war effort. In a letter to her former college roommate, Mrs. Charlotte Babcock Sills, she offered an explanation for publishing unpolished, "hastily written and hotheaded" verse—often against her better aesthetic judgment: "I have one thing to give in the service of my country,—my reputation as a poet. How many more books of propaganda poetry containing as much bad verse as this one does, that reputation can withstand without falling under the weight of it and without becoming irretrievably lost, I do not know—probably not more than one. But I have enlisted for the duration."[53]

Of *Make Bright the Arrows*, Babette Deutsch wrote in the *New Republic* that "when she turns to political themes, the gay impudence of her girlhood, the sensitive curiosity of her more mature work, are lost in the shriek of a helplessly angry woman . . . here is a Jeremiah feminized and shrill." For Deutsch, the impact of any poet in a wartime situation would be minimal, and certainly the reading public would agree that "hysteria is *ersatz* prophecy, and notes a poor substitute for poetry." In short, she deplored the "poetic journalese."[54] Louise Bogan in the *New Yorker* objected to the "noble tone" of indignation and "stock sentiment" of the volume: "That this sentimentality should at this particular moment appear in full force in American writing is a cause for concern and regret."[55] In a review for the *New York Times Book Review*, Peter Monro Jack found the volume to be consistent with a Millay style that had been used in some of her previous volumes—a style that captured "the free and ready speech of the moment." In Jack's opinion, this style had "a vitality and integrity . . . [a] passion and momentum." Even more stunningly, Jack praised the work as "direct and decisive" propaganda that joined a noble tradition of such verse as it was written in the past by John Milton, William Wordsworth, and Rupert Brooke: "Miss Millay matches them, and belongs with their company."[56]

The Murder of Lidice was anti-Nazi propaganda that was written hastily for the Writers' War Board in 1942. In ballad form, Millay focused on a young village couple whose marriage plans and whole way of life are destroyed on the very same day. The work was broadcast on the NBC radio network on 19 October 1942, with Paul Muni's voice lending luster to the reading. A review in *Theatre Arts* attested to the emotional impact on the audience: "So now radio drama has done what the movies have already done successfully—picked up an item of news out of the current war and made it at once into effective art."[57] Leon Whipple in *Survey Graphic* evaluated the work in its hardcover format. He appreciated the gesture toward communal poetry that Millay's verse-drama represented. Although some of the lines were touched with "beauty and compassion," others were "often forced and over-colored." In his opinion the work failed because Millay was "mastered by her emotions, not master of them."[58]

Millay's sister, Norma Millay Ellis, completed the editorial tasks necessary to publish *Mine the Harvest* in 1954 and *Collected Poems* in 1956. A return to close observation of the natural world is a distinguishing hallmark of *Mine the Harvest*. Hints of mystical experience and a positive affirmation of life are also characteristics of Millay's final poetic vision. Somewhat surprisingly, several reviewers found *Mine the Harvest* to be too intellectualized and too lacking in emotional sensibility. Katherine Bregy in *Catholic World* concluded that "Ecstasy is rare enough in the present collection." Besides some nature poems, she noted, there were reflections on "problems of man and of art in the world today." For Bregy this collection of poems from the last ten years of Millay's life was "a poetry of thought rather than feeling."[59] Sara Henderson Hay also expressed regret that in this volume Millay had moved away from "the intensely personal and emotional vein of her [earlier] poetry to a wider expression of a more universal and intellectualized scope and passion."[60] John Ciardi was delighted that Millay had dropped her "save-the-world rhetoric" in this volume, but he still objected to some poems that were, in his judgment, "self-intoxicated" or "self-dramatizing"—"the coy if fervent posturing" of a strolling player. Regrettably, he concluded, "When she aspires to be high serious, she is least successful."[61] Only the *New Yorker* reviewer, Louise Bogan, praised the volume; in it she found that Millay expressed "signs of a more energetic irony" as well as "her true lyric talent, her moments of perception, and her love of human values."[62] Robert Hillyer in the *New York Times Book Review* hailed the work as "the finest of Edna Millay's books." He praised the "clear sayings" and "the sure and unpretentious metrical technique," concluding that the volume was a testament to her genius for self-criticism because it effectively eliminated affectation and propaganda. "The results of this liberation," he wrote, "give to these poems of her last decade a variety, spontaneity and depth that surpass all her previous collections."[63]

Collected Poems drew a wide range of responses from reviewers. Francis Hackett in the *New Republic* hailed the book as "a monument to straightness and singleness of soul."[64] That the collection had a cumulative power could not be denied: Paul Engle in the *New York Post* remarked that "All her sonnets are gathered into one sequence in this volume, making a solid weight of excellence unsurpassed."[65] One of America's preeminent critics of poetry, Karl Shapiro, expressed a haunting prophecy: "I look in vain for the time when men will be so civilized as to appreciate this poet who wrote so voluminously and so passionately and so expertly, almost to no avail."[66] To Winfield Townley Scott the collection represented a mixed achievement: it demonstrated "her mastery of the music of verse"; however, "the trouble is her mastery is intermittent."[67] In a unique approach, Howard Zahniser analyzed *Collected Poems* from the perspective of Millay's intricate and on-going awareness of the natural world about her.[68]

Millay's achievements in the areas of drama, short fiction, and translation were certainly in evidence throughout the 1920s and 1930s. During the 1920s, Millay was most active as a dramatist. Her most famous play on the subject of war, *Aria da Capo*, was first published in *Reedy's Mirror* (18 March 1920), then in *Chapbook (A Monthly Miscellany)* in August 1920, and as a book by Mitchell Kennerley in 1921. Writing in the *Freeman*, Henry David Gray said, "The author of this symbolic fantasy is a poet of unusual promise. She has much more than lyric charm and delicacy of touch; there is point, as well, in almost everything she writes."[69] Commenting on the Provincetown Players production, Alexander Woollcott considered the play "enigmatic" but nevertheless full of "riches of meaning" and "the most beautiful and most interesting play in the English language now to be seen in New York."[70]

The Lamp and the Bell was commissioned for the fiftieth anniversary of Vassar's Alumnae Association. A five-act verse play, it was completed in 1921. Mark Van Doren found the drama to be delightful and predicted that it would be "best remembered as a delicate riot of gay asides and impeccable metaphors, Elizabethan to the bottom yet not in the least derivative; it bubbles pure poetry."[71] Although John V. A. Weaver expressed distaste for the play's topic—"We do not care for Lesbianism, no matter how beautifully described"—he nevertheless praised the characterization and songs in the work.[72] Also published in 1921 was Millay's verse play *Two Slatterns and a King*. The reviewer in the *Boston Evening Transcript* lauded Millay's "gift for whimsicality" and the play's "bright and sparkling verse."[73]

The King's Henchman was published in 1927. The production at the Metropolitan combined the talents of Deems Taylor (as composer) and Millay (as librettist). For Henry Seidel Canby, the work was "a woman's drama": "This is an intensely feminine play. . . . This play is the story of a futile woman who sells love for excitement."[74] In a *Bookman* review entitled "Miss Millay Goes Over the Top," Charles W. Ferguson praised the play's intensity and called it a drama that is "great and wonderfully made." Ferguson appreciated the story that unfolded naturally and dramatically as well as "the richness of [the play's] humor and repartee."[75] Sean O'Faolain, writing of the play in the *Irish Statesman*, called it "rich in the lyric tone" and "full of natural magic." The work showed Millay's new display of "emotion sifted in tranquillity."[76]

The play *The Princess Marries The Page* (1932) was actually written when Millay was a student at Vassar, but it was not published until 1932. The reviewer for the *Bookman* called it a "pleasantly romantic comedy." Furthermore, according to this critic, the play had "none of the irony of *Aria da Capo*, but something of the same quality of fantasy."[77] For the reviewer in the *Boston Evening Transcript*, the play was a combination of both superficial events and accomplished verbal techniques: it was "slight" and a "bit of romantic fluff," but it had "charm and wit as well."[78] The reviewer for the *New York Times Book Review* felt that the work "offers more enjoyment to the young than it is likely to afford the more mature." The play was, in short, "a delightful child's whimsy."[79]

Reactions to Millay's collection of her Nancy Boyd stories in *Distressing Dialogues* (1924) were brief and few in number. The reviewer for the *Boston Evening Transcript* called the humor in this collection of short fiction "versatile, sparkling and at all times brilliant. Rarely does one meet with satiric wit which is at once as refreshing and as originally phrased."[80] John Franklin in the *New Statesman* identified the significant strain of "bitter recklessness behind American humour" and so evident in Millay's stories.[81] Henry B. Fuller in the *New Republic* found some of the stories to be "cleverly done," but on the whole did not welcome the collection because it permitted the "unsympathetic to view her as an impish vulgarian, and the loyal to regret the capricious and irresponsible exercise of a high talent on a lower plane."[82] In "O These Wits!" Herman J. Mankiewicz found the collection of stories "delightful" and "an excellent compilation of cynical humor." Overall, he thought the book was "splendid." However, one strain of unrelenting satire offended his sensibilities: "Mrs. Boyd is primarily a satirist, but with a passion for reform that she may well watch, lest it swallow her. Thus, early in the present volume, there is an 'All-American Almanac and Prophetic Messenger,' full of bitterly invective satire that is anything but funny and that at moments resembles annoyance, chiefly because of its relentless intensity. At times Mrs. Boyd scowls when she should leer."[83]

In the mid-1930s, Millay worked with George Dillon on a translation of Charles Baudelaire's *Flowers of Evil* (1936). George Dillon (1906–1968) was a poet and scholar. Born in Florida and reared in Kentucky, he later served for a time as editor of *Poetry* in Chicago. He won a Pulitzer Prize for a volume of his poetry in 1932. Arnold Whitridge in the *Yale Review* complained that the translators were too concerned with meter and form to do an effective job of conveying the "temper" of Baudelaire. In short, "they have sometimes sacrificed the rigor of his thought. Occasionally they have almost prettified him."[84] In his review, "Charles Baudelaire's Poems in English Dress," Cuthbert Wright called it an "admirable" translation, true to the form and meter of the original work. Wright dwelt on Baudelaire's love-and-hate attitude toward Paris and the complexities of his life.[85]

Millay's public presence before American audiences was augmented by the many public readings that she gave of her works. Just one account of such a performance should be mentioned here to help to record the aura of these events. In 1925 Clifford Orr in the *Boston Evening Transcript* reported on the excitement and energy associated with Millay's reading at Bowdoin College in Brunswick, Maine:

Memorial Hall fills again, but this time fills to overflowing. Ten minutes before Miss Millay appears, there is standing room only. . . . Suddenly a silence, and there is Edna St. Vincent Millay! . . .

She is dressed, as always at these readings of hers, in bronze and green— in dull green silk hand-painted in dull gold. The color blends with her eyes, sets off her reddish hair. The gown surrounds her simple lyrics with a spell as of the Middle Ages. It is rounded about the neck; it falls straight and long to the floor in front, concealing her golden slippers; it crawls behind her in a grateful train; it tapers to tiny tight sleeves with points at the wrists. In it she assumes a mood that is only one of her various selves. She reads clearly . . . [86]

Another glimpse at the "various selves" of Millay can be found in her sparkling conversation in interviews. Rather than draw from previously published interviews, this volume presents for the first time the record of a fictional exchange between Millay and her life-long friend and fellow poet, Arthur Davison Ficke. It is entitled "Interview De Luxe with Edna St. Vincent Millay." The date is unknown, although internal evidence suggests that its setting resembles Millay's Greenwich Village apartment, perhaps between 1918 and 1922. One of many writers and friends to testify to the radiant presence of Millay in personal conversation was Dorothy Thompson. In 1951, she wrote, "When she was happy, charmed or enchanted, she had an indescribable radiance. . . . She was a most exciting conversationalist, whose mind could roam through music, philosophy, art and even politics."[87]

SURVEY OF CRITICAL ESSAYS, 1950–1990

During her lifetime, Millay was the subject of several extended essays. Edmund Wilson surveyed a range of poets in his 1926 essay "The All-Star Literary Vaudeville." Even at this early point in Millay's career, he could see approaching cracks and pitfalls: "Miss Millay has now, in turn, grown so popular that she, too, is in danger of becoming unfashionable." He further remarked that her "inferior work has no embroidery to disguise it."[88]

It might be tidy and convenient to say that the reaction against Millay's reputation began to appear in criticism just a few months after her death in 1950. In actuality, however, the vanguard attack could be seen even earlier, and it came from that guru of the 1970s media phenomenon, Herbert Marshall McLuhan. His judgment was harsh and all-encompassing: "Edna Millay . . . has never been anything but a purveyor of cliché sentiment. She is an exhibitionist with no discoverable sensibility of her own. . . . Had there been responsible critics to consider her first work some direction might have been given to her talent."[89] John Ciardi's now famous essay in the *Saturday Review of Literature* (1950) in essence portrayed Millay's verse and value in terms of his own adolescent fantasies. He wondered if in maturity one did not come to discard Millay's youthful insights: "This is not an experience, we conclude; it is a pose. And poem after poem confirms this experience: there is always that element of the overdramatic about them, a fabrication of the words rather than of the feeling, of a posture rather than of an experience." He concluded, "It was not as a craftsman nor as an influence, but as the creator of her own legend that she was most alive for us. Her success was as a figure of passionate living." So much for the past; as for her reputation in future years, Ciardi is not optimistic: "And even at its best it is not likely that her work can be popular so long as poetry continues its present development toward the ambivalent consciousness and the pessimistic intellect. Perhaps her poems must be forgotten."[90]

The 1960s saw little rally in critical attention to Millay's works. Two critics opened the decade with lukewarm assessments. Although M. L. Rosenthal had been personally impressed with the poet's "shimmering stage presence" in his student days at the University of Chicago in the early 1930s, in his influential book *The Modern Poets*, he slighted her in a very brief comparison with Elizabeth Bishop: "In her poems about Negroes and the poor Miss Bishop can be sentimental; these and her love poetry have just the consistency of a typical Millay poem. Her perfectionism is not such as to keep her from expressing emotions spontaneously."[91] Harold Orel's 1960 essay focused on Millay's last works, but it really offers an assessment of her final status in the American poetry scene. His opening questions now seem somewhat ironic given the great upsurge of interest in Millay that took place in the late 1970s and continued through the 1980s: "Does anyone still discuss the work of Edna St. Vincent Millay as a serious contribution to modern poetry? The critics have done with her. The professors no longer write about her." To Orel, Millay's problems began with the volume *Conversation at Midnight*. Although he admitted that the work lacked "a focused subject-matter and its literary form was bastardized," he admired Millay's courage for "attempting to become a better artist by grappling with her environment." Unfortunately, she never again succeeded in rising to this challenge and thus, in Orel's opinion, her work declined steadily in the 1940s. This period was a phase of her career, "undertaken *knowingly*," but also it was part of a lifelong effort on her part to grow as a poet.[92]

Following closely on the heels of Orel's assessment was the reprinting in 1964 and in 1968 of a 1938 essay, "The Poet as Woman," by John Crowe Ransom. The devaluation of Millay by New Critics such as Allen Tate and Cleanth Brooks that had occurred in the 1930s resurfaced in new reprintings and new anthologies during the 1960s, as the New Criticism was establishing a throttle-grip on classroom instruction.[93] In Ransom's snide judgment, Millay was to be faulted for her failure to write verse that was sufficiently masculine. As a woman she was drawn to the emotional; to Ransom, her poetry lacked intellectual interest. Her place was not in the academic classroom, for she was "the best of the poets who are 'popular' and loved by Circles, Leagues, Lyceums, and Round Tables."[94]

Beginning with Elizabeth Perlmutter Frank's essay on Millay and Louise Bogan, which appeared in *Twentieth Century Literature* in 1977, articles that examined Millay's life and work from the perspective of feminist criticism began to appear in significant publications on a yearly basis. It was as though a renaissance of interest in Millay studies had blossomed overnight. Frank examined the girl figure in the poetry of Millay and Bogan. "Both of these poets," Frank argued, "used the fact of being female not merely as subject matter, but as a formal principle for invigorating and intensifying lyric speech. Through the medium of female personae, each poet developed a specific approach to the lyric past." With the persona of the Girl, Millay was able to achieve "the freshness and breadth of emotion" praised in her early volumes of poetry; by the 1930s, the persona of a mature woman described the rejuvenating power of romance and passion.[95] A fresh, feminist approach that offered sustained critical analysis of Millay's poetry was offered by Jeannine Dobbs's "Edna St. Vincent Millay and the Tradition of Domestic Poetry" in the *Journal of Women's Studies in Literature* (1979). Although Millay's domestic poems are few, they are notable. Dobbs argued that "a reassessment of Millay suggests that her greatest contribution and achievement lay in the poems she wrote of a personal, immediate nature—poems out of her own experience as a woman and out of her understanding of that experience on the part of other women." Dobbs focused on the seventeen-sonnet sequence, "Sonnets from an Ungrafted Tree" in *The Harp-Weaver*, and she made connections to poems by other women poets. Dobbs's essay is interesting for making a distinction between Millay's "shocking" and "feminist" verse (for which she was praised by reviewers) and her "domestic poems" which she wrote outside of that mode (and for which she was usually downgraded).[96]

Patricia A. Klemans, in " 'Being Born a Woman': A New Look at Edna St. Vincent Millay," offers fresh critical analysis and values the poet's feminist individuality. Klemans calls *Fatal Interview* "only one of the many beautiful and meaningful collections of poetry which speak particularly to a woman's experience." Millay was an important voice during her time period. She "spoke for a generation of young women who responded to her standards of sexual independence and feminine heroism. . . . her poetry is written with consummate skill and her message of feminine individuality is ageless."[97]

The year 1979 marked not only the appearance of Sandra Gilbert and Susan Gubar's masterpiece of feminist criticism, *The Madwoman in the Attic*, but also the publication of their coedited collection of essays, *Shakespeare's Sisters: Feminist Essays on Women Poets*. Jane Stanbrough in her essay stressed Millay's language of vulnerability as an expression of the anguish that all women feel as victims of a patriarchal society. Even gifted women are served up bitter doses of limitations, false expectations, and humiliations—as Millay herself experienced in a 1937 incident at New York University that is described in a letter.[98]

In 1937 Millay was invited to receive an honorary degree at New York University. Several men were also to be so honored, but they were invited to a special dinner at the Waldorf Astoria. Millay protested that she had been unfairly excluded from intellectual companionship with the other honorees on the basis of her sex. She felt humiliated and discriminated against because her invitation was confined to a dinner hosted by the chancellor's wife for a small group of ladies at a separate location. Stanbrough unravels the complexities of Millay's responses—"her linguistic distress signals"—to female vulnerability. As she points out, her "bravado" often disguises the intensity of her reaction against the subjection of women to assault, confinement, restriction, oppression, and victimization. As a study of tensions between violence and constraint in Millay's personal poems on the theme of women's vulnerability, Stanbrough's essay is a highly convincing exploration of the unrelenting dynamics of power and punishment.[99]

The year 1982 saw the second edition of Norman A. Brittin's biographical-critical study in the Twayne Author Series. In the preface to the revised edition, he explained his willingness "to augment and particularize the discussion of Millay as a feminist."[100] The pace of Millay criticism in the 1980s was set: two more outstanding essays from the feminist perspective appeared in 1986. Suzanne Clark's "Jouissance and the Sentimental Daughter: Edna St. Vincent Millay" explored issues of power and powerlessness in Millay's poetry as well as "the contradiction of the woman as poet." Clark applies the theories of Freud, Lacan, and Kristeva to assist her in explaining many of her insights. In her efforts to escape the confinement of the feminine, Clark pointed out, "Millay thought she was rebelling against the sentimental with her entire career." However, Millay's efforts "to escape the confinement of the feminine all seem to entail her abject return." Another dimension of Clark's essay is to illustrate the forms of enjoyment, the expressions of "jouissance" that Millay practiced. Some components were cross-dressing, the use of personae, and linguistic experimentation, including the use of baby talk in her poems and letters.[101]

Debra Fried in her award-winning article, "Andromeda Unbound: Gender and Genre in Millay's Sonnets" (1986), explored Millay's use of the sonnet form. With references to the use of the form by such masculine predecessors in the tradition as Petrarch, Shakespeare, Milton, Wordsworth, and Keats, Fried demonstrated how Millay revised the Romantic notion of the sonnet as a liberating prison and turned the form into a trope for her own struggles and conflicts as a woman poet. Fried posed larger questions concerning the underexplored topic of the relationship between gender and genre, with special reference to the history of the sonnet, arguing that Millay's famous sonnet "I Will Put Chaos into Fourteen Lines" openly "equates sexual and poetic dominance in its insistence on the control and compression required of the woman poet who seizes upon traditional forms in order to free herself from the forces that would deny her the power to order poetic forms—forces that include traditional male accounts of the need for poetic order." Millay's innovative use of enjambment was also given lively treatment: "Millay here makes enjambment positively sexy." Fried resoundingly demonstrated her intellectual convictions as well: she proved her point that "poetic forms and genres are not natural but ideological." Furthermore, her assertion that part of Millay's goal was "to reclaim the sonnet sequence for the voice of the woman" merits further study. [102]

Continued feminist work on Millay is further evident in a second essay by Suzanne Clark, "The Unwarranted Discourse: Sentimental Community, Modernist Women, and the Case of Millay," published in *Genre* (1987). The thesis of her essay is that "modernist poetics excluded female poets at the level of theory." Further, "modernism offers its own forms of repression." Much of her essay focuses on the question of "the sentimental" as applied to women in the history of writing. Close analysis of several poems reveals a new and sustaining dimension of Millay's writing, "how she negotiates the contradictory demands of a modernist art and the appeal to a powerful community of readers." [103]

Beekman W. Cottrell once praised Millay as a beacon of clarity on the wasteland scene of twentieth-century modernism. "Few have equaled her ability to capture the beauty she so unceasingly strove to record," he wrote. "She wrote lyric poetry in an age which doted upon academic, abstruse, allusive, and anti-emotional poems. . . . Her great concern—unlike that of many of her contemporaries—was for clarity and communication." [104] Gilbert Allen in his essay "Millay and Modernism," written for this volume, developed this line of argument in fruitful detail. The essay argues that Millay's presentation of the urban landscape in several poems in *A Few Figs from Thistles* (1920) places her "within the technically conservative wing of Popular Modernism." In his reading of Millay's *Collected Poems*, Allen found "many different, often contradictory Millays." Most of all, he admired her openness to experience, which he viewed as a special kind of courage. Joanne Veatch Pulley's essay, also written for this volume, offers commentary on a variety of Millay's short stories—labeled "hack writing" by some in the 1920s and largely ignored in recent critical discussions. It examines these stories in light of a feminist approach: how a woman of the twenties dealt with the social issue of abortion and tried to define the place of the artist in society after World War I. The final two essays, written for this volume, continue to address the theme of Millay's identity as an artist. Robert Wiltenburg's essay illuminates Millay's reading of various Renaissance poets and assesses the influence that they had on her own work, pointing out that her varied responses as a reader of these texts also helped define her own identity as a writer. Sandra Gilbert's essay deals with Millay's sexual and psychological experiences as a complex of private and public images is established. Thus,

Millay's strategic self-presentation as a "feminine" poet is discussed, along with the consequences such a presentation had for her art.

BOOKS ON MILLAY

In his provocative essay that assesses Millay's status in 1990, Robert Erwin maintained that one problem with her reputation is how she came to be presented in existing biographies and the collection of her letters, asking "how could Millay know that the publication of two very tame biographies and a collection of her letters in the twenty years after her death would if anything lower her reputation?"[105] So, it is true that as the centennial of Millay's birth arrived, the scholarly community lacked a definitive biography of Millay. Although Erwin does not mention it in his assessment, we also lack a major critical study of Millay's work. A brief survey of existing books on Millay should be noted here, with a corresponding assessment of their sometimes glaring inadequacies.

The earliest book on Millay appeared in 1936. Elizabeth Atkins in her *Edna St. Vincent Millay and Her Times* concentrated on analyzing literary influences on the poet. She also judged Millay to be an initiator, a leading force on the current literary scene. Her adulatory conclusion is that Millay is a major poet. With the exception of Karl Yost's bibliography of Millay's works that appeared in 1937, with an essay by Harold L. Cook, no monograph appeared until one year after Millay's death. In 1951, Vincent Sheean provided details of his acquaintance with Millay during the 1940s. His is a lightweight book entitled *The Indigo Bunting: A Memoir of Edna St. Vincent Millay* that conveys Millay's love of birds, Shakespeare, and skinny-dipping in the cold waters of her retreat on Ragged Island, Maine. A biography that focuses on her formative years and that was designed for adolescent readers appeared in 1957, Toby Shafter's *Edna St. Vincent Millay: America's Best Loved Poet*. The 1960s brought the greatest harvest of Millay monographs. Miriam Gurko's *Restless Spirit: The Life of Edna St. Vincent Millay* was a biography published in 1962. Although the analysis of Millay's poetry lacks depth in terms of rigorous modern critical standards, Gurko does trace a development in character and artistry over the several decades of Millay's career. Two books that were written for larger series in American literature appeared in 1967. James Gray's pamphlet for the University of Minnesota Press series views Millay as an essentially tragic figure, one whose early attainment of artistic maturity necessarily led to decline in the later years. He identifies her major theme as the search for individual integrity. Norman A. Brittin's title in the Twayne Author Series appeared in 1967. In its first edition, he devoted three chapters to biographical information. Other chapters cover her poetry and plays. The final chapter surveys the critical response. In his revised edition, published in 1982, he adds sections on her short stories and the impact of feminist criticism on assessing her reputation. Jean Gould's *Poet and Her Book: A Biography of Edna St. Vincent Millay* was published in 1969. Although it aims at a more mature reading public, it offers few new details or profound interpretations. Although technically not a complete book on Millay, Joan Dash's *A Life of One's Own: Three Gifted Women and the Men They Married* (1973) contains a long chapter that nevertheless should be consulted because of its psychoanalytical approach and its attention to her relationship with her husband. Dash concludes that Millay was "a neurotic woman, death-haunted, claustrophobic and sexually ambiguous."[106] Anne Cheney's *Millay in Greenwich Village* (1975) focuses on Millay's emotional and literary relationships with such important male writers and critics of the period as Floyd Dell, Edmund Wilson, Arthur Davison Ficke, and others. It attempts a psychological portrait of Millay in her most creative years. There is no corresponding study that defines the importance of Millay's connections to her mother and her sisters. However, her relationship to Elinor Wylie and other influential women writers is analyzed by Cheryl Walker in *Masks Outrageous and Austere* (1991). Another biography that was written primarily for young adults as part of Chelsea House's American Women of Achievement series is Carolyn Daffron's *Edna St. Vincent Millay* (1989). The short book's most attractive feature is its reproduction of over twenty-five photographs of Millay and her acquaintances over various decades from the files of the Vassar College Library. Nancy Milford has been granted the most complete access to the papers of Edna St. Vincent Millay. The scholarly world awaits her definitive biography.

There has been careful and adequate bibliographic attention to Millay studies—both in primary and secondary listings. The earliest and still standard primary bibliography is Karl Yost's *A Bibliography of the Works of Edna St. Vincent Millay* (1937). He lists collations in chronological order through 1936. He also has sections on "Appearances and Music," "Periodicals," and "Criticism," which includes books, periodicals, and portraits. The most helpful secondary reference tool is Judith Nierman's *Edna St. Vincent Millay: A Reference Guide* (1977). John J. Patton's "A Comprehensive Bibliography of Criticism of Edna St. Vincent Millay" (*Serif* 5 [September 1968]: 10–32) should also be consulted.

Popular acclaim for Millay is demonstrated convincingly in newsletters from the Book of the Month Club or newspaper items. In *Book News* (March 1990), the editor reported that in response to a previous column of poetry, members wrote to nominate their favorite poets. Edna St. Vincent Millay was among the leading choices, receiving many votes and commentaries. In *Book News* (January 1991), a special offer of Millay's *Collected Poems* in hardcover format was advertised.[107] That the musical and dramatic side of Millay's canon also receives periodic revivals can be witnessed in the recent performance of an absorbing thirty-seven-minute opera in one act entitled "Aria da Capo." Transformed by Brent Weaver as his doctoral dissertation, the premiere took place at Clayton State College in November 1990. A music critic called it a "persuasive" performance in which "wit abounds."[108]

FUTURE OF MILLAY STUDIES

In an interview in the *New York Times*, Norma Millay Ellis, the poet's sister who lived at Steepletop after Millay's death, observed: "You know, she was one of only three poets who made her living from poetry. Only Robert Frost and Ogden Nash did it, too. Her royalties have helped me live for the last twenty-four years." She further remarked: "Those who love Millay are legion. I call them her private public, those who come and say they started to write because of her."[109] The existence of a large and enthusiastic contingent of Millay admirers is constantly demonstrated: witness, for example, the overwhelming response to the issuance of a special commemorative postage stamp in 1981 or the large attendance at benefit concerts in New York City on each anniversary of her birth. Then, too, there is the flourishing Millay Colony for the Arts, directed each year since 1973 by Ann-Ellen Lesser. The Millay Colony gives residencies for one month to writers, composers, and visual artists at the Steepletop site. In the centennial year of 1992, a major conference on Millay was held at Skidmore College. Most importantly, Millay's works continue to be studied in college classrooms and over the last decade she has been the subject of at least a dozen doctoral dissertations. As access is gained to more of her papers, discoveries that will unlock new dimensions of one of the most gifted and complex American women writers of the twentieth century loom on the horizon of scholarly understanding.

ACKNOWLEDGEMENTS

Many individuals have provided technical and inspirational assistance during the many months of preparation needed to compile this book. First and foremost I am indebted to Joanne Veatch Pulley. Her sparkling, never-ending enthusiasm for Millay's life and works only increased during the two years that we worked together on this project. That we could work together was due to the generosity of the University of South Carolina. South Carolina College (the Honors College) provided funds in the form of an undergraduate student research fellowship for two years. The Office of Sponsored Programs and Research also provided funds to underwrite her library efforts and to fund a research trip of mine to libraries on the East Coast with important Millay holdings. The English Department deserves gratitude for providing some Xerox and postage assistance. Also, three English Department graduate assistants—James Boyce, Elizabeth Harris, and especially Becky Lewis—

offered invaluable services in the final stages of this project. My colleagues, Professors Ashley Brown, Matthew J. Bruccoli, Judith James, and Joel Myerson, offered helpful advice on various aspects of this project. At Thomas Cooper Library, professional and untiring assistance was rendered to us by the following individuals: Faye Chadwell, assistant reference librarian; Dan Boice, assistant head of the reference department; Jens Holley, interlibrary loan librarian; Cathie Gottlieb, library technical assistant in interlibrary loan; Jo Cottingham, library technical assistant in interlibrary loan; Laurie Preston, assistant reference librarian; and the remainder of the reference department staff. In microfilm services, Victoria Reese, documents assistant, Lester Duncan, head of documents and microforms, and Deborah Yerkes, assistant documents librarian, offered patient and professional advice to us. Joyce Shuler, photoduplication department, handled each Xerox reproduction with efficiency and care. James Nagel and various editorial staff members at G. K. Hall—Melissa Solomon and Sylvia Miller— have provided invaluable editorial assistance and advice over several months. Special gratitude is extended to Elizabeth Barnett, Millay's literary executor.

WILLIAM B. THESING
University of South Carolina

Notes

1. Ellen Bryant Voigt, "Poetry and Gender," *Kenyon Review* n.s. 9, no.3 (Summer 1987): 138, 137, 139.

2. Robert Erwin, "The Case of the Missing T-Shirt" in his *The Great Language Panic and Other Essays in Cultural History* (Athens: University of Georgia Press, 1990), 122, 124.

3. Edna St. Vincent Millay, *Letters of Edna St. Vincent Millay*, ed. Allan Ross Macdougall (New York: Harper, 1952), 94.

4. Millay, *Letters*, 102–3.

5. John Haynes Holmes, "Ten Women Named as Greatest Living," *New York Times*, 18 May 1931, 19.

6. Millay, *Letters*, 358.

7. Michel Mok, "Poetic Strife Begins at 42 for Edna St. Vincent Millay," *New York Post*, 5 December 1934, 5.

8. Norman A. Brittin, *Edna St. Vincent Millay* (Boston: Twayne, 1982), 15, 139.

9. Millay, *Letters*, 34.

10. Millay, *Letters*, 106.

11. Anonymous, "Edna St. Vincent Millay Found Dead at 58," *New York Times*, 20 October 1950, 27.

12. Michel Mok, "Edna St. Vincent Millay Sings Again," *New York Post*, 15 July 1937, 15.

13. Millay, *Letters*, 315–16.

14. Beekman W. Cottrell, "Edna St. Vincent Millay," *Carnegie Series in English* 2 (1955): 41. For her forthcoming biography, Nancy Milford has compiled new medical evidence concerning the circumstances of Millay's death. (Milford, "The Last Chapter," Skidmore College Millay Conference, keynote address, February 21, 1992.)

15. Harriet Monroe, "First Books of Verse," *Poetry*, 13 (December 1918): 167–68.

16. Louis Untermeyer, "Why a Poet Should Never Be Educated," *Dial* 64 (14 February 1918): 146.

17. Jesse B. Rittenhouse, *"Renascence", Bookman* 46 (February 1919): 682.

18. Anonymous, "Briefer Mention," *Dial* 71 (September 1921): 373.

19. Frank Ernest Hill, "Edna St. Vincent Millay," *Measure*, March 1921, 26.

20. Padraic Colum, "Miss Millay's Poems," *Freeman*, 2 November 1921, 189.

21. Maxwell Anderson, "Second April," *Measure*, September 1921, 17.

22. Anonymous, *"Second April," Times Literary Supplement*, 1 September 1921, 567.

23. John Gould Fletcher, "Sentiment and Anti-Sentiment," *Freeman*, 30 January 1924, 502.

24. Anonymous, "Miss Millay's Poems" [Review of *The Harp-Weaver*], *Times Literary Supplement*, 26 June 1924, 401.

25. Genevieve Taggard, "Her Massive Sandal," *Measure*, April 1924, 12.

26. Babette Deutsch, "Alas!", review of *The Buck in the Snow*, *New Republic* 56 (7 November 1928): 333–34; Louis Untermeyer, "Song from Thistles," *Saturday Review of Literature* 5 (13 October 1928): 209.

27. Louis Untermeyer, "Song from Thistles," *Saturday Review of Literature* 5 (13 October 1928): 209.

28. Percy Hutchison, "Miss Millay's New Lyrics Are More Deeply Serious," *New York Times Book Review*, 7 October 1928, 2.

29. Max Eastman, "A Passing Fashion," *Nation* 127 (5 December 1928): 628.

30. Frederick E. Pierce, "Three Poets Against Philistia," *Yale Review* 18 (December 1928): 365.

31. Harriet Monroe, "Miss Millay's New Book," *Poetry* 33 (January 1929): 210–14.

32. Edd Winfield Parks, "Edna St. Vincent Millay," *Sewanee Review* 38 (January–March 1930): 42–49.

33. Allen Tate, "Miss Millay's Sonnets," *New Republic* 66 (6 May 1931): 335–36.

34. Katherine Bregy, Review of *Fatal Interview*, *Catholic World* 133 (August 1931): 628.

35. Anonymous, "Sonnets from the States" [Review of *Fatal Interview*] *Morning Post* (London), 10 November 1931, 4.

36. Percy Hutchison, "Edna St. Vincent Millay's Grave New Book of Poems," *New York Times Book Review*, 4 November 1934, 2.

37. Louise Bogan, "Conversion Into Self," *Poetry* 45 (February 1935): 277–79.

38. Philip Blair Rice, "Edna Millay's Maturity," *Nation* 139 (14 November 1934): 568, 570.

39. Chauncey B. Tinker, "The Spirit of the Age," *Yale Review* 24 (Winter 1934): 413–15.

40. Basil Davenport, *"Conversation at Midnight," Book-of-the-Month Club News*, August 1937, 7; Peter Monro Jack, "Conversation of Our Time: Edna St. Vincent Millay's Tapestry of Contemporary Themes," *New York Times Book Review*, 25 July 1937, 1, 12.

41. See John Peale Bishop, "A Diversity of Opinions," *Poetry* 51 (November 1937): 99–104; John Gilland Brunini, "Light Verse." *Commonweal* 26 (27 August 1937), 425; and William Plomer, Review of *Conversation at Midnight*, *Spectator* 159 (15 October 1937), 646, 648.

42. Anonymous, "About Books and Authors: Edna St. Vincent Millay's Poetic Melange About Seven Men at Midnight," *Newark Evening News*, 22 July 1937, 12.

43. Edmund Wilson, " 'Give That Beat Again.' " *New Republic* 91 (28 July 1937): 338–40.

44. Robert Hillyer, review of *Conversation at Midnight*, *Atlantic Monthly* 160 (September 1937): unnumbered page.

45. Groverman Blake, "Turning the Pages," *Cincinnati Times-Star*, 21 July 1937, 32.

46. John Holmes, "A Poet Who Often Converses at Midnight," *Boston Evening Transcript*, 7 August 1937, 2.

47. Anonymous. "Critics Vote on Best Books of 1937 in Country-Wide Poll," *Saturday Review of Literature* 17 (2 April 1938): 8–9.

48. Burton Rascoe, "Miss Millay," *Newsweek*, 22 May 1939, 40.

49. Robert Francis, review of *Huntsman, What Quarry?*, *Virginia Quarterly Review* 15 (Autumn 1939): 646–47, 649.

50. Burton Rascoe, "Miss Millay," *Newsweek* 22 May 1939, 40.

51. John Holmes, "Millay's Poems in Last Collection Glitter, but Are Only Partly Gold," *Boston Evening Transcript*, 24 May 1939, 13.

52. Paul Rosenfeld, "Under Angry Constellations," *Poetry* 55 (October 1939): 47–50.

53. Millay, *Letters*, 311–12.

54. Babette Deutsch, "Mme. Jeremiah," *New Republic* 103 (2 December 1940):761.

55. Louise Bogan, review of *Make Bright the Arrows, New Yorker* 16 (28 December 1940): 62.

56. Peter Monro Jack, "Miss Millay's Poems for Our Time," *New York Times Book Review*, 1 December 1940, 6.

57. Anonymous, review of *Murder of Lidice, Theatre Arts* 26 (December 1942): 733–34.

58. Leon Whipple, review of *The Murder of Lidice, Survey Graphic*, 31 (December 1942): 599.

59. Katherine Bregy, review of *Mine the Harvest, Catholic World* 179 (September 1954): 478.

60. Sara Henderson Hay, "The Unpersuadable V.," *Saturday Review* 37 (5 June 1954): 20.

61. John Ciardi, "Two Nuns and a Strolling Player," *Nation* 178 (22 May 1954): 445–46.

62. Louise Bogan, review of *Mine the Harvest, New Yorker* 30 (29 May 1954): 104.

63. Robert Hillyer, "Of Her Essential Heart and Spirit," *New York Times Book Review*, 25 April 1954, 5.

64. Francis Hackett, "Edna St. Vincent Millay," *New Republic* 135 (24 December 1956):22.

65. Paul Engle, "Edna Millay: A Summing-Up of Her Work." *New York Post*, 25 November 1956, M-11.

66. Karl Shapiro, review of *Collected Poems, Prairie Schooner* 31 (Spring 1957): 13.

67. Winfield Townley Scott, "A Handful of Living Flowers," *Saturday Review* 40 (5 January 1957): 18.

68. Howard Zahniser, "Edna Millay, Nature Poet," *Nature Magazine* 50 (April 1957): 172–73.

69. Henry David Gray, "Three Plays from Provincetown," *Freeman*, 9 June 1920, 308.

70. Alexander Woollcott, "Second Thoughts on First Nights: There Are War Plays and War Plays," *New York Times*, 14 December 1919, sec. 8, p. 2.

71. Mark Van Doren, "Women of Wit," *Nation* 113 (26 October 1921): 482.

72. John V. A. Weaver, "Personally Conducted: Edna St. Vincent Millay and Charlotte Mew," *Brooklyn Daily Eagle*, 20 August 1921, 8.

73. Anonymous, "A Moral Interlude: A Dramatic Episode Involving Two Slatterns and a King," *Boston Evening Transcript*, 26 August 1922, sec. 4, p. 7.

74. Henry Seidel Canby, " 'Stand Back, Pretty Lady,' " *Saturday Review of Literature* 3 (19 March 1927): 661.

75. Charles W. Ferguson, "Miss Millay Goes Over the Top," *Bookman* 65 (March 1927): 83–85.

76. Sean O'Faolian, review of *The King's Henchman, Irish Statesman* 8 (3 September 1927): 620.

77. Anonymous, review of *The Princess Marries the Page, Bookman* 77 (January 1933): 99.

78. Anonymous, review of *The Princess Marries the Page, Boston Evening Transcript*, 7 January 1933, 2-X.

79. Anonymous, "Edna Millay's Delightful Child's Whimsy," *New York Times Book Review*, 18 December 1932, 8.

80. Anonymous, "Distressing Dialogues," *Boston Evening Transcript*, 15 November 1924, 4.

81. John Franklin, "New Novels," *New Statesman* 24 (22 November 1924): 205.

82. Henry B. Fuller, "Dialogues and Spotlights," *New Republic* 41 (7 January 1925): 180.

83. Herman J. Mankiewicz, "O These Wits!" *New York Times Book Review*, 2 November 1924, 12.

84. Arnold Whitridge, "Baudelaire in English," *Yale Review* 25 (June 1936): 822, 823.

85. Cuthbert Wright, "Charles Baudelaire's Poems in English Dress," *New York Times Book Review*, 3 May 1936, 4, 18.

86. Clifford Orr, "New Literary Era Confronts the Old," *Boston Evening Transcript*, 9 May 1925, part 6, p. 3.

87. Dorothy Thompson, "Woman Poet," *Ladies' Home Journal* January 1951, 12.

88. Edmund Wilson, "The All-Star Literary Vaudeville," *New Republic* 47 (30 June 1926): 161.

89. Herbert Marshall McLuhan, "The New York Wits," *Kenyon Review* 7 (Winter 1945): 18.

90. John Ciardi, "Edna St. Vincent Millay: A Figure of Passionate Living," *Saturday Review of Literature* 33 (11 November 1950): 8, 9, 77.

91. Personal interview with M. L. Rosenthal, Chapel Hill, North Carolina, 28 June 1990. Also, M. L. Rosenthal, *The Modern Poets: A Critical Introduction* (New York: Oxford University Press, 1960): 254–55. It should also be pointed out that in their classic study, *The Modern Poetic Sequence: The Genius of Modern Poetry* (New York: Oxford University Press, 1983), M. L. Rosenthal and Sally M. Gall offer no discussion of Millay's accomplishments in the sonnet form.

92. Harold Orel, "Tarnished Arrows: The Last Phase of Edna St. Vincent Millay," *Kansas Magazine* 1 (1960): 73–78.

93. See John Crowe Ransom, "The Poet as Woman," *Southern Review* 2 (Spring 1938): 783–806; reprinted 1964. See also Allen Tate, "Miss Millay's Sonnets," review of *Fatal Interview New Republic* 66 (6 May 1931): 335–36; reprinted in *The Poetry Reviews of Allen Tate, 1924–1944*, ed. Ashley Brown and Frances Neel Cheney (Baton Rouge: Louisiana State University Press, 1983), wherein Tate claims that Millay's "success with stock symbolism is precariously won" and that "she is not an intellect but a sensibility"; and Cleanth Brooks's "Edna Millay's Maturity," *Southwest Review* 20 (January 1935): 1–5, wherein he claims that a poem such as "Apostrophe to Man" "reveals her immaturity clearly and cruelly" (p. 2).

94. Ransom, 786.

95. Elizabeth Perlmutter Frank, "A Doll's Heart: The Girl in the Poetry of Edna St. Vincent Millay and Louise Bogan," *Twentieth Century Literature* 23, no. 2 (May 1977): 157.

96. Jeannine Dobbs, "Edna St. Vincent Millay and the Tradition of Domestic Poetry," *Journal of Women's Studies in Literature* 1 (Spring 1979): 89–106.

97. Patricia A. Klemans, " 'Being Born a Woman': A New Look at Edna St. Vincent Millay," *Colby Library Quarterly* 15, no. 1 (March 1979): 18.

98. Millay, *Letters*, 289–91.

99. Jane Stanbrough, "Edna St. Vincent Millay and the Language of Vulnerability," in *Shakespeare's Sisters: Feminist Essays on Women Poets*, edited by Sandra M. Gilbert and Susan Gubar (Bloomington: Indiana University Press, 1979): 183–99.

100. Brittin, *Millay*, iii.

101. Suzanne Clark, "Jouissance and the Sentimental Daughter: Edna St. Vincent Millay," *North Dakota Quarterly* 54 (Spring 1986): 85–108.

102. Debra Fried, "Andromeda Unbound: Gender and Genre in Millay's Sonnets," *Twentieth Century Literature* 32 (Spring 1986): 11, 12, 17, 20.

103. Suzanne Clark, "The Unwarranted Discourse: Sentimental Community, Modernist Women, and the Case of Millay," *Genre* 20 (Summer 1987): 133, 134, 142.

104. Cottrell, "Edna St. Vincent Millay," 39.

105. Erwin, 126.

106. Joan Dash, "Edna St. Vincent Millay," in her *A Life of One's Own: Three Gifted Women and the Men They Married* (New York: Harper and Row, 1973), 116–227.

107. Bridgitte Weeks, "From the Editor-in-Chief" (column), *Book of the Month Club News* (March 1990), 30, and "Special Dividend Offer," *Book of the Month Club News* (January 1991), 21. In a less favorable light, Millay's problems with alcohol addiction are detailed in *Co-starring Famous Women and Alcohol* by Lucy Barry Robe (Minneapolis, Minnesota: CompCare Publications, 1986), 279–80, passim.

108. Derrick Henry, "Classical Music Notes: Opera with the Power of Poetry Sets Stage for Young Composer," *Atlanta Journal and Constitution,* 25 November 1990, N-8.

109. Harold Faber, "Millay Farm Becoming an Arts Colony," (interview with Norma Millay Ellis), *New York Times*, 20 February 1974, 26.

BOOK REVIEWS

Renascence and Other Poems

◆

Why a Poet Should Never Be Educated [Review of *First Offering* by Samuel Roth; *Renascence and Other Poems* by Edna St. Vincent Millay; and *First Poems* by Edwin Curran.]

Louis Untermeyer

These three first volumes, with their curious kinship and even more curious contrasts, furnish a variety of themes. They offer material for several essays: on "What Constitutes Rapture"; on "The Desire of the Moth for the Star"; on "The Growing Tendency among Certain Publishers to Ask One Dollar and Fifty Cents for Seventy Pages of Verse"; on "A Bill for the Conservation of Conservative Poetry"; on "Life, Literature, and the Last Analysis"; on "Why a Poet Should Never be Educated." One cannot deal with all these fascinating considerations, but I hope to suggest the crippling effect the college usually has on the embryonic poet; how imagination is slurred over and form is magnified; how rhapsody is tuned down to rhetoric and regularity; how poetry, in short, emerges not as an experiment, a record of varied days, meditations, and adventures, but as an orderly procession of standard thoughts, a codified treatise, a course in pattern-making. Take these three books, for instance. Mr. Roth has been brought up at a university, and its formal stamp is over all his pages. Miss Millay wrote two of the most fresh and beautiful lyrics which contemporary American poetry can boast—before she went to Vassar. Since that time she has produced nothing that has more than a trace of her initial spontaneous quality; her subsequent poems strain to make up in intellectual concepts what they have lost in naïveté. . . .

Reprinted from the *Dial* 64 (14 February 1918): 145–47.

It is impossible to tell how far the universities are (from a literary point of view) responsible for so many sudden blossomings and so many early deaths. But everyone can name at least half a dozen examples. Was it not less precocity than the hot-house atmosphere of Harvard which made John Hall Wheelock bloom too quickly—a forced growth that almost sapped him for a sturdier flowering? And, at the other extreme, (to change the metaphor) was it not the universities that almost succeeded in extinguishing Robert Frost's guarded flame with their damp disapproval? Perhaps it was not so much disapproval that they exhibited as, what was worse, a ponderous indifference to what did not conform to the curriculum of prescribed beauty. It was this placid unconcern which made Frost realize that these halls of learning (he attended and left two of them) were built not to prepare the future but to perpetuate the past. The list of ruined or rejected originators might be extended to the back cover of this magazine; every reader might add his own quota. But catalogues are tiresome and unsatisfactory as evidence. I shall return to my trio and particularize.

Turning to the second volume is like opening a window in a musty class-room. Here is air and motion, sunlight and the reflection of cloud-driven skies—even though the shadows are sometimes seen upon charted walls. For the greater part, these pages vibrate with an untutored sincerity, a direct and often dramatic power that few of our most expert craftsmen can equal. Turn, for instance, to the opening poem that begins like a child's thoughtless rhyme or a scrap of nonsense verse:

> All I could see from where I stood
> Was three long mountains and a wood;
> I turned and looked another way,
> And saw three islands in a bay.
> So with my eyes I traced the line
> Of the horizon, thin and fine,
> Straight around till I was come
> Back to where I'd started from;
> And all I saw from where I stood
> Was three long mountains and a wood.

An almost inconsequential opening, but as the poem proceeds, one with a haunting and cumulative effect. "Over these things I could not see / These were the things that bounded me," it goes on. And then without ever losing the simplicity of the couplets, it begins to mount. There is an exquisite idyllic passage beginning:

> The grass, a-tiptoe at my ear,
> Whispering to me I could hear;
> I felt the rain's cool finger-tips
> Brushed tenderly across my lips,

> Laid gently on my sealéd sight,
> And all at once the heavy night
> Fell from my eyes and I could see—
> A drenched and dripping apple-tree,
> A last long line of silver rain,

and suddenly, beneath the descriptive rapture, one is confronted with a greater revelation. It is as if a child playing about the room had, in the midst of prattling, uttered some shining and terrific truth. This remarkable poem is, in parts, a trifle repetitious, but what it repeats is said so poignantly that one thinks of scarcely any lesser poet than Blake when one begins the ascending climax:

> I know the path that tells Thy way
> Through the cool eve of every day;
> God, I can push the grass apart
> And lay my finger on Thy heart!

Or witness the first of the unnamed sonnets, that has a similar mixture of world sadness and a painful hunger for beauty, a hunger so great that no delight is great enough to give her peace:

> Thou art not lovelier than lilacs—no
>   Nor honeysuckle; thou art not more fair
>   Than small white single poppies—I can bear
> Thy beauty; though I bend before thee, though
> From left to right, not knowing where to go,
>   I turn my troubled eyes, nor here nor there
>   Find any refuge from thee, yet I swear
> So has it been with mist—with moonlight so.

Elsewhere (as in "The Suicide") the tone is more sophisticated. The results of reading begin to show. In "Interim" we see the intrusion of foreign accents; echoes of other dramatic monologues disturb us as the poem wanders off into periods of reflection and rhetoric. And there are pages where all that was fresh and native to this young poet seems to have turned to mere prettiness and imitation. "Ashes of Life" might have been written by Sara Teasdale in a weak moment; "The Little Ghost" lisps sweetly after Margaret Widdemer. After the preceding exhibits such lapses are doubly distressing. The inclusion of these merely pleasant pieces is all the more surprising when one notes the inexplicable omission of "Journey" from this volume—a youthful poem, but sharpened and illuminated with a succession of original touches. Here is a part of it:

> Cat-birds call
> Through the long afternoon, and creeks at dusk

Are guttural. Whip-poor-wills wake and cry,
Drawing the twilight close about their throats;
Only my heart makes answer. Eager vines
Go up the rocks and wait; flushed apple-trees
Pause in their dance and break the ring for me . . .
Round-faced roses, pink and petulant,
Look back and beckon ere they disappear.

First Books of Verse

HARRIET MONROE

Here is a very exceptional first book, a book which is achievement rather than promise. One would have to go back a long way in literary history to find a young lyric poet singing so freely and musically in such a big world. Almost we hear a thrush at dawn, discovering the ever-renewing splendor of the morning.

Renascence gave me the only thrill I received from Mr. Kennerley's 1912 anthology, *The Lyric Year*. It was so much the best poem in that collection that probably it's no wonder it didn't receive any one of the three prizes. Reading it once more, after six years' discipline in modern poetry, I am thrilled again. The surprise of youth over the universe, the emotion of youth at encountering inexplicable infinities—that is expressed in this poem, and it is a big thing to express. Moreover, it is expressed with a certain triumphant joy, the very mood of exultant youth; and the poet gets a certain freshness and variety into a measure often stilted. The poem is too compact for quotation—it should be read entire. Possibly its spiritual motive is summed up in the couplet: "God, I can push the grass apart / And lay my finger on Thy heart!"

This poem is much the biggest thing in the book; indeed, one almost sighs with fear lest life, closing in on this poet as on so many others, may narrow her scope and vision. It requires a rare spiritual integrity to keep one's sense of infinity against the persistent daily intrusions of the world, the flesh and the devil; but only the poet who keeps it through the years can sing his grandest song.

But even without *Renascence* the book would be exceptional. Not so much for *Interim*, though its emotion is poignantly sincere and expressed without affectation, as for some of the briefer lyrics. Such songs as *Kin to Sorrow, Tavern, The Shroud*, are perfect of their very simple and delicate kind; and one or two of the sonnets are admirable—*Time does not Bring Relief* and *Bluebeard*. A few of the best songs were first printed in POETRY, though we find no acknowledgment of this fact in the book; (which, by the way—let me heap coals of fire on the publisher's head—is beautifully designed and

From *Poetry* 13 (December 1918): 167–68. Copyright by The Modern Poetry Association and reprinted by permission of the Editor of *Poetry* and by courtesy of Dr. and Mrs. Edwin S. Fetcher, St. Paul, Minnesota.

printed.) Among the poems unfamiliar to our readers perhaps *God's World* is typical of the poet's mood and manner:

> O world, I cannot hold thee close enough!
>   Thy winds, thy wide grey skies!
>   Thy mists, that roll and rise!
> Thy woods, this autumn day, that ache and sag
> And all but cry with color! That gaunt crag
> To crush! To lift the lean of that black bluff!
> World, World, I cannot hold thee close enough!
>
> Long have I known a glory in it all,
>   But never knew I this—
>   Here such a passion is
> As stretcheth me apart. Lord, I do fear
> Thou'st made the world too beautiful this year.
> My soul is all but out of me—let fall
> No burning leaf; prithee, let no bird call.

A Few Figs From Thistles

♦

Edna St. Vincent Millay

FRANK ERNEST HILL

One may as well admit that Edna St. Vincent Millay is just now the most interesting person in American poetry. Unfortunately a great many have begun reading her verse not because they were seeking good art, but because F.P.A. made nursery rhymes about her name, or because of her frank professions of impropriety. They have been confused as to what she is and means. Probably Frank Shay's first Salvo, containing fifteen poems by Miss Millay, has not cleared their minds.

Nevertheless, this pamphlet-booklet defines Miss Millay pretty well. For one thing, it reveals clearly her artistic attitude. It is a collection of lyrics, but one leaves it realizing as never before the dominance of the dramatic in almost everything that Miss Millay has done.

It is unnecessary to seek for this in pieces that are frankly objective, in *She Is Overheard Singing, Daphne, The Beanstalk,* and *Aria da Capo.* In these, of course, aside from the personal experience and personal philosophy which legitimately underlie any art, the ego does not intrude. But the quality of these is after all little different from the quality of Miss Millay talking about herself. Even when she becomes confessional it is to build up pictures. One is told of her emotions, but only, as with dramatis personae, through her actions. These lyrics are, in fact, dramatic monologues in which the author is spying upon herself.

> Grief of grief has drained me clean,
>   Still it seems a pity
> No one saw,—it must have been
>   Very pretty,

Reprinted from the *Measure: A Journal of Poetry* 1 (March 1921): 25–26.

she wrote in her first volume. There is the point of view. The best poem in *A Few Figs From Thistles* is probably a sonnet beginning

> I think I should have loved you presently
> And given in earnest words I flung in jest;
> And lifted honest eyes for you to see,
> And caught your hand against my cheek and breast,

and these four lines show as well as anything one could quote how the point of view is utilized. Miss Millay is a poet who externalizes her own soul, saying not "I shall feel thus," but "I shall do that."

She carries this dramatization pretty far. Probably her minute dramatic sense has made meter a minor concern with her. It is hard to explain the acceptance of conventional forms by so individual a poet on any other ground. And certainly it affects her diction, making it vehicular only. There is no fine phrasing in anything of Miss Millay's except in a few girlish poems. She never uses a revealing adjective; she prefers the revealing gesture. On this account she is never colorful, and she will seem sterile to some readers when she does not seem shocking to them. From the standpoint of color even *Renascence*, as someone remarked in conversation, is just rain. The later sonnets and lyrics have in their objective accuracy the white and gray of marble or running water. To one who likes purple in his poetry this is unsatisfying, but with re-reading he will get a peculiar satisfaction in the very thing which has made her forsake color for action, painting for sculpture. It dignifies the rather conventional music of her work. To the theme of disillusion and the tone of irony which are now Edna St. Vincent Millay's it brings a fullness of active content which calls one back to re-read, to ponder, to repeat.

Second April

♦

Second April

Maxwell Anderson

When poetry is perfect and moving there is little to be said about it except that it is so; a reviewer can quote it and point to it, and there, unless he should try to rewrite it in prose and thereby make himself ridiculous, his function ends. Not that Edna St. Vincent Millay's *Second April* is above criticism. In common with all other poets of the period she often searches in vain for a subject and at last contents herself with a theme too slight or too fantastic to be worth handling. There is small excuse for *The Blue-Flag in the Bog* or *The Bean-stalk*—none in fact, save the artistry wasted on them. The theme of *Doubt No More That Oberon* is so hackneyed that one is left flatly wondering why it should have been printed. The *Ode to Silence*, the longest venture in the volume, is an artificial ecstasy; exquisite treatment cannot save it.

But *Inland, Wild Swans*, the *Elegy*, and the third of the twelve sonnets are powerful, humanly moving, perfectly touched, said as only a first-class artist could say them. There are other things of nearly equal excellence, and the whole book rises above the tin-pan procession of the usual by virtue of an almost flawless sensitiveness to phrase. Miss Millay, also, is one of the most clear-headed poets who ever put pen to paper. She is akin to Burns in the definiteness of her object and the astonishing accuracy with which she finds the exact homely image to clinch her meaning. This from *Exiled*, for example: "Always I climbed the wave at morning, / Shook the sand from my shoes at night."

Second April resolves a doubt, too, a doubt that the brilliant child of *Renascence* would ever grow up. That she has taken on a woman's stature is best proved by the sonnets. I have space to quote but one:

Reprinted from *The Measure: A Journal of Poetry* 7 (September 1921): 17.

Not with libations, but with shouts and laughter
We drenched the altars of Love's sacred grove,
Shaking to earth green fruits, impatient after
The launching of the colored moths of Love.
Love's proper myrtle and his mother's zone
We bound about our irreligious brows,
And fettered him with garlands of our own,
And spread a banquet in his frugal house.
Not yet the god has spoken; but I fear
Though we should break our bodies in his flame,
And pour our blood upon his altar, here
Henceforward is a grove without a name,
A pasture to the shaggy goats of Pan,
Whence flee forever a woman and a man.

Aria da Capo

♦

Second Thoughts on First Nights:
There Are War Plays and War Plays

ALEXANDER WOOLLCOTT

The week just brought us a pretty good musical comedy, a spiritualistic war play, and a delightful light opera.

A PRETTY GOOD MUSICAL COMEDY

Miss Millions is the name of the aforesaid musical comedy. Arriving Tuesday night at the miniature Punch and Judy, it is the work of R. H. Burnside and Raymond Hubbell, a librettist and composer more accustomed to providing entertainment for a somewhat larger theatre known as the Hippodrome. The Hubbell score from "Miss Millions" is engaging and the company includes Miss Valli Valli of "Dollar Princess" and Cohan revue memories. Miss Valli Valli can act and dance considerably better than she sings.

The Phantom Legion was the war play, which came on Wednesday to the Playhouse—a well-meant piece by Anthony Paul Kelly. It is a spiritualistic drama based on the idea that the allied soldiers were not discharged by death, but that their undemobilized spirits remained on duty to keep up morale and govern their survivors by suggestion. They had ghostly liaison officers and spectral top-kicks and everything. This dreary notion is made dreadful by its sepulchral performance, the arm-waving, hollow-voiced, I-am-thy-father's-ghost performance given at the Playhouse enough to dissipate utterly the considerable store of sentiment the first act accumulates.

Monsieur Beaucaire, the Tarkington romance transformed into a delightful light opera by André Messager, arrived at the New Amsterdam on Thursday night, and proved to be a cause for rejoicing. So graceful and melodious a score does not come to us more than once in a decade, and it is sung almost as well as it deserves to be.

A Fine War Play

When, as with the Provincetown Players, inscrutability is one of the chief props of the establishment, the reviewer's task is likely to grow a trifle complicated. Indeed, in any theatre which can count on comparatively cerebral audiences, a passion for the cryptic is bound to manifest itself from time to time. So in each Macdougal Street bill there are bound to be pieces, which provoke certain low persons in the audience to such mutinous disrespect as greeted Browning's "Sordello," that gorgeously enigmatic poem which Jane Carlyle read with great interest, without, however, being quite sure whether Sordello was a man or a city or a book. Tennyson said that the first line of the poem: "Who will, may hear Sordello's story told," and the last line, "Who would, has heard Sordello's story told," were the only two lines in the poem that he understood and that they were lies. Then there is the story Chesterton tells of its terrible effect on Douglas Jerrold. Poor Jerrold was just turning the corner in a long illness and, having at last wrung from his doctors permission to read a bit each day, chanced upon "Sordello" as his first book. No sooner had he read a little way—than he turned deadly pale, put down the book, and cried: "My God! I'm an idiot: My health is restored, but my mind is gone. I can't understand two consecutive lines of an English poem."

It is with some such sense of a tottering world that our more solid citizens, bred in a laboriously obvious theatre, sometimes grope their way out into the Macdougal Street night, the while the true villagers flutter and twitter entertainingly and sigh with gusty rapture. So it was with the complacent, bottomless mystifications of "Three from the Earth" in the last bill, and so, in a measure, it is with the fairly enigmatic piece called "Aria da Capo," which is the mainstay of the present one. But in this case there are riches of meaning just a little way below the surface. You should see this bitterly ironic little fantasy by Edna St. Vincent Millay. It would not be difficult to defend the statement that, aside from its limitations of production and performance, this is the most beautiful and most interesting play in the English language now to be seen in New York.

It is a study of heart-breaking tragedy considered as an interlude between the laughters of fluffy satiric comedy. Very likely it would pass over the heads of the average unthinking audience, but surely no mother from a gold-starred home, who saw the war come and go like a grotesque comet and who now hears the rattlepated merriment of her neighbors all the more distinctly because of the blank silence in her own impoverished home—surely no such mother will quite miss the point of "Aria da Capo."

The scene is A Stage, which, according to a playwright somewhat greater than any yet produced in Macdougal Street, all the world is. The rising curtain discloses a jolly, harlequinade setting of black and white, with Pierrot and Columbine at table together—toying with their food and their existence. Their idle chatter sets the play going.

COLUMBINE: Pierrot, a macaroon—I cannot live
            Without a macaroon!

PIERROT: My only love,
            You are so intense! * * * Is it Tuesday, Columbine?
            I'll kiss you if it's Tuesday.

COLUMBINE: It is Wednesday
            If you must know. * * * Is this my artichoke,
            Or yours?

PIERROT: Ah, Columbine, as if it mattered. Wednesday. Will it be Tuesday
            then tomorrow
            By any chance?

COLUMBINE: Tomorrow will be * * * Pierrot.
            That isn't funny.

PIERROT: I thought it rather nice.
            Well, let us drink some wine and lose our heads,
            And love each other.

Thus the prattle purls along between the pretty pair—not altogether idle chatter at that, as you may note when, for instance, Pierrot cries out:

            Don't stand so near me,
            I am become a Socialist. I love
            Humanity; but I hate people. Columbine.
            Put on your mittens, child, your hands are cold.

COLUMBINE: My hands are not cold.

PIERROT: Oh, I am sure they are,
            And you must have a shawl to wrap around you
            And sit by the fire!

COLUMBINE: Why, I'll do no such thing;
            I'm hot as a spoon in a teacup.

PIERROT: Columbine.
            I'm a philanthropist. I know I am,
            Because I feel so restless. Do not scream
            Or it will be the worse for you.

COLUMBINE: Pierrot,
            My vinaigrette! I cannot live without

My vinaigrette!

PIERROT: My only love, you are
So fundamental! How would you like to be
An actress, Columbine? I am become
Your manager.

COLUMBINE: Why, Pierrot, I can't act.

PIERROT: Can't act! Can't act, La, listen to the woman!
What's that to do with the price of furs? You're blonde,
Are you not? You have no education, have you?
Can't act! You underrate yourself, my dear.

And so on and so on. It is such random shooting as this which is interrupted by the sudden entrance of Cothurnus as Tragedy, who, prompt-book in hand, bids the pair begone while two youths, Thyrsis and Corydon, are summoned reluctant from their dressing rooms to play their scene. Theirs is a tragedy which begins in pastoral amity. But trouble enters soon.

CORYDON: What say you, Thyrsis, shall we make a song
About a lamb that thought himself a shepherd?

THYRSIS: Why, yes—that is, why no—(I have forgotten my line).

COTHURNUS: "I know a game worth two of that."

THYRSIS: (Oh, yes.) I know a game worth two of that.
Let's gather rocks and build a wall between us,
And say that over there belongs to you
And over here to me.

CORYDON: Why, very well,
And say you may not come upon my side
Unless I say you may?

THYRSIS: Or you on mine!
And if you should, 'twould be the worse for you.

Thus laggard and disinclined, the young players prepare the way for the quarrel, for which they are so indisposed by nature that they must needs be prompted always by the invisible director. Mark how the suggestion comes. Hear Thyrsis say naïvely:

Corydon, after all, and in spite of the fact
I started it myself, I do not like this
So very much. What is the sense of saying
I do not want you on my side of the wall?
It is a silly game. I'd much prefer
Making the song you spoke of making
About the lamb, you know, that thought himself
A shepherd. What do you say?

CORYDON: (I have forgotten the line.)

COTHURNUS: "How do I know this isn't a trick?"

CORYDON: (Oh, yes.) How do I know this isn't a trick
To get upon my land?

THYRSIS: Oh, Corydon,
You know it's not a trick. I do not like
The game, that's all. Come over here, or let me
Come over there.

CORYDON: It is a clever trick
To get upon my land.

Thus, fed from without, the quarrel waxes and at last they slay each other and lie, a limp, pathetic heap, upon the floor, when Columbine and Pierrot come prancing back to play their scene again. It is Columbine who sees the bodies and screams with fear. It is Pierrot who bids Cothurnus drag them out. He and Columbine can't very well sit down and eat with two dead bodies lying under the table, you know. The audience, he explains, would hardly stand for it. Then Cothurnus makes answer:

What makes you think so? Pull down the tablecloth
On the other side, and hide them from the house
And play the farce! The audience will forget.

So they cover up the bodies with the gay table cloth, take their old places, and begin again:

COLUMBINE: Pierrot, a macaroon! I cannot live
Without a macaroon!

PIERROT: My only love.
You are so intense. Is it Tuesday, Columbine?

And so on and so on, as the curtain slowly falls, the same old idle chatter, over and over again, forgetful of the dead youths lying there under the table.

The Lamp and the Bell

◆

Women of Wit [Review of *Poems* by Marianne Moore; *The Lamp and the Bell* by Edna St. Vincent Millay; *Second April* by Edna St. Vincent Millay; and *The Contemplative Quarry and the Man with a Hammer* by Anna Wickham.]

MARK VAN DOREN

For better or for worse these women have contracted marriages with wit, have committed themselves to careers of brains. Seventeenth-century England, where all of the three would have been at home, would have prized them well. Twentieth-century England and America will not do badly to accept their poetry now for better or for worse, since by many a sign it is here to stay a while; almost certainly more of its sort remains to be written and read. It is independent, critical, and keen, a product oftener of the faculties than of the nerves and heart; it is feminine; it is fearless; it is fresh.

The improvement between Miss Millay's first volume of serious poems and her last is remarkable because it has been effected through deliberate exercise of the wits. There never has been any doubt that Miss Millay was a fine poet, but "Renascence" in 1917 had soft spots—a little obscurity, a little sentimentality, a little pose. That "Second April" has virtually none of those things cannot be accounted for merely by the fact that Miss Millay is four years older; she has lived those years brightly and clearly, has done brisk, profitable labor. Her one-act play, "Aria Da Capo," was essentially serious, but it was saved from solemnity by a harlequin-cloak of charming, irresponsible banter which she flung completely around it. Her pamphlet of poems last year, "A Few Figs from Thistles," had sparkle in its passion,

Excerpted from the *Nation* 113 (26 October 1921): 481–82. Reprinted by permission of *The Nation* magazine/The Nation Company, Inc.

even a little smartness. "The Lamp and the Bell," a tragedy, will be best remembered as a delicate riot of gay asides and impeccable metaphors, Elizabethan to the bottom yet not in the least derivative; it bubbles pure poetry. No wonder, then, that "Second April" is intelligent and acceptable; though nothing, of course, can precisely explain its poise, its temper, its sensitive music, and its general justness of feeling. In it sings the voice of a Cavalier for the moment subdued . . .

Two Slatterns and a King. A Moral Interlude

◆

[Review]

BOOKLIST

A fanciful, one-act play in verse, first produced at Vassar college, in which the jade Chance causes the king to marry a slattern instead of the tidy bride he desired. Slight but amusing.

Reprinted from *Booklist* 18 (June 1922): 324.

The Harp-Weaver and Other Poems

◆

Sentiment and Anti-Sentiment

JOHN GOULD FLETCHER

How far a poet can afford to indulge his sentiment in his verses is a question that criticism has not yet answered. It is obvious that every form of sentiment, whether it be the bourgeois one of love for home, mother, wife and children, or the highly Bohemian one of love for one's pipe, glass and mistress, is capable of being stretched to a point where it becomes sentimentality; but where this point lies is a ticklish question. There is a narrow gulf between, let us say, "The Old Oaken Bucket" and "To a Field-Mouse whose Nest Was Turned up by the Plough"—a gulf the perception of which is largely a matter of taste. Poetry, more than any other art except perhaps music, depends upon degrees of feeling which are exceedingly difficult to state in exact terms.

The present generation, especially in its most radical and alert members, has a tendency to pride itself on its lack of sentiment; but I am rather inclined to suspect that anyone who fears and shuns a particular quality is precisely the man who secretly cherishes it to the point of excess. This reflection has been strengthened by the examination of three recent volumes of verse, two of which seem to me to be sentimental, however much they may protest to be otherwise. Curiously enough, it is precisely these two volumes which have won, in contrast to many books of the older generation, a more immediate recognition among the small number of persons who usually read and discuss poetry.

The curious reader, who is capable of overcoming any shock of surprise caused by Mr. E. E. Cummings's syntax, spelling and punctuation, will find this poet's ancestry readily traceable. Here are echoes from Swinburne, Rossetti, the earlier Elizabethans and, above all, the earlier "romantic" manner of Mr. Pound. Mr. Cummings is, I think, more variously gifted

Reprinted from *The Freeman* 8 (30 January 1924): 502.

than Mr. Pound is or was, and could he overcome his desire to startle and mystify, would be considerably a poet: but he is a sentimentalist. Or, to put it in another way, he is a sensualist. All poets, and all other persons, business men or others, whose weakness is that they yield too readily to the appeal of the flesh, are born sentimentalists. Witness Byron. Mr. Cummings, whose volume leads off with an epithalamium which is disorganized Swinburne mated to inchoate Elizabethanism, and who concludes his book with the line "Then you will slowly kiss me," is even more sentimental than Byron. Despite his ingenuity in concealing the fact, he has only one subject and this is woman in her carnal aspect. "Tulips and Chimneys" is an attempt to go over the ground already covered by the first series of "Poems and Ballads"; and like that volume it suffers from an appalling monotony of theme, thought and style.

Miss Edna St. Vincent Millay is as well known among ordinary amateurs in poetry as Mr. Cummings is among the narrower circle of the elect. Yet she, too, is a sentimentalist, though she wears her rue with a difference. The difference is that Miss Millay prefers to appear more ingenuous, more direct, than Mr. Cummings. Where he is a tortured fantast, performing acrobatics on the tightrope of his sensibility, she slides along the string as if she were walking the ground. Take the "Ballad of the Harp-Weaver" for example. Here is, if you like, conscious *naïveté*—the unforgettable rhythm of Mother Goose, the verbal utterance of a primer—all used to deal out an idea which is wishy-washy to the point of intellectual feebleness; an idea without backbone, without integrity. We are deluded by the use of memotechnic devices into reading something that prostitutes our minds to its level. Yet three strong-headed and, for aught I know, highly masculine males proceeded to give this very poem the Pulitzer prize in succession to Mr. Robinson! Truly, sentiment pays.

It is a relief to turn from such works as these to Mr. Bodenheim's latest volume. Here is a ferocious antisentimentalist. I am not sure how much of a poet Mr. Bodenheim is. What I am sure of is that his work is honest—honest to the point of mocking at its own honesty—and that it never mistakes a state of sentiment for one of intense feeling. It does not, like Mr. Cummings, deck out a meretricious attitude in complex phrases, nor like Miss Millay strip the same attitude to pseudosimplicity. Mr. Bodenheim is, as the stinging acidity of his style betrays, less concerned anyway with feeling than with thought. Life is to him a boundless paradox, an irony of defeat, a bitter act of treachery. Alike in his method of writing, his attitude to society at large, and his defiant individualism, he reveals the poet preoccupied with moral, rather than aesthetic, values. Perhaps for that very reason he seems more vital and important when he attempts the lunge and thrust of the eighteenth-century couplet than when he writes in the looser, more diffuse form of free verse.

Distressing Dialogues [by Nancy Boyd]

◆

Dialogues and Spotlights

Henry B. Fuller

A thing may be right enough in one place, yet not so right in another. To apply this truism specifically, a string of pieces may do well enough in a monthly periodical, yet rather less well in the pages of a book. A closer application still: these Dialogues might very satisfactorily have been left uncollected and these Spotlights unfocused.

"Nancy Boyd" is understood to be another manifestation of Miss Millay herself. In the pages of *Vanity Fair* her brief bits produced an effect—they were sprightly and tricksy, even if now and again a trifle earthy. Between covers they are less to be relished. Miss Millay is, of course, capable of exhibiting herself in various phases. Depending on her milieu, which might be a woman's club, a bourgeois drawing-room, or an assembly in the "Village" or in Montparnasse, she has appeared to different observers in different lights: as an angel child, as "a chorus-girl on a holiday," as a "society girl" outdoing society itself, or as the languid and morbid product of a decadent civilization. The present collection permits the unsympathetic to view her as an impish vulgarian, and the loyal to regret the capricious and irresponsible exercise of a high talent on a lower plane. Everything is cleverly done—even here and there with spurts of the inexplicable thing which must be called genius; yet one would be as well pleased if it hadn't been done at all.

The dozen or so writers shepherded by Mr. Farrar of *The Bookman* display wide differences in age, taste, equipment and discretion. The volume shows little unity of texture or of tone. Mr. Farrar's contributors are a discrepant lot: they rise to real criticism; they fall to mere gossip; they sink, far too often, to dubious personalities. The book, while varied and readable, by no means attains a distinguished average, and often displays more knowingness than taste.

From the *New Republic* 41 (7 January 1925): 180–81. Reprinted by permission.

Both these books, to tell the truth, are lively and entertaining enough. But the country is suffering from a surfeit of youthful spirits, facetiousness and facile chatter. The skittish and the jaunty do well enough on occasion, but ought not to be depended upon much longer in our formation of a national attitude.

The King's Henchman

◆

"Stand Back, Pretty Lady"

HENRY SEIDEL CANBY

The gusts of experiment blow through poetry, stirred up by the spinning modern world where beauty grows hard and geometric and ugly mediocrity takes on such significance as to mould verse to its likeness. Poetry, like music, acquires harshness in order to escape the suavity of mere imitation, and clash and clang come back into poetical sound, not echoing the metallic clank of the barbaric age but, like its verse, simulating a reality where noise is excitement and living beautifully is not to live at all. We have moods of realism in our poetry, and rightly; we have disjointed, broken rhythms, which synchronize, though unwittingly, with the partial, disconnected generalizations of science that flash truths but never truth. We write poetry of reminiscence in moulds whose patterns are long since shattered, charming the fancy but feeding the imagination on mist wreaths and perfumed smoke. This is the history of poetry and the "way of development" and "the inevitable sequence"—with its most unwelcome novelties often nearest, perhaps, to the curve of hope, and its pleasing memories no more substantial than those faint echoes of an age of energy in the last of the brood of Tennyson.

But the lyric emotion is timeless. The ideas which stir it up into the light, and also its mood, are temporal, but not its essential quality of beauty made personal. And the true lyricists of every period are a brotherhood separated in time but so alike in the source of their emotion that the symbols which they use for the life about them are interchangeable without loss of reality. Keats can sing of Provençal mirth, and Tennyson of chivalry, and Housman can be Latin in his brevity; and Masefield moves from Tyrian galleys to dirty British traders and back again to the Roman legions.

Miss Millay's play, which is probably a better play than a libretto—it is too good line for line to be lost in opera—belongs to lyric poetry of the

From the *Saturday Review of Literature* 3 (19 March 1972): 661. Reprinted by permission.

timeless order. The scene is Anglo-Saxon, the diction is as pre-Norman and pre-French, and pre-Latin as she could make it; not a hint of the modern world does she allow herself in scene, character, or language. But as literature it is no more Anglo-Saxon than Shakespeare's "Antony and Cleopatra" is Græco-Roman, the English of it is closer to Wycliffe than to Cynewulf, the characters, if they are placed historically at all, belong in love-sick Provence of the twelfth century rather than in England of the tenth. The legend she borrows from England of the dark ages, the ethics from the great love tradition of the medievals, the spirit is her own.

I do not mean that the restrictions of language and scene that she has accepted are unimportant. The modern who finds his way into the true fairyland of the eternal lyric cry, must bind his eyes and follow a narrow path. Shakespeare, the greatest of lyric dramatists in English, has hung like the curse of greatness past over most modern attempts to suck sweetness and poignancy from legend and history. They have all written like him who have felt pure song for lyric action—even Browning when most lyrical. Some intuition warned Miss Millay, and by forswearing all the piled up riches of the tongue acquired through nine centuries, and writing in words which in their own day made only rough prose or barbaric music, she has achieved a style which is by no means Anglo-Saxon, but unShakespearian; neither modern (as a lyric should never be) nor archaic either.

> The turn of thy head, thy speaking,
> Is like a thing found,
> To a man seeking.

Or

> Lost, lost,
> Forgotten and lost,
> Out of sight, out of sound!
> Letting the sun ride by, with his golden helmet,
> And all his flashing spears and his flags outstreaming,—
> Ride by, ride by, ride by,
> Shaking the ground!

Or

> Oh, Cæsar, great wert thou!
> And Hadrian was thy name!
> Thine eye did itch till a Roman ditch
> Was dug in British shame!
> But I would not stand in thy stead,
> For I'd liefer be quick than dead!

Cæsar thy day is done!
While ours is but begun!

The idea of the singing song last quoted is quite unhistorical, impossible either in mood or in conception to an Anglo-Saxon; that of course is of little importance; the language is as far from the Anglo-Saxons as the thought, but it *is* the language of the timeless lyric, traditional, expressive, personal all in one. There is no better instance of freedom gained by the refusal of liberty.

I have implied, and should say outright, that Miss Millay's poetry in "The King's Henchman" has the quality of a classic and should be judged as such. One does not look for nuances of modern feeling in it, nor new tones expressive of new notes in the industrialized world. She has endeavored to write in the diction understood of those to whom the twelfth century and the Ming dynasty are as real as the Concord of Emerson or the Pennsylvania Terminal, and it seems that she has succeeded.

The extent of her success is a different question. The exigency of writing for music and the slow drama of an opera have not harmed her play. The melody of language is her gift, and the simplicity required by song has not driven her to flatness as would be the case with many another poet. Indeed, one suspects that she has given way nowhere, and that many of her lines have a crispness in the reading that the music must necessarily mar and be marred by. Nor are the broad brush strokes of opera characterization unfavorable to a lyric drama, poignant but not subtle, unless in its inner meanings. A full expression of a simple lyric emotion is what she aimed at and what she has achieved.

If there are limitations that derogate, they are her own and not assumed. This is an intensely feminine play. Ethelwold, the woman-hating hero, terrible in battle, is bemisted in an instant of magic night into a lover who is a woman's ideal, and indeed a woman. Only Eadgar the King is right masculine and his lines were laid down by a hundred romances. This is a lyric weakness, excusable in opera, where sentiment is at a premium, yet a dramatic loss. As so often in modern literature, where women are beginning to contribute the most finely wrought fiction, the man suffers, embodying the woman's wish rather than male necessity. If Ethelwold has been a princess rival instead of a traitorous henchman, Miss Millay's drama would have a better right to place among the great. She cannot do a man as Shakespeare could do Juliet or Cleopatra.

Yet, essentially, "The King's Henchman" is a woman's drama. This is its link with time, our own time, and specifically Miss Millay's time, which, like all good lyric, it transcends but does not escape.

This play is the story of a futile woman who sells love for excitement. It is as much a story of modern futility as Hemingway's "The Sun Also Rises," though so much less explicit and so much more complete in expressiveness. The medieval theme, which Chaucer would have understood, is of Iseult who risked all for love of a man, or Cresseid who destroyed herself for love of many men. But Ælfrida is a different breed. Her emotions are more esthetic than biological. She yields herself to a magic moonlight and the poetic need of a lover, but to show herself beloved and beautiful is soon a stronger motive; she must go to Ghent where the fashions are new, she cannot be ugly even to save her husband's life, her heart is too narrow for a great love, and her spirit too restless for a present happiness. Her candle must burn at both ends, and hence she is ruinous to men; she fouls their blood; she is beautiful but at the end nothing; the play leaves her to bewail the better dead.

"The King's Henchman" is the tragedy of a neurotic woman. Friendship of men, it says, is worth more than the lyric love, half angel and half bird, which flits so eerily through the moonlight but turns to vanity in the sun. Yet if this is the dramatic weakness of a play which gives us woman's loves in man's guises, it is its lyric strength, for there is that fragile intensity in the climactic love making of Æthelwold and Aelfrida, which gives to poetry the note of beauty not to be held which the lyric always seeks. And behind the poetry is the beautiful scorn and beautiful regret of a person, alive, in time, who sings for herself and to relieve her own *saeva indignatio* a timeless story in timeless verse.

So much for stricture and interpretation. For the great beauty of "The King's Henchman" we can only be thankful.

The Buck in the Snow

◆

Song from Thistles

LOUIS UNTERMEYER

This, Miss Millay's first collection of poems in five years, is her thinnest volume physically and, alas, poetically. Not that her technique fails—Miss Millay does not know how to write a bad poem—but there is a change in pitch that may be ascribed to a tenuousness of mood or a thinning of timbre. The rich sonority of "Renascence" and "Second April," that warm vibration which stirred the air with the first syllables of the unnamed sonnets, has dwindled to a music that no longer celebrates eager dawn or headlong day but is tuned, with wry resignation, to the beginning of evening. The key, for the most part, is minor; the lines pronounce it over and over. "Gone, gone again is Summer the lovely." "We have forgotten where we are." "Only the bobolink . . . knows my heart, for whom adversity has not a word to say that can be heard above the din. . . . The rain has taught us nothing." "Now goes under, and I watch it go under, the sun that will not rise again." "Here where the rain has darkened and the sun has dried so many times." "Forever over now, forever, forever gone. . . ." Never has Miss Millay plucked so insistently on the autumnal string; never has she been so preoccupied with the water darkening, with the ceaseless "action of waves and the action of sorrow," with the lonely self and "the wind at the flue."

This is also the most uneven of the poet's volumes. I have said that Miss Millay could not write a bad poem, but here once in a while (as in the third-rate Housman "The Road to Avrillé) she almost succeeds. "The Buck in the Snow" shows evidences of a not too critical inclusiveness, even of a repetition of effects as well as material. "Mist in the Valley" is a throw-back; with "These hills to hurt me more that am hurt already enough" the anger attempts to summon the same poignance of "God's World" in which the hurt of beauty was exceeded only by its overpowering radiance.

From the *Saturday Review of Literature* 5 (13 October 1928): 209. Reprinted by permission.

But, apart from determining worst and best, there is something here that will surprise Miss Millay's admirers and interest her fellow-craftsmen. And that is Miss Millay's experiments in a (for her) new technique. The most obvious of these is the lengthening and increased flexibility of her line. No longer confined to tight couplets and casual quatrains, the lyricist has achieved an unusual set of suspensions and cadences by combining free verse and, occasionally, prose rhythms with balanced measures. Rhyme is dropped into these passages like an unexpected largesse. The result is a delightful—and definite—accomplishment. Merely as an example, the title-poem proves this:

> White sky, over the hemlocks bowed with snow,
> saw you not at the beginning of evening the antlered buck
>   and his doe
> Standing in the apple-orchard? I saw them. I saw them
>   suddenly go,
> Tails up, with long leaps, lovely and slow,
> Over the stone wall into the wood of hemlocks bowed
>   with snow.
>
> Now he lies here, his wild blood scalding the snow.
>
> How strange a thing is death, bringing to his knees, bring-
>   ing to his antlers
> The buck in the snow.
> How strange a thing,—a mile away by now, it may be,
> Under the heavy hemlocks that as the moments pass
> Shift their load a little, letting fall a feather of snow—
> Life, looking out attentive from the eyes of the doe.

Less noticeable but no less worthy of notice is the way the poet repeats, twists, and half turns the same phrase so that the words (as in Mac Leish's later poems and in the longer ones of Eliot) add to their literal quality a bell-like insistence. "Dirge without Music" and "The Cameo" are particularly skilful in their distribution and shifting of emphasis. Lastly—still speaking from the narrow technical angle—there is the broadening of this poet's musical gamut. She has begun to sound the possibilities of assonance and "slant" rhymes. In the quaint "Counting-Out Rhyme" the triplets revolve about "sallow-yellow-willow," "maple-apple-popple," "moonbeam-barn-beam-hornbeam." The last two verses of "The Hardy Garden" felicitously mingle dissonance and a final full rhyme:

> See here the phlox and the iris, and establish
>   Pink and valerian, and the great and lesser bells;

But suffer not the sisters of the year to publish
  That frost prevails.

How far from home in a world of mortal burdens
  Is love that may not die and is forever young!
Set roses here: surround her only with such maidens
  As speak her tongue.

If I imply that Miss Millay has grown detached, it is not to suggest that her ecstasy is abstract in the essential way that Léonie Adams's is abstract. Miss Millay's metaphysics remain personal; she is still too much in love with lost love and the frail hawkweed, with the shards of a broken pot, the memory of dusty almonds and a world forgotten, the trodden grape and the minutiæ of the unrelinquishing mortal mind. Even so "general" a poem on death as the lengthy "Morituris" proceeds from a sense of personal struggle. A concluding segment is indicative of the mood:

Withstanding death
  Till life be gone,
I shall treasure my breath,
  I shall linger on.

I shall bolt my door
  With a bolt and cable;
I shall block my door
  With bureau and table;

With all my might
  My door shall be barred.
I shall put up a fight,
  I shall take it hard.

With his hand on my mouth
  He shall drag me forth,
Shrieking to the south
  And clutching at the north.

But exception must be made in the case of a small portion of the volume, especially the group which brings the book to its ascending close. These seven sonnets justify all that has gone before; a reputation might be built on "The Pioneer," the powerful and ironic "Sonnet to Gath," the moving "Grow not too high, grow not too far from home," and the magnificent "On Hearing a Symphony of Beethoven." In the last, Miss Millay has done the impossible: she has not only written that rarest of things, a successful poem on a symphony, she has held, in fourteen lines, the music, the orchestra, the audience, and the triumphant catharsis which is Beethoven. I quote it as climax:

Sweet sounds, oh, beautiful music, do not cease!
Reject me not into the world again.
With you alone is excellence and peace,
Mankind made plausible, his purpose plain.
Enchanted in your air benign and shrewd,
With limbs a-sprawl and empty faces pale,
The spiteful and the stingy and the rude
Sleep like the scullions in the fairy-tale.
This moment is the best the world can give:
The tranquil blossom on the tortured stem.
Reject me not, sweet sounds! oh, let me live,
Till Doom espy my towers and scatter them,
A city spell-bound under the aging sun,
Music my rampart, and my only one.

This is a double victory. Here the poet fixes and subjugates her evanescent material—and overcomes her own limitations. The triumph is complete in every way: the sonnet rises above its almost fatal first line, its inversions, its generalities. Even its rhetoric, instead of a handicap, becomes an integrating tone in the composition.

It is such authority of idea and utterance that makes one forget the too easily accomplished verse-making, the only half-illuminated concepts. It is the complete realization of something beyond the shaping of words that puts permanence into at least a score of Edna St. Vincent Millay's best. Had she written nothing but "Renascence" and "God's World," with which she made her startling debut, the "Elegy" of her college period, the somewhat later "Wild Swans" and "The Poet and His Book," three or four of the Shakespearian sonnets (among which the Beethoven would stand second) and the comparatively little known "Aria da Capo," she would be sure of her distinguished (and much worshipped) niche not only in America but in English letters. Such poetry reflects the paradox of its being: it is immediate and it is immutable.

Fatal Interview.
Sonnets by Edna St. Vincent Millay

◆

Miss Millay's Sonnets

ALLEN TATE

More than any other living American poet, with the exception possibly of T. S. Eliot, Miss Millay has puzzled her critics. Contrary to the received opinion, her poetry is understood even less than Eliot's, in spite of its greater simplicity, its more conventional meters and its closer fulfilment of the popular notion of what the language of poetry should be. Of contemporary poets whose excellence is beyond much dispute, she is the most difficult to appraise. She is the most written about, but her critics are partisans: they like her too well or not enough. There is something like worship here, patronage or worse there; both views are unjust; and what is worse, they are misleading. Less interested readers of her verse are tired of violent opinion; the more skeptical, perhaps, are put off by her popularity in an age of famously indifferent taste.

This, too, is misleading. Apart from her merit as a poet, Miss Millay is, not at all to her discredit, the spokesman of a generation. It does not behoove us to enquire how she came to express the feelings of the literary generation that seized the popular imagination from about 1917 to 1925. It is a fact that she did, and in such a way as to remain as its most typical poet. Her talent, with its diverting mixture of solemnity and levity, won the enthusiasm of a time bewildered intellectually and moving unsteadily towards an emotional attitude of its own. It was the age of The Seven Arts, of the old Masses, of the Provincetown Theatre, of the figure and disciples of

From the *New Republic* 66 (6 May 1931): 335–36. Reprinted by permission. "Leda and the Swan" reprinted with permission of Macmillan Publishing Company from THE POEMS OF W. B. YEATS: A NEW EDITION, edited by Richard J. Finneran. Copyright 1928 by Macmillan Publishing Company, renewed 1956 by Georgie Yeats.

Randolph Bourne. It has been called the age of experiment and liberation; there is still experiment, but no one is liberated; and that age is now dead.

Miss Millay helped to form that generation, and was formed by it. But she has survived her own time. Her statement about those times, in "A Few Figs from Thistles" and "Second April," was not, taken philosophically, very profound; morally, it has been said, it did perceptible damage to our young American womanhood, whose virgin impatience competed noisily with the Armistice and the industrial boom. There were suicides after "Werther" and seductions after "Don Juan." Neither Byron nor Miss Millay is of the first order of poets. They are distinguished examples of the second order, without which literature could not bear the weight of Dante and Shakespeare, and without which poetry would dry up of insensibility.

Being this kind of poet, Miss Millay was not prepared to give to her generation a philosophy in comprehensive terms; her poetry does not define the break with the nineteenth century. This task was left to the school of Eliot, and it was predictable that this school should be—except by young men who had the experience to share Eliot's problem—ignored and misunderstood. Eliot penetrated to the fundamental structure of the nineteenth-century mind and showed its breakdown. Miss Millay assumed no such profound alteration of the intelligence because, I suppose, not being an intellect but a sensibility, she was not aware of it. She foreshadowed an age without bringing it to terms. Taking the vocabulary of nineteenth-century poetry as pure as you will find it in Christina Rossetti, and drawing upon the stock of conventional symbolism accumulated from Drayton to Patmore, she has created, out of shopworn materials, a distinguished personal idiom: she has been able to use the language of the preceding generation to convey an emotion peculiar to her own.

The generation of decadence—Moody, Woodberry and Louise Imogene Guiney—had more than Miss Millay has; but she has all that they had which was not dead. By making their language personal she has brought it back to life. This is her distinction. It is also her limitation. As a limitation it is not peculiar to her, her age or any age, but common to all; it is the quality that defines Collins and Gray, and, in the next century, poets like the Rossettis and Tennyson. Poets of this second order lack the power of creation in the proper sense in which something like a complete world is achieved, either in the vast, systematic vision of Milton, or in the allusive power of Webster and Shakespeare where, backed only by a piece of common action, an entire world is set up in a line or even in a single phrase. In these poets the imaginative focus is less on the personal emotion than on its substructure, an order of intellectual life, and thus their very symbolism acquires not only a heightened significance but an independent existence of its own. Not so with Miss Millay; we feel that she never penetrates to the depth of her symbols, but uses them chiefly as a frame of reference, an adornment to the tale. It has been frequently and quite justly remarked that Miss Millay uses her classical symbols perhaps better than any other living poet; we should add, I believe, that she uses them conventionally better. She takes them literally, subtracting from them always only what serves her metaphor; whereas even a modern like Yeats is capable, in his sonnet "Leda," of that violent addition to the content of the symbol as he finds it which is the mark of great poetry.

Miss Millay's success with stock symbolism is precariously won. I have said that she is not an intellect but a sensibility: if she were capable of a profound analysis of her imagery she might not use it: such an analysis might disaffect her with the style that she so easily assumed, without necessarily leading her, as Yeats was led in mid-career, to create a new style of her own. The beautiful final sonnet of the sequence is a perfect specimen of her talent; and it is probably the finest poem she has written:

> Oh, sleep forever in the Latmian cave,
> Mortal Endymion, darling of the moon!
> Her silver garments by the senseless wave
> Shouldered and dropped and on the shingle strewn,
> Her fluttering hand against her forehead pressed,
> Her scattered looks that trouble all the sky,
> Her rapid footsteps running down the west—
> Of all her altered state, oblivious lie!
> Whom earthen you, by deathless lips adored,
> Wild-eyed and stammering to the grasses thrust,
> And deep into her crystal body poured
> The hot and sorrowful sweetness of the dust:
> Whereof she wanders mad, being all unfit
> For mortal love, that might not die of it.

We have only to compare this, magnificent as it is, with Mr. Yeats's "Leda" to see the difference between the two kinds of symbol that I have described. The difference is first of all one of concentration and intensity; and finally a difference between an accurate picture of an emotion and an act of the imagination:

> A sudden blow: the great wings beating still
> Above the staggering girl, her thighs caressed
> By the dark webs, her nape caught in his bill,
>
> He holds her helpless breast upon his breast.
> How can those terrified vague fingers push
> The feathered glory from her loosening thighs?
> And how can body, laid in that white rush
> But feel the strange heart beating where it lies?
> A shudder in the loins engenders there

> The broken wall, the burning roof and tower
> And Agamemnon dead.
>
> Being so caught up,
> So mastered by the brute blood of the air,
> Did she put on his knowledge with his power
> Before the indifferent beak could let her drop?

In an age which, in Mr. Pound's phrase, has "demanded an image"; an age which has searched for a new construction of the mind, and has, in effect, asked every poet for a chart of salvation, it has been forgotten that one of the most valuable kinds of poetry may be deficient in imagination, and yet be valuable for the manner in which it meets its own defect. Miss Millay not only has given the personality of her age, but has preserved it in the purest traditional style. There are those who will have no minor poets; these Miss Millay does not move. The others, her not too enthusiastic but perhaps misguided partisans, have seen too much of their own personalities in her verse to care whether it is great poetry or not; so they call it great.

It is doubtful if all of Miss Millay's previous work put together is worth the thin volume of these fifty-two sonnets. At no previous time has she given us so sustained a performance. Half of the sonnets, perhaps all but about fifteen, lack distinction of emotional quality. None is deficient in an almost final technique. From first to last every sonnet has it special rhythm and sharply defined imagery; they move like a smooth machine, but not machine-like, under the hand of a masterly technician. The best sonnets would adorn any of the great English sequences. There is some interesting analysis to be made of Miss Millay's skillful use of the Shakespearean form, whose difficult final couplet she has mastered, and perhaps is alone in having mastered since Shakespeare.

The serious, austere tone of her later work must not deceive us: she is the poet of ten years ago. She has been from the beginning the one poet of our time who has successfully stood athwart two ages; she has put the personality of her age into the intellect and style of the preceding one, without altering either. Of her it may be said, as of the late Elinor Wylie, that properly speaking she has no style, but has subtly transformed to her use the indefinable average of poetic English. We have seen the limitations of this order of talent. When the personal impulse lags in a mind that cannot create a symbol and invent a style, we get the pastiche of "The Buck in the Snow": the defects of such a talent are defects of taste, while the defects of Blake are blunders. Let us say no more of it. Miss Millay is one of our most distinguished poets, and one that we should do well to misunderstand as little as possible.

The Princess Marries the Page

♦

[Review]

TIMES LITERARY SUPPLEMENT

This little play was written, Miss Millay tells us, when she was an undergraduate at Vassar College and was actually begun several years before. It is, therefore, one of her earliest literary efforts. As such it is extraordinarily deft and accomplished and reveals how precocious was the verbal mastery which she has applied in her later lyrics to the emotional conflicts and experiences of adult life. The conflict in this play and its resolution is quite artificial, but it is charmingly contrived. The Page who seeks sanctuary in the Princess's room is in fact the son of a neighbouring and hostile king and he has been sent to spy out a secret entrance to the castle and let the enemy in. But love for the Princess has stayed his hand and her love for him saves his head. Their innocent love-making is delightfully childish, and both of them have just sufficiently stepped out of a fairy-story to be at once enchanting and natural. The dialogue is light and vivacious and comedy frequently sweetens romance. That the play is actable is proved by four successful productions, but its quality is best suggested by Miss Millay's own comment on re-reading it after thirteen years—"It was unmistakably a youthful work, and very slight, but I thought it rather pretty."

From *Times Literary Supplement* (London) (29 December 1932): 990. Copyright 1932 and reprinted by permission of Times Newspapers Limited.

Wine from These Grapes

◆

Conversion Into Self

LOUISE BOGAN

The phenomenon of conversion in the artist has increased in frequency and desperate intention within our time. In any period, at maturity, the break between the artist's early instinctive adjustment or lack of adjustment to a limiting world, and his later more conscious and rational choices, bred out of experience, must be accomplished. The poet, particularly, as he matures, is faced with the antagonisms of complexity and loss: if he is capable of any growth he has more intimations to synthesize and more disorganization to bear, while comforting delusion softens the brutality of each new crisis, as it arises, with lessened power. Our time presses this individual battle into an unbearably tight compass and gives it no aid. The once nourishing and adaptable systems of worship are reduced to the flatness of myth or the mania of superstition; the current social order collapses, as it arose, without dignity; a new order forms based on rigid mass dogma, inimical to isolation and sensitive individual variation alike. The poet realizes only too clearly how diminished he appears, seen against the general let-down and break-up, if he keeps to his proper arena; and it is natural that, in many cases, he turns in panic from his natural place and seeks asylum in the general turmoil.

It is possible, however, now as always, for the poet to fight it out within the field of his own work, to express himself and his period within his own function, skirting the evils of escape and absorption. The conversion into his later, out of his earlier, self, without reference to modern or ancient idiocies, continues to be a problem worthy of his entire powers. Yeats is the great example of a poet who fronted the grappling world, yet kept his eye, his mind, and his hand free for the act of continual maturing creation. In her latest book, *Wine from These Grapes*, Edna Millay at last gives evidence that

From *Poetry* 45 (February 1935): 277–79. Copyright 1935 by The Modern Poetry Association and reprinted by permission of the Editor of *Poetry* and with permission of Ruth Limmer, literary executor.

she recognizes and is prepared to meet the task of becoming a mature and selfsufficing woman and artist. It is a task she never completely faced before, in spite of the maturity-beyond-her-years which her remarkable endowment threw, from time to time, into the current of her work. And it is a task from which, in *Fatal Interview*, she definitely fled away. Those sonnets, extraordinary in execution as they were, she based on the immature impulse to experience beyond the limits of experience, to inflate the mortal passion of love into extravagant proportions. Malraux, in *La Condition Humaine*, defines this tendency in one of his characters: ". . . il ne pouvait vieillir: l'âge ne le menait pas à l'experience humaine mais à l'intoxication . . . où se conjugueraient enfin tous ses moyens d'ignorer la vie."

In *Wine from These Grapes* maturity sounds strongly, though intermittently. The accent chagrin and desperation, both resolved and unresolved, is there—the sound of bitter thought, of meditation, of solitude, of the clear, disabused and unexcited mind. To this tone we can give our whole attention and respect. Miss Millay's native and inalienable power over meter and epithet retains its force; her lapses into mere lyrical prettiness are more infrequent. One feels, as always, that she has included poems merely experimental, in order to fill up the bulk of a book. But she has crossed the line, made the break, passed into regions of cold and larger air. If this reviewer scants the critical duty of definiteness, and neglects to give chapter and verse for this claim, it is because the book exists and deserves to be consulted as a whole. Briefly, the *kind* of intimation and mood felt and projected in *The Return, From a Train Window, Desolation Dreamed Of, How Naked, How Without a Wall,* and *The Oak Leaves* is neither young nor transitional, but grown. And the sonnet sequence, *Epitaph for the Race of Man*, figures forth at length a mature disaffection which Miss Millay has never before sustained.

Flowers of Evil [Translation from the French of Charles Baudelaire, with George Dillon]

◆

Baudelaire in English

Arnold Whitridge

When Sainte-Beuve accused Baudelaire of "Petrarchising on the horrible" he was really laying his finger on the quality in Baudelaire that has endeared him to posterity. Certainly no French poet has had such a lasting influence on foreign literature. Racine is too exclusively French to be universal; he defies translation altogether. La Fontaine can be translated but the result is very small beer. Victor Hugo brings little into English literature with which it is not already familiar. It is only Baudelaire who actually gains in prestige when he crosses the frontier. He gathered flowers where no one had ever looked for flowers before, and if the perfume is acrid it is all the more satisfying to generations that have grown weary of the conventional sweetness of romantic poetry.

The best proof of Baudelaire's vitality is that poets as different as Aldous Huxley, T. S. Eliot, and Edna St. Vincent Millay all find in him a confirmation of their own attitude towards life. "In 'Les Fleurs du Mal' " says Huxley, "the modern finds all his own sufferings described—with what incomparable energy, in forms how memorably beautiful!" T. S. Eliot is attracted to Baudelaire because "he gave new possibilities to poetry in a new stock of imagery of contemporary life," which is precisely what Eliot himself has done, and also because, again like Eliot, "he perceived that what really matters is sin and redemption."

Miss Millay is impressed by a slightly different aspect of Baudelaire's genius. For her he is primarily "a poet of the intellect, a lover of order, of perfection in form, . . . a poet who proposed to conquer ugliness by making

From the *Yale Review* 25 (June 1936): 821–23. Copyright 1936 by Yale University and reprinted by permission.

beauty of it." These are the aspects of his poetry that are reflected in the present translation. Of the 129 poems of the 1861 edition, the last to be published in Baudelaire's lifetime, the present translation contains 72, of which 37 are signed by Miss Millay and 35 by Mr. Dillon. Not merely have they translated the bulk of "Les Fleurs du Mal" but they have attempted to reproduce in every instance the metre and form used by Baudelaire in the original poem. By this means the authors believe that though individual poems may have been pretty roughly handled "the anatomy at least is still intact." The result is certainly interesting though it may be questioned whether the anatomical structure of a poem is ever the same after the poem has been hauled out of its native habitat, however carefully the rhyme schemes and stresses are preserved in the new surroundings. After all, the genius of a language is not to be denied. An alexandrine in English is very different in its effect upon the ear from an alexandrine in French, and no matching of stresses can make it the same. Certainly Miss Millay and Mr. Dillon have produced some lovely poetry but in their determination to maintain Baudelaire's outward appearance they have sometimes sacrificed the rigor of his thought. Occasionally they have almost prettified him. Baudelaire's "le corps brulé de secrètes chaleurs" is metamorphosed into "a slim body secretly aflame for love." In the same way the ghastly prayer, "Ah! Seigneur! donnez-moi la force et le courage/De contempler mon coeur et mon corps sans dégoût!" becomes "Almighty God! Give me the courage and the power/To contemplate my own true image without disgust!"—which somehow misses the naked intensity of the original. No one can complain that these translations are inaccurate but the temper of them is not the temper of Baudelaire.

"Les Fleurs du Mal" is the product of an intellectual aristocrat, of a dandy who had lost himself in Bohemia. If he chose to masquerade as Satan he was always a very exquisite Satan who impressed his contemporaries with his lofty politeness and his "froideur britannique." This is a side of him that Miss Millay and Mr. Dillon are too much inclined to ignore. To translate "Ce pays nous ennuie, ô Mort! Appareillons!" as "We've seen this country, Death; We're sick of it! Let's go!" is to make him too modern. It suggests that Baudelaire was a rollicking good fellow who might at any moment have slapped you on the back, whereas actually he would have shuddered at any such familiarity. Nor would he ever have said "We all have our weak moments, eh?" which is Mr. Dillon's translation for "Nous sommes tous plus ou moins fous!" The Baudelaire of this translation is altogether too easygoing. In his English dress he never makes us feel as he did his friend Barbey d'Aurevilly, that there were only two courses open to him—either he must blow his brains out or become a Christian.

This is not to say that the translators have failed. Some of their renderings, in particular the translation of "La Cloche Fêlée" and "Le Gout du

Néant," are extraordinarily beautiful. Nevertheless, those of us who believe that Edna St. Vincent Millay is one of the greatest lyric poets of our day will begrudge the time she has spent conveying Baudelaire into English. The author of "Fatal Interview" is too vivid, too individual a genius, to act as a conductor for another poet, even when that poet happens to be Baudelaire.

Conversation at Midnight

◆

Conversations of Our Time: Edna St. Vincent Millay's Tapestry of Contemporary Themes

PETER MONRO JACK

The admirers of Miss Millay's early "personality" poems and the designed perfectitude of her later sonnets may not take easily to this new book of hers. It is a sparkling piece of writing, worldly, mature, objective and dramatic; but it is extremely irregular in form and obviously quite inconclusive in its argument. It is very far indeed from the seacoast of her first Bohemia and it has little to do with the somewhat arrogant eloquence of her "Epitaph for the Race of Man." It is neither naïvely philosophical nor philosophically naïve, as her earliest and latest poems have tended to be. It offers no easy solution in romantic adventure or surrender or protest or disillusion. It does not "sing," it does not always rhyme, it does not invariably delight the senses, and it often offends one's carefully cultivated and proprietary taste in poetry. It is as modest in its aims as it is intelligent in its direction; and still it takes its place—for the first time, perhaps, in Miss Millay's spectacular career—easily and well in the logic of contemporary poetry.

As a conversation piece its variety of character and colloquialism suits contemporary poetry admirably. The time is the present, the place is New York, the scene is a house in Tenth Street, the hour is after dinner— Bourbon, Scotch, Irish, or wine—and the persons are: a stockbroker, a painter, a successful writer of short stories, a poet who is also a Communist, a Roman Catholic priest, a young man in the advertising business, and a liberal and agnostic host who may, *ad lib.*, be Miss Millay herself, and who allows the talk to take whatever turn it chooses.

From the *New York Times Book Review*, 25 July 1937, Sect. 7, pp. 1 & 12. Copyright 1937 by The New York Times Company. Reprinted by permission.

The conversation runs yet deviously and discontinuously and yet with
a sense of purpose through the subjects that any seven men might discourse
on (one should note that Miss Millay avoids any absolute professionalism—
there is no philosopher or scientist in the group, no one who could settle
deductively or inductively the rights of the argument: the discourse is a
free-for-all on a strictly amateur basis, always with the exception of the
Communist), and the subjects are in turn hunting and fishing, women,
religion and politics, music, art, anecdotes, acquaintances in common, business, and again politics. None of the characters makes any great headway
with his knowledge or rhetoric. It is the variety that counts, the dramatic
interplay of contemporary opinion, neither too ignorant nor too specialized,
the one man's meat and the other man's poison, vividly and immediately
realized in conversation, liberally and agnostically, and sometimes despair-
ingly, described in character.

The stockbroker, Merton, is the character who rides most easily through
the book. He is very fairly pictured as a representative of the capitalistic
class, wealthy, oldish, energetic, well read, reasonable but set in his opinions.
His most charming moments are when he remembers a river he has fished,
but he is very alert when it comes to an argument. Carl, the Communist,
considers him as his natural enemy. So far as there is a real clash in the
conversation it is between the capitalist and the Communist. The conversation ends at 2 in the morning with both nearly coming to blows, though
the amenities are preserved, of course, by the host. But the one knows what
he has and the other knows what he wants. Each has the other's number,
exactly, and in no uncertain terms. Merton says:

> Oh, God, why live, to breathe a prescribed and rationed air!—All free
> Opinion, all interchange of vigorous thought, suffocated
> By the poisonous motor-exhaust of motor minds!
> Passion regimented; curiosity regimented; endeavor regimented;
> Culture, and grace, and all the things I cared for
> Equally divided among the mob, and sauced to their taste!

And Carl promptly answers:

> You, an individual?—you, you regimented mouse?
> You Harvard Club, Union Club, white tie for the opera, black tie for
>   the theatre,
> Trouser legs a little wider this year, sir,
> I would suggest dark blue instead of black, sir,
> Pumps are no longer worn, sir,
> Mah-Jongg, cross-word, anagram, backgammon, whist, bridge, auction,
>   contract, regimented mouse!
> Why, you're so accustomed to being flanked to right and left by people
>   just like yourself

That if they ever should step aside you couldn't stand up! . . .
You, an individual?
You salad for luncheon, soup for dinner,
Maine for Summer, Florida for Winter,
Wife-pampering dog-worshiper!

Between these extremes, in which the verse breaks into a noisy bick-
ering, is the patient faith of the priest which can convince no one and who
leaves early, unable to stem or abide the rising tide of argument; the gentle
manners of the host, Ricardo, who has no hope for the world, a gentler
Jeffers, who says, "Let us abdicate now; let us disintegrate quietly here,
convivially imbibing / The pleasanter poisons" the earthy splendor of Pygmalion, the successful writer of short stories who has his bawdy stories to tell
and his many conquests to make before he gives up anything for a hypothetical
next world, on this planet or another; the wistful desires of John, the painter,
who would like to believe in the gods that have been taken from him; the
clouded vision of the clear-eyed advertising man whose present trouble is the
lack of love: between the extremes of political panaceas Miss Millay inserts,
deftly and at the same time defiantly, the recognizable routine of life that
makes life livable. It is neither the fascism in us, nor the communism, that
rules our lives, but the liberalism that reconciles both and makes possible a
host like this Ricardo, who will hear all sides, hoping and waiting for the
best, dreading and awaiting the worst, but still certain that his uncertainty
is the best future for the world.

This is not to say Miss Millay's attitude. But the excellence of her
present poetry is that it has almost entirely freed itself from the nice or neat
egotism that has beset her sonnets like a good fairy's blessing, and that it
has brought a privateness of feeling into a world of thought. Her public talk
is a necessary test of present-day poetry, and we dare to say that it takes its
place, in its own way, with Pound's "Cantos," Eliot's "The Waste Land,"
Crane's "The Bridge," Auden's "The Orators," Wyndham Lewis's "One-
Way Song," MacLeish's "Frescoes for Mr. Rockfeller's City," or with "The
Secret" of Arthur Davison Ficke (to whom the volume is dedicated) and the
"Nightmares" (in "Burning City") of Stephen Vincent Benét.

All of these for the moment have given up the narrow and personal
dictatorship of the lyric and have attempted to give poetry a meaning beyond
their pleasure in sound and sense effect. Of course Miss Millay has done this
before, notably in her poems of social protest, but always with herself as
protagonist. Here, apart from some prerogatory feminine touches of decora-
tion, is a participation in the contemporary intelligence, rather than a considered partition of herself from it.

The style too is a delightful recognition of Miss Millay's virtuosity,
hitherto almost entirely confined to a re-rendering of Shakespeare's sonnets
or A. E. Housman's stanzas. It spreads over pages of witty and beautifully

stylized free verse, or concentrates in a random sonnet or two, or descants on a theme in the manner of Ogden Nash, or outdoes Sandburg in colloquial sauciness, or it fetches in an Elizabethanism by the way, or dresses itself formally in careful quatrains: but almost everywhere and whatever it does it makes its point as a poem of our times, accurately rendering the stress and distress of our present living, an imperative book of the year, in or out of poetry.

"Give That Beat Again"

Edmund Wilson

This new book of Edna Millay's I have found a little disappointing.

For the first twenty five pages or so, "Conversation at Midnight" is stimulating. Seven men of different kinds are brought together and made to talk about love, religion, communism, fascism, war and other subjects of current interest—with interludes on hunting, fishing, racing and mushroom-collecting. The poet is plunging with her ready intelligence into the confusion of cross-currents of the time, and the reader is put on the *qui vive*: he is expecting a revelation. But the discussion doesn't seem to come to much. It covers familiar ground, and the people—the stockbroker, the Communist, the liberal, the Roman Catholic, the artist, the sensualist, the advertising man—say many of the clever things that people usually say, without arriving at very many of the illuminating things which people do not usually say but which the poet ought to make them say. We expect it to gather momentum, but during the latter part it rather bogs down. At the very end, it mounts to a climax with an increasingly acrimonious altercation between the stock-broker and the Communist—each of whom accuses the other of submitting slavishly to regimentation—to which the liberal host puts an end by offering both the parties a drink.

But the dialogue is rarely allowed to penetrate to the fundamentals of the problems on which it touches. There are insights of considerable vividness—the picture of secularized man howling at night over the grave of God, the picture of the atheistic Communist rejecting the advances of Faith when it presents itself to his face only to succumb to an assault from the rear; but the really great forces which are upsetting the world somehow do not get squarely on the stage. What is really involved, for example, in such an argument as that between the radical and the stockbroker is the conflict between the classless and the class ideal; and Miss Millay has sidestepped this by making the pretenses of both parties ridiculous.

It may be that this part of the discussion has been blurred by Miss Millay's having lost her first manuscript and having been obliged to write the poem over. The worst developments of the Stalin dictatorship in Russia, with the new phase of the Stalin-Trotsky quarrel, which figure in this second

From the *New Republic* 91 (28 July 1937): 338–40. Reprinted by permission.

version, had not yet taken place when the first one was written. And it may be that in the year which has elapsed since the first manuscript was destroyed by fire, Miss Millay has felt obliged to make her imaginary Communist more fanatical and less convincing in his desire to see his fellows happy and free, as the real Communists have been going in that direction. In one of her most revealing flashes, she makes the liberal address the Communist as follows:

> Russia under Lenin is so many light-years away,
> Its noble beam approaches you but now;
> You stand transfigured in the golden light today
> Of a star that, even while you bask in its bright ray,
> Blackens, and disappears.
> We must allow,
> Perhaps another nineteen years,
> Before you see what's happening in Russia now.

And the debate in "Conversation at Midnight" cannot have failed to be confused by all this. Yet there are larger issues involved in all these questions of religion and socialism, fascism and democratic ideals, which go deeper than the passing events of politics as they go deeper than the prejudices and emotions of such individuals as Miss Millay has imagined. And I do not see that Miss Millay has kept them in sight. For her the whole upshot of the matter seems to be that both the stockbroker and the radical hanker only after the status of obedient cogs in a smoothly operating machine. But is this what they are fighting about in Spain? Miss Millay probably does not really think so, as she has contributed to a volume of translations of Spanish poems published for the benefit of the loyalist cause; but you would never find it out from "Conversation at Midnight." Nor, failing a real dramatization of the issue of the democratic versus the capitalist society, does she focus the various opinions and types from any other clear point of view.

I believe that the fundamental trouble here is that Miss Millay lacks the dramatic imagination—that is, that it is not natural for her to identify herself with imaginary characters. Of her plays, "Aria da Capo" was an eclogue, highly charged and deeply disturbing, like all her best work of that time; but the characters—as was quite suitable—were pure abstractions. "The King's Henchman," which had some beautiful poetry in it, was a poem like the plays of Yeats. But in "Conversation at Midnight" she has tried to animate and keep distinct a number of different people and points of view; and her own very strong personal point of view turns out not to lend itself so easily to this kind of dissociation. She is attempting a sort of thing not unlike some of Bernard Shaw's plays and very much like J. Lowes Dickinson's "Modern Symposium"; but, failing their expertness in the analysis of ideas, she ought to, and tends to, get out of such a subject effects of emotional conflict of a kind quite alien to Dickinson or Shaw. Yet these emotional chemical reactions do not, to my mind, really occur. What does happen is that, on the one hand, she is either consciously satirizing her characters' banalities or commenting on them from a long way off, while, on the other hand, her own peculiar pessimism, with its noble magnanimity and bitterness, is always trying to rise to the surface but is never allowed to emerge. We keep listening instinctively through the chatter and chaff for the voice we are accustomed to hear, and now and then we think it is speaking:

> Ricardo said, "Whatever the case for God, the
>   splendor of Man
> Cannot be questioned.
> This Music, this proud edifice erected
> Out of reach of the tide
> By drowning hands,
> This deathless, this impeccable, projected
> By peccant men, who even as they labored sank
>   and died,
> Irrefutable witness to that splendor stands.
>
> It speaks more loud
> Than the waves that batter
>
>> The wild bluff:
>> There is no God.
>> But it does not matter.
>> Man is enough.

But compare this to Miss Millay's marvelous sonnet, "On Hearing a Symphony of Beethoven." For anyone capable of that, this was hardly worth doing at all. And in the meantime, the dramatized points of view of Miss Millay's fictitious personalities never give rise to any conflict half so real as the conflicts within the poet herself as she has expressed them directly in her own person: "Pity me that the heart is slow to learn / What the swift mind beholds at every turn."

The interchange of "Conversation at Midnight" mostly falls into a vein to which Miss Millay has not given play for some time, which she has, in fact, developed hitherto only in the pseudonymous dialogues and sketches which she was writing about fifteen years ago. "Conversation at Midnight" is worldly and witty in a way different even from "Figs from Thistles." Here is a chorus of males speaking antiphonally on the subject of women:

> "Yes, there's a long list of items to that bill by the time you come
> to foot it,
> Me lad," Pygmalion continued. "As Ogden Nash might put it:

They're always wanting attention, and if you don't feel like kissing
them every minute of the day it's a misdemeanour:
And right in the middle of the season they send your shooting
clothes to the cleanour.". . .

MERTON: And when you get your bath-towel wet wiping your hair
They put it back in the bathroom with a patient smile and show
you the mark it made on the back of the chair. . . .

MERTON: And they use your last razor-blade and get it dull and don't tell
you a word about it.

LUCAS: And when you ask them what they did with your old white
sweater you can tell by their guilty look they've given it to the
Good Will but they pretend they've never heard about it.

PYGMALION: And they're always saying, "Now don't interrupt me!" and always
interrupting, and they can't let anything drop.
And they insist on telling long stories, which they do very badly,
because they never know what to leave out or where to stop. . . .
And they leave lipstick on cigarette-butts and napkins and all
around your mouth and on your collar.

MERTON: And when they buy something for 2.98 instead of 3 they think
they've saved a dollar. . . .
And when you think they look nice and say, "Is that a new dress?"
they exchange glances with some other woman.
And they pride themselves on having a masculine mind when as a
matter of fact they're hardly human.

She used to do this sort of thing in the prose of "Nancy Boyd"; but she
has now developed a new semi-verse medium which is something like a
combination of Ogden Nash and Robinson Jeffers, but which in her hands is
much more flexible as it follows a quicker and subtler play of the intelligence.
"Conversation at Midnight" is really very witty; and the imagery, as is usual
with Edna Millay, provides an element of excitement and surprise through
its power to intensify realistic observation presented with a daring baldness:

Corruption, too, is a kind of development—it depends
on the viewpoint. . . .
To the buzzard under his shabby wings appraising the
beach from above, the whip-ray
Till he be stranded and the land soldier-crabs have
taken his eyes out
Has not achieved maturity.

But Nancy Boyd is not Edna Millay; and this group of ventriloquial figures
does not bring her very much closer to being so. Not that Nancy Boyd isn't
good in its way, and not that this book isn't all right in its way. But the

best of the impersonal poems in the volume called "The Buck in the Snow," are more truly philosophical than the whole of this long discussion.

As for the verse, this reviewer has been prophesying for years about the obsolescence of verse technique and the gradual victory of prose; but now he finds himself a little dismayed at the rapidity with which the process is going forward. Little did we think in our youth, when the line of Milton still seemed irrefrangible and when we used to laugh in our innocence at W. S. Gilbert's rhymed but meterless ballad of "The Lost Mr. Blake," as Gilbert intended us to, that we should live to see the day when its interminable lines that look and sound like paragraphs of prose would be the type of much serious poetry. The beat of English verse has been so sprung, broken, muted, loosened, that it might almost as well be abandoned altogether. Compare MacNeice and Auden with Yeats and Housman; Robinson Jeffers with John Masefield; the early Eliot with "Murder in the Cathedral"; Ogden Nash with Franklin P. Adams. And now Miss Edna Millay, one of the sole surviving masters of English verse, has gone to pieces, too. She was beginning to handle her metrics negligently in the volume called "The Buck in the Snow," and she produced some very successful poems in this way; then she went further in "Wine from These Grapes." But it was in her translations from Baudelaire that the ravages of the mischief became alarming. Instead of rendering the ringing alexandrines of Baudelaire in English meters equally accurate and emphatic, she fell into what seemed a fallacy entirely uncharacteristic, of assuming that the effect of the French could be conveyed by trying to write French verse in English—that is, by dropping the English stress and letting the verses go loose. But the result was not a bit like Baudelaire: it was merely inferior verse for Miss Millay.

Now in "Conversation at Midnight," you see metrics in full dissolution. The stress is largely neglected; the lines run on for paragraphs; sometimes the rhymes fade out. Sometimes poor little sonnets, like souls from the Platonic overworld that want to be born again, flutter into the all-liquefying flux; but they find themselves simply carried along by the stream of the conversation and become filled with its miscellaneous content, to which their form has no special appropriateness and to which it is powerless to give symmetry or point. This is all quite distinct from the *vers libre* of some years ago, which, though prosy, was sharp and precise or had the rhythms of the Whitmanesque chant. But the rhythms are weary now: as Max Eastman says, they almost amount to a joke on disciplined writing itself.

I am not complaining about this state of affairs: I know that it is all on the cards. And "Conversation at Midnight" is highly entertaining, in any case. Edna Millay at her most relaxed is livelier than most of our poets at their brightest. But I miss her old imperial line.

Huntsman, What Quarry?

◆

Under Angry Constellations

PAUL ROSENFELD

Edna St. Vincent Millay may be thought to bear an amusing resemblance
to the great Napoleon: Austerlitz has proved to be anything but her Water-
loo. This, the secluded field of action of our wildfire poet, has become the
scene of no mean victories. Felicitous volume after volume emerges from the
upstate farm; and the latest of them, a collection of her recent ballads and
song-like short poems expressing personal emotion, reiterates the truth the
others affirm: that of her poetic powers' fine capacity for self-renewal. The
majority of the lyrics in *Huntsman, What Quarry?* communicate feeling with
all her former fancy, piquancy, verve, but also in instances with a powerful
style and a plangent music not without sublimity.

In passing, it must also be remarked that Miss Millay may be thought
to bear a resemblance to the little Napoleon as well as to his great uncle,
for this reason: it appears that the continuation of her entanglements in
international politics must very directly lead to her Sedan. Among the poems
in the new volume failing to approach in tone and imagery the truth and
force of some reality—they are a minority—the series reflecting the late
Czecho-Slovakian and Spanish tragedies is unhappily conspicuous. Her feelings seem to have little or no intuition of the forces underlying these political
catastrophes. The imagery of *Say That We Saw Spain Die* verges dangerously
on the sheerly decorative. The attempt exhibited by the sonnet-sequence
From a Town in a State of Siege—to extract from the state of bombarded open
towns imagery incisively representative of the uncertain, threatened condition
of life—was singularly fruitless.

The realities which in the present instance have given the poetry greatest
substance and weight, far more than "this brutal age" in which "the foul

From *Poetry* (October 1939): 47–50. Copyright 1939 by The Modern Poetry Association and reprinted
by permission of the Editor of *Poetry*.

supplants the fair, / The coarse defeats the twice-refined" are forces with a purely subjective station: those which during the tragic fifth decade of human life seem to slow down the body's motion and press on the heart. Eminent among them is the refinement and sublimation of desire which in this second adolescence of the human being victimizes the sensuous and the personal life. The "huntsman" who, in the perfectly rounded little ballad lending the book its title, forever chases "the hot pads that ever run before . . . the pointed mask that makes no reply", and crying "Hoick!" abandons the lady, the warm supper and the bed, to slay "the red brush of remembered joy": what is he more definitely than desire which ambitiously has taken truth, the infinite, for its object; and robs the senses of their delights and casts down the walls of illusions hiding the ghastly actuality? The lantern

> For want of whose ill-trimmed, aspiring wick
> More days than one I have gone forward slowly
> In utter dark, scuffling the drifted leaf,
> Tapping the road before me with a stick

—what is that but the power to love and waken its responses, become a vital necessity at a period when desire, demanding perfection, has rendered the world doubly bare of opportunities for comfort and fulfillment? As for the autumn and "cold of the sun's eclipse", and its moods of melancholy and feelings of approaching death and their music which penetratingly pervade the book (it is noteworthy that of all the poems only one takes its imagery from spring—it is an "occasional" ballad, evidently written for a sick English friend and his American wife—and at least thirteen derive theirs from the world "between day and evening in the autumn"): we can only feel *it* to be the chilly climate perpetually facing the setting sun, into which a desire that would harmonize the world and finds itself balked of its object and predestined to defeat by chaos and lack of necessary time, drives its possessors.

Accessions of new courage are also vocal; moods of stubborn allegiance to the apparently hopeless human and poetic quest:

> I am the convoy to its cloudy end
> Of a most bright and regal enterprise.
>
> . . . I have heroes to beget
> Before I die.

Grief nonetheless prevails. Failure seems predestinate. The "bright and regal enterprise" set forth

> under angry constellations, ill-
> Mounted and under-rationed and unspurred.

Despair perceives the leader, the inner imperative,

> Duped and delivered up to rascals; bound
> And bleeding, and his mouth stuffed; on his knees;
> Robbed and imprisoned; and adjudged unsound.

In the sunset, the evening star seems "the first riding-light in the calm harbor", which alone offers release from an unequal, tragic struggle.

Again, a capricious, wayward, excited play of fancy provides certain of the sharp symbols that communicate these moods. "Rolled in the trough of thick desire", she feels pity for the poor

> Who bail disaster from the boat
> With a pint can . . .
> Who never came into the wind,
> Who took life beam-on from the start.

Her musical patterns almost invariably are faithful to these moods. What occasionally interferes with the transmission is a certain nervous instability of fancy, possibly abetted by the imperatives of the rhyme-scheme. To the mind of the present reviewer, the impressive sonnet commencing "Count them unclean, these tears that turn no mill" is damaged by the circumstance that its octet derives the symbol of creative action from the agricultural sphere and its sestet from the military. The conflict blurs the picture and tends to place the sincerity of the mood in question. But in many instances the vision has been clear (two or three of the sonnets in the volume are magnificent evidences of the fact). And in combination with a sustained music and a strong, almost monumental diction, it has perfectly transmitted such elevated moods as the one in which this poet recaptures Schopenhauer's serene conception of the Artist's death:

> Thou famished grave, I will not fill thee yet,
> Roar though thou dost, I am too happy here;
> Gnaw thine own sides, fast on; I have no fear
> Of thy dark project, but my heart is set
> On living—I have heroes to beget
> Before I die; I will not come anear
> Thy dismal jaws for many a splendid year;
> Till I be old, I aim not to be eat.
>
> I cannot starve thee out; I am thy prey
> And thou shalt have me; but I dare defend
> That I can stave thee off; and I dare say,
> What with the life I lead, the force I spend,
> I'll be but bones and jewels on that day,
> And leave thee hungry even in the end.

Make Bright the Arrows; 1940 Notebook

◆

[Review of *Make Bright the Arrows*]

Louise Bogan

Poetry, in a truly creative epoch (such as existed in Europe from 1918 to the early thirties), is distinguished by the variety of surprising and delightful sounds made by the poets who produce it. Uniformity of tone is a sure sign of something going to seed. In America, the poets active in what was roughly called the poetic Renaissance, which started around 1912, have lapsed into uniformity. These poets are now widely accepted and read. They are winners of Pulitzer Prizes, members of the American Academy of Arts and Letters, pillars of literary society, and wearers of the official palm. But, in their progress through these honors, they have come to sound almost exactly alike. They are, moreover, not only more or less indistinguishable from each other but also practically indistinguishable from the poets contained in Stedman's "Victorian Anthology" or from Victor Hugo. It is so difficult and exasperating to think up something to say about poets who exemplify this condition that one puts off the task as long as possible. In consequence, the books dealt with here are being reviewed late.

Reading such books, one is reminded of what happens to certain highly cultivated flowers after cultivation ceases. They revert to magenta, a debased hue, neither one thing nor the other. Beneath the level of truly creative expression, in any period, in all arts, runs this level of coloring. It is the natural, middle, uniform tone beneath human expression; a little sad, a little sentimental, self-indulgent, vain, quite rhetorical, and very, very "stock." It is easy and academic to call this state post-Romantic or whatnot. It is a state at once too simple and too complex to be thus summarily described. Flaubert called it middle-class. It is a state and the level of Salieri as opposed to that of Mozart; of Greuze as opposed to Delacroix. It is the level above

From the *New Yorker* 16 (28 December 1940): 62. Reprinted by permission and by courtesy of Ruth Limmer, literary executor.

which the artist raises himself, almost unconsciously, by the very power of his idiosyncrasies. In poetry, as in other art forms, the power and the glory come in with the unique sound of the individual exploring all emotion through the unique emotion of his individual mind and heart.

Yes, it would have been difficult, in 1915 or so, to foresee the day when, for example, Conrad Aiken and Edna Millay would come to sound much alike. Aiken, who once had his own accent and method, in 1940, in a new book, a sequence of forty-three sonnets entitled "And in the Human Heart," almost completely loses them. Mr. Aiken, in maturity, can write on any subject. He absorbs time, space, human love, eternity, the weather, and nature in all its varied manifestations. He absorbs these and (the sure sign of sentimentality, that magenta of the spirit) he feels himself able to cope with them. Before the fluency and the rhetoric of Mr. Aiken's sonnets, all obstacles melt away. The sonnet form, which must be kept formal and stern if it is not to become a bloated literary exercise, serves in Mr. Aiken's case to accentuate the immaturity of his matter. For the mature poet does not soar above tragedy. He accepts, examines, and describes it, in spite of the fact that in our day it is particularly difficult to remain disciplined and thus accept, examine, and describe.

We now come to Miss Millay's new book, "Make Bright the Arrows." This volume was written, according to her publishers, at high speed and with great indignation. It appears coincidentally with Miss Millay's announcement in the press that she is through with "art" for the duration. In these poems, she expresses the utmost horror and disgust at what is going on in Europe, and advocates that everyone immediately set about sharpening weapons, in both the spiritual and material sense, in order to go into action to make a better world. That it is a sincere book goes without question. What strikes the reader is that here is a new war, different in almost all respects from wars which have preceded it, being urged upon people in exactly the same way that it was urged in 1914. The noble tone, the stock sentiment, which post-1918 poetry, in all European languages, depreciated and made tiresome and unreadable, reappear. Apollinaire, the best exponents of Dada, Eliot, Rilke, Yeats, and Auden, who parodied and analyzed this tone, have gone for nothing. That this sentimentality should at this particular moment appear in full force in American writing is a cause for concern and regret. And as for Miss Millay's farewell to "art," is it not better for a player, in a crisis, to close his instrument than to dedicate himself to the rendition of sentimental waltzes, or even to pounding it with his fists?

The Murder of Lidice (1942)

♦

[Review of *The Murder of Lidice*]

THEATRE ARTS

Enthusiasm for the radio as a medium for drama was quickened recently through the broadcast of Edna St. Vincent Millay's dramatic poem, *The Murder of Lidice*. The interest centred not only in the poem itself and its performance but in the emotional impact on the audience, reported over and over again. The poem was said to have been written more or less at top speed for the Writers' War Board. With a writer usually as meticulous as Miss Millay it might have been expected to have had some of the faults of 'occasional' poetry. Perhaps it had. If so, this will show in the printed version which Harper's are soon to publish. But the only matter of importance to us is that as broadcast drama the poem was entirely successful. It had all things in its favor. It was prefaced skilfully by Alexander Woollcott; the almost unequalled eloquence of Paul Muni's voice added to the lustre of the reading; but there is no doubt that it was the theme of the poem and the poet's dramatic attack on that theme that created the effect.

So now radio drama has done what the movies have already done successfully—picked up an item of news out of the current war and made it at once into effective art. The theatre works more slowly. It takes so many processes and so many techniques before a play can be written, financed, designed, cast, rehearsed, produced. It labors under an adverse critical attitude which is prone to decry 'journalism' in drama. And yet the theatre, too, has done in this war what it has not done before. It has made mordant theatre out of war facts, first with *There Shall Be No Night*, then with *Watch on the Rhine* and *The Moon Is Down*, and now this season with *The Eve of St. Mark*.

Reprinted from *Theatre Arts* 26 (December 1942): 733–34.

Letters of Edna St. Vincent Millay
[Edited by Allan Ross Macdougall]

♦

[Review of Millay Letters]

WILLARD THORP

The publication of these two volumes of letters is an event of great importance for scholars and critics concerned with American literature. Though
their paths never crossed, Hart Crane and Edna St. Vincent Millay were both
wonder-children of the 1920's. Taken together their careers tell the story of
the literary renaissance of their time.

The generation which their lives epitomize was discreet about its private
affairs, however much the public was titillated by what supposedly was going
on in Greenwich Village and the Rue Montparnasse. Now it can be told,
and the telling, as these revealing letters from two camps show, will only
increase our wonder at the artistic integrity of this generation which, far
from being "lost," was trying honestly and with hard work to create a new
American literature.

So different in most ways, Crane and "Vincent" Millay both possessed
the intense desire for personal freedom characteristic of the writers and artists
who were their contemporaries. Each risked much to have this freedom. Yet
their recklessness was more often a form of courage than mere defiance.
Both were amazingly precocious, scarcely serving their apprenticeship before
writers already established were eager to accept them as peers. Here the
resemblance ends. Miss Millay, almost from the beginning, was *the* American
poet for large numbers of readers, while, in spite of the constant efforts of
his friends, Crane was scarcely known at all beyond his immediate circle. He
had been tagged with that damning word obscurity, a vice from which some
who knew him best tried to dissuade him. Yet, in their exit from life, the

From *American Literature* 25 (May 1953): 240–43. Copyright 1953 by Duke University Press, Durham,
N.C. Reprinted by permission.

similarities converge. Apparently not even Crane's closest friends know why he committed suicide, but his letters show that he was deeply troubled because for two years he had written almost no poetry except "The Broken Tower." In a strangely similar strain, Miss Millay, having suffered many cruel blows in her private life, again and again in her last letters assures her friends that she will regain the power and skill she once possessed.

For what they reveal in their vividness and in style, Crane's letters are much superior to Miss Millay's. She cared little for letter writing. For Crane communication was indispensable to existence. The patient arguments with his father and mother are the ground bass of his letters. Though they never understood the strange child they had produced, each fought the other through him and ceaselessly sought his acquiescence and affection. Though he saw through them and at times despised them, he could never break with them. (The psychologists will have to explain why.) It may be that a clean break would have been best for him, but if it had occurred we should not have these letters of self-justification in which he tries over and over again to tell C. E. and Grace Crane what it was to be Hart Crane.

From his friends, the Allen Tates, Gorham Munson, Waldo Frank, Malcolm Cowley, Slater Brown, and the others (and there were many others), Crane held back nothing, not even discreet references to his homosexual affairs which he did not otherwise obtrude into his friendships. Everything is here: the delight of the young man from the provinces before the wonders of New York, and later of Paris and Mexico; the patient self-justification of the kind of poetry he must write; the minute and helpful criticism of the work of others; the gossip of the coteries; the literary quarrels; in sum, the "secret history" of a literary generation. As the chaos of his private life contrasts strangely with the artistic control evident in his poetry, so do the horrors hinted at in these letters contrast with the maturity of his judgments of people (including himself) and even of public affairs. The double alienation from which he suffered, both as man and artist, made him the more acutely observant of the normal life of his times.

Except for some sloppiness of proofreading, Mr. Weber's editing is satisfactory. In so far as he could, or it was important to do so, he has explained references to Crane's sexual excursions. Allusions to poems and obscure events are well footnoted. It might seem that Mr. Weber's greatest achievement was his success in persuading so many of Crane's friends to permit his letters to them to be printed, for Crane could be nasty when he was in a vengeful mood. But this consent was actually the final act of generosity. While he was alive, they all tried to save him from self-destruction. The record of their affection and admiration, obliquely set down in the letters, is not the least notable fact which emerges from them.

Though Hart Crane and Edna St. Vincent Millay plunged into the literary life of New York at about the same time, 1916–1917, the groups they moved in barely touched. The circle of her early friendships with Witter Bynner, Arthur Davison Ficke, and the Charles Rann Kennedys, widened through the years to include Deems Taylor, Franklin P. Adams, George Dillon, and a host of others who were devoted to the vivacious, mercurial, stubborn, successful girl from Camden, Maine, and Vassar, who had published "Renascence" at the age of twenty and had become famous in a day. The names of her friends tell us something at once. They were not, like Crane's friends, nourishing their art on Donne and Laforgue, Joyce, and Eliot. They were closer to the American average. Some of them, indeed, could speak to millions and be understood. Some of them, it must be admitted, were not very serious about their art; and they were certainly not participants in the "revolution of the word," as were Crane and his friends. They still wrote sonnets and talked about Beauty.

Is it because many of her friends were not deeply concerned about literature, though they produced it, that there is so little technical talk about poetry in these letters and so little theorizing about it? Only in her last months, when Miss Millay regretted the propaganda poetry she had written during the Second World War and was vexed because her publishers seemed to be exploiting her name and reputation unduly, does she write at length about her art. The great majority of the letters in this volume are filled with the kind of vivid personal news which one's family and one's friends desire to have. The best letters are those in which her vein of satire flashes: a superb one to Floyd Dell in 1933, ragging him for his prim objections to the amount of drinking indulged in by "presumably intelligent people"; and another, to her husband, about the woes of the lady poet on the lecture circuit. There are other high moments, as in the letter to Governor Fuller about Sacco and Vanzetti and the letter to the League of American Penwomen rebuking them for attempting to honor her after their "recent gross and shocking insolence" to Elinor Wylie.

But if we miss in these letters the accent of a great poet we cannot fail to understand why Vincent Millay's friends thought her a great person. She was generous and self-reliant and brave. (In the end much bravery was required of her. She despised pretense and hated injustice. Her fame never went to her head. She should have been a greater poet.

Mr. Macdougall, who was a friend of Miss Millay's from 1919, has edited her letters carefully and usually with sufficient annotation. Now and then he fails to explain some important allusion or event which was only too well known in her circle. It is good to have, for example, her stout words to the League of American Penwomen alluded to above, but what readers now will recall how it had insulted Miss Wylie?

These two volumes of letters greatly enrich the small body of primary materials having to do with the literary life in the fabulous twenties. They will go on the shelf with Cowley's *Exile's Return*, Conrad Aiken's *Ushant*,

Arthur Mizener's biography of F. Scott Fitzgerald, Carlos Baker's recent study of Hemingway, and March and Tambimuttu's *T. S. Eliot: A Symposium*. Small in number though these books are, we can already see, through them, how much more creative and influential this literary generation was than that of the 1890's in England, with which it has too often been compared.

Mine the Harvest

◆

Two Nuns and a Strolling Player

JOHN CIARDI

Norma Millay, the poet's sister, has gathered together a last harvest of sixty-six poems unpublished at the time of Edna Millay's death. One is delighted to note in them that the save-the-world rhetoric of Miss Millay's poems of the thirties is largely gone from these. And especially delighted to find flashes of power. The talent, nevertheless, remains self-dramatizing. One cannot doubt the fervor and charm of Miss Millay's private personality. What else could have driven her—deliberately, as her letters reveal—to write bad poetry to the high causes of World War II? But the poet must be judged in the poems, and there is no escaping the conviction that a poet more devoted to the poem—Miss Adams and Miss Bogan will do as examples—would not have tolerated such dreary lines as "Ah, no; ah, no; poor female bird," such readiness to fall into June-noon rhymes, such self-intoxicated absurdities as "The apple-trees bud, but I do not" (a damn good thing, I'd say).

None of which is to deny the joys that are. "The Strawberry Shrub" is superbly managed in the three central stanzas, and there are moments of other poems that flash and go in a way of fire. The impression remains, however, that Miss Millay's strengths and weaknesses are both elocutionary. When she aspires to the high serious, she is least successful, for what emerges is not the true high serious but only its elocutionary manner. The fact is that whatever Miss Millay's intellectual achievements as a human being—and many who have known her have testified that they were impressive—her poetic gift was no vehicle for the intellectual. The poems offer not Minerva but an actress playing Minerva—a charming and talented actress, to be sure, but the difference remains. When the poem offers Miss Millay an opportunity

From the *Nation* 178 (22 May 1954): 445–46. Reprinted by permission of the *Nation* magazine / The Nation Co., Inc.

for her dramatic or self-dramatizing urge—as it emphatically does in, say, the first of the Tristan poems—then the result is splendid. When the best it can come up with is that poor female bird, or the coy if fervent posturing of "The Journal," then it is nowhere at all.

Collected Poems

◆

Edna Millay: A Summing-Up of Her Work

PAUL ENGLE

What is untrue of most poets was beautifully true of Edna St. Vincent Millay—her poems were as well-turned as her own slim ankle.

That delightful fact gave an extra life to the poetry when she was alive for Miss Millay seemed to be not merely a person writing skillfully in verse. She was the very presence of the art of poetry itself. If poems could ever take a human form, then this is what they would look like.

But how do the lines stand up in plain type, silent on the page, without that lyrical personality breathing motion into them?

Many things come finely clear when one reads through the life's work. Miss Millay was usually at her best the greater the formality of her verse.

In the loose-lined poems the rhythm wavers and rhetoric foams over the page. But in the tight forms, there is an achieved intensity which makes the poem radiant.

Thus, she is one of the great makers of sonnets in this century. All her sonnets are gathered into one sequence in this volume, making a solid weight of excellence unsurpassed.

Another fact quickly appears—the more private and personal the motivation, the better the poem; the more public and generalized, the feebler the poem.

Miss Millay's war verse is among the weakest here, whereas some of her early things with, perhaps, a slighter motivation, are much more moving.

Some of the poems sound curiously outworn now, the lines languishing in a tired vocabulary: "That, sickening, I would fain pluck thence"; "the

Reprinted from the *New York Post*, 25 November 1956, p. M-11.

long festive board prinked out in prodigal array, the very monster which they sailed forth to conquer and to quell."

These moments are so full and inexpressive as to drag down the poems, and there are far too many of them.

There is a small group of poems not included in any previous volume. As is so often the case, they add little that is new, and largely confirm this reader's view that the author was too often content with the easy phrase and the trite word.

But a final judgment must be this: here is a heavy weight of light lyrics. Not "light" in a bad sense of lacking substance, but rather of having fineness of motion and alertness of language.

Here are certain sonnets which will be read with devotion as long as there are readers devoted to perfected sound. On a further reading, "Renascence" stands up still as one of the moments in American poetry when a sudden new talent flared in the literary sky. All through this volume one has the feeling—Edna St. Vincent Millay, her book, her unique and shining book.

Edna St. Vincent Millay

FRANCIS HACKETT

The poems of Edna St. Vincent Millay have up to the present existed in more than twenty volumes. Now the poet's sister, Norma Millay Ellis, has gathered into a single volume, which includes sixteen poems not previously published, the corpus to be known as definitive. It makes a big book. The type is handsome, the paper heavy, and the cover, though its sharply pointed corners dig into your palms, is attractive. No dates are attached to the different sections, and all the sonnets are grouped together, but it is easy to write in the dates from Who's Who, though "Mine the Harvest" is not listed in that reference book.

This is obviously a book to live with. Anyone who comes late to the poet, with nothing personal to go on except the photograph on the wrapper— in which the stoical features have a tragic, almost an Indian, starkness— cannot complain of scant material. Its poetic form should defy the worm, and its feeling is never prinked or smartened after the first timid and propitiating pages. It is full of the courage the poet ascribed to the mother she loved, "rock from New England quarried."

When Edna St. Vincent Millay was not so very far from "the wasteman's little daughter in her First Communion dress," Santayana was giving his talk in California on "The Genteel Tradition in American Philosophy," which made this relevant discrimination: "The American Will inhabits the sky-scraper; the American intellect inhabits the colonial mansion. The one is the sphere of the American man: the other, at least predominantly, of the American woman. The one is all aggressive enterprise; the other is all genteel tradition." And from there he went on crisply, deftly, maliciously, to define the "agonized conscience" of Calvinism which was to be found in the early New England communities. "Calvinism, essentially, asserts three things: that sin exists, that sin is punished, and that it is beautiful that sin should exist to be punished." Yet "serious poetry, profound religion (Calvinism, for instance), are the joys of an unhappiness that confesses itself; but when a genteel tradition forbids people to confess that they are unhappy, serious poetry and profound religion are closed to them by that."

From the *New Republic* 135 (24 December 1956): 21–22. Reprinted by permission of *The New Republic* © 1956, the New Republic, Inc.

Santayana left Melville out of consideration here. He also left the Civil War out of consideration. Wasn't it that war which cut off Melville's work and which started American men on the rampant "aggressive enterprise" that was to shunt women, not into intellect so much as into a thin refinement that for raw liquor tried to substitute cambric tea? The bloodiest war of the Nineteenth Century did not agonize male conscience, it hardened it. It generated savagery. War hailed down on the flowering of New England, and blasted the Hawthornes. It drove the women to soften as best they might, by the aid of whatever chivalry they could elicit, an era of cutthroat barbarism, mitigated by philanthropy and hush-money.

Walt Whitman and William James, both mentioned by Santayana, did strive for the inner life thus truncated. Whitman strove to build on the fraternity of the war, and to transcend the genteel. James tried to curb the savagery behind "aggressive enterprise" at the same time that he revolted against the hush-hush of Chatauqua. He did not wince half as much at the vulgarity in democracy as at the parching conservatism, the compromise and fear, which was and is the blight on any culture.

By the time Edna St. Vincent Millay finished her post-graduate course in Greenwich Village—she wrote the Baccalaureate Hymn, Vassar College, 1917—she came of age. The tradition that had lapped her youth, the "fine worm-eaten shroud which breaks to dust when once unroll'd," she no longer clutched to herself. She wanted what the Negroes had wanted, Emancipation. The vote was part of it, the latch-key, free love, free speech. This time, after another war, women were tired of the pedestal, they wanted the play of their limbs and the play of their minds. And this poet wanted to rear a Tower to Beauty:

> Such as I am, however, I have brought
> To what it is, this tower; it is my own;
> Though it was reared To Beauty, it was wrought
> From what I had to build with: honest bone
> Is there, and anguish: pride; and burning thought;
> And lust is there, and nights not spent alone.

What impassioned her and made her vulnerable, was the idea Walt Whitman and William James had both possessed, a large sense of America. Edna St. Vincent Millay was a true daughter of Maine. She had its Calvinist sense of sin to begin with, a fear of death, a fear of man, and a fear of the male that is God. But while she kept coming back to native astringency, and reluctantly quitted its coast and heavy seas, she grappled with her fears. One tradition of femininity she could not unlearn, that of her mother's loving kindness, but the pride and intrepidity of her stock carried her through an intensely painful evolution, one which issued her into a state that included but was wider than the state of Maine, or than these United States. "Upon this age, that never speaks its mind," she poured her burning thought, and so emancipated herself. The lacerations of one who could love too well had to be endured. She scorned evasion. No hedge could keep death from slipping in, though it might be the death of love. It could rape from her the beings who were more to her than herself, but what saved the poet in her was a reverence for life, extending out and beyond all sentient individual beings to sentient national beings, and so to universal being, which, by reason of the "obsequious greed" in man, "the red triumphant child" that is spewed "upon this world from the collective womb," gave her the tragic sense of life that inheres in universal being.

With America she was not at war, merely at sea, re-inventing a compass. Under inhospitable stars, facing abrupt incidents and experiencings that would have to be grasped if one was to keep foothold and a steering wheel, she could navigate alone, as her sonnet sequence, "Epitaph for the Race of Man," made explicit. This, together with "Modern Declaration" and "Not For a Nation," can take us as far beyond the prescribed limits of collectivity as, say, St. Gaudens does when in a Washington cemetery, by a stroke of the imagination, he indicates the mystery that enfolds arrival and departure.

But along with her New England stoicism we have certain concomitants of reverence for life, indignation at its gross abuse. The murder of Lidice, the murder of Sacco and Vanzetti, the murder of Hiroshima, "logic alone, all love laid by," connect themselves with a score of poems that capture her heart. "And on the gravel crawls the chilly bee."

This bee, the sparrow, the thrush, "The Fawn," "The Dragonfly," the snake, "Sky-Colored Bird," "When the tree-sparrows with no sound," the hawkweed, the blue iris, the pigeons, "The Buck in the Snow"—all these and more are so poignantly made one with her as the unloved husband's dying in "Sonnets from an Ungrafted Tree" is flawlessly realized, without hiding its rigor. Intense feeling goes with "chastity of soul," and the humblest of details, like the commonest of creatures, win dignity from the art they incite, both to very great height and to equally great depth.

"If I die solvent," the poet could afford to say at the last, not casting away "wit, courage, honor, pride," "when loping Death's upon me in hot sooth,"

> 'Twill be that in my honored hands I bear
> What's under no condition to be spilled
> Till my blood spills and hardens in the air:
> An earthen grail, a humble vessel filled
> To its low brim with water from the brink
> Where Shakespeare, Keats and Chaucer learned to drink.

This is the great, not the genteel, tradition. Varied, felicitous, sustained, Edna St. Vincent Millay explores the tragic sense of our time and "the joys of an unhappiness that confesses itself." Hers is the serious poetry, the profound affirmation, that the genteel tradition forbade. New England is in it, "clean cliff going down as deep as clear water can reach." "There, thought unbraids itself, and the mind becomes single." This book is a monument to straightness and singleness of soul.

[Review of *Collected Poems*]

KARL SHAPIRO

This is a seven-hundred-page edition of the collected poems of Edna St. Vincent Millay. Her plays and translations are not included in this work, but there are a few unpublished poems. (I have not gone to the trouble to find out which.) Edmund Wilson, who knew her, has so far written the best essay about her poetry; it seems unlikely that anyone who did not belong to her circle can say anything to the point.

The poems have an intimacy which makes the reader recoil, even if he is susceptible to this flirtation. What is worse, it is the intimacy of the actress and (off-stage) the *femme fatale*. All this has been said before, and it is said best in the poems. The center of her experience is love, but it is the most desperately middleclass love poetry one can imagine, with neither rough-and-tumble nor courtliness nor high sacrifice. But it rings so true—that makes it worse—and it is so well said, with all its horrid mannerisms; it is such a parody of the great love poets that one is dissolved in tears.

It is really wicked to talk about *her* "social conscience" which she raged about later on. Love poets always fall in love with *society* at a certain age.

I look in vain for the time when men will be so civilized as to appreciate this poet who wrote so voluminously and so passionately and so expertly, almost to no avail.

Reprinted from *Prairie Schooner* 31 (Spring 1957): 13, by permission of the University of Nebraska Press. Copyright 1957 University of Nebraska Press.

ARTICLES AND ESSAYS

◆

The Literary Spotlight:
Edna St. Vincent Millay

BOOKMAN

Edna St. Vincent Millay is a slim young person with chestnut-brown hair shot with glints of bronze and copper, so that sometimes it seems auburn and sometimes golden; a slightly snub nose, and freckles; a child mouth; a cool, grave voice; and grey-green eyes.

With these materials, she achieves a startling variety of appearances. When she is reading her poetry, she will seem to the awed spectator a fragile little girl with apple blossom face. When she is picnicking in the country she will be, with her snub nose, freckles, carroty hair, and boyish grin, an Irish "newsy." When she is meeting the bourgeoisie in its lairs, she is likely to be a highly artificial and very affected young lady with an exaggerated Vassar accent and abominably overdone manners. In the basement of the Brevoort, or in the Café de la Rotonde in Paris, or the Café Royal in London, she will appear a languid creature of a decadent civilization, looking wearily out of ambiguous eyes, and smiling faintly with her doll's mouth, exquisite and morbid. A New England nun; a chorus girl on a holiday; the Botticelli Venus of the Uffizi gallery. . . .

She is all of these and more. A contradictory young person! And the real Edna St. Vincent Millay, beneath all these disguises? That is hard to say. She does not give you any help by what she tells you of herself. Her speech is another series of disguises—of fictions, if you will. In the last few years there has grown up an Edna St. Vincent Millay legend, a sort of Byronic legend, which the younger generation is pleased to believe in. She accepts it; doubtless she is flattered by it—as any of us would be, the more flattered, the more untrue it was!—and perhaps she tries after a fashion to live up to it. She is certainly not the person to spoil a good story, especially if it is about herself, by prudish denials. As to that, she has a proud maxim: "I am that I am." Yes, she is what she is. Which leaves the matter where, doubtless, she prefers it to remain—in mystery.

The Edna St. Vincent Millay legend is based on her poems—or, to speak more exactly, upon one particular book of poems, the one entitled "A Few Figs from Thistles." Its title gives an indication of its cynical optimism.

Reprinted from *Bookman* 56 (November 1922): 272–78.

Previous to this volume she had been known as the author of "Renascence," and had gained the devout admiration of a few poetry lovers, but no popular audience. With the publication of "Figs from Thistles," she became the poet laureate of the younger generation. The first poem in the volume is as follows:

> My candle burns at both ends;
>   It will not last the night;
> But ah, my foes, and oh, my friends—
>   It gives a lovely light!

The second poem utters the same gospel of impulse:

> Safe upon the solid rock the ugly houses stand:
> Come and see my shining palace built upon the sand!

The younger generation is not excessively interested in literature as such; and in spite of its aesthetic pretenses, beauty of a high order can pass by without its acclaim. The postwar state of the young mind is individualistic and egocentric. If these boys and girls hail Edna St. Vincent Millay as their poet, it is because she seems to be writing about them. The postwar youth, who cherishes no illusions as to his own stability, honesty, or fidelity, is glad enough to find this comparison of himself with the tame old fashioned kind of lover:

> Oh, Prue, she has a patient man,
>   And Joan a gentle lover,
> And Agatha's Arth' is a hug-the-hearth,—
>   But my true love's a rover!
>
> Mig, her man's as good as cheese
>   And honest as a briar,
> Sue tells her love what he's thinking of,—
>   But my dear lad's a liar!
> · · · · · · · · · · · · · · · · · · ·
> Cold he slants his eyes about,
>   And few enough's his choice,—
> Though he'd slip me clean for a nun, or a queen,
>   Or a beggar with knots in her voice. . . .
>
> Joan is paired with a putterer
>   That bastes and tastes and salts,
> And Agatha's Arth' is a hug-the-hearth,—
>   But my true love is false!

The postwar mood of girlhood, the mood of freedom which was dramatized outwardly by bobbed hair and knee length skirts, finds itself pleasantly expressed in this volume:

> And if I loved you Wednesday,
>   Well, what is that to you?
> I do not love you Thursday—
>   So much is true.

It is a mood of freedom gaily maintained even in the midst of what might seem an emotional bondage:

> Now it may be the flower for me
>   Is this beneath my nose;
> How shall I tell, unless I smell
>   The Carthaginian rose?

Or, as it is more earnestly but not less gracefully put in another poem:

> Oh, think not I am faithful to a vow!
>   Faithless am I save to love's self alone.
> Were you not lovely I would leave you now:
>   After the feet of beauty fly my own.

This attitude toward life is summed up in the sonnet with which the volume appropriately ends: "If you entreat me with your loveliest lie, / I will protest you with my favorite vow."

Not every poet can have a legend. There must be something in his personality, as well as in his poetry, to stimulate the imaginations of his fellows and make them project their own wishes, sensationally, upon him. Yet it is not his fault; and it may be his misfortune. The Edna St. Vincent Millay legend has distracted attention from work of hers that is more beautiful and more deeply sincere. Some of these poems, just quoted, are after all a kind of *vers de société*, not less so because the society with whose emotions these poems politely and playfully deal is the bohemian society of fellow artists. Here are, truly enough rendered, the superficial emotions of a creative artist at odds with life and love, half fearful of some desperate and fatal trap, half proud of his escape. But this light laughter has a forced note in it, and this pride of escape is a regretful and at best a grim pride. Love is dealt with more honestly, even though cruelly, in another poem, the concluding sonnet of "Second April"—in which the poet repudiates with cold anger the lover's "mouth of clay, these mortal bones against my body set," and "all the puny fever and frail sweat of human love."

In this fierce Manichæan denunciation of the body and the poor joys it has to offer, we find the real attitude that underlies these frivolities—and it is far from being a frank acceptance of the facts of life. It is not modern, it is something very ancient—an austere religious idealism, none the less austere and none the less a religion because it now has artists for its priests. It is a belief in something beyond this mortal life—the immortality, in this instance, of art. And it is not as a woman that the poet speaks here, but as a human being and a creative artist. Her mortal lover, with his dream of a warm earthly happiness to which she as woman must minister, is pushed aside. "You shall awake," he is told,

> from dreams of me, that at your side,
> So many nights, a lover and a bride,
> But stern in my soul's chastity, have lain,
> To walk the world forever, for my sake,
> And in each chamber find me gone again!

In a sense it is a rebellion against sex, and—since women are by social custom more the servants of their sex than men—against being a woman: a triumphant escape into an impersonal realm of art, which resembles heaven in that there is no marrying nor giving in marriage. Another woman poet, Anna Wickham, has expressed quaintly the same rebellion: "I hide my breast in a workman's shirt, / And hunt the perfect phrase."

But it is, as found in real life, not so austere a state of mind as might be imagined. In these feminist days it is not unusual to talk to a girl in forgetfulness of the fact that she belongs to the other half of the human race; but it is nevertheless not yet so commonplace that one does not feel a thrill to discover in a girl the capacity for such a broadly human relationship. Edna Millay is, eminently, such a person, the most delightful of companions—a gay and whimsical comrade, heartfree if not carefree, keen, generous, and braveminded.

The poetic scorn of mere human nature has its origin, of course, in the fact of the transiency of life. Life is pitiful because—as poets more than other people are given to reminding themselves—it comes inevitably to an end. "This flawless vital hand, this perfect head, this body of flame and steel"— shall die like any other: "it mattering not how beautiful you were."

Meanwhile, awaiting death, the poet has brave things to say: "the sands of such a life as mine run red and gold even to the ultimate sifting dust" . . .

> In me no lenten wicks watch out the night;
> I am the booth where Folly holds her fair,
> Impious no less in ruin than in strength . . .

But still the thought of death recurs. Therefore—

> Suffer me to take your hand.
> Suffer me to cherish you
> Till the dawn is in the sky.
> Whether I be false or true,
> Death comes in a day or two.

And again, for a more sufficient solace against the thought of death, comes the hope of that immortality which art offers to those who serve her well:

> Ah, when the thawed winter splashes
> Over these chance dust and ashes,
> Weep not me, my friend!
>
> Me, by no means dead
> In that hour, but surely
> When this book, unread,
> Rots to earth obscurely,
> And no more to any breast,
> Close against the clamorous swelling
> Of the thing there is no telling,
> Are these pages pressed!

It is in such poems as these, in which the thought of death makes life more sweet, more beautiful, and more to be cherished moment by moment, that Edna Millay is at her best and loveliest. She has the gift of seeing things as though with her last living look. Her poem "Renascence" embodies the strange fantasy of one dying and coming alive again to look once more upon the earth. Another poem, "The Blue Flag in the Bog," relates a still stranger fantasy—the destruction of the earth, and of one sadly watching it burn, from heaven. "Now forevermore good-bye, all the gardens of the world!" In both poems it is a child who sees the beauty of earth so poignantly; and it is thus that Edna Millay sees it, always, with the eyes of a child—and thus that she salutes it, as one who is about to take leave of it forever.

All her early life was spent on the coast of Maine, and her young mind seems to have been filled with an infinity of impressions of the sea: "The sticky, salty sweetness of the strong wind and shattered spray"; "the loud sound and the soft sound of the big surf that breaks all day." She began to write poetry as a child, encouraged by her mother, who is a poet of real if unfulfilled talent, and a woman besides of vivid, humorous, and tolerant personality. But it wasn't of these familiar scenes that Edna as a child wrote; it was, as in a poem to be found in the files of "St. Nicholas," of "the road to romance"! It was only, perhaps, when she had trodden the road away from childhood that she looked back and found it so beautiful:

> Always I climbed the wave at morning,
>   Shook the sand from my shoes at night,
> That now am caught beneath great buildings,
>   Stricken with noise, confused with light.

It was the child who climbed the wave at morning, and not the adult wearied with city noise, who wrote "Renascence." That poem, comparable in its power and vision to "The Hound of Heaven," was written during her eighteenth and nineteenth years. It was submitted in a prize poem contest and published among other poems in "The Lyric Year," in 1912. It is now generally remembered as having won the prize; the fact is that it was passed over altogether in the awards.

This strange, lovely, mystical poem aroused in literary circles curious speculations as to its author, who was imagined as a child mystic. A poet, now better acquainted with her, wrote a solemnly congratulatory letter such as he might have written to young Christina Rossetti, or to Santa Teresa herself. He was much puzzled by the irrelevant and frivolous missive he received in return—dealing chiefly with the elated purchase of a pair of red dancing slippers. She was, it seemed, a real nineteen year old girl!

The year following she entered Vassar. She graduated in 1917 with an A.B. and a reputation for brilliant scholarship. She had written two plays at college and acted in them—"The Princess Marries the Page" and "Two Slatterns and a King." And now her first volume of poems was to appear.

The volume, "Renascence," included together with the title poem some quietly notable new ones. These showed no signs of influence by any of the jazzy contemporary movements in poetry; they were not cubistic nor postimpressionistic, they were not in free verse, nor intended to be chanted to revival tunes; the lines were chiseled, the rhythms classical—she was so old fashioned, even, as to write sonnets. The new poems contained nothing so astonishing as "Renascence," but they showed a marked individual talent, and they maintained for her the respect of lovers of poetry.

She came from college, ambitiously, to New York, and settled in Greenwich Village, where rents were—in those days—low; in a very tiny room on Waverly Place, hardly large enough for a bed and a typewriter and some cups and saucers; a room, however, with the luxury of a fireplace, for which Joe the Italian brought, every few days, staggering up the stairs, a load of firewood at ten cents a precious stick. Here, on the floor, hugging the fire, she sat, remembering the coast of Maine: "the green piles groaning under the windy wooden piers"; "robins in the stubble," and "brown sheep upon the warm green hill" . . . remembering these, and making of such images poignant poems, only, as always happens with young poets, to get them back again from magazine editors who were "already overstocked with poetry."

A poet can, of course, live almost exclusively upon tea and coffee. But one must have cigarettes once in a while. Also, it is pleasant to have real cream, instead of condensed milk, in one's coffee. So, remembering her acting experience at Vassar, she went to the theatrical agencies, seeking a job. She was sent to the Provincetown Theatre of Macdougal Street, and acted in a number of comedies, and presently had some of her own plays put on. But the Provincetown Theatre, at that time, was very much an art-for-art's sake institution, paying neither actors' salaries nor authors' royalties. It was a happy moment when she was given a small "part" in one of the Theatre Guild productions, and a salary.

But there were no more "parts," and no more salary; and meantime she lived on bread and coffee, or, for a change, bread and tea; except when, according to the happy bohemian custom of the Village, someone dropped into her tiny room on Waverly Place with a delicatessen dinner of pickles, olives, cold roast beef, potato salad, and, if he were a true friend, a bottle of cream—honest-to-God cream!—or on those other exceptional occasions when somebody had the money to pay for a dinner in the basement of the Brevoort.

When they dropped in, laden with packages from the delicatessen, or with the elate air of one who is going Brevoorting, they might find her crouched brooding on the floor of an unswept and disorderly room. She was not brooding over some shattered romance—for romances are always shattered, so why trouble about a thing like that?—but over a batch of manuscripts just come back from some magazine. . . . She *ought*, no doubt, to make use of her knowledge of shorthand and get a job as a stenographer; or even go to work at the ribbon counter of a department store. If people didn't want beautiful poetry why should she starve writing it? A fair question! . . . But to go to work, in that dull mechanical sense, would be a final surrender of her pride as a creator; it meant giving up being a poet. It would be spiritual suicide; and if it came to that, why accept the ignominy of doing drudgery for people who don't care for poetry? Why live in such a world at all?

On the other hand, why not? She had had no illusions about the world. It was an ugly and absurd place. She had never supposed otherwise, nor had any serious hope of its ever being made much better by her revolutionary friends. But, ugly and absurd as it was, the poet could find beauty in it. That was what poets, apparently, were for—to squeeze this toad of a world with unflinching fingers until it gave up the jewel, of which—as all children who read fairy tales know—it is the venomous guardian! Perhaps she had better stick it out—which, upon further consideration, she decided to do.

In this tiny room might be seen, at times, her charming younger sisters, Norma, who had also come to New York, and Kathleen, on her vacation from Vassar—and sometimes the three of them could be persuaded to "harmonize" an old song of their own, Edna taking a throaty baritone:

> Oh, men! Men! Men!
> Oh, men alluring,
> Waste not your hour
> (Sweet hour!)
> In vain assuring.
> For love, though sweet,
> (*Oh, tho thweet!*)
> Is not enduring.
> Ti-di-dee and ti-di-da!
> We must take you as you are,
> Etc.

A pleasant scene to remember. . . .

Edna Millay's later career includes the publication of "Aria da Capo," a very remarkable play first presented by the Provincetown Players; "The Lamp and the Bell," which was the Vassar play for 1921; "A Few Figs from Thistles," already mentioned; and "Second April," in which her poetry has come to full bloom. "The Poet and His Book" is among the great lyrics of our language; and the volume contains, besides this poem, more than one that will go into the anthologies. In the meantime her work has happily found a wider recognition. She is at present in Europe, with her mother; she is finishing a fantastic prose romance, and—one learns with regret—is not anxious, in spite of the moth-eaten and rusty aspect of that part of the world, to return to her native land.

Edna St. Vincent Millay

Louis Untermeyer

In 1912, an anthology entitled *The Lyric Year* (Mitchell Kennerley) awarded three prizes to the contributions, none of which had appeared in any volume. Ten thousand poems (according to Ferdinand Earle, the editor) by nearly two thousand writers of verse were submitted and one hundred poems by as many poets were printed in this collection. Contrary to current belief, none of the three prizes was won by the outstanding poem in the book—a poem which has become one of the most famous in contemporary letters. Its author, totally unknown at the time, was little more than a child living on the seacoast of Maine, and it was not until her first book was published five years later that it became possible to appraise the work of Edna St. Vincent Millay.

The poem to which I have referred—the title-poem of her *Renascence and Other Poems* (Mitchell Kennerley, 1917)—was written when Miss Millay was nineteen years old; it remains possibly the most astonishing performance of this generation. But it is far more than a performance; it is a revelation. It begins like a child's aimless verse or a counting-out rhyme:

> All I could see from where I stood
> Was three long mountains and a wood;
> I turned and looked another way,
> And saw three islands in a bay.
> So with my eyes I traced the line
> Of the horizon, thin and fine,
> Straight around till I was come
> Back to where I'd started from;
> And all I saw from where I stood
> Was three long mountains and a wood.

After this almost inconsequential opening, the couplets develop into what first seems to be a descriptive idyl and then, growing out of a straightforward lyricism, mount into a rapt hymn to being. In this child's passion for identification with all of life, burns a splendor that attains nothing less than magnificence. She reaches up her hand and touches the sky, she sees

Reprinted from *American Poetry Since 1990* (New York: Henry Holt, 1923): 214–21.

"Immensity made manifold," she hears "The gossiping of friendly spheres, /
The creaking of the tented sky, / The ticking of Eternity."

The universe, "cleft to the core," is open to her probing senses. In her
desire for unity with all growth and suffering, the living earth surges through
her.

> A man was starving in Capri;
> He moved his eyes and looked at me;
> I felt his gaze, I heard his moan,
> And knew his hunger as my own.
> I saw at sea a great fog-bank
> Between two ships that struck and sank;
> A thousand screams the heavens smote;
> And every scream tore through my throat.
> No hurt I did not feel, no death
> That was not mine; mine each last breath
> That, crying, met an answering cry
> From the compassion that was I.
> All suffering mine, and mine its rod;
> Mine, pity like the pity of God.

This spiritual intensity drives her to the very heart of existence. In a
vision, she sees herself resting deep in the earth where consciousness becomes
still keener.

> The grass, a-tiptoe at my ear,
> Whispering to me I could hear;
> I felt the rain's cool finger-tips
> Brush tenderly across my lips,
> Laid gently on my sealèd sight,
> And all at once the heavy night
> Fell from my eyes and I could see!—
> A drenched and dripping apple-tree,
> A last long line of silver rain. . . .

It is a cumulative rapture in which the climax comes like a burst of
sudden trumpets; one is confronted by the revelation of forgotten magnificence. Mystery becomes articulate. It is as if a child had entered the room
and, in the midst of ingenuousness, had uttered some lucid and blinding
truth. There is a Blake-like poignance in the ever-ascending cadence, a
leaping simplicity which cries:

> O God, I cried, no dark disguise
> Can e'er hereafter hide from me

Thy radiant identity!
Thou canst not move across the grass
But my quick eye will see Thee pass,
Nor speak, however silently,
But my hushed voice will answer Thee.
I know the path that tells Thy way
Through the cool eve of every day;
God, I can push the grass apart
And lay my finger on Thy heart!

This lyrical mastery is manifest on all except a few pages (such as "Interim" and "Ashes of Life," which lisp as uncertainly as the hundreds of poems to which they are too closely related); it shines particularly in the unnamed sonnets, the light "Afternoon on a Hill," the whimsical "When the Year Grows Old" and the remarkable "God's World," in which Miss Millay has communicated rapture in a voice that no lyricist of her time has surpassed for beauty. In the fourteen lines of "God's World" this poet sounds the same hunger which intensified "Renascence." Here the spiritual passion is so exalted that the poet trembles with and voices the breathless awe of thousands caught at the heart by a birdnote or a sunset. But where the others are choked in the brief moment of worship, she has made ecstasy articulate and almost tangible.

O world, I cannot hold thee close enough!
    Thy winds, thy wide grey skies!
    Thy mists that roll and rise!
Thy woods, this autumn day, that ache and
    sag
And all but cry with color! That gaunt crag
To crush! To lift the lean of that black bluff!
World, World, I cannot get thee close enough!

Long have I known a glory in it all,
    But never knew I this:
    Here such a passion is
As stretcheth me apart, Lord, I do fear
Thou'st made the world too beautiful this year;
My soul is all but out of me,—let fall
No burning leaf; prithee, let no bird call.

It is something of a shock to turn from *Renascence*, possibly the most amazing first book of the period, to the succeeding *A Few Figs from Thistles* (Frank Shay, 1920; Revised Edition, Stewart Kidd Company, 1922). Here Miss Millay seems to have exchanged her birthright for a mess of cleverness;

it is nothing more than a pretty talent that gives most of these light verses the quality of a facile cynicism, an ignoble adroitness. This is the "first fig":

> My candle burns at both ends;
>   It will not last the night;
> But ah, my foes, and oh, my friends—
>   It gives a lovely light!

Only the dilettanti of emotion could relish, after the radiance of her first poems, the sophisticated smirk that accompanies "The Penitent," "Thursday," "She Is Overheard Singing," "The Merry Maid," and others of the same easy genre.

> And if I loved you Wednesday
>   Well, what is that to you?
> I do not love you Thursday—
>   So much is true.

> And why you come complaining
>   Is more than I can see.
> I loved you Wednesday,—yes—but what
>   Is that to me?

One resents such lines not because one feels the poet may lose her quality by playing with fire, but because she is merely setting herself off in theatrical fireworks and so is in danger of losing her soul. The author of "God's World" is the last person who should deck passion with tinsel.

But there are deeper penetrations even in this volume. When Miss Millay is less consciously irresponsible, less archly narcissic, *A Few Figs from Thistles* bear riper fruit. "Portrait by a Neighbor" is a clear and delightful picture—one cannot forget the scatter-brained dreamer who "weeds her lazy lettuce by the light of the moon," who "forgets she borrowed butter and pays you back cream!" "The Singing Woman from the Wood's Edge" (in the new edition) is no less playfully precise. And if, in *The Lamp and the Bell*, a tragedy in blank verse and five acts (Frank Shay, 1921), this gift of portraiture is strained beyond its power, there are many individual passages and several scenes of intensity on the theme of platonic love between two girl-companions. *Aria da Capo* (Mitchell Kennerley; the August, 1920, issue of Harold Monro's The Chapbook was devoted to its first appearance) is a much more poignant condensation; a tensely ironic one-act play in which the traditional Pierrot, Columbine, Corydon and Thyrsis are placed—the first pair frivolously, the two shepherds like protesting marionettes—against the terrible background of war.

Second April (Mitchell Kennerley, 1921) recaptures the earlier, concentrated ecstasy. There is little rhetoric here, no mere imitation of prettiness; the too-easy charm to which Miss Millay occasionally descends is replaced by a dignity, almost an austerity of emotion. Hers is a triumph not only of expression but above her idiom; she is one of the few living poets who can employ inversions, who can use the antiquated *forsooth, alack! prithee,* and *la,* and not seem an absurd anachronism. Possibly it is because Miss Millay is at heart a belated Elizabethan that she can use locutions which in the work of any other American would be affected and false. "The Blue-Flag in the Bog," a splendid sequel to "Renascence," contains this rapture undisguised; "The Bean-Stalk" reflects it in a lighter tone of voice. "The Poet and His Book" is almost as intensified, and "Journey," written in her 'teens, holds some of the loveliest lines Miss Millay has ever composed.

> All my life long
> Over my shoulder have I looked at peace;
> And now I fain would lie in this long grass
> And close my eyes.
> > Yet onward!
> > Cat-birds call
> Through the long afternoon, and creeks at dusk
> Are guttural. Whip-poor-wills wake and cry,
> Drawing the twilight close about their throats.
> Only my heart makes answer. Eager vines
> Go up the rocks and wait; flushed apple-trees
> Pause in their dance and break the ring for me. . . .
> Of round-faced roses, pink and petulant,
> Look back and beckon ere they disappear.
> Only my heart, only my heart responds.

Possibly the most haunting section of this volume is the "Memorial to D.C." These six lyrical epitaphs and dirges have a vibrancy which this poet has never surpassed, a pathos which is somber but in which bitterness has no part. "Prayer to Persephone" accomplishes the miracle of being pathetic and whimsical in the same breath; "Elegy," which the poet may well have addressed to herself, trembles with its own high notes. Its parts are so lyrically integrated that I risk the vandalism of detaching the conclusion of this poem:

> Cherished by the faithful sun
> On and on eternally
> Shall your altered fluid run,
> Bud and bloom and go to seed;
> But your singing days are done;
> But the music of your talk
> Never shall the chemistry

> Of the secret earth restore.
> All your lovely words are spoken.
> Once the ivory box is broken,
> Beats the golden bird no more.

The sonnets which occur in all of Miss Millay's volume, exhibit the same sensitive parsimony which is in the best of her lyrics. *Second April* contains twelve that have the bright phrasing cut down to the glowing core. Her highest achievement in this form, however, is, I believe, not here, but in the group "Eight Sonnets," which she contributed to *American Poetry— 1922* (Harcourt, Brace and Company). The first six of these are as arresting as anything Miss Millay has accomplished; the sixth, indeed, is as fine a sonnet as this age has produced. This is the passionate evocation of magic, brilliant in its stripped clarity.

> Euclid alone has looked on Beauty bare.
> Let all who prate of Beauty hold their peace,
> And lay them prone upon the earth and cease
> To ponder on themselves, the while they stare
> At nothing, intricately drawn nowhere
> In shapes of shifting lineage; let geese
> Gabble and hiss, but heroes seek release
> From dusty bondage into luminous air.
>
> O blinding hour, O holy, terrible day,
> When first the shaft into his vision shone
> Of light anatomized! Euclid alone
> Has looked on Beauty bare. Fortunate they
> Who, though once only and then but far away,
> Have heard her massive sandal set on stone.

It is such felicity of language that gives the poetry of Edna Millay the power of resonant speech; hers is a voice that is both intellectually thrilling and emotionally moving.

Youth and Wings:
Edna St. Vincent Millay: Singer

Carl Van Doren

The little renaissance of poetry which there have been a hundred historians to scent and chronicle in the United States during the last decade flushed to a dawn in 1912. In that year was founded a magazine for the sole purpose of helping poems into the world; in that year was published an anthology which meant to become an annual, though, as it happened, another annual by another editor took its place the year following. The real poetical event of 1912, however, was the appearance in *The Lyric Year*, tentative anthology, of the first outstanding poem by Edna St. Vincent Millay. Who that then had any taste of which he can now be proud but remembers the discovery, among the numerous failures and very innumerous successes which made up the volume, of *Renascence*, by a girl of twenty whose name none but her friends and a lucky critic or two had heard? After wading through tens and dozens of rhetorical strophes and moral stanzas, it was like suddenly finding wings to come upon these lines:

> "All I could see from where I stood
> Was three long mountains and a wood;
> I turned and looked another way,
> And saw three islands in a bay.
> So with my eyes I traced the line
> Of the horizon, thin and fine,
> Straight around till I was come
> Back to where I'd started from;
> And all I saw from where I stood
> Was three long mountains and a wood."

The diction was so plain, the arrangement so obvious, that the magic of the opening seemed a mystery; and yet the lift and turn of these verses were magical, as if a lark had taken to the air out of a dreary patch of stubble.

Nor did the poem falter as it went on. If it had the movement of a bird's flight, so had it the ease of a bird's song. The poet of this lucid voice

Reprinted from *Many Minds* (New York: Knopf, 1924): 105–19.

had gone through a radiant experience. She had, she said with mystical directness, felt that she could touch the horizon, and found that she could touch the sky. Then infinity had settled down upon her till she could hear "The ticking of Eternity." The universe pressed close and crushed her, oppressing her with omniscience and omnisentience; all sin, all remorse, all suffering, all punishment, all pity poured into her, torturing her. The weight drove her into the cool earth, where she lay buried, but happy, under the falling rain.

> "The rain, I said, is kind to come
> And speak to me in my new home.
> I would I were alive again
> To kiss the fingers of the rain,
> To drink into my eyes the shine
> Of every slanting silver line."

Suddenly came over her the terrible memory of the "multi-colored, multi-form, beloved" beauty she had lost by this comfortable death. She burst into a prayer so potent that the responding rain, gathering in a black wave, opened the earth above her and set her free.

> "Ah! Up then from the ground sprang I
> And hailed the earth with such a cry
> As is not heard save from a man
> Who has been dead, and lives again.
> About the trees my arms I wound;
> Like one gone mad I hugged the ground;
> I raised my quivering arms on high;
> I laughed and laughed into the sky."

Whereupon, somewhat quaintly, she moralized her experience with the pride of youth finally arrived at full stature in the world.

> "The heart can push the sea and land
> Farther away on either hand;
> The soul can split the sky in two,
> And let the face of God shine through.
> But East and West will pinch the heart
> That cannot keep them pushed apart;
> And he whose soul is flat—the sky
> Will cave in on him by and by."

Renascence, one of the loveliest of American poems, was an adventure, not an allegory, but it sounds almost allegorical because of the way it interpreted and distilled the temper which, after a long drought, was coming into American verse. Youth was discovering a new world, or thought it was. It had taken upon itself burdens of speculation, of responsibility, and had sunk under the weight. Now, on fire with beauty, it returned to joy and song.

2

Other things than joy and song, however, cut across the track of this little renaissance. There was a war. Youth—at least that part of it which makes poems—went out to fight, first with passion for the cause and then with contempt for the dotards who had botched and bungled. Gray Tyrtæuses might drone that here was a good war designed to end war, but youth meantime saw that it was dying in hordes and tried to snatch what ecstasy it could before the time should come when there would be no more ecstasy. Boys and girls who would otherwise have followed the smooth paths of their elders now questioned them and turned aside into different paths of life. Young men and maidens who would otherwise have expected little of love for years to come now demanded all that love offers, and demanded it immediately for fear it might come too late. The planet was reeling, or looked to be; all the settled orders were straining and breaking. Amid the hurly-burly of argument and challenge and recrimination a lyric had a good chance to be unheard; yet it was a lyrical hour, as it always is when the poet sees himself surrounded by swift moments hurrying to an end. Some sense of this in the air, even amid the hurly-burly, gave to the youth of the time that rash, impatient, wild ardor and insolence and cynicism which followed in such fleet succession, growing sharper as the war which was to have been good turned into the peace which was bound to be bad.

Miss Millay's *Aria da Capo*, like *Renascence*, has an allegorical sound, because it lays its finger so surely upon the mad sickness of the race during those futile years. The little play, now dainty with artifice and now racy with slang and satire, opens with Columbine and Pierrot skylarking in their pretty fashion, using, however, words with two sharp edges to each of them. But they are driven from the stage by tragedy, which sets the friendly shepherds Thyrsis and Corydon to playing a scene in which they divide their mimic field with colored ribbons, which they call a wall, find one of them mimic water on his side and the other mimic jewels, move on to a conflict which they did not mean or want and which they see is hardly so much reality as senseless acting, and in the end kill each other across the barrier, dying in each other's arms. Back come Pierrot and Columbine to resume, only a little disturbed by the dead bodies lying under their feet, the happy farce. Love among the ruins! Butterflies above the battle! Such folly as had been acted

by the nations, the play hints, belongs rather to the painted theater than to
the solid earth. There is not enough wisdom to understand it; there are not
enough tears to bewail it. It may be better to frolic and forget.

3

The decade since the little renaissance began has created a kind of symbol
for this irresponsible mood in the more or less mythical Greenwich Village,
where, according to the popular legend, art and mirth flourish without a
care, far from the stupid duties of human life. No one so well as Miss Millay
has spoken with the accents credited to the village.

> "My candle burns at both ends;
> It will not last the night;
> But ah, my foes, and oh, my friends—
> It gives a lovely light!"

Thus she commences in *A Few Figs from Thistles*. And she continues with
impish songs and rakish ballads and sonnets which laugh at the love which
throbs through them. Suckling was not more insouciant than she is in
Thursday:

> "And if I loved you Wednesday,
> Well, what is that to you?
> I do not love you Thursday—
> So much is true.
> And why you come complaining
> Is more than I can see.
> I loved you Wednesday—yes—but what
> Is that to me?"

With what a friendliness for wild souls she tells the story of the singing
woman "Whose mother was a leprechaun, whose father was a friar."

> "In through the bushes, on any foggy day,
> My Da would come a-swishing of the drops away,
> With a prayer for my death and a groan for my birth,
> A-mumbling of his beads for all that he was worth.
>
> And there sit my Ma, her knees beneath her chin,
> A-looking in his face and a-drinking of it in,
> And a-marking in the moss some funny little saying
> That would mean just the opposite of all that he was praying!

He taught me the holy-talk of Vesper and of Matin,
He heard me my Greek and he heard me my Latin,
He blessed me and crossed me to keep my soul from evil,
And we watched him out of sight, and we conjured up the devil!

Oh, the things I haven't seen and the things I haven't known,
What with hedges and ditches till after I was grown,
And yanked both ways by my mother and my father,
With a 'Which would you better?' and a 'Which would you rather?'

With him for a sire and her for a dam,
What should I be but just what I am?"

Speaking in this manner, Greenwich Village seems a long way from the village of Concord, heart of the old tradition, even though Hawthorne loved a faun when he met one, and Thoreau was something of a faun himself. In the classic village any such mixture as this of leprechaun and friar would have been kept as close a secret as possible, and conscience would have been set to the work of driving the leprechaun taint out. In Greenwich Village the friar is made to look a little comical, especially to the mother and daughter who conspire to have their fling behind his back.

4

This tincture of diablerie appears again and again in Miss Millay's verse, perhaps most of all in the candor with which she talks of love. She has put by the mask under which other poets who were women, apparently afraid for the reputation of their sex, have spoken as if they were men. She has put by the posture of fidelity which women in poetry have been expected to assume. She speaks with the voice of women who, like men, are thrilled by the beauty of their lovers and are stung by desire; who know, however, that love does not always vibrate at its first high pitch, and so, too faithful to love to insist upon clinging to what has become half-love merely, let go without desperation. A woman may be fickle for fun, Miss Millay suggests in various poems wherein this or that girl teases her lover with the threat to leave him or the claim that she has forgotten him; but so may a woman show wisdom by admitting the variability and transience of love, as in this crystal sonnet:

"I know I am but summer to your heart,
And not the full four seasons of the year;
And you must welcome from another part
Such noble moods as are not mine, my dear.
No gracious weight of golden fruits to sell

Have I, nor any wise and wintry thing;
And I have loved you all too long and well
To carry still the high sweet breast of spring.
Wherefore I say: O love, as summer goes,
I must be gone, steal forth with silent drums,
That you may hail anew the bird and rose
When I come back to you, as summer comes.
Else will you seek, at some not distant time,
Even your summer in another clime."

What sets Miss Millay's love-poems apart from almost all those written in English by women is the full pulse which, in spite of their gay impudence, beats through them. She does not speak in the name of forlorn maidens or of wives bereft, but in the name of women who dare to take love at the flood, if it offers, and who later, if it has passed, remember with exultation that they had what no coward could have had. Conscience does not trouble them, nor any serious division in their natures. No one of them weeps because she has been a wanton, no one of them because she has been betrayed. Rarely since Sappho has a woman voiced such delight in a lover's beauty as this:

"What's this of death, from you who never will die?
Think you the wrist that fashioned you in clay,
The thumb that set the hollow just that way
In your full throat and lidded the long eye
So roundly from the forehead, will let lie
Broken, forgotten, under foot some day
Your unimpeachable body, and so slay
The work he had been most remembered by?"

Rarely since Sappho has a woman written as outspokenly as this.

"What lips my lips have kissed, and where, and why,
I have forgotten, and what arms have lain
Under my head till morning; but the rain
Is full of ghosts to-night, that tap and sigh
Upon the glass and listen for reply;
And in my heart there stirs a quiet pain
For unremembered lads that not again
Will turn to me at midnight with a cry."

In passages like these Miss Millay has given body and vesture to a sense of equality in love; to the demand by women that they be allowed to enter the world of adventure and experiment in love which men have long inhabited. But Miss Millay does not, like any feminist, argue for that equality. She takes it for granted, exhibits it in action, and turns it into beauty.

5

Beauty, not argument, is, after all, Miss Millay's concern and goal. She can be somewhat metaphysical about it, as in her contention that

> "Euclid alone has looked on Beauty bare.
> Let all who prate of Beauty hold their peace,
> And lay them prone upon the earth and cease
> To ponder on themselves, the while they stare
> At nothing, intricately drawn nowhere
> In shapes of shifting lineage."

For the most part, however, she stands with those who love life and persons too wholly to spend much passion upon anything abstract. She loves the special countenance of every season, the hot light of the sun, gardens of flowers with old, fragrant names, the salt smell of the sea along her native Maine coast, the sound of sheep-bells and dripping eaves and the unheard sound of city trees, the homely facts of houses in which men and women live, tales of quick deeds and eager heroisms, the cool, kind love of young girls for one another, the color of words, the beat of rhythm. The shining clarity of her style does not permit her to work the things she finds beautiful into tapestried verse; she will not ask a song to carry more than it can carry on the easiest wings; but in all her graver songs and sonnets she serves beauty in one way or another. Now she affirms her absolute loyalty to beauty; now she hunts it out in unexpected places; most frequently of all she buries it with some of the most exquisite dirges of her time.

These returning dirges and elegies and epitaphs are as much the natural speech of Miss Millay as is her insolence of joy in the visible and tangible world. Like all those who most love life and beauty, she understands that both are brief and mortal. They take her round and round in a passionate circle: because she loves them so ardently she knows they cannot last, and because she knows they cannot last she loves them the more ardently while they do. Dispositions such as hers give themselves to joy when their vitality is at its peaks; in their lower hours they weep over the graves of loveliness which are bound to crowd their courses. Having a high heart and a proud creed, Miss Millay leaves unwept some graves which other poets and most people water abundantly, but she is stabbed by the essential tragedy and pity of death. Thus she expresses the tragic powerlessness of those who live to hold those who die:

> "Nor shall my love avail you in your hour.
> In spite of all my love, you will arise
> Upon that day and wander down the air
> Obscurely as the unattended flower,

It mattering not how beautiful you were,
Or how beloved above all else that dies."

Thus she expresses the pitiful knowledge which the living have that they
cannot help the dead:

"Be to her, Persephone,
All the things I might not be;
Take her head upon your knee.
She that was so proud and wild,
Flippant, arrogant and free,
She that had no need of me,
Is a little lonely child
Lost in Hell,—Persephone,
Take her head upon your knee;
Say to her, 'My dear, my dear,
It is not so dreadful here.' "

Are these only the accents of a minor poet, crying over withered roses
and melted snows? Very rarely do minor poets strike such moving chords
upon such universal strings. Still more rarely do merely minor poets have so
much power over tragedy and pity, and yet in other hours have equal power
over fire and laughter.

Miss Millay's Kinship to Keats

ARTHUR SYMONS

I have been reading the Poems of Edna St. Vincent Millay, in the beautifully printed edition of Mr. Martin Secker, with its bright green binding; finding in it, of course, much that is unequal, immature, and uninspired. Yet, on the whole, few books of modern verse, of verse written by women, have given me so much pleasure; only, I shall not say what Poe, by no means a good critic, wrote on Mrs. Browning. "Her wild and magnificent genius seems to have contented itself with points—to have exhausted itself in flashes—but in the profusion—the unparalleled number and close propinquity of these points and flashes render her book *one flame*, and justify us in calling her, unhesitatingly, the greatest—the most glorious of her sex." On the contrary, I would say that some of her verse reminds me of Poe's when he is most fantastically inhuman—and that here is an overconscious artist doing strange things with strange materials.

"The Poet and His Book" has in it a supreme sense of what Life and Death are, of one's possible survival, of the fortune or misfortunes of our most precious books—written by one's life-blood—of those revels, spirits, travelers, goblins, thieves, that have haunted and obsessed the imagination of some of the greatest poets, from Catullus to Villon, from Aristophanes to Baudelaire and Verlaine. This seems to me comparable with some of those of Beddoes, whose "Death's Jest-Book" is the most morbid and undramatic poem in our literature; Beddoes, who has written a new Dance of Death in poetry, who has become the chronicler of the praise and ridicule of Death; whose genius is made manifest in these lines:

> The moon doth mock and make me crazy,
>   And midnight tolls her horrid claim
>   On ghostly homage. Fie, for shame!
> Death, to stand painted there so lazy.
> There's nothing but the stars about us,
>   And they're no tell-tales, but shine quiet:
>   Come out, and hold a midnight riot,
> Where no mortal fool dare flout us.

Reprinted from *Literary Digest International Book Review* 2 (April 1942): 351–52.

That is *macabre*: so is this stanza of Miss Millay's:

> Down, you mongrel, Death!
>   Back into your kennel!
> I have stolen breath
>   In a stalk of fennel!
> You shall scratch and you shall whine,
>   Many a night, and you shall worry
>   Many a bone, before you bury
> One sweet bone of mine!

I have been reading "The Celtic Twilight," that beautiful and magical and exquisite and strange and bewildering volume of Yeats, where he says, after an invocation, how he had driven off the black clouds and how he had noticed that the man on his left hand had passed into a death-like trance, and that for some days he could not get over the feeling of having a number of deformed and grotesque figures lingering about him. "The Bright Powers are always beautiful and desirable, and the Dim Powers are now beautiful, now quaintly grotesque, but the Dark Powers express their unbalanced natures in shapes of ugliness and horror." I should not be surprised if these sentences might not have inspired Miss Millay in the creation of "The Singing Woman from the Wood's Edge," which has wild rhythm of its own, and which shows that one must have a depraved and an abnormal imagination to have written such verses as these. I might almost imagine myself with Huysmans in Paris in 1892, when he was writing "La-Bas," witnessing the monstrous tableau of the Black Mass—so marvelously, so revoltingly described in the central episode of the book—which is still enacted in our days. These verses are monstrous and yet humorous, devilish and malign:

> And who should be my playmates but the adder and the frog,
> That was begot beneath a furze-bush and born in a bog?
> And what should be my singing, that was christened at an altar,
> But Aves and Creeds and Psalms out of the Psalter?

> But there comes to birth no common spawn
> From the love of a priest for a leprechaun,
> And you have never seen and you shall never see
> Such things as the things that swaddled me!

> After all's said and after all's done,
> What should I be but a harlot and a nun?

This poem reminds me of a story of hers, "Louis-Philippe," printed in *The Century Magazine,* which, when I read it, seemed to me on the whole the most abnormal, insane, cruel and hallucinatory study in a well-known form of mental alienation, that I had ever read. One felt the horror and the intense abomination of the thing as if these minute incidents had happened in an opium-dream. Besides this, there is the evident influence on her of Poe and of Villiers de l'Isle Adam; for in this story, also, there is a sort of double irony, a crisscross and intertexture of meanings and suggestions, which, again, sound the note of horror.

"The Blue-Flag in the Bog," which has over forty stanzas, contains I know not what undercurrent of subtle sensations and of wild imaginings and of an almost ecstatic rapture. It is unlike anything I have read. There are, of course, touches in it of the Bible, of Blake, and of Meredith. These lines that reel, rush, spin, twist, have something in them of an actual hallucination. The poem is naked as air, as the evil naked nakedness of a snake. It shudders, and the Earth and the Flesh shudder, the waste grasses and the wild winds shudder: and there is always God—Father, Son and Holy Ghost—and there is the hand that, finally, rescues the fainting soul and the body that has forgotten all its grief. It seems impossible to quote many of these stanzas. Here are a few:

> God had called us and we came;
>   Our loved earth to ashes left;
> Heaven was a neighbour's house,
>   Open flung to us bereft.

> Withered grass—the wattles growing!
>   Aimless ache of laden boughs!
> Little things God had forgotten
>   Called me, from my burning house.

> And I listened for a voice;—
>   But my heart was all I heard;
> Not a screech-owl, not a loon,
>   Not a tree-toad said a word.

> And I peered into the smoke
>   Till it rotted like a fog:—
> Then, encompassed round by fire,
>   Stood a blue-flag in a bog!

> In a breath, ere I had breathed,—
>   Oh, I laughed, I cried, to see!
> I was kneeling at its side,
>   And it leaned its head on me!

Miss Millay in her "Ode to Silence" has chosen the singular but not lawless meter which Patmore used in "The Unknown Eros"; the form is derived from the Odes of Pindar. Swinburne said of the Ode on Athens and the

Ode on the Armada: "By the test of these two poems I am content that my claims should be decided and my station determined as a lyric poet in the higher sense of the term." There is no more likelihood of Swinburne going down to posterity as the writer of those two splendid poems than there is of Coleridge being remembered as the writer of the Ode to France rather than as the writer of the Ode on Dejection. The first is a product of the finest poetical rhetoric, the second is a growth of the profoundest poetical genius. There is a wonderful lyric growth—of rare flowers and of wasted weeds—in Miss Millay's Ode; which, founded as it is on Patmore's meter, is, in spirit and in execution, much more akin to Keats than to Patmore; and in these lines I find something of what I find in Keats: a waiting mood, a kind of electrically charged expectancy which draws its own desire out of the universe. She seems to have reincarnated something of the sense of the mystic soul of the Maenad, which to the Greeks meant as much as the myths of Dionysus, the god of intoxication, Apollo being the God of dreams; which meant as much as the image of Dionysus stained with wine-lees that I saw in Bologna on a famous Etruscan mirror; who, like Hades himself, is hollow and devouring, an eater of man's flesh: together with that other sense the Greek spirit had of the gulf of horror over which it seems to rest, suspended as on the wings of the condor.

> "She will love well," I said,
> "The flowers of the dead;
> Where dark Persephone the winter round,
> Uncomforted for home, uncomforted,
> Lacking a sunny southern slope in northern Sicily,
> With sullen pupils focussed on a dream,
> Stares on the stagnant stream
> That moats the unequivocal battlements of Hell,
> There, there, will she be found,
> She that is Beauty veiled from men and Music in a swound."
>
> I sought her down that dolorous labyrinth,
> Wherein no shaft of sunlight ever fell,
> And in among the bloodless everywhere.
> I sought her, but the air,
> Breathed many times and spent,
> Was fretful with a whispering discontent,
> And questioning me, importuning me to tell
> Some slightest tidings of the light of day they know no more,
> Plucking my sleeve, the eager shades were with me where I went.

The writer of verse like this has risen on the wings of her imagination to a height almost equal with the height of the last poem I have referred to. Only I find, as it were, "the flaming gulf" between them. There is in this Ode a limitless hunger and some of that wisdom which is the sorrowful desire of Beauty.

Comment: Edna St. Vincent Millay

Harriet Monroe

Long ago, when I was mooning and dreaming through the pig-tail period, I used to think how fine it would be to be the greatest woman poet since Sappho. The audacity of youth—of near-childhood—would have scorned any lower goal; and the young aspirant, gazing aloft and afar, seemed to detect a smile of encouragement on the inhumanly beautiful visage which glorified an imaginary shrine.

Well, failure is the lot of all—it were shame indeed for ardent youth to set up any attainable goal. The dream must outrun the fleetest foot, or else the trophy will wither in one's hand. "Success—there's no such thing!" I once made a "successful" man say in a play. It is more reasonable to take pride in the degree of one's failure than to measure with facile vanity one's achievement.

But I am reminded by that old dream to wonder whether we may not raise a point worthy of discussion in claiming that a certain living lady may perhaps be the greatest woman poet since Sappho. After all, the roll contains few names. Who are they, the woman-poets of the past twenty-five hundred years? Possessing few languages, I am incompetent in the search, but I can remember no names of importance in the Greek, Roman or mediaeval literature. Folk-lore may hide under its anonymity a few women—its motive and feeling are often feminine; but no one can search them out. POETRY'S wide shelf of more-or-less-modern anthologies—French, German, Italian, Russian, Jugo-Slavian, Armenian, Ukrainian, Swedish and others—all these contain few feminine names, and apparently none of importance. Two or three oriental ladies have been listed, but of their quality we cannot judge.

In short, the woman-poets seem to have written almost exclusively in the English language. Emily Bronte, Elizabeth Barrett Browning, Christina Rossetti, Emily Dickinson—these four names bring us to 1900. Differing profoundly each from the others, these women were alike in this—they were all recluses by instinct, leading shy lives more or less aloof from the world; three of them spinsters, and the fourth protected and enveloped by a singularly potent and sympathetic marriage.

From *Poetry* 24 (August 1924): 260–66. Copyright 1924 by The Modern Poetry Association and reprinted by permission of the Editor of *Poetry* and by courtesy of Dr. and Mrs. Edwin S. Fetcher, St. Paul, Minnesota.

Emily Bronte—austere, heroic, solitary—is of course the greatest woman in literature. Not even Sappho's *Hymn to Aphrodite* (ignorant of Greek, I speak timidly) can surpass *Wuthering Heights* for sheer depth and power of beauty, or match it for the compassing of human experience in a single masterpiece. But *Wuthering Heights*, though poetic in motive and essence, classes as a novel rather than a poem; and, if one omits that from the reckoning, Emily Bronte's rank as a poet, or more specifically as a lyrist, rests upon a single poem, the sublime *Last Lines* which made her faith in life immortal—for her other poems, some of them fine, are scarcely important. As a poet, she has not the scope, the variety, of Edna St. Vincent Millay, whose claim to pre-eminence we are considering.

Mrs. Browning?—well, some of the *Sonnets from the Portuguese*, another fine sonnet *Grief*, and lyric bits of longer (usually too long) poems, are beautiful and poignant, sincerely feminine in their emotional appeal. But they do not quite ascend to those higher levels which we are now trying to explore.

Nor Christina Rossetti. Religious poems like *Paradise* and *Marvel of Marvels* are finely fluted little altar-candles—burning rather pale, though, beside those of real ecstatics like Saint Teresa or Gerard Hopkins; and a few songs—*When I am dead, my dearest*, and others—are lovely in their sweet sincerity of renunciation. But these also breathe not that rarer air.

Emily Dickinson seems to climb higher than either Elizabeth or Christina. Her brief poems—many of them—have a swift and keen lyric intensity, a star-like beauty. They are sudden flashes into the deep well of a serene and impregnable human soul, sure of the truth in solitude.

✷Edna Millay is a very different person from any of these four. By no means a recluse, she has courted life and shunned none of its adventures. Her youth has been crowded with companions, friends, lovers; she has gone through college, earned her living at journalism, has travelled, acted, given readings, known poverty and comparative ease—in short, she has taken the rough-and-tumble of a modern American girl's life and has reached its usual climax, marriage. Beginning, before she was twenty and while still a little tomboy of the Maine coast, with *Renascence*, a poem of desperate faith, lithe as a faun in its naked search of the soul, the danger has been that life might lure her away from art. The complications of a hunted human soul in these stirring days—the struggle for breath, for food and lodging, the pot-boilers, the flirtations, the teasing petty trials and interruptions—how could the poet in her survive all these, and put out fresh flowers of beauty?

But the poet has survived and the flowers have sprung up richly along her path. If *Renascence* remains the poem of largest sweep which Miss Millay has achieved as yet—the most comprehensive expression of her philosophy, so to speak, her sense of miracle in life and death—yet she has been lavish with details of experience, of emotion, and her agile and penetrating mind has leapt through spaces of thought rarely traversed by women, or by men either for that matter.

For in the lightest of her briefest lyrics there is always more than appears. In the *Figs*, for example, in *Thursday, The Penitent, The Not Impossible Him* and other witty ironies, and in more serious poems like *The Betrothal*, how neatly she upsets the carefully built walls of convention which men have set up around their Ideal Woman, even while they fought, bled and died for all the Helens and Cleopatras they happened to encounter! And in *Aria da Capo*, a masterpiece of irony sharp as Toledo steel, she stabs the war-god to the heart with a stroke as clean, as deft, as ever the most skilfully murderous swordsman bestowed upon his enemy. Harangues have been made, volumes have been written, for the outlawry of war, but who else has put its preposterous unreasonableness into a nutshell like this girl who brings to bear upon the problem the luminous creative insight of genius?

Thus on the most serious subjects there is always the keen swift touch. Beauty blows upon them and is gone before one can catch one's breath; and lo and behold, we have a poem too lovely to perish, a song out of the blue which will ring in the ears of time. Such are the "little elegies" which will make the poet's Vassar friend, D.C. of the wonderful voice, a legend of imperishable beauty even though "her singing days are done." Thousands of stay-at-home women speak wistfully in *Departure*; and *Lament*—where can one find deep grief and its futility expressed with such agonizing grace? Indeed, though love and death and the swift passing of beauty have haunted this poet as much as others, she is rarely specific and descriptive. Her thought is transformed into imagery, into symbol, and it flashes back at us as from the facets of a jewel.

And the thing is so simply done. One weeps, not over D.C.'s death, but over her narrow shoes and blue gowns empty in the closet. In *Renascence* the sky, the earth, the infinite, no longer abstractions, come close, as tangible as a tree. *The Harp-weaver*, presenting the protective power of enveloping love—power which enwraps the beloved even after death has robbed him, is a kind of fairy-tale ballad, sweetly told as for a child. Even more in *The Curse* emotion becomes sheer magic of imagery and sound, as clear and keen as frost in sunlight. Always one feels the poet's complete and unabashed sincerity. She says neither the expected thing nor the "daring" thing, but she says the incisive true thing as she has discovered it and feels it.

Miss Millay's most confessional lyrics are in sonnet form, and among them are a number which can hardly be forgotten so long as English literature endures, and one or two which will rank among the best of a language extremely rich in beautiful sonnets. It is a pity that the poet ever broke up the series of *Twenty Sonnets* published in *Reedy's Mirror* during April and May, 1920, and afterwards scattered, all but two of them, through the volumes entitled *Second April, Figs from Thistles*, and *The Harp-weaver*. About three-fourths of the twenty belong together in a sequence which should be restored, a sequence which might be entitled *Winged Love* since it portrays the ecstasy and bitter brevity of passion. Among these are *Into the golden vessel of great song, Not with libations, Oh think not I am faithful to a vow, And you as well must die, Cherish you then the hope I shall forget*, and others in which verbal music, the winged phrase, the richly colored image, carry poignant emotion in triumph.

Beyond these, outside the love-sequence, the *Euclid* sonnet stands in a place apart, of a beauty hardly to be matched for sculpturesque austerity, for detachment from the body and the physical universe. Other minds, searching the higher mathematics, have divined the central structural beauty on which all other beauty is founded, but if any other poet has expressed it I have yet to see the proof. That a young woman should have put this fundamental law into a sonnet is one of the inexplicable divinations of genius. Those shallow critics who decry the modern scientific spirit as materialistic, who find no creative imagination in such minds as Willard Gibbs and Wilbur Wright, would do well to meditate upon this poem, one of the great sonnets of the language. If Miss Millay had done nothing else, she could hardly be forgotten.

But she has done much else. Wilful, moody, whimsical, loving and forgetting, a creature of quick and keen emotions, she has followed her own way and sung her own songs. Taken as a whole, her poems present an utterly feminine personality of singular charm and power; and the best of them, a group of lyrics ineffably lovely, will probably be cherished as the richest, most precious gift of song which any woman since the immortal Lesbian has offered to the world.

Edna St. Vincent Millay

GENEVIEVE TAGGARD

Women have borne poets and evoked poetry, but how few of them have written it! And for the simplest possible reason. We are coming to know that you cannot separate the creative fibre. All the nervous vitality that flows into a great poem begins in physical fertility, just where in the past it has almost always ended. In short, the creative woman before our time usually had twelve children; she seldom wrote poetry. After thirty, whatever her creative dimensions, she probably did not even read it. Children are tangible, insistent, appalling actualities, and their reality has a way of hushing the intensity that lies behind all abandon. Counting Sappho first, although she is really little more than a shadowy symbol, we find in consequence the meagre list in our own tongue Emily Brontë, Christina Rossetti and Elizabeth Barrett—none of them very adequate to our desire.

And then—suddenly, quite dazzlingly, in America, Emily Dickinson and Edna St. Vincent Millay.

I turn directly to Edna Millay to avoid, perhaps, all the temptation to contrast her with Emily Dickinson—a task so subtle and at the same time so full of pure generic extremes that nothing short of a long essay would suffice. Forgetting all likenesses and differences then, there remains one that is big and significant. Edna Millay is really the first woman poet to take herself seriously as an artist. Even Emily Dickinson, for all her strength and self-knowledge, refused to do that, except at midnight, when alone, like a burglar or a miser, she gloated over her riches.

Edna Millay is, if you love the truth of exaggeration, a new thing under the sun. Or at least the first of her sort for a long time. Perhaps in Crete before Sappho's day, in the large-minded matriarchate, there were women who achieved all the qualities of the artist that we now find ourselves calling masculine. But to get nimbly away from adjectives and vague speculation, let us look at some of this lyric poetry. Find, if you can, in another poet, a theme like this *Lament*:

> Listen, children:
> Your father is dead.

From *Equal Rights: The Magazine of the National Woman's Party* 12 (14 March 1925): 35. Reprinted by permission of The National Woman's Party.

From his old coats
I'll make you little jackets;
I'll make you little trousers
From his old pants.
There'll be in his pockets
Things he used to put there,
Keys and pennies
Covered with tobacco;
Dan shall have the pennies
To save in his bank;
Anne shall have the keys
To make a pretty noise with.

Life must go on,
And the dead be forgotten;
Life must go on,
Though good men die;
Anne, eat your breakfast;
Dan, take your medicine;
Life must go on;
I forget just why.

The first stanza of *Portrait by a Neighbor* runs in a well-known but hitherto unexpressed groove:

Before she has her floor swept
Or her dishes done,
Any day you'll find her
A-sunning in the sun!

The Poet and His Book turns sharply to the invisible audience often unconsciously addressed:

Women at your toil,
Women at your leisure
Till the kettle boil,
Snatch of me your pleasure,
Where the broom straw marks the leaf;
Women quiet with your weeping
Lest you wake a workman sleeping,
Mix me with your grief!

Miss Millay is what she asserts herself to be, nothing primarily but a poet, very busy and hard put to it to keep herself traveling light enough to suffer no dimunition of that complicated power. But because the world is still sifted deep with the old, out-grown conception, and because in the

English lady's past her poetry was often like her embroidery, we have an audience now that minimizes this lyricism. In an article a year ago in the *New Republic* Miss Amy Lowell lamented that the new school of poetry, of which Miss Millay is the chief figure, was essentially a feminine and minor affair, claiming for her own the adjectives major and masculine. Subjective poetry for Miss Lowell is, according to the article, always, or usually, minor. These distinctions are so curiously interwoven with all manner of popular synonyms and prejudices that they eventually take themselves off without a murmur of protest from me, even when later on in the article another related idea rears its head—Miss Millay lacks intellectuality! I console myself with the loss of this blue-stocking virtue and take down *Aria da Capo, The Lamp and the Bell,* or reread the *Sonnets from An Ungrafted Tree.*

Aria da Capo, written long before the existence of the American expressionistic play is, while small, perfect, of the age, and revolutionary.

An hour with this play makes it apparent that Miss Millay has no difficulty in being a poet when she is writing a drama. The next notable fact is that she is exceedingly dramatic throughout even her most gossamer poetry. Always it is the gesture, never a static picture. Even the massive sandal of Beauty is remembered as *set* on stone. *Prayer to Persephone* would be wrong and ruined without the gesture and the descending cadence of the last utterance:

> Be to her, Persephone,
> All the things I might not be;
> Take her head upon your knee.
> She that was so proud and wild,
> Flippant, arrogant and free,
> She that had no need of me,
> Is a little lonely child
> Lost in Hell,—Persephone
> Take her head upon your knee;
> Say to her, "My dear, my dear,
> It is not so dreadful here."

The common confusion of which Miss Lowell's remarks are an example comes from a misunderstanding of the driving force behind the whole lyric impulse. An eternal feud between centripetal and centrifugal forces sunders and reunites all magical expression. There is one impulse for control and its antagonistic impulse for abandon, one pressing inward, the other exploding at the center. This battle holds the little atom of creative intensity almost quiet because of its balance. If either gain the upper hand entirely, the moment of creation is destroyed. To despise lyric poetry or call it personal— and this, I think, is what many people are doing when they say subjective— is to miss the point of its being uttered at all. A Dionisian abandon, a sharp lyric cry may sum up all the slow-moving objective meanings and purposes.

Lyric poetry by its very fragility and singleness of voice can achieve an intimate universality that ponderous magnificent masses only build up to. With the Greeks the instinct for control and form perfected itself in their drama. At the end and peak of drama a song like this *Mariposa* (which was written for *The Lamp and the Bell*) is all that is left to be said:

> Butterflies are white and blue
> In this field we wander through.
> Suffer me to take your hand.
> Death comes in a day or two.
>
> All the things we ever knew
> Will be ashes in that hour,
> Mark the transient butterfly,
> How he hangs upon the flower.
>
> Suffer me to take your hand.
> Suffer me to cherish you
> Till the dawn is in the sky.
> Whether I be false or true,
> Death comes in a day or two.

The All-Star Literary Vaudeville

EDMUND WILSON

I have left the women lyric poets aside in order to discuss them as a group by themselves. On the average, though less pretentious, I think I find them more rewarding than the men: their emotion is more genuine and their literary instinct surer. Miss Reese, the dean of the guild, astonishes me by continuing to write, not only with the same distinction, but almost with the same freshness, as forty years ago. Sara Teasdale, the monotony of whose sobbing note rendered her rather unfashionable when a more arrogant race of young women appeared, has made real progress in her art since her earlier books of poems and has recently written some of her most charming lyrics. Miss Millay has now, in turn, grown so popular that she, too, is in danger of becoming unfashionable; but she remains the most important of the group and perhaps one of the most important of our poets. Like Mencken, the prophet of a point of view, she has, like him, become a national hero; nor, as in the case of certain other prophets, is her literary reputation undeserved. With little color, meagre ornament and images often commonplace, she is yet the mistress of deeply moving rhythms, of a music which makes up for the ear what her page seems to lack for the eye; and, above all, she has that singular boldness, which she shares with the greatest poets and which consists in taking just that one step beyond one's fellows which, by bringing poetry in fresh contact with moral reality, has the effect of making other productions take on an aspect of literary convention. Elinor Wylie, in the best of her verse and in her novel Jennifer Lorn, gives expression to a set of emotions quite different from those of Miss Millay, but one which has also its intensity and its typical interest. Her literary proficiency is immense: she is never at a loss for a witty reference or for a brilliant image; she commands the finest fabrics, the richest sensations, the choicest works of art, the most amusing historical allusions and the most delicious things to eat. And, as a consequence, her inferior work is almost as well written as her best; and her best work has both a style and a splendor of a kind very rare in America—where, even when these qualities do appear together, as they did to some extent in Amy Lowell, they too often remain hollow and metallic from a lack of a heart at the core. Edna Millay's inferior work has no embroidery to disguise

Excerpted from the *New Republic* 47 (30 June 1926): 161–62. Reprinted by permission.

it; and, save in her vein of classical austerity, she has for her best only the sorrel or mullein-stalk of the barren and rocky pastures, the purple wild sweet-pea dragging drift-wood across the sand, the dead leaves in the city gutters, the gray snow in the city street, the kettle, the broom, the uncarpeted stairs and the dead father's old clothes—grown strange and disturbing now, to this reader's sense, at least, as the prison-window of Verlaine or the common cross-roads of Catullus. Louise Bogan plucked one low resounding theme on a tensely strung steel string but they are its vibrations, rather than a development, which are still ringing in the air. Léonie Adams has published a most remarkable book, of which the language, seeming to branch straight from the richest English tradition of the seventeenth century, strikes music from the skies of the calm summer starbreak, the bright-washed night after rain and the blue translucence of evening, where a gull or a pigeon, rising alone, seeking freedom in that clarity and space, is lost in a celestial confusion of cloud and light. An anthology of these women writers of lyrics should contain, besides the poets mentioned above, the Cinquains of the late Adelaide Crapsey and the best of Miss Taggard, Miss Deutsch and a number of others, of whom the younger Laura Gottschalk may eventually prove one of the most interesting and in whose company Dorothy Parker, long known as a humorous writer, has recently, it seems to me, fully proved her right to belong.

Edna St. Vincent Millay

John Hyde Preston

I

It is remarkable in one who has done all her work within the last fifteen years—years of tremendous change and revolt in poetry—that she should bear away so little, so extraordinarily little, of the revolutionary hall-mark. And that fact by no means argues, on Miss Millay's part, any indifference to influence or a lack of sympathy with the main movements of her time. On the contrary, it speaks simply for her genuineness and courage in keeping staunchly by her own individual plan of life; for in this she represents a mastery of self that is rare always and doubly rare in these roaring days. Amid the striving and searching, so fashionable in our generation, for a false originality, Miss Millay has stood her own ground with the passionate will that belongs only to the strong of voice.

And yet it is very probable that she herself was scarcely conscious of her stand, for it was too natural, too inevitable to be designed. While such persons as Amy Lowell, Harriet Monroe, and Carl Sandburg—really important persons, beyond doubt—worked about her, preaching the "new poetry," she turned a deaf ear and went her own unavoidable way: not because she was thinking of their "manner" and modernity, and refuting them, but because she knew no other way to go and was too honest to hoodwink herself into believing that she did. A real artistic revolution has always some most salutary effects; it cleanses the air and swamps the weaker spirits who attempt to join the red-shirts when they do not naturally belong among them. Today the battlefield is strewn with the dead bodies of idiosyncratic bards who, in their anxiety to "express the age," let theory get ahead of their sense of beauty. Those rare beings in this country who could abide the pressure and the tides now stand the mightier for their sincerity—supreme among them, William Ellery Leonard, Edwin Arlington Robinson, and Edna St. Vincent Millay.

But to say that Miss Millay is apart from clique-movements is not by any means to say that she is not original; rather, she is exceedingly original, for the only real originality possible to man consists in setting down one's

From *Virginia Quarterly Review* 3 (July 1927): 342–55. Reprinted by permission.

own individual impressions and emotions, the whole matter lying in the potential expansiveness of one's soul. Whether one chooses to write free-verse or sonnets is of no moment. For the *poseur* is as old as Adam, and there is nothing very original about an insincere gesture, no matter how it may be accomplished. A lover of light and clarity, Miss Millay, with the instinct of the true poet, will allow nothing to come between her and her honest expression.

Perhaps the first impression that one receives from her poetry is that of an extraordinary range and interplay of moods, yet each one so distinctly a part of her mind that they seem sometimes to result from what appears to be, narrowly speaking, almost an excess of self-knowledge. That Miss Millay found herself early, is certain. And it is equally certain that she has always possessed what may be called "poetic instinct"—the ability to select from one's physical and mental experience the things that contribute most to the intensification of one's soul. A sensitive spirit on a romantic pilgrimage through an over-sophisticated civilization from which much of its romance has been robbed—this is the keynote of her work, as it is the keynote of many other modern poets not so finely tempered or so feverishly alert.

In words, not one of which can be divided from its context, she has celebrated an exquisitely personal reaction to a world that cannot draw her response in every of its various manifestations. That those intense and beautiful "high-moments" of life occur to us less directly in our modern times, that existence is larger and more difficult than it was for Spenser or Milton, for examples, is a fact that must lead to the development on our parts of a closer, more concentrated observation, together with the evolution of an immaculate craftsmanship, that we may express, as nearly as possible, all that we can snatch of beauty where we see it—or in other words, to convey what Pater has somewhere called "the impression of the individual in his isolation."

And thus it is that the good poet must needs become a "specialist," so to speak, in the sphere of beauty, dividing what is distinctly *his* from what he can neither claim nor let claim him. And as the entangled interests of modern life grow in range and breadth, so the poet must become more and more *selective*, reaching out his hand only to what pleases his soul; and much more, indeed, must he disregard, not because it is of less value in itself, but simply because it has not the same high level of appeal to his individual perception. This has been true of all ages, but it becomes increasingly true among the perplexities and "opposites" of our fast-changing civilization. That it is difficult, impossible for some to achieve, there is abundant testimony in our modern books of verse; for it requires above all else that the writer *know himself*, and such knowledge asks that rare broadness of soul to which we have, perhaps obscurely, assigned the term *genius*.

Amid this confusion of interests that appalls so many of us, Miss Millay has made her own choice, gone her own way. While her outlook upon life is one of sad delight and worship of beauty, one can detect, far beneath the surface that is so seldom bitter, a strong undercurrent of disenchantment and something of that pessimistic laughter that mixes the pride of youth with an almost premature life-wisdom. Hers is the wistful striving to recapture an unnamed and undefinable joy that has fled away—an afterall-hopeless effort to maintain an unalloyed exuberance, for as she says: "Growing old is dying young." Life she sees, with the rest of us, as too much in the fleeting order of things, mocking our attempts to hold it at its best, vanishing as it appears, along with its ecstatic little train of loveliness; and with that awful uncertainty fully realized, she expresses a passionate cry for the Absolute: "Euclid alone has looked on beauty bare," she says, not because she has any desire to see Euclid's peculiar kind of beauty, but because she craves a governing *definiteness* among the things of the world, that she may escape in a measure from that terrible sense of quick-lived wonder that leaves with us only a pang at our helplessness to hold or define it. And because hers is the longing for the eternal, "fixed" beauty that cannot pass with the momentary change of the senses, she envies those "Who, though once only and then but far away, / Have heard her massive sandal set on stone."

Over the frail surface of things Miss Millay lets play her extraordinarily wistful pity and irony—those two qualities which Anatole France saw as the most graceful attributes of man—and mingled with them is a strain of sad, yet almost pouting, humour. She has asked for the fullest intensity of life, if only to complete its otherwise faint meaning; and to see the vision depart is to bleed one's self.

> That April should be shattered by a gust,
> That August should be levelled by a rain,
> I can endure, and that the lifted dust
> Of man should settle to the earth again;
> But that a dream can die will be a thrust
> Between my ribs forever of hot pain.

To broaden our scope, to reach out for all things good and bad as parts of being, and to infuse into that being all that there is of mystery and wonder, is an ideal to be persistently sought after if we are ever to achieve fulfillment. And in "Renascence," that magnificent celebration of the individual consciousness—with its restriction or its freedom, as the soul makes choice—she has pointed to this with exquisite artistry.

> The world stands out on either side
> No wider than the heart is wide;
> Above the world is stretched the sky,—
> No higher than the soul is high.
> The heart can push the sea and land

Farther away on either hand;
The soul can split the sky in two,
And let the face of God shine through.
But East and West will pinch the heart
That cannot keep them pushed apart;
And he whose soul is flat—the sky
Will cave in on him by and by.

She carries, through fortune and misfortune, this same determination to "harvest beauty where it grows," even unto the dust, with a sweet fierceness.

Death, I say, my heart is bowed
Unto thine,—O mother!
This red gown will make a shroud
Good as any other!

But because so intensely alive, beauty must die and fade the farthest away; and Miss Millay knows its passing and the pain of its passing and the awful emptiness that haunts its shade.

Nor will my love avail you in your hour.
In spite of all my love, you will arise
Upon that day and wander down the air
Obscurely as the unattended flower,
It mattering not how beautiful you were,
Or how beloved above all else that dies.

And she knows, too, how it must torture and tear the heart that is responsive above others to it; how man must often hate with all his soul the very beauty that is his life and his shrine, and how he must turn from it sometimes as if in dread.

I am waylaid by Beauty. Who will walk
Between me and the crying of the frogs?
Oh, savage Beauty, suffer me to pass,
That am a timid woman, on her way
From one house to another!

II

As part of the sensuous paganism which is in her attitude towards life, she has sung boldly and beautifully of her woman's love of man, appreciating his peculiar beauty as can only women and Walt Whitman. The old inhuman days when women poets were forced to take up the disguise of Rosalind are gone now, and (may Heaven grant!) gone forever: for their assumed garb made them no more convincing in their rôles than did Rosalind's hose and doublet; and it is only within the reach of modern poetry (barring Sappho) that we can find women paying their direct and unconcealed tribute to their lovers, neither under the cloak of pseudonym nor with the insincerity of adopting the masculine point of view.

None has been more clear and honest—more amazingly honest sometimes—than Miss Millay. Sensitively, and with swift strokes, she has set down, if not the Odyssey of a heart, at least a record of all its poignant moments, its strange terrors, its little absurdities, and much, too, of its mocking emptiness. Love, speaking broadly, is her religion; and without it she would be as unconvincing as a wingless bird. No woman since Mrs. Browning has written love-sonnets that equal hers in sheer intensity and depth; and I believe that no English-speaking poet, either man or woman, within the memory of our generation, has brought to love a more exquisite and personal interpretation. Sara Teasdale has done beautiful lyrics, Arthur Davison Ficke some sonnets that bid for a hallowed name; but no one has achieved, in my view at least, the same insistence of passion, the same sadness born of joy, which Miss Millay has created in so delicate a music. What her personal life has been is, of course, no concern of ours; but it seems only obvious that she must have suffered deeply, for it is only through suffering that one can attain such richness and sweetness. Hers is no celebration of a pretty courtship or a sick caprice; it is the madness and fierceness of love, the horror and sudden hollowness of love, the love that kills while it satiates, that corrodes while it soothes, the love that drives men to ecstasy and to despair—

> . . . wherefore now let sing
> All voices how into my throat is thrust.
> Unwelcome as Death's own, Love's bitter crust.

It seems worth while to insist upon her love poems, because she has insisted upon them herself as the intensest part of her experience. Love (so-called) is a passion common to us all, and yet it is only the rare and great person who can love well and deeply—one's capacity for noble passions being always the measure of one's soul. Miss Millay is aware of this, I think, for her harping is upon the beautiful and terrible, scorning all that is stodgy and small of spirit. " 'Tis not love's going that hurts my days, / But that it went in little ways." Or again, in characteristic strain:

> Weep him dead and mourn as you may,
>   Me, I sing as I must:
> Blessed be Death, that cuts in marble,
>   What would have sunk in dust.

The secret of a life well-lived is simply the ability to intensify, to bring all that is rare and strange in humanity into one's own experience. The only failure is the failure to do this. Miss Millay knows that anything really great must be, in its essence, egotistic; and that love, the most essentially selfish of passions, is (in its broad sense) the highest exaltation we can reach. She knows, too, that the lover is the head and counterpoint of his own world, and that the beloved is only the spring, so to speak, of his flight. For the true lover, whether consciously or not, asks for nothing save his own ecstasy; and, little as he may guess it in the moment of his passion, he is forever paying his tribute, not to the divine one, but to the cruel and remorseless god of his own ego. As a kind of quintessence of Miss Millay's viewpoint, I quote in this place a sonnet in which she has given expression to this attitude with a beauty as subtle as it is courageous:

> What lips my lips have kissed, and where, and why,
> I have forgotten, and what arms have lain
> Under my head till morning; but the rain
> Is full of ghosts to-night, that tap and sigh
> Upon the glass and listen for reply,
> And in my heart there stirs a quiet pain
> For unremembered lads that not again
> Will turn to me at midnight with a cry.
> Thus in the winter stands the lonely tree,
> Nor knows what birds have vanished one by one,
> Yet knows its boughs more silent than before:
> I cannot say what loves have come and gone,
> I only know that summer sang in me
> A little while, that sings in me no more.

III

Miss Millay's first substantial achievement was, of course, "Renascence," written when she was barely nineteen and published in "The Lyric Year" for 1912; but her first poetry of length dates from a short decade ago when, as a senior at Vassar College, she wrote a lyric drama in five acts, "The Lamp and the Bell." As a production for the graduating class, it was distinguished from the mass of such by the fact that it was poetry and beautiful poetry, and that it can stand in good place in modern literature. The story is of Elizabethan times, celebrating the devotion of two women; but no matter how much the thing may be in the spirit of the sixteenth century, it never descends to imitation, but rather strikes an essentially modern note, embodying much of its author's accustomed "raciness" of language and thought. Of course it has its weaknesses—the greatest of which is a slight sentimentality—its technical deficiences, and here and there something of immaturity.

But that Miss Millay herself thinks well of it was said in the fact that she reprinted three of its loveliest lyrics in "The Harp-Weaver." She has written, also, a poetic fantasy in one act, "Aria da Capo"—a rather captivating but insignificant little thing which has no place in her best work. It shows emphatically a frivolous, frilly chord that worms its way into her other poetry now and then, along with a desire to be "pretty"—the most inexcusable of poetic faults, but one which she has apparently now outgrown.

But these two plays are interesting, not so much for themselves, perhaps, as in that they point a direction in her later work, and bring us to what is indubitably her greatest attainment, "The King's Henchman." All the deep maturity of her art is here, all its breath-taking beauty and delicacy. I believe it has surprised even her most fervid admirers, those who have been long confident of her powers. Its success as an opera, which has been almost unprecedented at the Metropolitan (thanks to Mr. Taylor's excellent music), is actually small beside its value as literature, which is inestimable. I do not exaggerate when I say that "The King's Henchman" is unapproachably the greatest lyric drama since Swinburne's "Atlantic"—and I am well aware of Flecker's "Hassan."

The tale itself is simple and colourful, a tragedy of tenth century England. The widowed King Eadgar, wishing a new bride to grace his state, sends, as his henchman, Aethelwold, his foster brother and bosom friend, to Devon to woo in his stead the beautiful Aelfrida, being himself unable to leave court because of tiresome business with the monks. Aethelwold, a courageous soldier, has had little experience with women and holds them almost in contempt:

> So many dry leaves in a ditch they are to me,
> These whispering girls,
> A little fairish and a little foulish,
> And all alike, and mightily underfoot—

so that Eadgar knows the wisdom of sending him.

Aethelwold and Maccus, his friend and serving-man, after travelling long, come at last one night into a deep wood, heavy with mist, thinking themselves yet far from their destination, though actually within calling distance of Aelfrida's house. Maccus goes off to hunt a road, while Aethelwold drops asleep. It is All Hallow's Eve which, according to legend, is the night upon which any maid that wanders forth will find her lover. Aelfrida comes softly into the wood, singing; and as the mist clears, the moonlight, "icy-sweet," falls upon the slumbering Aethelwold. Thinking him a vision of her dream, Aelfrida bends to kiss him, and he awakes. When they discover they are both flesh and blood, they find themselves already deeply in love. And this love-scene, which Miss Millay pens so sensitively, must take its place among those rare few in all literatures that are really poignant and exquisite.

Aethelwold is overcome by Aelfrida's radiant glory, still ignorant of who she
is.

> Oh, Godes Son,
> How wounding fair thou art!
> The sight of thee
> Is like a knife at the heart!
> Of thee the sight or the sound,
> The turn of thy head, thy speaking,
> Is like a thing found
> To a man seeking!

Aelfrida slightly fears the strangeness of the meeting, while Aethelwold
recognizes the depth of the spell:

> Oh, God, what aileth me?
> Thou—knowest thou aught of love,
> And how it taketh a man?
> Thinkest thou I am in love with thee?

Aelfrida gives herself into his arms, helpless: "I am lost—I am swept out to
sea—."

The scene moves on, deeply charged, to its tragic climax. It seems a
pity that Miss Millay should have marred it at its very height by two such
hackneyed-sounding lines as: "Drink, drink in haste my breath, / Ere it be
swallowed up by thievish Death!" Then Ase, the servant-nurse, calls her
mistress through the woods, "Aelfrida!" and Aethelwold, hearing the name,
is stricken down by grief and remorse. He tries to escape, but he cannot; his
passion is too fiercely upon him. He yields to the temptation to betray
Eadgar's trust, sending back word that the lady "is nothing fair . . . nothing
for the King"—

> And whereas Lord Aethelwold,
> Sparing the King's love . . .
> Sparing the King's love, hath little else beside,—
> The blessing of King Eadgar is besought
> Upon the wedding of Lord Aethelwold
> Unto the maid Aelfrida.

After their marriage they are lost in their love, but Aethelwold is forever
haunted by the thought of his foul play. Then the ominous sky finally crashes
down its storm when Eadgar comes to pay a friendly visit. Before his arrival
Aethelwold confesses to Aelfrida that she might have been Lady of all Britain
but for him; but begs her now, for his love to her, to put grey meal in her
hair and to appear bent and weather-weary to the King, that her husband

may not be found out. Aelfrida promises; but her narrow ambition to be Queen overpowers her mind, and she seals the tragedy of all three by suddenly coming before Eadgar in all her glorious beauty, bedecked with jewels. The King, his heart sore and sad, bitterly reproaches his friend:

My mind, that hath been fed so long on the sweet fare of utter trust in thee,
Smells at this meat,
And turns away—

while Aethelwold, unable to forgive his own treachery, stabs himself and stretches dead at Eadgar's feet. The drama comes to an end like the chanting of a momentous dirge—a deep-voiced song of beauty and sorrow.

Among her shorter work, Miss Millay has published some things which are perfectly negligible (good poets are not always discerning critics of their own poetry), others like "Sorrow" or "The Bean-Stalk" that have but a small and passing appeal. Such a piece as "The Suicide" is well enough for the pulpit, but I would claim nothing further for it. The "Ode to Silence" smacks of the school-room and lacks original inspiration. I heartily hope that on the distant day when she collects her poems, she will have the critical keenness to exclude things like "Indifference" and "The Return from Town"; that she will shorten "Interim" and delete the trite second stanza of "Ashes of Life."

"The Ballad of the Harp-Weaver," which won the Pulitzer Prize for poetry in 1923, is a pathetic, curiously wistful little thing, utterly apart from the tenor of anything else she has written. Speaking from my own experience, the quiet beauty and the pathos of it must rush upon one in the first reading, or not at all; the suddenness of its thrill and the terrible indictment of its meaning wear away after repeated perusals. The Ballad is important, of course, as another manifestation of a versatile spirit, but it falls, I think, slightly below the level of her best work. Still, the hand of the artist is there—certain, relentless, and operating with a subtlety that defies analysis.

But it is in her sonnets, according to my view of the matter, that she reaches the Alps of her shorter accomplishments. In all her books they stand out head and shoulders above the rest, and many approach the cool, Olympian beauty of "The King's Henchman." To this difficult and delightful form she has brought a touch most deft and exquisite, with that combination of simplicity and grandeur which her art commands so well. The more one goes over these sonnets (and their test is that they can bear innumerable readings), the more do they yield, like the plays of Shakespeare, of their inner kernel of thought and strength of human love. Their unity and swift music are a joy and a relief in a day when the sonnet, in so many cases, has become a sort of hoarse scream trying to penetrate a vacuum. (I do not speak of the "Sonnets from an Ungrafted Tree"; these are, to my mind, sadly disappointing). She possesses that rare gift which makes the fine sonneteer—the gift of carrying her meaning by rhythm and making one unconscious of the rhyme-words. The following quotation illustrates her almost magic handling of a single thought:

> When I too long have looked upon your face,
> Wherein for me a brightness unobscured
> Save for the mists of brightness has its place,
> And terrible beauty not to be endured,
> I turn away reluctant from your light,
> And stand irresolute, a mind undone,
> A silly, dazzled thing deprived of sight
> From having looked too long upon the sun.
> Thus is my daily life a narrow room
> In which a little while, uncertainly,
> Surrounded by impenetrable gloom,
> Among familiar things grown strange to me
> Making my way, I pause, and feel, and hark,
> Till I become accustomed to the dark.

IV

The woman who wrote "The King's Henchman," "The Poet and His Book," and "The Harp-Weaver," is vastly apart from her contemporaries. A master of a wide range, she can command the oldest as well as the newest forms with equal felicity. She has not the hard, cold, wellnigh Grecian beauty of H.D., not the polished, crystal-glass beauty of Elinor Wylie, nor the purple-trumpeted, battle-field beauty of Amy Lowell. Her beauty, on the contrary, while lacking something of their sharp precision, is yet much closer than theirs to flesh and blood, to life as it is lived on earth; and harkens back for strength to the great elemental things—mountains, the sea, simple people and the forces of pure nature. And above all, she has never betrayed her deep human sympathy by dragging it into the snare of words and theories.

She is a pure poet, in the sense that Keats and Shakespeare were pure poets. Knowing well that life is primarily a search after beauty (for all our efforts amount to this in the final reckoning), she is without prejudices, without dyspeptic "moralities," and asks only that, through its vicissitudes, the soul shall grow. She gives what she has, in a flood of light. As for the spring-time freshness of her style and mastery of language, there are no words; we can only wonder and be thankful.

Her final place, time and its advancing generations will determine. Posterity, that exacting gardener, will winnow her poetry for what is best in it—and the greater part is too sweet and clear to sour with the years. The smaller portion of chaff will be blown away. What of change and development another decade may bring to her, is not for us to prophesy. She is still a young woman—a very young woman when her fame and accomplishment are considered—and there is time ahead for even better work than she has done thus far—which is, I confess, saying a great deal.

She is a very vital, impulsive, and original spirit, I think—a lover of life and beauty for their own sakes, insisting always upon the sovereignty of emotions and the essential nobility of all that is human in man's days. Her position among the poets of our century is as secure as it is enviable. She stands out, a rich figure against the dull-coloured tapestry of modern verse. No one can approach her to-day without becoming aware of a lucid and subtle vision that seems to have penetrated far into all that there is of hope and fear, and love and dreams, in the rough architecture of our lives.

The New York Wits

Herbert Marshall McLuhan

It may indeed turn out that the present cleavage between popular and rational forms of entertainment will never be mended. The common reader with whom Dr. Johnson rejoiced to concur is as dead as Pan. And just how many centuries of intellectual ascesis concurred with centuries of homogeneous social life to produce him, we are now privileged to contemplate. As late as Crabbe and Jane Austen serious art could hold the same road as "good society," following the main march of the affections. Even putting aside Blake and Wordsworth, one could say that after Jane Austen no serious artist exists save in drastic opposition to his society. The practical reason of the artist involuntarily has come to indict the life around him as a sensual riot wilfully opposed to reason and order.

Even successful writers like Dickens and Thackeray preserved their line of popular communication with the taste of their time at the expense of their art. Their refusal to confront their experience critically meant that they never raised the material they worked with to the level of art. . . .

In the case of Alexander Woollcott and Dorothy Parker a more or less direct link with Swinburne, Wilde, and the 'nineties, and kinship with Edna St. Vincent Millay, are admitted. Real but less direct connections with the 'nineties exist also for such writers as Robert Benchley, James Thurber, Ogden Nash, and E. B. White. Thurber and Nash filter the revolutionary nihilism of a Wilde through the whimsy of Lewis Carroll and Edward Lear. They are avowedly less "caustic" than the formidable Woollcott and Parker. But taken together the Broadway Wits constitute our Bloomsbury and represent a tradition which has admitted authority in America. In fact it is hard to point to any other tradition which is at all comparable. Whether good or bad, there is no other national focal point for a whole complex of attitudes to current experience. Beneath this level is Hollywood and the chaotic world of best-seller narrative. To one side stands a tiny group of writers and readers of serious interests. But here is the meeting ground of highbrow and middlebrow. After thirty or more years *The New Yorker* continues to provide this ground today. Nobody could ask a more immediate evidence for this fact than Edmund Wilson's acceptance of his present job on the magazine.

Excerpted and reprinted from the *Kenyon Review* 7 (Winter 1945): 12–28.

Minority culture in America has mainly been concerned with the problem of absorbing European influences. From the beginning of American letters surprisingly little attention has been given to popular art and entertainment—a fact which betrays a radical flaw in minority culture. How little this attitude can afford to be indulged today should be clear if only from the fact of the great influence which American popular art has had abroad—particularly jazz and the movies. The failure of American writers to direct a strong critical light on popular art may be due to their own sense of futility, or it may proceed from a defect of political awareness—a failure to note that art and education, which include minority thought and feeling, are indivisible from the total life of the nation. From no point of view is such neglect defensible. The results are debilitating to high and popular art alike. The fact that the New York Wits have been immune from serious critical attention has meant a real loss to American letters and education. For here is a group of writers at once enjoying popular approval and a reputation for lively intelligence and artistic accomplishment. A major focus for critical effort presents itself.

A glance at some of the phrases which Louis Untermeyer applies to the "skin-tight" verse of Millay suggests their equal applicability to the verse of Dorothy Parker: "gay impudence," "pitched in the key of loss," "heel-and-toe insouciance," "celebrates eager dawn or headlong day," "preoccupied with the water darkening," "in love with lost love, with the shards of her broken pot." These notes are quite as apt for Dorothy Parker, for whom many would also claim the tribute Untermeyer bestows on Millay's *Renascence*: "It is as if a child had, in the midst of ingenuousness, uttered some terrific truth." The laughable ambiguity of this *mot* deserves treatment in a Thurber cartoon. But what are we to conclude from Mr. Untermeyer's omission of Mrs. Parker from his heavily padded *Modern American Poetry*? If derivative debility is the criterion of admission, as it seems to be for nine tenths of the exhibits, why isn't Mrs. Parker there? Miss Millay refracts her Shelleyan vehemence and wild emphasis through Mrs. Browning and a handful of Elizabethan epithets; Mrs. Parker refracts hers through the would-be austere naiveté of *Shropshire Lad*.

Both poets exploit long-established poetic fashions, appealing to a semi-alert audience which is glad to recognize hackneyed sentiment in a *chic* (that is, expensive) modern setting. Ever since being up-to-date has exerted the pressure of time-snobbery people have been as anxious to conform to the Zeitgeist in art and literature as in politics and morals. The net result has been a notorious time-lag and deadening of sensibility. Edna Millay, for example, has never been anything but a purveyor of cliché sentiment. She is an exhibitionist with no discoverable sensibility of her own. The pretentious rhetoric of the "unimpeachable body" variety won't stand a moment's scrutiny. Had there been responsible critics to consider her first work some direction might have been given to her talent. As it is, she is taken seriously in academic circles today. Vigorous and uncompromising criticism is indispensable to the fecundating of any kind of artistic ability. The lack of such criticism is not only indirectly fatal to the emergence of good work but permits every sort of humbug to flourish and to steal the soil which might nourish the real thing.

Mrs. Parker exhibits a mechanism of sensibility which is about as complicated as a village pump, though it masquerades as daring *avant garde* naughtiness and revolt. As she said of Katherine Hepburn, the Edna St. Vincent Millay of our stage, she "runs the gamut of emotions from A to B." Her lyrics are charged with masochism and self-pity, while her prose is uniformly sadistic like her famous social *persona*. So Woollcott's whimsical statement that she is a blend of Lady Macbeth and of Little Nell is an unintentionally deft but damaging analysis.

Edna St. Vincent Millay:
A Figure of Passionate Living

JOHN CIARDI

Political historians remember 1917 as the year in which the United States went to war to make the world safe for democracy. Literary historians recall it as a time of great stirring in American poetry. Ezra Pound and his followers were beginning to imagize. T. S. Eliot stood between "Prufrock" and "The Waste Land." Baudelaire was becoming an excitement in advance circles. Yeats was at the point of his best writing. Hopkins was about to be published. Joyce and Gertrude Stein had already brought their techniques far enough forward for E. E. Cummings, as a Harvard undergraduate, to have written an extremely perceptive assessment of their experiments and aims. In short, The Age of the Manifesto was upon us. Schools and movements were everywhere. The next ten years were to see them flower and fade quarterly, leaving behind them stacks of unread little magazines.

Into all this excitement and search for a new way of writing stepped twenty-five-year-old Edna St. Vincent Millay, who had just been graduated from Vassar and had just published a volume of verse called "Renascence." Miss Millay brought forth her ballad stanzas, her archaic embellishment, and her sonnets in the grand manner. Perhaps not surprisingly, even her traditionalism was enough to excite a school into being.

Edna St. Vincent Millay became a name for a kind of lyric to be imitated wherever the female heart beat fast.

Her popularity, easily won, was to continue through all the Twenties and—perhaps a sign of dangerous limitation or perhaps a sign of fundamental power—was to reach beyond the "literary" to something resembling the "public." Her reading appearances were to become triumphs of trailing gowns and far-flung gestures. The legend of her loves was to illuminate dreams from Keokuk to Salt Lick.

Now Edna Millay is dead, and somehow the Twenties, when some of you were very young and some of us were children, are suddenly sent splintering into antiquity. What a long way back it is to yesterday when Edna St. Vincent Millay was The Village and The Village was Edna St. Vincent Millay, and you went back and forth all night on the ferry, and I, still in

From the *Saturday Review of Literature* 33 (11 November 1950): 8–9, 77. Reprinted by permission.

knickers, read about it in Medford, Massachusetts, and daydreamed the wonders of the life being lived just off Washington Square.

Or else it was just silly and adolescent with shouting on street corners, and dreary recitals by bearded poets, and a great deal of very high level small-talk by flat-chested girls in excruciating dresses. But, silly or not, it was a time of tremendous vitality, and certainly no one lived it more passionately and beguilingly—or so at least it seemed to me, and so it must have seemed to thousands of adolescents like me—than Edna St. Vincent Millay.

There are always two of every poet: one a person, the other a presence contrived by the poems. Whatever the person is, the presence is something else, an aspect of the person or a series of aspects. The reader of Edna Millay is easily confused in this since the person and the presence seem so bound up together, the legend of her living so much a part of the poems. One reads the poems and thinks he could walk down the street and identify their author on sight.

It is impossible, of course, to say whether or not Edna Millay's poems will "survive"—whatever that means—but in the very immediacy with which one makes a person of the presence may lie the best testimony to a creative achievement. For it is not good enough simply to dismiss the issue by saying that the poems are autobiographical. Or if it is, it is only good enough if one realizes that autobiography is not transcribed so much as it is invented. No one can write all of himself; he must select aspects, and every selection invents. Whatever powers and whatever limitations are to be found in the poems, their achievement is that they invented Edna St. Vincent Millay.

Almost, one is tempted to say nostalgically, they invented a decade. One knows this is an absurdity and yet one half-thinks it. One may as well say the raccoon coat invented the plastic age. No, what I am thinking is that she invented it (or somehow brought it alive) to me and certainly to many of my generation busy at their first fumblings and exaggerations.

I must have been nearing fifteen, a happy prowler in the dark stacks of our public library, when I began to pull down poetry from the shelves. About all the poetry I had behind me was Kipling and I was not sure but what he was too "young"—by which I meant I had read him more than six months ago. Then I found "The Man with a Hoe." That was a wonderful discovery: "Who loosened and let down that brutal jaw?" I would demand of my sisters. "Spoon River" was another: "Petit the poet, tic-tic, peas in a dry pod"—it was enough to make me feel like a critic. Then one day I opened "The Harp-Weaver" and came on "The Goose Girl":

> Spring rides no horses down the hill,
> But comes on foot, a goose-girl still
> And all the loveliest things there be
> Come simply, so it seems to me.

If ever I said, in grief or pride,
I tired of honest things, I lied;
And should be cursed for evermore
With Love in laces, like a whore,
And neighbors cold, and friends unsteady,
And Spring on horseback like a lady!

Now there was a thing you could really recite: grief, pride, curses, whores! This was life! I began to read Millay avidly, to spout her endlessly. "What lips my lips have kissed." Mine hadn't kissed anything but the cheeks of aunts, but wasn't that part of the drama? "Euclid alone has looked on Beauty bare." How rich that was! "Let all who prate of Beauty hold their peace, / And lay them prone upon the earth, and cease . . ." What a sudden sense of life they released! Even the too-muchness was right. In retrospect, of course, one knows that it was exactly the too-muchness that was right, but what an excitement it was then to curl up with it in a corner of the stacks and wait for the time when you could recite it to a girl with the moon beside you or, perhaps more accurately, to the moon with a girl beside you. Certainly the moon comes first.

"The Goose Girl" still strikes me as the most typical of Edna Millay's poems, of the kind of presence she sought to invent. Its measure is cut to absolute simplicity; one thinks immediately of Housman, whose hand has surely touched Edna Millay's first poems. And immediately one senses a difference in the simplicity. "The Goose Girl" bears many surface resemblances to Housman's "Cherry Trees." The meter, the kind of language, the easy flow of the symbols, the imagery, all have a great deal in common. Yet Housman's poem remains convincing, and somehow "The Goose Girl" does not.

The difference occurs not in the way of saying but in the attitude of the saying, a point Robert Frost once made especially well in speaking of "the way the poet takes his subject, the way the poet takes himself." One is finally forced to distrust the way Edna Millay takes herself in this poem. One can believe without reservation that Housman wanted to walk out quietly to observe the cherry trees. His feeling for the false bloom of snow upon them is evoked beyond question. But can one feel the same conviction in the evocation of Spring as the Goose Girl and the Lady on Horseback, or is the author being consciously picturesque? And when we are told that "All the loveliest things there be / Come simply, so it seems to me," not only the archaic use of "be" but the knowledge of Miss Millay's archness in so many of her other poems makes us wonder if this is not simply another pose. We doubt, and immediately the poem confirms our doubt by the burst of rhetoric that fills up the next five lines. This is not an experience, we conclude; it is a pose.

And poem after poem confirms this experience: there is always that element of the overdramatic about them, a fabrication of the words rather than of the feeling, of a posture rather than of an experience. It is, one suspects, exactly this in the poems that once set twenty years of undergraduates to imitating them. Something in the overstatement of the poems fitted our own imbalance. Perhaps that explains why I fell violently in love as a sophomore at Bates College with our local Edna, or, more precisely, with the best of our local Ednas, for even at so small a school as Bates there were at least two dozen of them. Certainly something powerfully suited to our needs grew at that edge of bathos.

> I screamed, and—lo!—Infinity
> Came down and settled over me.

Or in the coy first hungering for great sophistication:

> After all, my erstwhile dear,
> My no longer cherished,
> Need we say it was not love,
> Just because it perished?

It swaggered with us like our first self-conscious cigarettes, an endless, very fine portrait of ourselves being very wise.

It seems impossible now that we could have been so moved by such lines. Or is it simply that we can never again be so moved by anything? Whatever the truth of it, we were moved, we were filled, we were taken.

Then somehow it was all over. The Twenties had ended even for those of us who were too young to do more than overhear the tail end of their legend. Symbolically, Edna Millay's power to thrill and carry the reader seemed to end with them. For what made the poems immediate was the passionate youngness of their author. And suddenly it was years later and the youngness had fled. One read Auden and Spender instead, and as each of the new Millay books appeared—"Wine from These Grapes," "Conversation at Midnight," "Huntsman, What Quarry?"—one wondered what had happened to the breathlessness and carry that used to be in the poems.

The simple fact seems to be that, having outgrown her youth, Edna Millay had outgrown the one subject she could make exciting. "Conversation at Midnight" was her attempt at intellectual reportage of an age, but it provided no subject for her gift. It seemed as if she had stopped living in order to talk—to talk endlessly and dully—about life. There is still here and there the intense preoccupation with herself, her body, the pose of her body, but where once we read of the body in love we now read:

> Over the sound of flushing water, which
> For some strange reason, science having gone so far,
> Even in the houses of the extremely rich

Still roars in a room, and everybody knows where you are . . .

Instead of bright children on MacDougal Street,

Sons-of-bitches at Hialeah
hacking their initials in the royal palms . . .

Instead of the endless energy of the girl, we are presented the matron posing before her dressmaker who turns her about and is made to cry: *"Que Madame est maigré."*

Then came the war, and the social consciousness that had first driven her to write some of her worst poetry in "Justice Denied in Massachusetts" (the Sacco-Vanzetti trial), betrayed her into such books as "Make Bright the Arrows." These are tragic books from which the last vestige of gift has disappeared; nobly to be sure, for reasons that all men of good will must be tempted to condone. But finally poetry must be protected from even the highest motives. Perhaps especially from the highest motives. Moral indignation is no substitute for art. In these poems, unfortunately, only that substitution speaks: line after line of exhortations from the vocabulary of humanism, page after page of moral platitudes, but not a phrase of poetry. We agreed that there were no islands left, we wept for Lidice, but the poems could not find our feelings. The facts themselves were so desperately more moving.

But to enumerate a poet's failures is not to judge him. A writer must be judged by his best. Edna Millay's best came at a time when many needed her excitement. Whether her capture of that audience was a good or a bad thing for the course of poetry one cannot say with any conviction. Certainly her intimate treatment of the frankly sensuous was some part of an age's contribution toward broadening the range of subjects permissible to poetry. That much is surely good. Certainly, too, the kind of poetry she set herself to write has found no followers except among the dim mediocrities of the Poetry Societies. And that cannot be good. But neither merit nor lack of merit defined her position in the poetry of the Twenties. It was not as a craftsman nor as an influence, but as the creator of her own legend that she was most alive for us. Her success was as a figure of passionate living.

Unfortunately, passion is nonreflective. At its slightest her passion made her the mother of the O-God-the-pain! girls, of the O-World-I-cannot-hold-you-close-enough! school. And even at its best it is not likely that her work can be popular so long as poetry continues its present development toward the ambivalent consciousness and the pessimistic intellect. Perhaps her poems must be forgotten. Or perhaps they will become like "The Rubaiyat" and the "Sonnets from the Portuguese," poems that generation after generation of the young will be swept away by, gorgeously, overwhelmingly swept away by, and then outgrow.

But today none of that seems to matter. One finds himself less inclined to criticism than to nostalgia. At least it will be so for all of us who were very young and very merry and aren't exactly that any more, but who once long ago opened those little black books with their titles pasted to the binding, and suddenly found the wind blowing through everybody's hair and a wonderful girl running to us through the wind. *"Que Madame est maigré."* But what a whirling all-night time it was!

My Friendship with Edna Millay

Max Eastman

It was during those years [the 1920s] that Edna wrote her greatest poetry. *The Buck in the Snow* came out in 1929. It was enthusiastically welcomed in England, although reviewed with a note of disappointment in America, the reason for this being, I think, that she had been silent long enough to become a myth, and it was the myth of a more lightly tuneful and less warmly thoughtful poet than she had grown up to be. There was more passion and less wit in these larger and freer rhythms. There were more thoughts and not perhaps so many bright ideas. I suppose it was a question what one had originally perceived as the essence of her genius. For those to whom it was her very great lyrical cleverness—that delicate skill as a grammatical engineer, which people who do not write poetry always admire so much and take for the very fluid of inspiration—for them, no doubt, the new warmth and thoughtfulness seemed a decline. And those super-modern critics who "babbled in the streets at night" over her immature verses—partly, one cannot help thinking, because that was the fashion—were off already on the trail of a new fashion. As one who remained, by the grace of God, in the earlier fashion, I can say that the title-poem of *The Buck in the Snow* seems to me one of the perfect lyrics in our language, a painting of life and death unexcelled, indeed, anywhere. It is completely her own; no one else that ever lived could have written it.

> White sky, over the hemlocks bowed with snow,
> Saw you not at the beginning of evening the antlered buck and his doe
> Standing in the apple-orchard? I saw them. I saw them suddenly go,
> Tails up, with long leaps lovely and slow,
> Over the stone-wall into the wood of hemlocks bowed with snow.
>
> Now lies he here, his wild blood scalding the snow.
> How strange a thing is death, bringing to his knees, bringing to his antlers
> The buck in the snow.
> How strange a thing,—a mile away by now, it may be,

Excerpted from *Great Companions: Critical Memoirs of Some Famous Friends* by Max Eastman. Copyright © 1942, 1959 by Max Eastman. Renewal copyright © 1987 by Yvette Sakay Eastman. Reprinted by Farrar, Straus and Giroux, Inc.

Under the heavy hemlocks that as the moments pass
Shift their loads a little, letting fall a feather of snow—
Life, looking out attentive from the eyes of the doe.

Epitaph for the Race of Man was also composed during the years of our close friendship, as well as the sonnet sequence *Fatal Interview*—another classic that the poet's adolescent admirers, in belittling her mature poetry, have managed largely to ignore. Neither of these magnificent works of genius is once mentioned by Horace Gregory and Marya Zaturenska in their *History of American Poetry*—1900–1940. This pretentious volume, supposedly a standard work of reference, sums up Edna St. Vincent Millay with the remark that "Her virtues are those of an effortless, seemingly artless charm of youth, and of lightly touched and quickly dispelled sorrow," and voices the prophecy that her verse will probably "introduce other generations of girls and young women to the phenomena of an adolescent self-discovery in terms of poetry." Unless it be personal pique, only the general decline of critical taste throughout the whole period can explain this astonishing fact.

Many who felt the heartbroken passion contained in the serenely controlled forms of *Fatal Interview* were puzzled by the idea that they were composed "when the author was living quietly with a husband of eight years standing." Elizabeth Atkins showed a manuscript containing this quoted phrase to Eugen, and reports that he responded "in a deeply bitten marginal comment" that the assumption it makes is a lie. I never discussed this question with either of my friends, but I can join my testimony to his that, passionately and admiringly as they loved each other, "living quietly with a husband of eight years standing" is far from a description of Edna's mind during those years. Nor would the corresponding phrase be a description of his. He never ceased to adore her and care for her with a unique devotion, less like a husband's than that of a nursemaid toward a child of whom she is enamored. But he was a man, and men are a nomad sex. He was, moreover, in principle opposed to possessiveness in marriage on either side. Freedom of emotional experience had been a cardinal item in the private marriage vows taken by him and Inez Milholland in the heyday of the feminist movement in America. Glorious Inez died too soon, alas, for their youthful dream of a new kind of partnership to undergo a crucial test, but I have no reason to suppose that Eugen offered to Edna a less openhearted love. That she, on her side, felt no need to be possessed or circumscribed will be obvious, I think, to anyone who lives a little with her poetry. . . .

A more deeply self-damaging result of the puritanical streak in Edna was her disastrously conscientious attempt, in the crises of World War II, to write popular propaganda in the form of poetry. She gave all that she received for this poetry, and the manuscripts of it, to buy ambulances for the Red Cross. She was tremendously sincere—sincere enough, had it occurred to her, to go to work in a munitions factory, or wrap packages, or knit socks for the soldiers. That would have been a better gift to the war effort than bad poetry. But it would not have been the sacrifice of self that New England's rigid moralism demands. Edna may have imagined her name to be so renowned that her poetry, diluted to newspaper copy, would be an important help in "rousing the country," but I find this hard to believe. Her statement, "I have one thing to give in the service of my country, my reputation as a poet," strikes me as one of the most aberrant products of the modern brain-disease of propaganda. It was righteousness on the rampage, the sense of duty gone mad. And it ended, naturally, in a nervous breakdown.

"For five years," she wrote, explaining her illness to Edmund Wilson, "I had been writing almost nothing but propaganda. And I can tell you from my own experience that there is nothing on this earth which can so much get on the nerves of a good poet as the writing of bad poetry."

In sending us her beautifully titled book, *Make Bright the Arrows*, she wrote on the fly-leaf an inscription that was painful to read: "To Max and Eliena, who will not like the many bad lines contained in this book, but who will like the thing it wants so much to help to do, and who will like the reaffirmation of my constant affection and love. . . ." Many American writers—most of them—have at times diluted the purity of their art in order to make money; Edna's sin, we can say at least, was of a nobler-seeming kind. But it was a sin no less. She acknowledged later that this debauch of self-sacrifice had been a mistake, and regretted it sadly. But then it was too late. She never recaptured her lost self. She never wrote a great poem after that. . . .

Tarnished Arrows:
The Last Phase of Edna St. Vincent Millay

HAROLD OREL

Does anyone still discuss the work of Edna St. Vincent Millay as a serious contribution to modern poetry? The critics have done with her. The professors no longer write about her. And those who think of her as the most authentic woman personality since Emily Dickinson must explain—sooner rather than later—the poetry of her last phase; some blushes are inevitable.

The fall from grace of Edna St. Vincent Millay is a serious matter, and the essay that follows attempts to explain how and why it happened. It hazards a guess, but perhaps no more than a guess is possible, and at least it will build on available evidence. Part of that evidence, unfortunately, must be *Make Bright the Arrows*, perhaps the most disastrous book ever published by a major American poet.

Think back to the year 1937, when Miss Millay, more than popular, always quoted, well loved, handsomely printed, had attained the stature of a classic. Karl Yost had even compiled *A Bibliography of the Works of Edna St. Vincent Millay*, and to it Harold Lewis Cook contributed an appreciative essay. The argument that Mr. Cook pursued (and which Miss Millay approved, because it avoided "major errors of interpretation") amounted to this: her work would never be read as history "except for the comment implied in the almost total absence of contemporaneous allusion." Her interests lay in Nature, love, and death; man amid the stars; man and God—but not in war, economic and social upheavals, theories, and movements.

Even by 1937, however, critics were arguing that Miss Millay needed new themes, that she was tightly chained to her individual emotions, and that (in a poetical sense) she was standing still. Mr. Cook had to cope with these remarks; he did so by pointing to "Epitaph for the Race of Man," published originally in 1928, as a "striking" departure from Miss Millay's "usual theme." This sonnet sequence, together with *Fatal Interview*, seemed to him to be "the crowning achievement of Miss Millay's work to the present time."

Hence, his answer to the criticism was indirect, nor did he venture

From *Kansas Quarterly* (Manhattan, Kansas) 1 (1960): 73–78. Copyright © 1960 *Kansas Quarterly* and Harold Orel. Reprinted by permission.

more than a vague prophecy that her poetry would develop "in new directions." And in 1937 one might legitimately wonder what new string she had for her bow.

Her poetic plays held little promise as a mode of development. Indeed, they had no commercial future. Nor did she deceive herself as to the merits of those plays she had already written. In a candid letter to Cass Canfield (written in October, 1947, but expressing a long-held point of view), she refused to encourage *Harper's* in its suggestion that the time had come for a volume of her collected plays. To her, the only consequential play she had written, her "one really good, serious play," was *Aria da Capo*.

Partially, 1937 answered the question: it marked the appearance of *Conversation at Midnight*, a poem that Miss Millay had reconstructed arduously from memory after a fire at the Palms Hotel on Sanibel Island destroyed the original manuscript. Miss Millay was strongly dissatisfied with many portions of the book, and admitted that they did not measure up to the quality of what had been lost; but the public could judge only what had been published. The book showed strong traces of strain and hurry. Miss Millay insisted that the work was best considered "in terms of the theatre," as a play, since there were "not more than about thirty lines of descriptive narrative in the entire book."

However kindly the reader came to *Conversation at Midnight*, he found much of it a crashing bore. The play did not move. The primary effect created by the "conversation" of the seven men was static; a series of set pieces did not constitute an organic poem, or a valid statement of the theatre.

The critics (whom Miss Millay read carefully) were rude. The gist of their comments was that Miss Millay, *their* Miss Millay, had no business with bastardized form. Edmund Wilson wrote in the *New Republic* (July 28, 1937), ". . . the discussion doesn't seem to come to much. It covers familiar ground, and the people . . . say many of the clever things that people usually say, without arriving at very many of the illuminating things which people do not usually say, but which the poet ought to make them say." John Holmes gibed at her in the Boston *Transcript* (August 7, 1937), ". . . she might better have gone the whole way and made the book a play instead of what it is, neither story, play, nor poem. And such a play would be something like Noel Coward's idea of Ogden Nash writing like Edna St. Vincent Millay." Robert Hillyer, in the *Atlantic* (September, 1937), referred to it as "a 122-page work which, to speak frankly, is unutterably dull—as dull as a dictaphone record."

What they ignored was the necessity which had called forth the form: Miss Millay's own conviction, implicit in the work, that something new had to be tried. She had become dissatisfied with the spectrum of themes that she had already recorded; better than the critics, she knew that she needed either to develop new ideas on the subjects of "Nature, love, and death," or to develop new themes. Hence, the fact that *Conversation at Midnight* failed as a work, and evoked so dismayed a response from even her most faithful admirers, should not distract our attention from Miss Millay's heroic effort to identify the subject-matter that would serve her in the years to come.

For the book does move away from her past. Love is no longer the heart of the matter. Part II begins with the emphatic cry of a twenty-five-year-old copy-writer named Lucas ("hard-boiled and idealistic," says Miss Millay in one of her curiously noninformative remarks about the characters): "I want to talk about love!" He then proceeds to tell a story about a nameless girl who was engaged to another man when he first met her. He tried not to fall in love with her. ". . . I wouldn't let myself go, because I knew / About this man, and I didn't want to get hurt / If I could help it. Well, that all fell through." Her kiss made impossible his continued reserve. It led to several dates, and to a belief that the girl intended to marry him. He was to learn otherwise. ". . . well, the other night / She called me up: her family had made a fuss, she said, / And she was marrying this chap. I said, 'O.K., go ahead.' " The story has no point. Miss Millay does not treat it with bitter-sweet irony (as she might have done at an earlier period). She does not exploit it as a revelation of Lucas's character. She just tells it. And the anecdote leads to a series of comments about women that reveal only a great weariness with the entire subject matter. "Women are poison," Pygmalion says. Merton adds that women keep watching to see where a friend "sets his glass down." And Lucas, wise beyond his years, contributes comments about how unreasonable women are. Several pages of insults about women follow. Carl summarizes the ennui of those present:

> We're about as through with this thing called
> Love as—what?—
> Plumes in our helmets, powder in our hair.
> Love's lazy, won't keep step, is all the time
> Swooning into a dozen lilies, or under a yew,
> Or looking backward, and bursting into tears
>   and rhyme;
> Holds everything up, just can't fit in, won't
>   do.

A line of poetry has been quoted, and the conversation drifts off into an attempt to identify the author. The female sex is a tiresome topic; it has been done to death. Love turns stale as familiarity breeds contempt.

Hence, Miss Millay's interest turns to other subjects. One is the possible usefulness of God in a secular age. Significantly enough, one of the speakers is Father Anselmo, a Franciscan who has developed artistic interests, and who debates God with people who run the "grave risk" of "being scorched by Faith." He knows that the people who have assembled in the drawing room of Ricardo's house cannot "contrive" to believe. Still, it is worth reminding them of the difficulties of mixing science and Jesus. And when he fails to make himself understood, he plays Bach on Ricardo's grand piano, building Peace "from felt, wire, ivory, and wood."

Another is the shoddiness of the cultural standards in the modern world. This may be illustrated not merely by Madison Avenue's brand of advertising, but by all the "many cunning amusements" that "this clever age affords." John's remark, "An artist is bound to be jealous when he considers that the public's being fooled / By a showy second-rater . . ." explains a good deal of the conversation: Miss Millay's jealousy of all the second-raters runs deep. She loves Greek and Latin literature, and on all sides she witnesses the cheapening of language, and of humane values. She believes that this topic is of legitimate concern to intelligent men in America's artistic capital.

A third problem of great concern is treated in the debate that rages between Merton, a very wealthy stock-broker, and Carl, a somewhat boorish poet. Miss Millay's prosy earnestness on the relative merits of capitalism and communism makes this whole section sludgy. Neither Merton nor Carl has the eloquence of Father Anselmo. The argument degenerates *ad hominem* at an alarmingly rapid pace in Part IV. It is not good poetry. But the political awareness, the knowing references to Trotzky, Stalin, *Das Kapital*, and the *Daily Worker*, the unsentimental statements to the effect that Russian progress has been purchased dearly at the price of liberty and of human dignity, mark Miss Millay as a careful reader of the stories contained in contemporary newspapers. And the book is prescient: war is coming. She does not make an educated guess; she is absolutely sure of it. "Don't be foolish," says Pygmalion, "it's catastrophe. And it's coming. If you want to outthink the thoughtless, you'll have to think faster."

Conversation at Midnight did not have a focused subject-matter, and its literary form was bastardized. But its author was attempting to become a better artist by grappling with her environment and by talking of the world she knew. The unkindness of the reviewers sent her back to the attic-chest for her next book, *Huntsman, What Quarry?* (1939), much of which went over material well known to her readers. Two years had passed, and the world had moved forward to the war she had predicted. The voice of Cassandra spoke in Part Two, where poems of a topical nature dealt with the agonies of China, Spain, and Czecho-Slovakia.[1] She found it impossible to return permanently to the patterns of the poetry which had made her famous. *Conversation at Midnight*, although unsatisfactory, had suggested methods of enlarging her subject matter; and to this impetus for the development of a new style was conjoined her patriotic impulse. She wanted America to know what she knew. She would help to save democracy through her poetry.

Make Bright the Arrows, subtitled "1940 Notebook," appeared at a time when Hitler had reached his apogee of power; its message should have had maximum meaning. But it contained an astonishing quantity of uncrafts-manlike poetry, and, far more than *Conversation at Midnight*, it shocked and depressed her readers.

One poem, "There Are No Islands Any More," was dated May, 1940, and carried the tag, "Lines Written in Passion and in Deep Concern for England, France, and My Own Country." It began baldly, "Dear Isolationist, you are / So very, very insular!" "It gets better," Irwin Edman commented dryly, "but not enough better to be poetry." For, although Miss Millay had at long last found her new subject matter, she had not learned how to transform headlines into poetry.

The catalogue of sins could be expanded. The extraordinary aspect of *Make Bright the Arrows* is that every time the war came into the lyric, the lyric died. The exhortations, the table-poundings, the tears, the oversimplified arguments, the sneers at "the old men of Vichy" and those who would give, "when the day comes, England to Germany," may have served an immediate purpose; but, within the covers of a book, they lost for Miss Millay her birthright as a poetess.

John Peale Bishop, writing in the *Nation* (December 7, 1940), said sadly, "In urging us to make bright the arrows, she has weapons in mind. It is only the martial arrows she has sharpened here. The arrows of Apollo lie neglected, tarnished, blunt." Louise Bogan was no kinder in the *New Yorker* (December 28, 1940): "The noble tone, the stock sentiment, which post-1918 poetry, in all European languages, depreciated and made tiresome and unreadable, reappear. That this sentimentality should at this particular moment appear in full force in American writing is a cause for concern and regret." Babette Deutsch deplored the "poetic journalese," and, in the *New Republic* (December 2, 1940), commented, "Few poets can hope to do more now than scribble Jeremiads in notebooks; but all who are honest with themselves and their public will admit that hysteria is *ersatz* prophecy, and notes a poor substitute for poetry." Unkindest cut of all came from Eugene Jolas, reviewing a separate edition of "There Are No Islands Any More" in *Living Age* (October, 1940): "We may dismiss [it] as the expression of a poet whose conviction and sincerity are obvious, but whose creative spirit has burned out."

These are representative comments. Miss Millay had tried to explore areas other than those she had made so familiar in her popular books of lyric poetry; she had been rebuffed; and there is no question but that the rebuffs were cruel. However, it should be pointed out that Miss Millay did not like her journalistic poems any better than the critics. She had written them but was under no illusions as to their worth. She had written them because she believed in what they were saying; she had written them because she was compelled to write them.

To George Dillon she wrote (November 29, 1940) that her book contained "not poems, posters," and that it was mostly "plain propaganda."

The few good poems included in the book were there because they happened to be propaganda too.

To Sister Ste. Helene, then Dean of the College of St. Catherine, St. Paul, Minnesota, she wrote (December 3, 1940) that her book contained "acres of bad poetry." She asked forgiveness for what she was trying to do and for what she was trying to help save.

Wretchedly ill, fighting for her health, she had to combat misunderstanding even among her friends. To Mrs. Charlotte Babcock Sills she wrote a long, tearful letter (January 2, 1941), asking that *Make Bright the Arrows* be re-read carefully. "Is it not unjust of you, my dear friend, to accuse me of trying to incite this country to send an army to fight on foreign soil just because my idea as to how best to keep this country out of war differs radically from yours?" She wanted, above all things, to keep America out of war by making it powerful and a "bowman" to be "feared." To that end, England had to be aided, and America had to arm for the sake of "its democratic ideals, its freedom, its individual liberties." Willingly she staked her reputation as a poet for the service of her country. It was the only sacrifice she might make. Unlike Mrs. Sills, she had no sons to be caught in the war. "How many more books of propaganda poetry containing as much bad verse as this one does," she wrote, "that reputation can withstand without falling under the weight of it and without becoming irretrievably lost I do not know— probably not more than one." She added: "But I have enlisted for the duration."

We are suggesting, in short, that the failure of Edna St. Vincent Millay, which the critics so angrily and immediately noted, was a phase of her career, entered into because she felt she had to grow as a poet; begun because she believed she could not be honest as a human being in any other way; undertaken *knowingly*. Her ruin as a creative poet began as a conscious act, and in that fact lies her tragedy. For twenty years she had been building her reputation as a perfectionist, and now it rested on a book of poetry "written in furious haste," "hot-headed," "faulty and unpolished," which (by her own confession) many "true lovers of pure poetry" would never forgive her for writing.

The worst came in 1941: America's involvement. After the declaration of war, she blurred all her enemies together as people who had "let Pearl Harbor happen." In December, 1941, she summed up her despair: "*Make Bright the Arrows*, of course, did no good at all."

Not once during the crowded, hectic war years did she delude herself that propaganda—however timely or useful—was worthy of her best talents. *The Murder of Lidice*, which moved Dr. Eduard Benes, had some good lines, but "not very many, and not very good," and she hoped that it would be allowed to die along with the war which provoked it. Her work for the Writers' War Board, Red Cross, and other organizations left her little time for creative thinking. It was financially unrewarding. It exhausted her emotionally. She worked as well as she could between bouts with doctors, hospital beds, X-rays. Her letters, edited by Allan Ross Macdougall (New York, 1952), indicate that her exasperation with matters beyond her control and her suspicion about her best work lying behind her were growing; that requests for new books, collections, and anthology selections upset her far more often than they pleased her. Her friends were dying: Eugene Saxton, John Peale Bishop, President Roosevelt, and then her husband, Eugen Jan Boissevain (August 30, 1949). She wrote less; she seemed to have less to say. In the letter to Cass Canfield already referred to, she said:

> I am writing. I have not many poems finished, but those that I have are good. The effect of writing so much propaganda during the war—from the point of view of poetry, sloppy, garrulous and unintegrated—is to make me more careful and critical of my work even than formerly I was, so that now I write more slowly than ever. But there will be a book. I am afraid even to suggest a possible date, lest I be caught again in that paralyzing nightmare of writing against time, which I so often experienced when writing for the radio during the war. If *Harper's* can be patient with me still, there will be a book.

The book, produced posthumously as *Mine the Harvest* (1954) and edited with loving care by Norma Millay, did not significantly change the picture; the critics were no longer interested. Now, too, the record is complete, with the publication of *Collected Poems* (New York, 1956), the definitive edition. It contains only a handful of poems from *Make Bright the Arrows*, the book that split a brilliant career into two unequal parts. But it contains also the poems that made Miss Millay's reputation, poems that sing, that may not be forgotten:

> Boys and girls that lie
> Whispering in the hedges,
> Do not let me die,
> Mix me with your pledges;
> Boys and girls that slowly walk
> In the woods, and weep, and quarrel,
> Staring past the pink wild laurel,
> Mix me with your talk,
>
> Do not let me die!

Notes

1. Mr. Cook's comment about "the almost total absence of contemporaneous allusion" was misleading. Miss Millay's social instincts had been in evidence before. The Sacco-Vanzetti

trial moved her deeply. About that event an important segment of *The Buck in the Snow and Other Poems* (1928) had been written: "Hangman's Oak," "Wine from These Grapes," "The Anguish," "Justice Denied in Massachusetts," and "To Those Without Pity." Miss Millay had even gone to the Governor of the Commonwealth of Massachusetts, attempting to stay the death sentence. She had willingly committed herself, had become engaged to fight for a belief. At the time her gesture seemed gallant, but unrepresentative of her major interests. Even her enthusiastic biographer, Elizabeth Atkins, wrote sternly in *Edna St. Vincent Millay and Her Times* (Chicago, 1936) that her "controversial mood, though it has given us much verse, has not given us much poetry."

Edna St. Vincent Millay

ROSEMARY SPRAGUE

"The problem about Vincent Millay," Marianne Moore has said, "is that she was popular for all the wrong reasons."[1] This perceptive comment by a great poet about one of her contemporaries provides an excellent starting point for any evaluation of Millay's achievement. With its usual proclivity for praising its own thoughts and ideas in print, a particular reading public— that of the Twenties and early Thirties—seized on Vincent's early poetry and perhaps gave it more praise than it deserved. But this same public, grown older and wiser, refused to accord the poet the same privilege, and became confused and resentful when she wrote more seriously. The war poetry seemed a betrayal of an image they had cherished, and her last and really finest volume was virtually ignored. *A Few Figs From Thistles* became a kind of mariner's albatross; like Swinburne, who was never permitted to forget that he had once written "Dolores," so her bright quatrains were quoted, anthologized, and perpetuated, until today almost everyone can quote "My candle burns" ad infinitum, while the remarkable love sonnets of *Fatal Interview* and other poems equally as fine remain unknown.

Her posthumous collection, *Mine The Harvest*, over which she worked long and carefully, has been published so recently (1954) that it makes a proper perspective difficult. But this may be just as well. Cold objectivity was not one of Vincent Millay's salient characteristics; she was emotional and subjective, and her poetry is far too personal to yield much to purely objective appraisal:

> Cruel of heart, lay down my song.
> Your reading eyes have done me wrong.
> Not for you was the pen bitten,
> And the mind wrung, and the song written.

This quatrain addressed "To Those Without Pity" was published in 1928. In *Mine The Harvest*, twenty-six years later, she again stated her criticism of the critics in no uncertain terms:

> It is the fashion now to wave aside
> As tedious, obvious, vacuous, trivial, trite,

Excerpted from *Imaginary Gardens: A Study of Five American Poets* (Philadelphia: Chilton, 1969): 168–73. Reprinted by permission of Chilton Book Company and Rosemary Sprague.

> All things which do not tickle, tease, excite
> To some subversion, or in verbiage hide
> Intent, or mock, or with hot sauce provide
> A dish to prick the thickened appetite;
> Straightforwardness is wrong, evasion right;
> It is correct, *de rigueur*, to deride.

For Vincent Millay believed that poetry must be honest, *and* intelligible—she described the writing of a sonnet by saying, "I will put Chaos into fourteen lines / and keep him there." In another poem, she says that a poet must have powers "such as must qualify a god," to create: ". . . not from dream, / No, not from aspiration, not from hope, / But out of art and wisdom. . . ." The word *art* refers to technical skill, what she called "the skill of the artisan, which every writer who has written for many years, at length acquires."[2] But the word may also be interpreted as that selective, utterly truthful view of reality which a poet achieves by putting "Chaos into fourteen lines"—by successfully verbalizing the inexpressible aspiration, hope, or dream. Greatness in poetry does not consist in putting reality on paper, but, through the power of language, giving the impression of reality—reality heightened and deepened, and all the more true, even though, paradoxically, the poetic reality is not actually "real." Vincent Millay possessed this gift in the highest degree, and achieved her finest poems by first writing down the inspiration the moment it came, and then by chipping away each superfluous word or unharmonious sound. Sometimes she would work for years over a poem, until it satisfied her highest standards.

And, once the poem was as perfect as she could make it, she would allow no changes:

> Any changes which might profitably be made in any of my poems, were either made by me, before I permitted them to be published, or must be made, if made at all, someday by me. Only I, who know what I mean to say, and how I want to say it, am competent to deal with such matters. Many of my poems, of course, are greatly reduced in stature from the majesty which I had hoped they might achieve, because I was unable, as one too often is, to make the poem rise up to my conception of it. However, the faults as well as the virtues of this poetry, are my own; and no other person could possibly lay hands upon any poem of mine in order to correct some real or imagined error without harming the poem more seriously than any faulty execution of my own could possibly have done.[3]

Her poetry reiterates this insistence upon the absolute integrity of the artist's work:

> Such as I am, however, I have brought
> To what it is, this tower; it is my own;

> Though it was reared to Beauty, it was wrought
> With what I had to build with:

the necessity of the poet's giving all he has to his work—

> Still as of old his being give
> In Beauty's name, while she may live. . . .

. . . his empathy with the suffering of the world—

> The anguish of the world is on my tongue.
> My bowl is filled to the brim with it; there is more
> than I can eat.

. . . his constant awareness of the beauty underlying the ugly, the sordid, and the mean—

> As sharp as in my childhood, still
> Ecstasy shocks me fixed.

. . . all qualities which make up his unique vision must, when they are finally given form in language, be allowed to stand as written, whether or not they are understood or appreciated. "I have learned to fail," Vincent Millay wrote with characteristic honesty, in "Lines Written in Recapitulation." But she also, at times, succeeded magnificently; that she refused to be influenced by "The Waste Land" and its imitations is rather more to her credit than otherwise.

For she could not imitate the gloom-filled, direly prophetic poetry which became the fashion after 1922. Although she wrote of grief and loneliness, though humanity sometimes disillusioned her, nevertheless her poetry is permeated with an unshatterable belief in the intrinsic goodness of the world. She clung, as all humanity must, to her ideal of the human spirit at its highest and best. From the first glad acceptance of "Renascence," to the last poems in *Mine The Harvest*, there is a recurrent appeal to man to rejoice in life, and to accept its challenge: "We, we the living, we the still alive—/ Why, what a triumph, what a task is here!" And the task? "To build our world; if not this year, next year." In one of her last poems, "Journal," she addresses herself to future generations in most persuasive words:

> Oh, children, growing up to be
> Adventurers into sophistry,

Forbear, forbear to be of those
That read the root to learn the rose;
Whose thoughts are like a tugging kite,
Anchored by day, drawn in at night.
Grieve not if from the mind be loosed
A wing that comes not home to roost;
There may be garnered yet of that
An olive-branch from Ararat.

She genuinely feared an over-rationalistic approach to life, lest it deaden the spirit:

We are clever,—we are clever as monkeys, and some of us
Have intellect, which is our danger, for we lack intelligence
And have forgotten instinct.

It was to the preservation of intelligence and instinct, and to the destruction of cynicism and *acidie* that poetry called her:

Yet I shall sing until my voice crack (this being my leisure, this my holiday)
That man was a special thing and no commodity, a thing improper to be
sold.

Life *is* transient and fleeting, but, so far as she was concerned, it should be lived "with all my senses, well aware / That this was perfect, and it would not last." Sorrow must be accepted, for in it strength can be found; even death can be kind, "reminding us how much we dared to love." Perhaps Edna St. Vincent Millay's vision can best be summed up in the final stanza of "Small Hands, Relinquish All":

Only the ardent eye,
Only the listening ear
Can say, "The thrush was here!"
Can say, "His song was clear!"
Can live, before it die.

The new reader, encountering her poetry for the first time, can agree with the comment of Edmund Wilson: "One never forgot the things she noticed, for she charged them with her own intensest feeling. This power of enhancing and ennobling life was felt by all who knew her."[4] In an age when there is so much chatter about idealism and the inviolability of the human spirit, it may be that the poetry of Edna St. Vincent Millay may prove a delightful, heartening discovery.

Notes

Unless otherwise noted, all references are to Miriam Gurko, *Restless Spirit: The Life of Edna St. Vincent Millay*, Crowell, 1962 (Gurko), and to *Letters of Edna St. Vincent Millay*, edited by Allan Ross Macdougall, Grosset and Dunlap, 1952 (Letters).

Poems taken from *Collected Poems: Edna St. Vincent Millay*, edited by Norma Millay, Harper & Row, 1956.

1. Marianne Moore, conversation with author.
2. Letters, 341.
3. Ibid., 329.
4. Edmund Wilson, *The Shores of Light* (Farrar, Straus and Young), 1952, 475.

A Doll's Heart:
The Girl in the Poetry of Edna St. Vincent
Millay and Louise Bogan

ELIZABETH PERLMUTTER FRANK

There are good reasons to compare the early work of Louise Bogan with that of Edna St. Vincent Millay, for it was in the work produced in their twenties that both poets used the fact of being female not merely as subject matter, but as a formal principle for invigorating and intensifying lyric speech. Through the medium of female personae, each poet developed a specific approach to the lyric past. Millay, assuming the existence of fixed conventions in lyric poem from its temporary submersion in the twin sloughs of Victorian sentiment and modernist gloom, while Louise Bogan sought in the variety, complexity, and rigor of traditional lyric verification and diction a means of forging an elemental lyric. She was from the outset of her career decidedly modernist in her commitment to reducing the lyric to its essentials, and to redefining its sources in emotion, whereas Millay intended only that her poems "measure up" to the lyric past by approximating traditional lyric uses of voice, diction, and theme. Both poets, however, were precocious adepts in the craft of lyric versification, and in the early 1920s it would have been difficult to differentiate their styles and poetic purposes.

Although the young Louise Bogan had nourished herself from late childhood with the work of William Morris, Swinburne, Dante Gabriel Rossetti, Christina Rossetti, and the French symbolists, and while in maturity she would enjoy deep poetic identification with Yeats and with Rilke, at the time that she first began to publish, in 1921, she was compelled to come to terms with the formidable presence of Edna St. Vincent Millay in order to free herself from adolescent taste and habit. The process of confrontation was neither rapid nor, from the outset, hostile. In fact, when in 1923 Edna Millay published her fourth book, *The Harp-Weaver and Other Poems*, and Louise Bogan her first, *Body of This Death*, they appeared to be members

All quotations of Edna St. Vincent Millay's work are from *Collected Poems*, Harper & Row. Copyright 1917, 1921, 1923, 1928, 1946, 1949, 1951, 1955 by Edna St. Vincent Millay and Norma Millay Ellis. From *Twentieth Century Literature: A Scholarly and Critical Journal* 23, no. 2 (2 May 1977): 157–79. Reprinted by permission. "Pyrotechnics," "Words for Departure," and "Betrothed" reprinted by permission of Ruth Limmer, literary executor.

179

in good standing of an unbroken tradition of lyric poetry by American women beginning with Emily Dickinson and continued by Louise Imogen Guiney, Lizette Woodworth Reese, Adelaide Crapsey, Sara Teasdale, and Elinor Wylie. It extended beyond Millay and Bogan into the middle and late 1920s with the work of Louise Townsend Nicholl and Abbie Huston Evans, finally becoming something very much like major art with the work of Léonie Adams and Marianne Moore.

Arriving in New York in 1920, aged 23, and five years Millay's junior, Louise Bogan would inevitably have discovered Edna St. Vincent Millay as the contemporary standard-bearer of that tradition. Indeed, with the publication of *Renascence* in 1917, it became clear to the New York literary world that Edna Millay was preeminently the poet who offered an alternative to the "new" poetry, and whose work could serve as a rallying point for the rejection of free verse, imagism, and Prufrockian ennui. When in 1921 she made the daring announcement in *A Few Figs from Thistles* that her candle burned at both ends, she was hailed as the quintessential woman poet: high-minded and high-handed, passionate, erotic, vulnerable, yet indomitable, lodestar for post-World War I youth who, world-and-war weary as they may have been, craved intense, feelingful experience even more than bleak, sullen, or dadaist confrontation with "a botched civilization." For Louise Bogan, then as always listening for the individual voice amidst the cries of a generation, Millay must have offered through the attitudes and forms of her verse the compelling spectacle of a poet who had dared both to resist what "the age demanded" and to resuscitate such recently rejected forms as the sonnet and rhymed-stanzaic lyric from the dust of late nineteenth-century and Georgian sentimentality. In just those ballads, quatrains, rhymed stanzas, and sonnets to which Louise Bogan from childhood had been irresistibly attracted, and to whose formal demands she had made herself wholly answerable, Edna Millay was triumphant, to the immense gratitude of a popular audience desirous of impassioned feeling and a thumping beat.

In retrospect, Millay's actual achievement, which was not inconsiderable, was to conserve, in her early volumes, the melodic simplicity of the combined pastoral and personal lyric by breathing into it a hybridized diction we must ruefully call "poetic." That is, starting with her earliest verses, Millay's style was a resplendent pastiche of Sapphic simplicity, Catullan urbanity, homeless Chaucerian idiom, uprooted Shakespearean grammar, Cavalier sparkle, Wordsworthian magnanimity, Keatsian sensuousness, and Housmanian melancholy, not of course compounded all at once in a single lethal draught, but lightly dispersed here and there throughout her songs and sonnets. Such diction soon came to represent poetry at once fresh and yet "as the ancient world understood it, poetry with metaphors and phrases that were at the same time lovely and new—metaphors and phrases as like and yet as unlike those of earlier poetry as a new-springing tree is like and unlike an older one."[1] Here was no fragmented, estranged, crumbling world, which to Millay's ears and eyes seemed more depressing than it actually was in the work of Eliot, Pound, and Aiken, but a universe to which the Aeolian strings of the poet's heart could still vibrate, her fingers all the while plucking an ancient lyre:

God's World

O world, I cannot hold thee close enough!
　　Thy winds, thy wide grey skies!
　　Thy mists, that roll and rise!
Thy woods, this autumn day, that ache and sag
And all but cry with colour! That gaunt crag
To crush! To lift the lean of that black bluff!
World, World, I cannot get thee close enough!

Long have I known a glory in it all,
　　But never knew I this:
　　Here such a passion is
As stretcheth me apart,—Lord, I do fear
Thou'st made the world too beautiful this year;
My soul is all but out of me,—let fall
No burning leaf; prithee, let no bird call.[2]

In the long-familiar guise of the poet aching with the world's beauty, Millay uses an equally commonplace "poetic diction" of apostrophe and grammatical inversion, with touches of archaism ("thou" and "prithee") to construct a speaker at once reverent, breathless, and naïve. This persona becomes more fully rendered in the volumes following *Renascence* as the Girl, who as the analogue of the young, girlish poet herself, becomes the vehicle of the most "poetical" features of Millay's lyric diction.

By the time she came to define the lyric reaches of Millay's verse, the Girl had behind her an ancient and honorable past. She had been addressed and sometimes assumed for voice by Sappho, and had prevailed in the maiden-song of folk and ballad tradition, as the shepherdess in both high and low forms of pastoral, and in the various incarnations of Portia, Beatrice, and, especially for Millay's purposes, in the trembling virginity and mad songs of Ophelia. While Millay in both early and late verse was often to compare herself to Dido, Cleopatra, Cressida, or Elaine, these comparisons were understood as deliberate similes, obvious extravagances meant to varnish or overlay the fragile Girl who stood as the "real" speaker of Millay's songs and sonnets, and who hovered forever between betrothal and betrayal, the promise of experience and its denouement in disillusion and despair. For the Girl, love—whether chaste or erotic, passionate or quiescent—was the whole of existence, subsuming her impetuous high-spiritedness and her thirst for intense sensation and meaning. Yet equally essential to the Girl's character was her self-abandon, and self-neglect. She would too often recklessly bestow herself upon some heartless lad who would, inevitably, betray her. Only then would she find at the very moment of heartbreak, at the very crisis of anguish, a terrible strength that would allow her to grieve but not to die. This combination of weakness and strength, of erotic susceptibility and unsuspected will, provided Millay's Girl with a basic affective strategy in which disappointment could change suddenly to ennui, and high lyric lamentation to shrugging colloquial gloom. Indeed, Millay's Girl was essentially a theatrical persona, a medium for the expression of sudden shifts in tone and implied bodily gestures. This mercurial quality is particularly noticeable in "The Shroud," where the poet melodramatically draws attention not to her words or even to her experience as such, but to the "picture" she makes in actually uttering the poem:

> Death, I say, my heart is bowed
>   Unto thine,—O mother!
> This red gown will make a shroud
>   Good as any other!
> (I, that would not wait to wear
>   My own bridal things,
> In a dress dark as my hair
>   Made my answerings.
> I, to-night, that till he came
>   Could not, could not wait,
> In a gown as bright as flame
>   Held for them the gate.)
> Death, I say, my heart is bowed
>   Unto thine,—O mother!
> This red gown will make a shroud
>   Good as any other!³

Exploiting the simplicity of ballad form not so much to ennoble the Girl's grief as to introduce the sinful symbols of red gown and red hair, the poem achieves a disarming pictorial quality that may indeed have been enhanced in oral delivery by the fact that Millay actually had red hair. The poem's real purpose is to shock and thrill the audience with sexual innuendo, not to utter a cry of the heart for lost innocence. Through the vividly compressed ballad diction Millay's readers or hearers would discern once again the modern Girl confessing that sex has led to shame and ruin. Horace Gregory and Marya Zaturenska rightly call Millay's gifts "histrionic" in *A History of American Poetry: 1900–1940*;⁴ her poetry drew attention to itself as an instrument for the swift alteration of mood, inviting swings in response from an audience thereby flattered into interpreting her volatile diction as depth of emotion. A corollary feature of Millay's theatrical mode was the power to make the audience share in the Girl's self-pity without appearing to cheapen that emotion. In "Scrub," a poem published in *The Harp-Weaver and Other Poems* (1923), the poet as ingenue views her fate as blasted and blighted, like a scrub oak destroyed by wind and storm, a stance she assumed in many other poems in which she likened her soul or her feelings to gnarled trees, budding seeds, or seasons and weathers in various stages of fervor and instability. By these means Millay's Girl bit to the core of the poet's lyric *donnée*—erotic and poetic exhibitionism—with "adorable" flair and considerable shrewdness. She spoke, that is, of her love affairs, not with Sappho's brevity, nor with Catullus's candor, but with an allusiveness indebted to both and a coyness both would have shunned. Using a rhetoric of swift changes of mood, the Girl could turn the lightsome measures of impulse and intimacy into the acrid dismissals and recriminations of scorn and ennui, becoming in the process "no mere girl at all, but a woman who had already grown weary of sin."[5]

Capable of moving readers and hearers, the skillful, charming verse through which the Girl had life was even so too dependent on implied gesture to be taken seriously as meant speech. If Millay's Girl defamed the "beautiful," or hinted at the improper, if in her excesses of feeling she occasionally rhymed bathetically or slithered around and over her meters, all it pointed to was her very modern right to say or do anything she pleased. Emancipation was a matter of mood, not conviction. Hence, in "Spring" she sulks and grumbles and finds April the cruelest month, not because it is agonizing to the torpid spirit to reawaken to life, but presumably because she has had a bad time of it romantically. In poem after poem, the formula or leitmotiv that identified Millay's Girl was the insouciant manner with which she turned grief to cynicism, often achieving a novel prestige by being the agent of the sexual rejection:

Passer Mortuus Est

Death devours all lovely things:
    Lesbia with her sparrow
Shares the darkness,—presently
    Every bed is narrow.

Unremembered as old rain
    Dries the sheer libation;
And the little petulant hand
    Is an annotation.

After all, my erstwhile dear,
    My no longer cherished,
Need we say it was not love,
    Just because it perished?[6]

Coolly, cleverly, the Girl slays with a Catullan sleight of hand her own naïve romanticism and the boyfriend's too. This is Edna St. Vincent Millay's

Girl at her best, the unflappable flapper whose sophistication has taken her beyond libertinage and rebellion toward an epicurean balance of urbanity and lyricism. Yet, within the volume in which it appears and in relation to the whole Millay canon, even such a polished poem as "Passer Mortuus Est" represents merely another mood-swing in the permanently inconsistent soul of the Girl. She could just as easily become the abandoned housewife, throwing off silk pajamas and donning instead a bedraggled apron:

Alms

My heart is what it was before,
    A house where people come and go;
But it is winter with your love,
    The sashes are beset with snow.

I light the lamp and lay the cloth,
    I blow the coals to blaze again;
But it is winter with your love,
    The frost is thick upon the pane.

I know a winter when it comes;
    The leaves are listless on the boughs;
I watched your love a little while,
    And brought my plants into the house.

I water them and turn them south,
    I snap the dead brown from the stem;
But it is winter with your love,
    I only tend and water them.

There was a time I stood and watched
    The small, ill-natured sparrows' fray;
I loved the beggar that I fed,
    I cared for what he had to say,

I stood and watched him out of sight;
    Today I reach around the door
And set a bowl upon the step;
    My heart is what it was before,

But it is winter with your love;
    I scatter crumbs upon the sill,
And close the window,—and the birds
    May take or leave them, as they will.[7]

In this poem wistful and resigned, in another brazen and proud, the Girl sang, as Millay had her say in "The Singing Woman from the Wood's

Edge," in the accents of "a harlot and a nun." In Millay's sonnets, especially, the Girl rode a seesaw of theatrical, gestural alternation. High-mindedness turned quickly to flirtation, poetic rapture to jazzy suggestiveness. In "Oh, think not I am faithful to a vow!" and "I shall forget you presently, my dear," both published in 1920 in *A Few Figs from Thistles*, the Girl attempts a Shakespearean density of phrasing to give a "high-toned" nonchalance to the declaration of concupiscence, while in "Into the golden vessel of great song," published the following year in *Second April*, sexual passion becomes at once legitimate and trivial when regarded as the force that joins the two lovers, both poets, in the far more important ecstasy of inspiration. Most often, the Girl played upon a range of emotional extremes in those poems where, as in "Passer Mortuus Est," she coolly ended the affair. In these we see an extraordinary coordination of explicitly verbal and implicitly physical gestures. In the following sonnet, for example, the Girl dismisses and eulogizes her boyfriend, all the while smoking a cigarette (its gray rings presumably circling her bobbed red hair):

> Only until this cigarette is ended,
> A little moment at the end of all,
> While on the floor the quiet ashes fall,
> And in the firelight to a lance extended,
> Bizarrely with the jazzing music blended,
> The broken shadow dances on the wall,
> I will permit my memory to recall
> The vision of you, by all my dreams attended.
> And then adieu,—farewell!—the dream is done.
> Yours is a face of which I can forget
> The colour and the features, every one,
> The words not ever, and the smiles not yet;
> But in your day this moment is the sun
> Upon a hill, after the sun has set.[8]

It is all so staged, so visible, so temporary, and it was what the literary world into which Louise Bogan was gaining entry in the early 1920s considered rich, sustaining fare. In the first issue, in March 1921, of the "little" New York poetry magazine, *The Measure*, coeditor Frank Ernest Hill, reviewing *A Few Figs from Thistles*, called Millay "just now the most interesting person in American poetry."[9] The same issue contained work by Conrad Aiken and Wallace Stevens, and in subsequent issues work by Robert Frost, Hart Crane, Louise Bogan and Léonie Adams would also be found. While each member of *The Measure's* group of revolving editors considered himself critically autonomous, there was remarkable unanimity in the appraisal of Millay. Maxwell Anderson called her poetry "perfect" in his review of *Second April*,[10] and in a long review of *The Harp-Weaver and Other Poems*, Genevieve Taggard, one of *The Measure's* most vocal contributors, pronounced Millay "one of the poets of all time," crediting her poetry with making "all other utterance almost banal."[11]

Other members of *The Measure's* editorial core, in addition to Hill, Anderson, and Taggard, included Agnes Kendrick Gray, Carolyn Hall, David Morton, Louise Townsend Nicholl, and George O'Neil, and it was to this group that Louise Bogan firmly attached herself soon after her poems began appearing in the magazine's pages in April 1921. She eventually assumed one of its revolving three-month editorships, between December and February of 1924–25, by which time she had already published her first book of poems, *Body of This Death*, and had achieved considerable stature not only among her colleagues at *The Measure* but also at *The New Republic*, where she published verse and reviews. She had, no doubt, been attracted to *The Measure* for its determined advocacy of what Maxwell Anderson described in the first issue as "the musical and rounded forms" over "the half-said, half-conceived infantilities and whimsicalities of the dominant American school."[12] Complaining frequently of the formlessness of imagism and vers-libre, and the "negativism" of what they otherwise frankly acknowledged as the vaster ambitions of Eliot and Pound, the editors of *The Measure* upheld Edna Millay as the leading voice in the pursuit of poetic quality they believed had dwindled away from Harriet Monroe's *Poetry* as it wearily reached the end of its first decade. Anderson pointed out in his statement of *The Measure's* editorial policy that while the magazine would probably never publish a great poem, the age being inimical to great poetry,

> *Poetry*, of Chicago, has come out uninterruptedly for ten years without doing it. This is not the fault of the editors of *Poetry*. If there had been masterpieces to print they would have printed them. There have been none. But the ten years of *Poetry's* history have been useful, fruitful, interesting. Miss Monroe and her band have pioneered well, and if the near future should actually hold a poetic revival in merit as well as in bulk, it will be due largely to their efforts.[13]

Thus neither strictly *derrière* nor *avant-garde*, *The Measure's* editors and contributors were mustered together in the name of rhyme, meter, stanzas, lyric smoothness, pure diction, of all, in short, that they considered essential to "form." By publishing in *The Measure*, Louise Bogan identified herself with the cause of form, and thereby placed herself, deliberately or not, in Millay's league; if not on her team. In the April 1921 issue, Bogan's poem, "Words for Departure," appeared in a group of "Nineteen Poems by Americans of the Younger Generation," whose members included Robert Hillyer, David Rosenthal, Eda Lou Walton, Kathryn White Ryan, Archie Binns, Hortense Flexner, Lola Ridge, and Dare Stark. Nearly every one of these poems was short, rhymed and stanzaic, the three keys to the kingdom currently ruled by Edna St. Vincent Millay. By her own predilection for poems in "form," by her alliance with *The Measure*, and by the linked facts of being female and a poet of immense natural gifts, Louise Bogan was virtually catapulted into an aesthetic confrontation with the imposing, slightly older poet.

That the confrontation took place, over time, there can be no doubt. It is less easy to say of what it was elemented. At first, however, from an epigram Bogan published in *The Liberator*, in 1923, it would appear to have been no less than direct imitation:

> *Pyrotechnics*
>
> Mix prudence with my ashes;
>   Write caution on my urn;
> While life foams and flashes
>   Burn, bridges, burn![14]

To anyone familiar with Edna Millay's "First Fig," the resemblance would have been unmistakable:

> My candle burns at both ends;
>   It will not last the night;
> But ah, my foes, and oh, my friends—
>   It gives a lovely light![15]

Similar echoes persisted in *Body of This Death* in poems peculiarly reminiscent in their themes and handling of certain poems of Millay's. From the outset, however, Bogan's actual workmanship differed tellingly from Millay's and just as "Pyrotechnics" possessed a crisper, more forceful linguistic texture than "First Fig," those poems in which Bogan shared or even derived subject matter from Edna Millay turned out to be those in which she developed a wholly separate mode of diction from that of her predecessor. It was as if a fastidious younger sister had stepped into the elder's well-worn clothes, only to find them costumes of net and lace, and slightly soiled satin, with trick seams and zippers for quick changes, broad gestures, and hints of knee and breast. Even though much of Louise Bogan's early poetry took as its lyric *donnée* the experience of the Girl as Millay had defined it, it simply would not do to have it revealed through display, in the language and cadence of implied gesture and mood-change as these had characterized Millay's work. Temperamentally and aesthetically hostile to display, yet equally unwilling to refine and condense emotion into the Victorian and Georgian inanities that Millay had so effectively avoided, Bogan worked in her early poems toward a diction of extreme seriousness, in which speech was not only expressive of the moment, but binding through time. Where Frank Ernest Hill had praised Millay for being "a poet who externalized her own soul,

saying not 'I shall feel thus,' but 'I shall do that,' "[16] Bogan seized not upon
the theatrical occasion of that vow but upon the linguistic form of vows in
themselves, and upon similarly powerful acts made in and by language alone,
as the foundation for a speech more binding, more essential, and thus more
whole than that found in Millay's verbal caprice. It would be speech that
contained itself without implying bodily movement, facial expression, into-
nation, projection, or props in a setting (such as a cigarette or red hair). The
difference is clearly illustrated in the statements and sighs comprising "First
Fig" as opposed to the imperatives of "Pyrotechnics." Vows, commands,
promises, warnings, and other performative or approximately performative[17]
expressions soon came to represent in Bogan's poetry the foundation of her
lyric diction, strengthening it with the distinctive capacity to resist the
ambiguity and doubtful sincerity so characteristic of Millay's verse. Moreover, when Louise Bogan occasionally did insert a dramatic antithesis or
reversal into the structure of a poem, it served only to enrich the texture of
speech already made firm by the logical clarity and serious purpose of explicit
and semi-explicit speech acts. By contrast, the logical membrane of Millay's
verse was extremely thin.

The consequence of the emerging difference in diction is that whereas
Millay's lyric language continued to conjure a make-believe, theatrical world,
with the poet spotlighted as mere-slip-of-a-Girl, Bogan's language was uttered by a Girl increasingly intent upon subordinating her personality and
experience to the discipline of language itself. Hence Bogan's Girl began to
speak more strongly, more bitterly, with greater pride and larger forgiveness
than Millay's, becoming in the process a poetic persona capable of celebrating
alike the piercing complexity of experience and the supple freshness of language. Where, for example, the end of the affair for Millay's Girl was reduced
to the formula of a toss of the head, a curl of the lip, and a Catullan allusion,
it became for the Girl in Bogan's poetry a rite de passage into the knowledge
of all endings, not to be contained by a quip or defined by received wisdom,
but savored, endured, and shaped through speech into dignity and finality.
What is gestural, momentary, and dependent on mood in "Only until this
cigarette is ended" is engraved on the mind and ennobled as ceremony in
Bogan's "Words for Departure":

Nothing was remembered, nothing forgotten.
When we awoke, wagons were passing on the warm summer pavements,
The window-sills were wet from rain in the night,
Birds scattered and settled over chimneypots
As among grotesque trees.

Nothing was accepted, nothing looked beyond.
Slight-voiced bells separated hour from hour,
The afternoon sifted coolness

And people drew together in streets becoming deserted.
There was a moon, a light in a shop-front,
And dusk falling like precipitous water.

Hand clasped hand,
Forehead bowed to forehead—
Nothing was lost, nothing possessed,
There was no gift nor denial.
2. I have remembered you.
You were not the town visited once,

Nor the road falling behind running feet.
You were as awkward as flesh.
And lighter than frost or ashes.

. . . .

3. You have learned the beginning;
Go from mine to the other.

Be together; eat, dance, despair,
Sleep, be threatened, endure.
You will know the way of that.

But at the end, be insolent;
Be absurd—strike the thing short off;

Be mad—only do not let talk
Wear the bloom from silence.

And go away without fire or lantern.
Let there be some uncertainty about your departure.[18]

Beginning with its title, the poem unfolds as an explicitly verbal act: not the hand waving goodbye, but the mind and voice together solemnizing departure. Neither disdainful nor crushed, the Girl who speaks throughout the poem evokes the scene of estrangement, summarizes the vanished richness of the affair, and goes on to issue a series of commands that, taken together, constitute an effort to establish distance, clarity, and integrity. Absent is the toying with nostalgia and cynicism so characteristic of Millay's Girl; so untheatrical, in fact, so complete is the capacity of Bogan's Girl to endure the separation that she hints that perhaps this certainty or finality itself discloses a flaw, an excessive stoicism. Thus she even counsels the lover to end his next affair with an arbitrary gesture: "Be absurd—strike the thing short off," so that the irreversibility of the formal farewell might be softened.

The middle section of "Words for Departure" is especially effective in suggesting the essential difference between Millay's superficial selection of experience as opposed to Bogan's surrender to the grain and savor of finality and limitation. Millay's Girl picks and chooses what she wishes to take from experience: "Yours is a face of which I can forget / The colour and the features, every one, / The words not ever, and the smiles not yet . . ." Rejecting the involuntary impingement of memory, Millay's Girl consciously selects keepsake impressions, willfully fragmenting the past. But Bogan's yields to the past with figures of rich completeness: "You were the rind, / And the white-juiced apple, / The song, and the words waiting for music."

Here are bitterness, consummation, joy, and frustration, each condensed in metaphor, each an act of memory, a recitation "by heart," as Bogan was later to call it in "Song for the Last Act," of the essence of the "erstwhile dear," as Millay's Girl would have called him. But Bogan's Girl refrains entirely from "emancipated" tones, although it is perfectly clear from the first section that the lovers have not only experienced a sexual relation, but even a degree of dissipation. A certain irony nevertheless exists that for the freedom of the poem's subject Bogan was most certainly indebted to the posturings of Millay.

As both Edna Millay and Louise Bogan no doubt keenly understood, the Girl of lyric tradition represented a figure of enchantment, poised briefly by the course of nature between maidenly hope and womanly disillusionment. In their early verse, both poets attempted that lyric set piece, the betrothal song, so familiar in both classical and European lyric tradition, with its mingling of the erotic and the elegiac. Not surprisingly, Millay pointed hers toward sexual innuendo and cynicism:

The Betrothal

Oh, come, my lad, or go, my lad,
And love me if you like.
I shall not hear the door shut
Nor the knocker strike.

Oh, bring me gifts or beg me gifts,
And wed me if you will.
I'd make a man a good wife,
Sensible and still.

And why should I be cold, my lad,
And why should you repine,
Because I love a dark head
That never will be mine?

I might as well be easing you
As lie alone in bed
And waste the night in wanting
A cruel dark head.

You might as well be calling yours
What never will be his,
And one of us be happy.
There's few enough as is.[19]

Thinly veiling a sexual proposition in the folk accents of this bitter ballad, the poem's quaint "easing you" reduces the Girl's unhappiness to a gesture again, a seductive shrug in which she grimly offers herself to a lad she doesn't love, just as she might hope to be thus pitied by the rejecting dark-haired lover. The sophisticated, risqué pastoral barely conceals the complacent mixture of helplessness and self-pitying "toughness" that supplied the formula for so many of Edna St. Vincent Millay's lyrics of erotic disillusionment. The ballad form itself, with its capacity to achieve dramatic simplicity and pure, condensed feeling, was similarly treated as a formula in Millay's art, as the vessel into which the slightly polluted waters of Millay's lyric reservoir could be poured and made to taste like the fresh stream of English undefiled. Millay's treatment of ballad stanza and lyric diction was too often arbitrary and vehicular, rather than felt and organic. It disguised an essential vulgarity that strove for "effect" and used tradition cosmetically, as mere varnish, though it did achieve a fine simplicity. Keeping this latter virtue in mind as the chief beauty of traditional maiden-song, Louise Bogan in "Betrothed" turns an elegy for the romantic wishes of girlhood into an acknowledgment and acceptance of change and uncertainty:

You have put your two hands upon me, and your mouth,
You have said my name as a prayer.
Here where trees are planted by the water
I have watched your eyes, cleansed from regret,
And your lips, closed over all that love cannot say.
 My mother remembers the agony of her womb
 And long years that seemed to promise more than this.
 She says, "you do not love me,
 You do not want me,
 You will go away."
In the country where I go
I shall not see the face of my friend
Nor her hair the color of sunburnt grasses;
Together we shall not find
The land on whose hills bends the new moon
In air traversed of birds.
What have I thought of love?
I have said, "It is beauty and sorrow."
I have thought that it would bring me lost delights, and splendor
As a wind out of old time . . .
But there is only the evening here,

And the sound of willows
Now and again dipping their long oval leaves in the water.[20]

Even though its syllables are, strictly speaking, arrayed in a solemn vers-
libre, in its feeling "Betrothed" is more responsive to its ancestry in maiden-
song than Millay's more explicitly musical phrasing in "The Betrothal." In
Bogan's poem, speech in the form of slow declaration empowers the Girl to
probe the rhythms of time and change that have prompted her misgivings.
She must forsake her mother, she must give up her girlhood friend, she must
question the meaning of love, even as she savors the lover's kiss and the rich,
peaceful landscape, not far from the Claude Lorrain-inspired[21] vines and
wharves of the later masterpiece, "Song for the Last Act." Bogan has sought
and found in the tradition of betrothal lyric a fusion of form and language
where simplicity represents an immense compression of feeling and an effort
to overcome fear and conflict. For Louise Bogan, the balance, measure, and
above all the compressed simplicity of virtually all shorter lyric forms were
synonymous not just with high artifice, but with clarity and integrity of
attitude: the lyric was the occasion for essential speech. Her Girl, like
Millay's, finds life a bitter disappointment. But where Millay's Girl lashes
out in petulant rage, as in "Spring," or takes her revenge in sexual cynicism
varnished as Catullan irony, as in "Passer Mortuus Est," Bogan's Girl accedes
to the moment of pain as a source of mystery and of renewal, if not of
complete affirmation:

Knowledge

Now that I know
How passion warms little
Of flesh in the mould,
And treasure is brittle,—
I'll lie here and learn
How, over their ground,
Trees make a long shadow
And a light sound.[22]

Turning grief away from the self, the poem affirms time, nature, and
peace. In another poem perhaps more clearly competitive with Edna Millay,
Bogan's Girl rejects theatrical gesture in a deliberate counterstrategy against
defeat:

My Voice Not Being Proud

My voice, not being proud
Like a strong woman's, that cries
Imperiously aloud
That death disarm her, lull her—

Screams for no mourning color
Laid menacingly, like fire,
Over my long desire.
It will end, and leave no print.
As you lie, I shall lie:
Separate, eased, and cured.
Whatever is wasted or wanted
In this country of glass and flint
some garden will use, once planted.
As you lie alone, I shall lie,
O, in singleness assured,
Deafened by mire and lime.
I remember, while there is time.[23]

In its first seven lines the poem offers an affront of the sensibility discoverable, for example, in Millay's "The Shroud," with its melodramatic plea for death as the release from the pain of betrayal. It continues, however, not as an example of merely another style of heartbreak, but as a determined resolution to resist the "strong woman's" histrionic and self-deceiving flirtation with death. The disciplined voice in Bogan's poem vows that desire will end, with the vows themselves acting to restore the self-possession threatened with disintegration by the easier hysteria of the Millay-like scream. Then, cautious lest the series of vows become just another pose, the speaker catches herself powerfully short with the qualifying afterthought, "I remember, while there is time." Though the will can do much, it cannot do all. The voice that issues vows rather than cries tries thereby to save the endangered soul, the whole, suffering, moral self that trusts to speech and speech alone to wrench herself away from the urge toward self-destruction.

Both Bogan and Millay encouraged their Girls to play upon the strength concealed in weakness, the weakness concealed in strength. Millay's tarnished virgin could become a "tough cookie," Bogan's proud lady could become ineffably sad. Millay took the lead in using "pure" lyric diction to dissemble complex sexual ironies, but it was left to Bogan to heighten this approach by turning the innocent measures of the carol in the following poem to a darkling cry of loss:

Chanson Un Peu Naive

What body can be ploughed,
Sown, and broken yearly?
She would not die, she vowed,
But she has, nearly.
    Sing, heart sing;
    Call and carol clearly.
And, since she could not die,
Care would be a feather,

> A film over the eye
> Of two that lie together
>   Fly, song, fly,
>   Break your little tether.
> So from strength concealed
> She makes her pretty boast:
> Pain is a furrow healed
> And she may love you most.
>   Cry, song, cry,
>   And hear your crying lost.[24]

Even "strength concealed" conceals from itself most dangerous sight of its own limitations. The Millay-Girl's mixture of weakness and strength, ingenuousness and shrewdness is lightly mocked, though the mockery is not lightly meant, in the trope of mutual deception, "Of two that lie together," which Bogan uses here almost exactly as she had in "My Voice Not Being Proud." By representing the Girl simultaneously summoning and denying psychic pain, Bogan implicitly alludes to a pattern occurring frequently in Millay's verse, as in "The Merry Maid," from *A Few Figs from Thistles:*

> Oh, I am grown so free from care
>   Since my heart broke!
> I set my throat against the air,
>   I laugh at simple folk!
> There's little kind and little fair
>   Is worth its weight in smoke
> To me, that's grown so free from care
>   Since my heart broke!
> Lass, if to sleep you would repair
>   As peaceful as you woke,
> Best not besiege your lover there
>   For just the words he spoke
> To me, that's grown so free from care
>   Since my heart broke.[25]

The Opheliesque lightness of the heart nearly crazed with grief and bitterness in this poem is even more concentrated in the pathetic sophistry of "Chanson Un Peu Naive," while the sexual self-destruction implicit in so many of Millay's lyrics is also present when the "she" of whom Bogan's poem speaks now takes another lover, flattering him and herself with the false strength and false ardor of a heart dangerously close to having burnt itself out. The paradox is driven deeper than Millay ever cared to go: license is a lie, and the candle burning at both ends goes out in madness before oblivion.

Thus, in Louise Bogan's first two books of poems, the task of deepening and extending the implications of the Girl's experience became identical with that of defining and strengthening Bogan's range and skill as a poet. By 1929, when her second book, *Dark Summer,* appeared, Louise Bogan had completed the task of establishing her own distinctive voice. In a poem appropriately titled "Girl's Song," Bogan seems almost to have taken the refrain of Millay's "Alms," "But it is winter with your love," and transformed it into an involuted conceit that shapes the poem as the quintessential Millay-derived lyric of Bogan's early career, yet marks as well the full transition of the Girl to Woman:

> Winter, that is a fireless room
> In a locked house, was our love's home.
> The days turn, and you are not here,
> O changing with the little year!
>
> Now when the scent of plants half-grown
> Is more the season's than their own
> And neither sun nor wind can stanch
> The gold forsythia's dripping branch,—
>
> Another maiden, still not I,
> Looks from some hill upon some sky,
> And since she loves you, and she must,
> Puts her young cheek against the dust.[26]

Unlike the Girl of "The Merry Maid," who protects herself from truth with a madcap lightness, and warns the next girl of her lover's perfidy, the Girl speaking now in "Girl's Song" has completed the cycle of innocence and betrayal, and sees in the sensuous lushness of spring and in the turning of the seasons the same inexorable law by which hope is destroyed. Not as a victim, but as a witness in full possession of the bitter fruits of time does the Girl here see both herself and her rival with the clear, unavenging detachment which marks the growth beyond girlhood to maturity.

Although Millay never quite outgrew the Girl, there is evidence that she tried to put her aside. In 1928, Millay wrote curiously, in "To a Young Girl," of the emotional artifice of that creature:

Shall I despise you that your colourless tears
Made rainbows in your lashes, and you forgot to weep?
Would we were half so wise, that eke a grief out
By sitting in the dark, until we fall asleep.

I only fear lest, being by nature sunny,
By and by you will weep no more at all,

And fall asleep in the light, having lost with the tears
The colour in the lashes that comes as the tears fall.

I would not have you darken your lids with weeping,
Beautiful eyes, but I would have you weep enough
To wet the fingers of the hand held over the eye-lids,
And stain a little the light frock's delicate stuff.

For there came into my mind, as I watched you winking the tears down,
Laughing faces, blown from the west and the east,
Faces lovely and proud that I have prized and cherished;
Nor were the loveliest among them those that had wept the least.[27]

It is one of Millay's stronger poems, without theater, without implicit gesture, with gentle irony toward the performing ingenue of her earlier work. Yet the poem did not mark a permanent step for Millay in the direction of reflective detachment; the persona of the Girl was outgrown more for the sake of propriety than conviction. The woman who chronicled the raptures of *Fatal Interview* in 1931 never stopped believing in the rejuvenating power of romance and passion, of simple sex and simple love for poetry's simple sake. In *Wine from these Grapes* (1934), *Huntsman, What Quarry?* (1939), and *Make Bright the Arrows* (1940), Millay turned increasingly to set pieces, political lyrics, and love poems still composed in the Girl's pastiche diction, though too many of them failed to achieve the freshness and breadth of emotion that the Girl had provided as a symbol in her earlier efforts.

In Bogan's verse, the Girl became the Woman only to be reborn, quite suddenly, as the Child. Not satisfied with regarding the flawed world of love as an unquestionable fatality, Louise Bogan sought to discover the sources of loss and betrayal, and found them not in the pangs of adolescence, but in the obsessions of childhood, in the refusal to relinquish early wants and hungers, and in the tyranny of unacknowledged childhood memories. The Child soon became for Bogan the source of rage, both justifiable and unjustifiable, an emotion virtually absent from earlier poems which had represented the Girl as speaker. The Child lived within the adult Woman, locked away and silent, until forced by circumstances, betrayal, or time itself to disrupt, intrude, and clamor for recognition. In one of her most powerful poems, "The Sleeping Fury," published in 1937 in the book of the same title, Louise Bogan regards her tormented alter ego as just this Child, "Who, after rage, for an hour quite, sleeps out its tears," and addresses her in the seventh stanza:

You uncovered at night in the locked stillness of houses,
False love due the child's heart, the kissed-out lie, the embraces,
Made by the two who for peace tenderly turned to each other.

And in the last stanza:

> Beautiful now as a child whose hair, wet with rage and tears
> Clings to its face. And now I may look upon you,
> Having once met your eyes. You lie in sleep and forget me.
> Alone and strong in my peace, I look upon you and yours.[28]

The Child, with its desire for justice, its supreme vulnerability, its unanswerable demands, had to be reclaimed and integrated within the self of the Girl if she were to achieve the wholeness, strength, and renewal of maturity. Yet the Child could not be allowed to tyrannize the process of growth. Thus, in "Kept," Bogan puts to rest the clamoring, unsatisfied Child, substituting once again command for cry:

> Time for the wood, the clay,
> The trumpery dolls, the toys
> Now to be put away:
> We are not girls and boys.
> What are these rags we twist
> Our hearts upon, or clutch
> Hard in the sweating fist?
> They are not worth so much.
> But we must keep such things
> Till we at length begin
> To feel our nerves their strings,
> Their dust, our blood within.
> The dreadful painted bisque
> Becomes our very cheek.
> A doll's heart, faint at risk,
> Within our breast grows weak.
> Our hand the doll's, our tongue.
> Time for the pretty clay,
> Time for the straw, the wood.
> The playthings of the young
> Get broken in the play,
> Get broken, as they should.[29]

Having been fully experienced, both Child and Girl are effectively silenced, not to emerge again for nearly thirty years when, in "Little Lobelia's Song," written late in Louise Bogan's life during a period of extreme emotional pain, the Child cries out to become once again part of the whole person:

> Each day, at dawn,
> I come out of your sleep;

I can't get back.
I weep, I weep.[30]

To go this deeply, this painfully into the psyche Millay was unwilling and unprepared. Yet without the precedent, and the challenge of Millay, Bogan might not have gained access to her full resources as a poet as swiftly, as assuredly, and as powerfully as she did. As Bogan and Millay discovered, the Girl was a lie, a doll, yet one essential to poetic identity and growth. The Child was more enduring, though finally peace, reconciliation, honor, and even joy came only to the Woman, the adult who had fought her way clear to detachment, and, no longer "faint at risk," had put her dolls away.

Writing to Edmund Wilson, in May of 1923, after Wilson had left some of Bogan's poems with her, Millay asked: "Who is this person? I never even heard of her. I was quite thrilled by some of the poems. Isn't it wonderful how the lady poets are coming along? 'Votes for women' is what I sez!"[31]

In 1951, a year after Millay's death, Louise Bogan wrote in *Achievement in American Poetry* that Millay

formulated for a new generation of young women a standard of sexual defiance and "heroism" which, in spite of its romantic coloring, was marked by truth and pathos. A certain hampering nihilism, as well as a close attachment to literary fashion, apparent in Miss Millay from the outset, prevented her from breaking through to impressive maturity; but even her later work is filled with distinguished fragments. She often succeeded in transcending her worst faults. Many of her sonnets are in the great tradition; and that she was, by nature, a lyric poet of the first order, is an incontestable fact.[32]

The little petulant hand had become an annotation—mere footnote to the era that had taken her for text.

Notes

1. Elizabeth Atkins, *Edna St. Vincent Millay and Her Times* (Chicago: Univ. of Chicago Press, 1936), p. 113.
2. Norma Millay, ed., from *Renascence* (1917) in *Collected Poems* (New York: Harper, 1956), p. 32. All subsequent citations of poems by Edna St. Vincent Millay are from this edition.
3. *Ibid.*, p. 43.
4. Horace Gregory and Marya Zaturenska, *A History of American Poetry: 1900–1940* (New York: Gordian Press, 1969), pp. 265 ff.
5. *Ibid.*, p. 268.
6. Millay, from *Second April* (1921) in *Collected Poems*, p. 75.
7. *Ibid.*, p. 88.
8. *Ibid.*, p. 575.

9. Frank Ernest Hill, rev. of *A Few Figs from Thistles,* by Edna St. Vincent Millay, *The Measure,* No. 1 (Mar. 1921), p. 25.

10. Maxwell Anderson, rev. of *Second April,* by Edna St. Vincent Millay, *The Measure,* No. 7 (Sept. 1921), p. 17.

11. *The Measure,* No. 38 (Apr. 1924), pp. 11–12.

12. *The Measure,* No. 1 (Mar. 1921), p. 23.

13. *Ibid.,* p. 25.

14. Louise Bogan, "Pyrotechnics," *The Liberator,* Ser. 61, 6, No. 5 (May 1923).

15. Millay, from *A Few Figs from Thistles* in *Collected Poems,* p. 127.

16. Hill, p. 26.

17. I use the term *performative* as it occurs in J. L. Austin, *How To Do Things with Words* (New York: Oxford Univ. Press, 1965), to mean acts actually constituted in and by language.

18. Louise Bogan, *Body of This Death* (New York: Robert M. McBride & Co., 1923), pp. 10–11.

19. Millay, from *The Harp-Weaver and Other Poems* (1923) in *Collected Poems,* pp. 173–74.

20. Bogan, *Body of This Death,* p. 9.

21. I am indebted for this insight to William Jay Smith, "The Making of Poems," in *The Streaks of the Tulip: Selected Criticism* (New York: Delacorte Press, 1972).

22. Bogan, *Body of This Death,* p. 13.

23. *Ibid.,* p. 16.

24. *Ibid.,* p. 28. Line 15 in this edition contains a misprint, "Plain," corrected to "Pain" in later editions.

25. Millay, from *A Few Figs from Thistles* in *Collected Poems,* p. 145.

26. Louise Bogan, *Dark Summer* (New York: Scribner's, 1929), p. 9.

27. Millay, from *The Buck in the Snow* (1928) in *Collected Poems,* p. 238.

28. Louise Bogan, *The Sleeping Fury* (New York: Scribner's, 1937), pp. 27–29.

29. *Ibid.,* pp. 38–39.

30. "Little Lobelia's Song," in "Three Songs," *The Blue Estuaries: Poems: 1923–1968* (New York: Farrar, Straus & Giroux, 1968), pp. 132–33.

31. Allan Ross Macdougall, ed., *Letters of Edna St. Vincent Millay* (New York: Harper, 1952), p. 173.

32. Louise Bogan, *Achievement in American Poetry* (Chicago: Henry Regnery Co., 1951), pp. 79–80.

"Being Born a Woman": A New Look at Edna St. Vincent Millay

Patricia A. Klemans

I, being born a woman and distressed
By all the needs and notions of my kind,
Am urged by your propinquity to find
Your person fair, and feel a certain zest
To bear your body's weight upon my breast:
So subtly is the fume of life designed,
To clarify the pulse and cloud the mind,
And leave me once again undone, possessed.
Think not for this, however, the poor treason
Of my stout blood against my staggering brain,
I shall remember you with love, or season
My scorn with pity,—let me make it plain:
I find this frenzy insufficient reason
For conversation when we meet again.[1]

This sonnet, written by Edna St. Vincent Millay, was first published in *The Harp-Weaver and Other Poems* in 1923. It is an excellent place to begin in looking at Millay as not only an important poet but also as a poet with contemporary appeal.

The subject matter obviously proclaims a feminist philosophy. While a passionate woman might be ruled at times by her natural sexual impulses, she has not necessarily lost her reason or powers of discrimination. Men have been proclaiming this philosophy—and practicing it—for centuries, but it was news when a woman said it. The terse conclusion, "I find this frenzy insufficient reason / For conversation when we meet again," characterizes a woman who refuses to conform to society's dictates. Millay, like the persona of her sonnet, was an independent spirit. Whether she was resisting a new style in poetry or philosophy, or insisting on her own life-style, she remained an individualist until she died.

From *Colby Library Quarterly* 15, no. 1 (March 1979): 7–18. Reprinted by permission. L. Robert Lind's poem "Ad Feminam Tristem, Sed Poetam" first published in the *Sewanee Review*, vol. 43, no. 1, Winter 1935. Reprinted with the permission of the editor.

Edna St. Vincent Millay shocked many people with the sexual honesty in her poetry and in her personal life. By 1923, when this poem appeared, she was one of the best known literary personalities in America. She had made a name for herself at the age of twenty when her first serious work, *Renascence*, was published in *The Lyric Year*, to great critical acclaim. The attention precipitated by the poem led to a scholarship to Vassar as well as many contacts with the literary leaders of the time. After graduating from college she headed for Greenwich Village where, becoming involved in acting as well as writing, she became an influential member of the contemporary art scene. With the publication of *A Few Figs from Thistles*, Millay became a sensation. The verse from that collection,

> My candle burns at both ends;
> It will not last the night;
> But ah, my foes and oh, my friends—
> It gives a lovely light!

seemed to epitomize the sexual defiance of the post-war generation. Millay's poetry suggested that she was a hedonist and her life-style seemed to confirm this view. Because of her many love affairs and avoidance of marriage, as well as her physical attractiveness and dramatic abilities, she was a subject of great interest and criticism. Her fans loved her and couldn't wait for her next volume of poems; her critics dismissed her as being frivolous, narrow, and tradition bound in her poetic forms.

In 1923, after returning from a year in Europe and publishing *The Harp-Weaver*, Millay became the first woman to win the Pulitzer prize and she married Eugen Boissevain, the widower of the suffrage leader, Inez Milholland. The poet of "I, being born a woman" was not only a woman of perception, as all poets must be, but also of experience. She had, by the age of thirty-one, led a life of personal and sexual freedom generally reserved only for men in our society. Her poetry presents this new viewpoint to literature—the liberated woman's view. In the nineteenth century we have the idealization of Elizabeth Barrett and Christina Rossetti and the obliqueness of Emily Dickinson to explore a woman's emotional life. In Millay we get a different view of "the needs and notions of my kind."

The work which best illustrates this unique contribution to literature is *Fatal Interview*, a sequence of fifty-two Shakespearean sonnets. The title is taken from John Donne's "Elegy 16": "By our first strange and fatal interview, / By all desires which thereof did ensue."[2] Published in 1931, Donne's tercentenary year, *Fatal Interview* not only relies a great deal on Donne's love poetry for its imagery and philosophy, but more importantly, presents a persona which is the first female counterpart to Donne's sophisticated lover. Millay's speaker is a realist; she is a woman of experience who presents her observations honestly, devoid of romanticizing or rationalizing. Unlike the 1923 sonnet, which describes a passionate but casual sexual encounter, *Fatal Interview* is concerned with the all-important love in a woman's life—a love that not everyone experiences personally, but one that everyone can relate to vicariously through reading this superb group of poems.

The critical response to "Fatal Interview" at its publication was generally favorable. Although Millay's popularity had ebbed somewhat since its high point in the early Twenties, a new book by her was still greeted with great interest. Harriet Monroe in *Poetry* began her review with these words: "This book is the record of emotional experience, done in terms of precise and measured beauty. It would be impossible to over-praise the consummate art with which Miss Millay has taken over the much-practiced form of the Shakespearean sonnet and made it her own as no other poet has, perhaps, since Shakespeare himself."[3] Allen Tate said in the *New Republic:*

> It is doubtful if all of Miss Millay's previous work put together is worth the thin volume of these fifty-two sonnets. At no previous time has she given us so sustained a performance. Half of the sonnets, perhaps all but about fifteen, lack distinction of emotional quality. None is deficient in an almost final technique. From first to last every sonnet has its special rhythm and sharply defined imagery; they move like a smooth machine, but not machine-like, under the hand of a masterly technician. The best sonnets would adorn any of the great English sequences. There is some interesting analysis to be made of Miss Millay's skillful use of the Shakespearean form, whose difficult final couplet she has mastered, and perhaps is alone in having mastered since Shakespeare.[4]

And finally, Genevieve Taggard ends her review in the *New York Herald Tribune Books* by saying: "We remember always a poet's best, his high water mark—his poorest vanishes like mortal speech. Her best is in the world of Shakespeare's sonnets, and, in her own field—she cannot be excelled. Immortality here is defined, served and achieved."[5]

Although all three of these critics agree without reservations that Millay is a master of the Shakespearean sonnet form, they do not all agree on the total worth of this collection. Miss Monroe's review is the most glowing in its praise of *Fatal Interview*. She calls it "one of the finest love-sequences in the language" but also makes the following comment:

> Because we have, in Miss Millay, a poet of very unusual scope and power—moreover, a woman poet of an epoch which no longer verifies Byron's line, "Man's love is of man's life a thing apart, / 'Tis woman's whole existence—" because of these facts which make a demand upon her, we have a right to feel in *Fatal Interview* her scope has narrowed from the broad ranges of her youth; and her power, however intense, however creative of perfection, accepts lower ground for its exercise.[6]

This criticism by a woman of a woman is very revealing. Monroe's choice of Byron's line suggests that she wants a woman poet of her "epoch" to deal with topics which are worldly, philosophical, "masculine." By Millay's choosing to write a book about love, a traditionally "feminine" preoccupation, the poet had, in Monroe's estimation, betrayed her early promise. One of the most frequent comments made about *Renascence* was that it was unbelieveable that it was written by a young woman. Its subject, a poet's vision of the world's grief and her reconcilement with the universe, as well as its great poetic proficiency, seemed beyond the range of a twenty year old girl from a small town in Maine. Monroe sees, therefore, *Fatal Interview* as a narrowing, an acceptance of "lower ground." Unfortunately, Monroe was unable to recognize how truly innovative the work was in presenting a feminine view of a subject for which the ground rules had been set by men. Instead she has reservations about how important a woman's love affair might be to the rest of the world.

Allen Tate makes it clear how important he feels it to be—not very. He damns Millay with faint praise, then compares her unfavorably with T. S. Eliot who he believes "penetrated to the fundamental structure of the nineteenth century mind and shows its breakdown." He continues, "Miss Millay assumed no such profound altercation of the intelligence because, I suppose, not being an intellect but a sensibility, she was not aware of it."[7] Tate's review is primarily an essay about his poetic tastes rather than an analysis of *Fatal Interview*. He spends more time discussing Eliot and Yeats than Millay, who is of course in his eyes a "sensibility" rather than an "intellect," whatever that means.

Genevieve Taggard's review, on the other hand, focuses on Millay and her poems but it too makes some ambiguous statements. After praising her for her skill as a sonnet writer, Taggard criticizes Millay for the very reasons that she has said she was effective. She says:

It seems to me that Miss Millay worships only one thing—perfection. Such a worship throws difficulties in the path of human love, but it suits the ardors of the sonnet-writer and the lover of beauty alike. She does not value uniqueness, she has no patience with rebel esthetics, new forms, naturalism which loves irregularity, which everywhere opposes logic and the almost machine-like perfection of detached art. Odd insights are awkward to her. Her preferences are for those elegiac and harmonious gestures of the greatest Greek sculptures. I should even dare to push the statement further and say that Miss Millay is interested in perfection, not people, in art, not in life—her courage and self scorn testify to her own self-rejection for the sake of her first principle. Is it not natural then that Miss Millay should choose the sonnet form which demands in the very act of writing, this attitude?[8]

Taggard undoubtedly got carried away with her own rhetoric. Given the known facts of Millay's life, her many and varied experiences, her close personal relationships with her family and friends, as well as the very personal and moving quality which characterizes *Fatal Interview*, it was certainly inaccurate and unfair to accuse her of being uninterested in life and in people. One wonders if Taggard would have charged Petrarch, Spenser, or Shakespeare with this attitude. Or is it the woman who Millay characterizes in her poems that bothers this critic? A woman of pride and principle; a woman of courage and arrogance; a woman some would find difficult to sympathize with. Millay's speaker rejects the games that lovers play and in doing so undoubtedly antagonizes some, including women.

In looking at the reviews of these contemporaries of Millay we can see reflected the tastes of the time. Millay was writing perfect love sonnets at a time when love seemed trite and the sonnet was "out." In 1923 Millay won the Pulitzer prize for *Second April* and Eliot won the Dial prize for *The Waste Land.* The great difference in these two books marks the great parting of the ways for Millay and Eliot. In 1920, both poets were expressing a philosophy of despair and were greatly attracted to the Elizabethans, especially Donne and Webster, for their ironic, worldly view. By 1923, however, Eliot had turned to nihilism as a philosophy, and symbolism and fragmentation as a technique. Millay took a different road. Her view of the world was not more optimistic than Eliot's. She too saw the disintegrating forces of her times but unlike him, she turned to nature and the past to form a defense against them. Instead of reflecting the disintegration in her poetry, her object was to "put Chaos into fourteen lines / And keep him there."

In *Fatal Interview* she puts the chaos of a love affair into fifty-two tightly constructed, interwoven sonnets; she also illustrates her personal poetic philosophy. She believed that her poetry, like herself, must be honest and intelligible. In Sonnet CLXV from *Mine the Harvest,* published in 1954, four years after her death, she expresses her views on contemporary poetry:

> It is the fashion now to wave aside
> As tedious, obvious, vacuous, trivial, trite,
> All things which do not tickle, tease, excite
> To some subversion, or in verbiage hide
> Intent, or mock, or with hot sauce provide
> A dish to prick the thickened appetite;
> Straightforwardness is wrong, evasion right;
> It is correct, *de rigueur,* to deride.
> What fumy wits these modern wags expose,
> For all their versatility: Voltaire,
> Who wore to bed a night-cap, and would close,
> In fear of drafts, all windows, could declare
> In antique stuffiness, a phrase that blows
> Still through men's smoky minds, and clears the air.

During her lifetime, poetic taste swung toward Eliot and experimentation and away from Millay and tradition. These three reviewers reflect this swing in their granting her skill yet being blind to the truly innovative aspects of the poems contained in *Fatal Interview*.

The sequence tells a moving story. The speaker, who first appears in Sonnet II, finds herself in the grips of a passion which she foresees from the very beginning as being ultimately disastrous. Although unable to free herself from her obsession, she refuses to conform to the expected behavior patterns associated with the woman's role in a love affair. She refuses to use guile to capture her lover and says in Sonnet III:

> Liefer would I you loved me for my worth,
> Though you should love me but a little while,
> Than for a philtre any doll can brew,—
> Though thus I bound you as I long to do.

And, in Sonnet VI, the speaker becomes very assertive when she chides her lover for finding it safer to love the women of literature, Cressid, Elaine, and Isolt, than to respond to her in whom passion pounds all day long. Here, and throughout the sequence, the woman is an initiator, honest and fearless. No coy mistress she; it is the man who seems to require the urging. In Sonnet XI she insists that the lover's relationship will be honest and direct, "Love in the open hand, no thing but that, / Ungemmed, unhidden, wishing not to hurt."

The affair runs a passionate and tumultuous course with the speaker's emotions alternating between ecstasy and despair. Even at the risk of losing her lover she will not compromise her principles. She says in Sonnet XXIII:

> I know the face of Falsehood and her tongue
> Honeyed with unction, plausible with guile,
> Are dear to men, whom count me not among,
> That owe their daily credit to her smile;

This woman Millay characterizes is a new personality in love poetry. She is no innocent virgin, religious zealot, shrinking violet, or scheming man-hunter. She is direct and forthright with a personal morality she will not compromise. When the inevitable break between the lovers comes, in Sonnet XXXIX, she again offers her lover her hand, but this time it is to say farewell. She internalizes her pain and accepts the inevitable.

The final poems trace the process the speaker must go through to regain the self-esteem she has temporarily lost in her abandonment to love. In Sonnet XL she says:

> You loved me not at all, but let it go;
> I loved you more than life, but let it be.

> As the more injured party, this being so,
> The hour's amenities are all to me—

The suffering is long and intense but she is a survivor. In Sonnet L she reflects that it has been a half year since her heart "broke in two; / The world's forgotten well, if the world knew."

This account of a love affair from a passionate woman's point of view creates a rich and illuminating experience for the reader. Each poem of the sequence leads logically into the next while being itself a lyric expressing a particular theme. Read independently, each poem is a complete experience; read in context, it is part of a complex design. *Fatal Interview* offers something new expressed in the framework and terms of the old. It presents love from a woman's point of view, yet it treats love as an ageless and natural experience. The poems are extremely personal, yet not private. Millay accomplishes this universality by interweaving the woman's experience with classical myth, traditional love literature, and nature.

The framework of the sequence is the legend of Selene and Endymion. The first and final sonnets have as their speaker the moon goddess who fell hopelessly in love with a shepherd. Unable to have him for her own, Selene enchanted him with eternal sleep and suffered the pain and anguish of mortal love forever. There are direct references as well as echoes of the tale throughout the work. Other characters from mythology are also present. In the poem celebrating the consummation of passion, Sonnet XII, the lover is likened to Jove when the speaker says:

> Olympian gods, mark now my bedside lamp
> Blown out; and be advised too late that he
> Whom you call sire is stolen into the camp
> Of warring Earth, and lies abed with me.

This passage is also reminiscent of the story of Cupid and Psyche in which Psyche is not allowed to see her lover and must extinguish her lamp when Cupid comes to her bed. Cupid and his mother, Venus, are directly referred to in Sonnet XV when the speaker says, "My worship from this hour the Sparrow-Drawn / Alone will cherish, and her arrowy child." This sonnet uses myth to emphasize the desperate plight of one who has abandoned herself to love. She says of Venus and Cupid:

> How have I stripped me of immortal aid
> Save theirs alone,—who could endure to see
> Forsworn Aeneas with conspiring blade
> Sever the ship from shore (alas for me)
> And make no sign; who saw, and did not speak,
> The brooch of Troilus pinned upon the Greek.

The effectiveness of this passage depends on the reader's knowledge of the stories of Aeneas and Dido and Troilus and Cressida. Millay assumes that her reader will know two of the greatest love stories of our culture and so she uses this comparison to emphasize the agelessness of her plight as well as the indifference of the universe.

Structuring her sequence on myth gives it a pagan base. The afterlife in Millay's sonnets only appears in a dream of the Elysian fields where the speaker meets the women who have been raped by Jove. The Gods which the speaker invokes are those of Greek mythology. Millay's world is pre-Christian and the Gods she acknowledges are indifferent to the plight of mankind. Her speaker does not have a personal deity who cares for her or promises her eternal life. She has no such consolation and so is as isolated from religious comfort as early pagans or twentieth century atheists.

There is a link in the poems with Christianity, of course, because that too is part of tradition. Millay alludes directly or indirectly to the literature of all ages but there is a particularly heavy emphasis on Donne and other metaphysical poets for the philosophy and imagery of the poems. It is not necessary that the reader of *Fatal Interview* be familiar with seventeenth century love poetry, but it adds a fascinating dimension to the sequence if one has such knowledge. The metaphysical poets are characterized by their wit—an ingenuity in literary invention, an ability to discover clever, surprising, or paradoxical figures. Millay is witty in that she uses the images of these early poets to create her own unique view of the subject. In Sonnet III she employs the compass image that Donne had made famous as a symbol of the perfect relationship between lovers. In "A Valediction Forbidding Mourning" he had likened himself and his love to a compass: "Thy soule the fixt foot, makes no show / To move, but doth, if the other doe." The woman is the fixed foot which only moves to follow the bent of the man.

Millay's compass is of a different variety and the woman is doing the moving. The speaker says:

> My needle to your north abruptly swerved;
> If I would hold you, I must hide my fears
> Lest you be wanton, lead you to believe
> My compass to another quarter veers,
> Little surrender, lavishly receive.

Here, instead of using the compass as the symbol of true love, Millay dramatizes man's propensity for wanting what is hard to get. The entire concept of the woman's character is changed from one of fidelity and dependency to one of experience and independence. Donne's compass encloses space; Millay's determines directions.

In Sonnet XI, Millay seems to be conversing with Donne. In "The Token" he had asked his lover to "Send me some token, that my hope may live" and concludes, "Send me not this, nor that, t'increase my store, / But swear thou thinkst I love thee, and no more." Millay's sonnet seems to be a reply to Donne's poem. She denies this request, deprecating his wish for a pledge of any sort. She offers, "Love in the open hand, no thing but that."

To the literary minded, Millay's sonnets abound with allusions to the immortals. Echoes of Chaucer, Virgil, Ovid, and the seventeenth century dramatists abound. Reading Millay's sonnets can, therefore, become a kind of game for literary buffs—just the kind of game that intrigued the seventeenth century mind but one which few modern readers have the background to participate in.

It is not necessary, however, for the reader of *Fatal Interview* to be familiar with myth or literary history to enjoy and to feel empathy with Millay's moving love sonnets. The poems are firmly connected and supported by a body of references common to all, that of nature. The fifty-two sonnets parallel the fifty-two weeks of the year during which time there is for all things, a season. It is autumn when the speaker first sees her lover; the consummation of the affair occurs in winter. The love blooms in spring, smolders through the summer, and is touched by frost in early fall. As the love affair ends the speaker longs for winter. She says:

> Freeze up the year; with sleet these branches
>   bend
> Though rasps the locust in the fields around.
> Now darken, sky! Now shrieking blizzard,
>   blow!—
> Farewell, sweet bank; be blotted out with snow.

The speaker, throughout the sequence, refers to herself as being close to nature. She knows from the very beginning of the affair that nothing can remain the same. In Sonnet XLVI she says:

> Even at the moment of our earliest kiss,
> When sighed the straitened bud into flower,
> Sat the dry seed of most unwelcome this;
> And that I knew, though not the day and hour.
> Too season-wise am I, being country-bred,
> To tilt at autumn or defy the frost:
> Snuffing the chill even as my fathers did,
> I say with them, "What's out tonight is lost."

This acceptance of the order of things, this resignation, is her way of maintaining her sanity. In her desolation she remembers the "island women" of Matinicus who stood alone in autumn "In gardens stripped and scattered peering north, / With dahlia tubers dripping from the hand" (Sonnet XXXVI). She finds some consolation in the thought that she has shared these common experiences. Like the women, she must accept change. Having experienced great joy, she must now endure the suffering—that is the balance of her world.

Gardens appear in many of the poems. When the affair is over, the speaker's garden is ruined, and the once still marigolds and sturdy zinnias are but "pale and oozy stalks." These details are Millay's observations of her immediate world. She grew up on the coast of Maine and lived on a farm in upper New York state after her marriage. These are rugged areas with early frosts and short summers. The gardens in Millay's world are strong and colorful but short-lived, like the brief but tumultuous love affair she describes.

The sea is even more important and pervasive in this sequence than the garden. The water imagery creates much of the sensuality of the poetry, as in Sonnet VII when she combines two of her favorite metaphors, the sea and night:

> Night is my sister, and how deep in love,
> How drowned in love and weedily washed ashore,
> There to be fretted by the drag and shove
> At the tide's edge, I lie—these things and more:
> Whose arm alone between me and the sand,
> Whose voice alone, whose pitiful breath brought near,
> Could thaw these nostrils and unlock this hand,
> She could advise you, should you care to hear.
> Small chance, however, in a storm so black,
> A man will leave his friendly fire and snug
> For a drowned woman's sake, and bring her back
> To drip and scatter shells upon the rug.
> No one but Night, with tears on her dark face,
> Watches beside me in this windy place.

In this poem, while using nature imagery to describe an emotional state, Millay creates in her female persona a bond with another female, Night. She carries this idea through the sonnets with her many references to women. The only ones who can understand the speaker's love are Selene, Leda, Danae, and Europa; the women of the Irish and Trojan coasts; the women of Matinicus; and perhaps the women reading this poetry. This affinity with women is unusual in any literature but very rare in love poetry where women are usually portrayed as rivals.

The lover in *Fatal Interview* does not leave the speaker for another woman; he leaves because he cannot love with an intensity and constancy equal to hers. The speaker says in this poem, "Small chance, however, in a storm so black, / A man will leave his friendly fire and snug / For a drowned woman's sake." She suggests that men are not capable of the depth of emotion which women are but are more concerned with comfort and security. This difference between the male and female lover is epitomized in the Selene-Endymion legend. Unlike the Keats poem which pities Endymion, Millay's sympathies are with Selene. The Goddess is devastated and wanders over the sky, distraught over losing her love; the Mortal sleeps, oblivious to all the pain and anguish he has caused.

Still, Millay is not suggesting that only women can love completely and passionately. She refers to Troilus who broke his heart when Cressida gave his love token away. In this legend it is the man who loved too well. In addition, the close parallels to Donne's love poems in many of these sonnets suggest that Millay considered Donne a soulmate, despite their different points of view. They are certainly in agreement on the effect of a tragic love affair. Donne wrote in "The broken heart":

> And now as broken glasses show
> A hundred lesser faces, so
> My ragges of heart can like, wish, and adore,
> But after one such love, can love no more.

Millay says much the same in Sonnet L: "The heart once broken is a heart no more, / And is absolved from all a heart must be."

Obviously, love is an emotional experience common to both men and women. Most of the great love poetry, however, has been written by men and not until Millay do we have the experience of seeing a personal examination of an affair from a woman's point of view. This view was not easily accepted by some. The following poem by L. Robert Lind, published in 1935 in the *Sewanee Review*, is an interesting reaction:

AD FEMINAM TRISTEM, SED POETAM
(After Reading Edna St. Vincent Millay's "Fatal Interview")

> O come away at last from this lorn love
> That will not hear, however sad you speak;
> O brood no more for him, you hurt wild dove,
> Seeking the lost that comes not though you seek.
> Were man so to be longed for and in truth
> The inmost object of your grave desire,
> And more than merely puppet in the booth
> Of sonnet-music, moved by a singing wire,
> You could not so your sorrow still rehearse
> And ring the changes in one mournful measure,
> Exhaust the resolutions of your verse,
> Or find in repetition such wry pleasure:
> You could but, woman-like, grieve without a word;
> Yet, being poet, your mourning must be heard.[9]

Granting that Mr. Lind's main purpose in writing this poem was to exhibit his wit rather than to offer any serious critical insights, it does reveal an attitude that is not uncommon in men's reactions to women's work. He makes the writing of poetry by a woman, at least love poetry, a sort of "Catch-22" situation. If she were really sincere, he says, she would grieve "woman-like" and not write at all. Since she persists in writing, then she cannot be sincere. This attitude supports Millay's speaker who believes that a man is incapable of understanding the passion of a woman.

No one disputes that *Fatal Interview* contains perfectly written sonnets. Many, however, have failed to perceive that the poems are unique and innovative in their presentation of a feminine viewpoint on love. Millay reversed the masculine-feminine traditional stances while working within the traditional forms. Today we have many women poets who are speaking frankly about a woman's nature. In 1931, we had Edna St. Vincent Millay. The unfortunate fact is that many have overlooked the message while appreciating the medium. A Millay poem looks traditional—in form it is. But her characterization of a woman who is initiator, aggressor, and controller as well as victim, sufferer, and survivor is unique. The woman of the poems contains within herself the knowledge and experience of the ages. In this sense she is Mother Earth. But she is also a human being with an intellect. Through experience and introspection, she comes to terms with life, finding her truths in nature and its order.

The time has certainly come for a second look at Millay's work, which is both impressive and varied. *Fatal Interview* is only one of the many beautiful and meaningful collections of poetry which speaks particularly to a woman's experience. Millay belonged to the generation which saw women finally get the right to vote, a time of feminine idealism which lionized Amelia Earhart for crossing the Atlantic Ocean by plane. Millay spoke for a generation of young women who responded to her standards of sexual independence and feminine heroism. Pushed to the back shelves for so many years, Millay's books deserve a new reading. Millay can speak to the women and men of today as well as to those of the Twenties and Thirties, because her poetry is written with consummate skill and her message of feminine individuality is ageless.

Notes

1. Edna St. Vincent Millay, *Collected Poems* (New York: Harper & Row, 1956), p. 601. All subsequent quotations from Millay's poetry are taken from this edition. The poems are copyright 1923, 1931, 1951, 1954, 1958 by Edna St. Vincent Millay and Norma Millay (Ellis), and are reprinted by permission of Norma Millay (Ellis).

2. *Donne: Poetical Works*, ed. Herbert J. C. Grierson (New York: Oxford Univ. Press, 1971), p. 99. All subsequent quotations from Donne's poetry are taken from this edition.

3. "Advance or Retreat?," *Poetry,* XXXVIII (July 1931), p. 216.

4. "Miss Millay's Sonnets," *New Republic*, XLVI (May 6, 1931), p. 336.

5. "A Woman's Anatomy of Love," *New York Herald Tribune, Review of Books*, April 19, 1931.

6. "Advance or Retreat?," p. 219.

7. "Miss Millay's Sonnets," p. 335.

8. "A Woman's Anatomy of Love."

9. Vol. XLIII (Jan.–Mar. 1935), p. 104. Reprinted by permission of the editor.

Edna St. Vincent Millay
and the Language of Vulnerability

JANE STANBROUGH

In 1917, when Edna St. Vincent Millay moved to Greenwich Village, her image as a woman of spirit and independence was already legendary. Previously, at Vassar, Millay had become a notorious public figure. She was a publishing poet, an impressive actress, and a dramatist of growing reputation. She had all along flaunted her independence impudently, smoking against the rules, cutting classes that were boring, earning a severe faculty reprimand which nearly deprived her of participation in her graduation ceremonies. This image of defiance was enhanced by her move to Greenwich Village, known as a hotbed of free-thinking radicals, and by her publication of five poems under the heading "Figs from Thistles" in *Poetry* in 1918, poems which vivified her inclination toward bohemianism and promiscuity. The famous first fig—"My candle burns at both ends;/It will not last the night;/But ah, my foes, and oh, my friends—/ It gives a lovely light!"— immortalized her public image of daring and unconventional behavior. It came as no real shock, then, when in 1920 she published an entire volume of poetry (including the first five figs) entitled *A Few Figs from Thistles*, dominated by a narrative voice that irreverently mocked public opinion and public morality, that scorned imposed values and prescribed behavior. This image of liberation and self-assurance is the public image Millay deliberately cultivated, the self-projection that stole the show, demanded applause and attention, suited a loud and raucous jazz-age temper. For half a century it has captivated readers and critics and minimized or veiled entirely a private anxiety-ridden image of profound self-doubt and personal anguish with which Millay contended all her life. The braggadocio of the public image is, in fact, contradictory to experience as Millay inwardly felt it and is belied by both the language and the form through which she reflected her deepest sense of that experience. Although the poetry in *Figs* solidified that public image of defiance and independence, it did so in language and structural patterns that divulge a private image of submission and constriction. The dominant tone of

From *Shakespeare's Sisters: Feminist Essays on Women Poets*. Edited by Sandra M. Gilbert and Susan Gubar. (Bloomington: Indiana University Press, 1979): 183–99; 327–28. Reprinted by permission of Indiana University Press and Jane Stanbrough.

the body of her work—the tone of heart-rending anguish—is apparent when she works at flippancy. Millay is unquestionably a woman who suffers, and the greatest source of her suffering seems to lie in an overwhelming sense of personal vulnerability—and ultimately of woman's vulnerability—to victimization by uncontrollable conditions in her environment.

This sense of vulnerability provides one of the richest linguistic patterns in her poetry, for in spite of her efforts to repress and protect a part of her emotional life, Millay is exposed and betrayed through a language pattern which calls attention to the emotional conflicts and tensions, the psychic realities of her existence. This pattern of self-revelation appears consistently throughout her work, though sometimes disguised by attitudes associated with the public image. "Grown-up," for example (from *Figs*), seems to be merely a cute, little versified cliché about the disillusioning process of growing up.

> Was it for this I uttered prayers,
> And sobbed and cursed and kicked the stairs,
> That now, domestic as a plate,
> I should retire at half-past eight?[1]

Notice the violence in the verbs; aptly, they do evoke an image of an unruly child, but they also suggest the strength of the frustration of the narrator for something absent from her life. The contrasting image, domestic as a plate, is perfectly appropriate to imply the flatness and brittleness and coldness that condition her existence. Growing into adult domesticity for this woman has been a process of subduing the will and shrinking the soul. The last line carries the shrinking image to its ultimate conclusion: oblivion, implied by the verb "retire." The woman is painfully aware of the disparity between her childhood hopes and the realities of her adult experience, a theme Millay treats at length in "Sonnets from an Ungrafted Tree." Here, the emptiness of the woman's life is made explicit by the fact that she retires at half-past eight, when for many the evening's activities have barely begun. This poem is a strong statement of protest against the processes that mitigate fulfilling and satisfying experience. Certainly, the poem might be read simply as a statement of the inadequacy of experience to measure up to the imaginative conception of it. But it is more. It is a specific statement about woman's experience. "Domestic as a plate" is an image that fits woman into her conventional place at rest on a shelf and out of the way. The poem reflects Millay's fears of her own fate and aids our understanding of the poet's excessive urge to proclaim herself a free and unconfined spirit.

Other poems in the *Figs* volume seem just as adolescently superficial as "Grown-up" but under closer analysis corroborate this deep sense of confinement and frustration. Both "The Unexplorer" and "To the Not Impossible Him" employ a central metaphor of limited travel to suggest the nature of the oppression and restriction felt by the narrators. In "The Unexplorer," the child-narrator is inspired to "explore" the road beyond the house, but on the basis of information provided by her mother—"It brought you to the milk-man's door"—she has resigned herself to confinement. She rather wistfully explains, "That's why I have not travelled more." The implications of familial repression in the socialization process of the female are rather grim. In "To the Not Impossible Him," while the tone is light and the pose coyly provocative, the issue again is serious. The last stanza concludes:

> The fabric of my faithful love
> No power shall dim or ravel
> Whilst I stay here,—but oh, my dear,
> If I should ever travel!
>
> (130)

Confining the female, denying her experience, the narrator suggests, is the only sure way of forcing her into the social mold. Millay says a great deal more about this process in *Fatal Interview,* a collection of fifty-one sonnets published in 1931.

The structural simplicity and childlike narrative voice are techniques Millay used frequently in her early work. "Afternoon on a Hill," published in 1917, appears to be too simple a poem to give a serious reading. In imitation of childhood speech and thus childhood experience, its regular meter and rhymed quatrains, its childlike diction and sentence structure effectively convey the notion of woman as child. The stanzas, significantly without metrical variation, measure out their syllables as repetitiously as the child's days:

> I will be the gladdest thing
> Under the sun!
> I will touch a hundred flowers
> And not pick one.
>
> I will look at cliffs and clouds
> With quiet eyes,
> Watch the wind bow down the grass,
> And the grass rise.
>
> And when lights begin to show
> Up from the town,
> I will mark which must be mine,
> And then start down!
>
> (33)

Though appearing to lack subtlety and complexity, the poem does create a tension through an ironic disparity between the directness in tone and structure and the implications of the experience. The speaker seems to symbolize childhood's innocence and freedom. But the freedom, in fact, is artificial, for the child is regulated and restrained. She reaches out; she withdraws. "I will touch a hundred flowers," she decides, but then promises obediently: "And not pick one." The passivity outlined in this poem—looking, watching, obeying—again ends with the narrator's total retreat. It is, on the surface, an innocent-looking action. But it is a form of surrender. Throughout the poem one hears the promises of the "good little girl." She will do what is expected of her; she will watch quietly and disturb nothing.

Psychological experiences merely hinted at in this poem are verified directly and harshly in later poems. In "Above These Cares" Millay's narrator nearly screams out her recognition of her state:

> Painfully, under the pressure that obtains
> At the sea's bottom, crushing my lungs and my brains
> (For the body makes shift to breathe and after a fashion flourish
> Ten fathoms deep in care,
> Ten fathoms down in an element denser than air
> Wherein the soul must perish)
> I trap and harvest, stilling my stomach's needs;
> I crawl forever, hoping never to see
> Above my head the limbs of my spirit no longer free
> Kicking in frenzy, a swimmer enmeshed in weeds.
>
> (307)

The woman's vulnerability is absolute because she is so helplessly ensnared. Her feelings of oppression and spiritual suffocation are excruciatingly described, and she craves a numbing of her consciousness to dull the pain of her awareness. The psychological disintegration resulting from thwarted experience shown in this poem is further displayed in "Scrub," where the disillusioned narrator reflects bitterly on the meaning of her oppression and recognizes its origins in childhood:

> If I grow bitterly,
> Like a gnarled and stunted tree,
> Bearing harshly of my youth
> Puckered fruit that sears the mouth;
> If I make of my drawn boughs
> An inhospitable house,
> Out of which I never pry
> Towards the water and the sky,
> Under which I stand and hide
> And hear the day go by outside;
> It is that a wind too strong
> Bent my back when I was young,

It is that I fear the rain
Lest it blister me again.

(160)

Made vulnerable by its natural inclination to stretch and grow, the tree is thus subjected to attack and mutilation by forces in its environment; it is bent and blistered into submission. Terrorized and intimidated in the process, the woman—like the child who reaches to touch the flowers—makes a complete withdrawal inside "An inhospitable house, / Out of which I never pry / Towards the water and the sky, / Under which I stand and hide. . . ." Imagining herself like the tree to be deformed and grotesque, the mutilated narrator bemoans the psychological crippling of denied opportunities and punitive restrictions.

Millay found the child-narrator device very suggestive of woman's susceptibility to intimidation. In her vulnerability to victimization, the child in "Afternoon on a Hill" is psychologically parallel to the terrorized woman of "Assault," a poem first published in 1920 in *The New Republic*.

I had forgotten how the frogs must sound
After a year of silence, else I think
I should not so have ventured forth alone
At dusk upon this unfrequented road.

I am waylaid by Beauty. Who will walk
Between me and the crying of the frogs?
Oh, savage Beauty, suffer me to pass,
That am a timid woman, on her way
From one house to another!

(77)

Here, ostensibly, is the narrator's expression of her sensitivity to and appreciation for the beauties of nature. But the word choice and the ideas evoked call into question so superficial a reading. The speaker describes the experience as an ambush where she is assaulted, "waylaid," forced by a savage attacker into terrified submission, an image obviously suggestive of rape. The woman is confused as well as terrified, and her bewilderment is apparent in the ambiguity of her perceptions. She calls her assailant Beauty, suggesting a benign, even attractive attacker. Yet, she describes the attack as savage and further qualifies its nature by defining Beauty in the shape of frogs. She thinks she hears them crying, and in a spontaneous outburst of identification with their pain, she too cries, "Oh, savage Beauty, suffer me to pass." The choice of "suffer" is brilliantly placed to capsulize the poem's theme, which is a vivid description of the author's sense of vulnerability and the suffering that accompanies it. The speaker feels isolated, unprotected, intimidated. In this poem Millay has cleverly succeeded in defining woman's sense of her true condition by capitalizing on a common assumption about the excessive emotional nature of women. At the same time, she has implied that woman's oppressor is a deceptively disguised external force.

Millay's insistent use of verbs of assault and bombardment is an index to her concept of reality. She may title a poem "Spring," but she really sees the brains of men eaten by maggots; she may claim that she sorrows over the "Death of Autumn," but she portrays a malign force controlling the world, for the autumn rushes are "flattened"; the creek is "stripped"; beauty, "stiffened"; the narrator, crushed. All around her in the systematic operation of the elements Millay perceives the processes of barbaric intrusion and fatal attack. Millay's use of nature, which seems to depict typical romantic disillusionment with the transience of beauty, is in fact loaded with psychological and social implications. In "Low-Tide," the tide's movements, like the conditions of her existence, are inexorable. There are beautiful surfaces, but treacherous realities: "No place to dream, but a place to die." Here, again, the figure of a child qualifies the state of vulnerability. The narrator lacks knowledge and experience. Trusting and unsuspicious, she is susceptible to betrayal. This childlike susceptibility is consciously rendered in "Being Young and Green":

> Being young and green, I said in love's despite:
> Never in the world will I to living wight
> Give over, air my mind
> To anyone,
> Hang out its ancient secrets in the strong wind
> To be shredded and faded. . . .
> Oh, me, invaded
> And sacked by the wind and the sun!
>
> (222)

Millay's use of "ancient secrets" is highly suggestive of the private self she wishes to protect, but neither consciousness nor will is a strong enough defense against attack and exposure. The words "invaded and sacked," like "waylaid" in "Assault," indicate both the treacherousness of the assailant and the devastation of the attack. Fearing ridicule as well as exposure, the narrator tries to forearm herself, but she is helpless against the assaulting invisible powers, which she names here as wind and sun. The intrusion is forced and, in a social context, implies the act of rape. The intensity of Millay's sense of personal violation is felt in the imagery of "Moriturus":

> I shall bolt my door
>   With a bolt and cable;
> I shall block my door
>   With a bureau and a table;

With all my might
   My door shall be barred.
I shall put up a fight,
   I shall take it hard.

With his hand on my mouth
   He shall drag me forth,
Shrieking to the south
   And clutching at the north.
                  (206–207)

    The attacker in this poem is identified as death, but for Millay the horror of the experience is not in the idea of dying, but in the vision of the brutalizing attack by which she is forced to a complete surrender. Millay's narrator is vulnerable to attack and to exploitation because of some basic inferiority, and, as the rape image implies, it lies in her sexuality.

    When Millay left Vassar in 1917 to do whatever she liked with the world, as President MacCracken had assured her she could, she must soon have been stunned and distressed at the world's reception of her. She tells her family: "Mrs. Thompson, a lovely woman who helped put me through college wants me to come & be her secretary for a while—. . . but I just don' wanna! . . . Of course, I feel like the underneath of a toad not to do what she wants me to do—but I can't make up my mind to address envelopes and make out card catalogues all fall . . . be called on to answer the telephone and make appointments & reject invites. I might have been governess to the Aults, except for a similar feeling about my independence."[2] Professionally, at graduation, she wanted more than anything to be an actress. She hoped also to continue to write plays and poetry. She believed in her own genius, and "The Bean-Stalk," published in 1920 in *Poetry*, seems to reflect the *Figs'* public image of self-confidence:

Ho, Giant! This is I!
I have built me a bean-stalk into your sky!
La,—but it's lovely, up so high!

This is how I came,—I put
Here my knee, there my foot,
Up and up, from shoot to shoot—
                  (71)

The possibilities are exhilarating: "What a wind! What a morning!—" But imagery in a middle section of the poem counteracts that sense of exhilaration and faith with a description of the real effects of the climb and the wind upon the climber. Even the first line's intention to emphasize the speaker's identity is undercut by the notion of "giant." The climber becomes suddenly

insecure and uncertain in her position; she realizes that she is open to the
wind, vulnerable to attack. She may even doubt her talent:

> . . . bean-stalks is my trade,
> I couldn't make a shelf,
> Don't know how they're made,
>
> (73)

The wind, first viewed as an exhilarating force, is soon felt as an assailant
which nearly dislodges her, an assailant which she can neither see nor combat:

> And the wind was like a whip
> Cracking past my icy ears,
> And my hair stood out behind,
> And my eyes were full of tears,
> Wide-open and cold,
> More tears than they could hold,
> The wind was blowing so,
> And my teeth were in a row,
> Dry and grinning,
> And I felt my foot slip
> And I scratched the wind and whined,
> And I clutched the stalk and jabbered,
> With my eyes shut blind,—
> What a wind! What a wind!
>
> (72)

The blowing, whipping, cracking force of the wind strips her to a skeleton.
Though the experience is terrifying and the climber confounded by the
violence of the attack and the wind's capriciousness, the climber holds her
position, struggling to resist the devastating power of her adversary. It is a
tentative position, however, for the wind is a treacherous force, invisible,
deceptive—an excellent symbol for the undefined powers which seem to
impede Millay's efforts and cause her such suffering, powers she ultimately
associates with social oppression and political tyranny.

Millay did not become an actress. She wrote few plays. She spent her
life struggling for survival as a poet. This may be difficult for readers to
understand who know that Millay was a Pulitzer Prize winner, a popular
lecturer, a well-known and sought-after personality whose poems were published, reviewed, and read. But we are not dealing with external data merely;
we are examining the poetry for insights into the truth of Millay's inner
sense of herself and her achievements. The language pattern of vulnerability
suggests strongly that Millay saw herself as a misfit and a failure and that
she believed that some external forces in her life impeded her development
and inflicted permanent injury. An untitled poem in her posthumous collec-

tion, *Mine the Harvest*, conveys an understanding of the power and insidi-
ousness of the enemy and a resignation to her fate. Again the verb pattern
defines the sense of vulnerability and impending disaster felt by the narrator;
the image of the overpowering force of the wave summarizes a lifetime of
futile effort to transcend and resist a society which she feels has conspired to
destroy her.

> Establishment is shocked. Stir no adventure
> Upon this splitted granite.
>
> I will no longer connive
> At my own destruction:—I will not again climb,
> Breaking my finger nails, out of reach of the reaching wave,
> To save
> What I hope will still be me
> When I have slid on slime and clutched at slippery
>   rock-weed, and had my face towed under
> In scrubbing pebbles, under the weight of the wave
>   and its thunder.
> I decline to scratch at this cliff. *If* is not a word.
> I will connive no more
> With that which hopes and plans that I shall not survive:
> Let the tide keep its distance;
> Or advance, and be split for a moment by a thing very
>   small but all resistance;
> Then do its own chore.
>
>   (503)

Here Millay identifies the malignant force assailing her as the establishment,
and the causes for her deep sense of victimization are less opaque. She feels
outside the establishment, in opposition to social tradition and authority.
She had sensed as a young woman that the world was "no fit place for a child
to play." She had discovered that for women, as for children, the beautiful
things were out of reach. For Millay, the realities of her life were found in
the rigidly structured patterns of social behavior: you must not smoke at
Vassar; you must not be an actress if you want Lady Caroline's financial
assistance; you must consider being a social secretary if you really seek
employment; you must marry; you must have children; you must not offend
conventional morality if you want recognition; you must be male if you want
serious criticism of your poetry.[3]

Millay concedes in this untitled poem that society does not tolerate its
individualists; especially does it not tolerate its independent women. To be
a nonconformist is to be exposed and intimidated, like the woman in "Assault"; it is to feel like the lone traveler in "How Naked, How Without a
Wall," chilled by the night air, struck by sharp sleet, buffeted by wind,

vulnerable to the wolf's attack. The social ramifications are explicit in this poem. For this traveler, since he chooses to venture "forth alone / When other men are snug within," the world is a terrifying place of loneliness, alienation, inevitable catastrophe. Most people, Millay feels, are vulnerable to social pressures; some will compromise. Some will suffer self-betrayal rather than isolation, as another of Millay's travelers does in "On the Wide Heath," surrendering himself to a loud shrew, a poaching son, a daughter with a disdainful smile:

> Home to the worn reproach, the disagreeing,
>   The shelter, the stale air; content to be
> Pecked at, confined, encroached upon,—it being
>   Too lonely, to be free.
>
> (301)

The imagery of confinement and attack offer an unbearable alternative to the individual who is forced to acknowledge, as this narrator does in that haunting statement of vulnerability: "it being / Too lonely, to be free."

For Millay, reality is oppression and victimization, and she feels attacked by forces that tyrannize, whether she names them sun and wind, as she does in her early poetry, or hangmen and huntsmen, as she does later. The shift in focus is significant, for it marks a deliberate attempt by Millay to explain her sense of victimization in a larger context of social injustices. She sees that justice is denied in Massachusetts and that the huntsman gains on the quarry.

Victimization by totalitarian powers is subtly suggested in "The Buck in the Snow," where we see death, as in slow motion, "bringing to his knees, bringing to his antlers / The buck in the snow." Horrified, with the narrator, we witness the capitulation, the ultimate defeat of beauty and freedom and life. The buck, vulnerable, defenseless, goes down before an invisible, armed, socially sanctioned slaughterer. In "The Rabbit," the speaker, suffering excruciatingly for her greater awareness of reality than the rabbit has, screams a warning to the rabbit:

> 'O indiscreet!
> And the hawk and all my friends are out to kill!
> Get under cover!' But the rabbit never stirred;
>   she never will.
> And I shall see again and again the large eye blaze
> With death, and gently glaze;
> The leap into the air I shall see again and again,
>   and the kicking feet;
> And the sudden quiet everlasting, and the blade of
>   grass green in the strange mouth of the
>   interrupted grazer.
>
> (326–27)

The real significance of the whole range of verbs of assault is crystalized here in the verb "kill." Millay's victims are all alike: innocent, helpless, unsuspecting, unarmed, in every way vulnerable. And they are all embodiments of Millay, the anguished, writhing, defenseless, and finally defeated victim. Millay's profound suffering and her constant rendering of personal vulnerability become increasingly comprehensible in the context of her imagery of woman as victim.

Virginia Woolf understood the agonies and stresses of gifted women struggling against conditions of oppression. "For it needs little skill in psychology," she wrote in *A Room of One's Own*, "to be sure that a highly gifted girl who had tried to use her gift for poetry would have been so thwarted and hindered by other people, so tortured and pulled asunder by her own contrary instincts, that she must have lost her health to a certainty."[4] Millay's personal feelings of oppression and the realities of social restrictions imposed on her own professional ambitions and desires are poignantly stated in Section V of "Not So Far as the Forest," where the figure of the wounded and confined bird suggests an authentic self-projection:

> Poor passionate thing,
> Even with this clipped wing how well you flew!—though
>   not so far as the forest.
>
>   (339)

The bird initially presents an appearance of freedom and capability, striking for the top branches in the distant forest. But the bird's weakness, his vulnerability to defeat, invisible at first in his attempted flight, is ultimately disclosed. It is his ambition, described in the poem as "the eye's bright trouble," that has made him vulnerable. He has been victimized by "the unequal wind," that seductive environmental force with its seeming beneficence but real destructive power; and he has been chained by a human hand:

> Rebellious bird, . . .
> Has no one told you?—Hopeless is your flight
> Toward the high branches. . . .
>
> Though Time refeather the wing,
> Ankle slip the ring,
> The once-confined thing
> Is never again free.
>
>   (339)

Millay responded passionately and deeply to visions of suffering victims, from the starving man in Capri to the war victims of Lidice. These visions correspond closely to her view of herself as victim, and her use of language patterns of vulnerability take on greater significance as she develops her understanding of herself as a woman in a world where women's values and feelings are either predetermined or discarded. Millay's frequent use of the childlike narrator is increasingly understandable in the context of her vulnerability to the world's view and treatment of her as a woman. The nature of her existence, like the nature of her vulnerability, is thus qualified by the fact that she experiences the world as a woman.

"The Fitting" is well titled to suggest Millay's sense of woman's social conditioning to fit the narrow role prescribed for her. Through verbs that attempt to mask the degree of harm inflicted in the process, the narrator bitterly expresses her sense of personal violation. She submits to the fitting in a state of mannikin-like paralysis.

> The fitter said, 'Madame, vous avez maigri, '
> And pinched together a handful of skirt at my hip.
> 'Tant mieux,' I said, and looked away slowly, and
>   took my under-lip
> Softly between my teeth.
>
>   Rip—rip!
> Out came the seam, and was pinned together in
>   another place.
> She knelt before me, a hardworking woman with a
>   familiar and unknown face,
> Dressed in linty black, very tight in the arm's-
>   eye and smelling of sweat.
> She rose, lifting my arm, and set her cold shears
>   against me,—snip-snip;
> Her knuckles gouged my breast. My drooped eyes
>   lifted to my guarded eyes in the glass, and
>   glanced away as from someone they had
>   never met.
>
> 'Ah, que madame a maigri!' cried the vendeuse,
>   coming in with dresses over her arm.
> 'C'est la chaleur,' I said, looking out into the sunny
>   tops of the horse-chestnuts—and indeed it
>   was very warm.
>
> I stood for a long time so, looking out into the
>   afternoon, thinking of the evening and
>   you. . . .
> While they murmured busily in the distance,
>   turning me, touching my secret body, doing
>   what they were paid to do.
>   (342–43)

The narrator suffers both indignity and depersonalization in the fitting process. For one moment only—in a single line in the poem—does Millay allow
the imaginative escape to seem a possibility. This emphasis is quite different
from that of "The Bean-Stalk," where fantasized possibility is the poem's
overriding effect.

Two of Millay's best and longest sonnet sequences, *Fatal Interview* and
"Sonnets from an Ungrafted Tree," dramatize further through metaphors of
love and marriage the fatality of woman's vulnerability to social conditioning.
Fatal Interview is an extended metaphorical illustration of the consequences
to women of their limited range of experience and their susceptibility to
emotional exploitation. "Women's ways are witless ways," Millay states in
a *Figs* poem and *Fatal Interview* dramatically narrates how woman is trained
to react emotionally to her environment and how devastating the results of
such training are. The title suggests the nature of the results. Sonnet xvii of
the sequence portrays woman's naiveté and lack of preparation for such an
"interview" as she encounters:

> Sweet love, sweet thorn, when lightly to my heart
> I took your thrust, whereby I since am slain,
> And lie disheveled in the grass apart,
> A sodden thing bedrenched by tears and rain,
> . . . . .
> Had I bethought me then, sweet love, sweet thorn,
> How sharp an anguish even at the best,
> When all's requited and the future sworn,
> The happy hour can leave within the breast,
> I had not so come running at the call
> Of one who loves me little, if at all.
>
> (646)

An innocent believer in the value of her feelings, the woman opens herself
to her lover's thrust. The sexual implications of "thrust" give emphasis to
the irony of the woman's willing surrender to rape and murder. Through the
image of happy submission to her slayer, Millay sharply renders the utter
pathos of woman's susceptibility. Too late she discovers the insignificance of
her self, her life. The sequence dramatizes the spiritual disintegration that
must occur through the social conditioning that explains woman's nature as
essentially emotional and her greatest need as love. The entire sequence is
relentless in its presentation of love's ravaging and immobilizing effects upon
women whose lives are so isolated and confined. Sonnet lxxi epitomizes the
victim's scarred state:

> This beast that rends me in the sight of all,
> . . . . .
> Will glut, will sicken, will be gone by spring.

. . . . .
I shall forget before the flickers mate
Your look that is today my east and west.
Unscathed, however, from a claw so deep
Though I should love again I shall not go. . . .
(631)

Throughout the sonnets, the narrator exposes her emotional vulnerability to assault, humiliation, abuse, abandonment, annihilation.

How drowned in lover and weedily washed ashore,
There to be fretted by the drag and shove
At the tide's edge, I lie—. . .
. . . . .
Small chance, however, in a storm so black,
A man will leave his friendly fire and snug
For a drowned woman's sake, and bring her back
To drip and scatter shells upon the rug. . . .
(636)

Brutalization and victimization characterize woman's existence.

In "Sonnets from an Ungrafted Tree" the New England woman narrator poignantly and unforgettably reveals how she has been trapped by her illusions of romance and by her dreams of beauty into a relationship which strangles her emotionally and spiritually. One of Millay's most brilliant images of woman's spiritual suffocation is found in Sonnet xi of this sequence:

It came into her mind, seeing how the snow
Was gone, and the brown grass exposed again,
And clothes-pins, and an apron—long ago,
In some white storm that sifted through the pane
And sent her forth reluctantly at last
To gather in, before the line gave way,
Garments, board-stiff, that galloped on the blast
Clashing like angel armies in a fray,

An apron long ago in such a night
Blown down and buried in the deepening drift,
To lie till April thawed it back to sight,
Forgotten, quaint and novel as a gift—
It struck her, as she pulled and pried and tore,
That here was spring, and the whole year to be
    lived through once more.
(616)

Representing woman's condition, the apron, confined to the clothesline, is contrasted to the figure of clashing armies, suggestive of her imagined dreams of adventure and romance—dreams fulfilled only in a masculine world. The apron, obviously an article of domestic servitude, is a symbol for the woman's relinquished self, "Board-stiff," "blown down and buried" years before. Even then, this woman had half perceived the futility of her dreams and had gone out reluctantly to pull and pry and tear at the apron to try to resurrect it. Ultimately, the woman surrenders

> . . . her mind's vision plain
> The magic World, where cities stood on end . . .
> Remote from where she lay—and yet—between,
> Save for something asleep beside her, only the
> window screen.
>
> (617)

The restrictive realities of her life—something asleep beside her and the window screen—are stark contrasts to the waning dreams of her imagined self.

It is understandable why Millay's two extended narratives of woman's psychological disintegration are presented in sonnet sequences. Millay persistently resorts to the constraints of traditional verse forms. Given her time and place in the history of American poetry and given the external evidence of her unconventional childhood and youthful radicalism, one would expect to find her in the company of the avant-garde of American poetry. But Millay is no true Imagist. She eschews the freedoms of form which Ezra Pound had defined as essential to the new poetry. The sonnet, her best form, is a fit vehicle to convey her deepest feelings of woman's victimization. Through it, Millay imaginatively reenacts her constant struggle against boundaries. The wish for freedom is always qualified by the sense of restriction; couplets and quatrains suit her sensibility.

In Millay's poetry, women, in their quiet lives of fatal desires and futile gestures, are tragic and heroic. She identifies herself with suffering women, women whose dreams are denied, whose bodies are assaulted, whose minds and spirits are extinguished. She states her consciousness of the universality of women's vulnerability and anguish in "An Ancient Gesture," contrasting Penelope's tears with those of Ulysses:

> I thought, as I wiped my eyes on the corner of my apron:
> Penelope did this too.
> And more than once: you can't keep weaving all day
> And undoing it all through the night;
> Your arms get tired, and the back of your neck gets tight;
> And along towards morning, when you think it will never be light,
> And your husband has been gone, and you don't know where, for years,
> Suddenly you burst into tears;
> There is simply nothing else to do.

And I thought, as I wiped my eyes on the corner of my apron:
This is an ancient gesture, authentic, antique,
In the very best tradition, classic, Greek;
Ulysses did this too.
But only as a gesture,—a gesture which implied
To the assembled throng that he was much too moved to speak.
He learned it from Penelope . . .
Penelope, who really cried.

(501)

From the earliest volume, *Renascence*, where even her youthful awakening is accompanied by its grief-laden songs of shattering, through her posthumous harvest of mature experience, Millay records, unrelentingly, her life of pain and frustration. If she too loudly insisted on the public self's claims for freedom to love and think and feel and work as she pleased, she nevertheless quietly throughout her work continued to send out her linguistic distress signals. It is her profound insight into her self's inevitable capitulation that makes Millay ultimately so vulnerable and her poetry so meaningful.

Notes

1.   Edna St. Vincent Millay, *Collected Poems*, ed. Norma Millay (New York: Harper & Row, 1956), p. 138. All poetry citations are from this edition, and page numbers are indicated in the text following the quotations.
2.   Allan Ross Macdougall, ed., *Letters of Edna St. Vincent Millay* (1952; rpt. Westport, Ct.: Greenwood Press, 1971), p. 77.
3.   Critical treatment abounds which fails to perceive either the scope of her subject matter or the real intentions of her work and which denies her the serious critical perspective so vital to art. See, for example, James M. Dabbs, "Edna St. Vincent Millay: Not Resigned" (*South Atlantic Quarterly*, 37, January 1938), who finds her quarrelsome; John Crowe Ransom, "The Poet as Woman" (*The World's Body*, 1938; rpt., Port Washington, N.Y.: Kennikat Press, 1964), who faults her for failure to write more like a man; Louis Untermeyer (cited in Dabbs), who associates the pangs of love in her poetry with pettiness; Edmund Wilson, "Epilogue, 1952: Edna St. Vincent Millay" (*The Shores of Light: A Literary Chronicle of the Twenties and Thirties*, New York: Farrar, Straus and Young, 1952), p. 778, who regrets that she had "no children to occupy her, to compel her to outgrow her girlhood."
4.   Virginia Woolf, *A Room of One's Own* (New York and Burlingame: Harcourt, Brace and World, 1957), p. 51.

Andromeda Unbound:
Gender and Genre in Millay's Sonnets

Debra Fried

In a critical climate in which we are rediscovering the powerful experiments of American women poets in the modernist era, the tidy verses of Edna St. Vincent Millay have remained something of an embarrassment. Tough-minded as they can be about sex, betrayal, and the price of being a woman who can write candidly about such matters, Millay's poems, particularly her sonnets, can often seem like retrograde schoolgirl exercises amidst the van-guard verbal dazzle of H. D., Mina Loy, Gertrude Stein, and Marianne Moore. In revising the history of modernism to make more central the achievements of these innovative poets, it has been convenient to dismiss Millay's work as copybook bohemianism. Millay may rightly be judged as a minor star in this constellation, but this is not, I think, why there have been so few serious investigations of Millay of late. Our silence attests rather to a failure to ask the right questions about how traditional poetic forms such as the sonnet may serve the needs of women poets.[1] Why does a woman poet in this century elect to write sonnets? What sort of gender associations can a poetic form such as the sonnet accumulate, and how may such associations, and consequent exclusions, make that genre an especially lively arena for the revisionary acts of women's poetry? What model of the relation between generic restraints and expressive freedom is suggested by the sonnet? How does genre shape the meanings of allusion within a sonnet, particularly allusions to other sonnets? And, most centrally for thinking about Millay, how has the sonnet historically implied connections between formal (generic, metrical, rhetorical) constraints and sexual ones?

Instead of asking such questions, we have tended to assume that we know just how and why a poet like Millay must use circumscribed, traditional poetic forms: to rein in her strong, unruly feelings. This idea is a common-place in earlier writing on the poet, as in Jean Gould's observation in her popular biography that Millay "found security in classical form: the sonnet was the golden scepter with which she ruled her poetic passions."[2] We can

From *Twentieth Century Literature: A Scholarly and Critical Journal* 32, no. 1 (Spring 1986): 1–22. Reprinted by permission. Winner of the 1986 *Twentieth Century Literature* Prize in Literary Criticism.

find similar claims in two recent essays on Millay's poetry. Jane Stanbrough caps a persuasive analysis of the deep sense of submission and constriction that lies behind Millay's seemingly defiant, unharnessed poetry with the observation that Millay's sonnets and sonnet sequences illustrate her tendency to "resort to the constraints of traditional verse form": "The sonnet, her best form, is a fit vehicle to convey her deepest feelings of woman's victimization. Through it, Millay imaginatively reenacts her constant struggle against boundaries. The wish for freedom is always qualified by the sense of restriction; couplets and quatrains suit her sensibility."[3]

This claim, sensible as it sounds, calls for considerable scrutiny. What poetic "sensibility," we may ask, is not in some degree suited to the strictures of poetic form? (Isn't that what it would mean to have a poetic sensibility?) The identification of sonnets with a creative temperament that both needs boundaries and needs to strain against them is by no means applicable exclusively to Millay or to women poets. Too many assumptions go untested in Stanbrough's implication that in Millay's dependence on poetic constraints to embody the drama of vulnerability and resistance we witness a particularly female response to lyric form. A full declaration of those assumptions would require an inquiry into the ways a potentially stifling poetic form may amplify—give pitch, density, and strength to—a poet's voice. If we are to isolate the particular resources, if any, with which a woman poet may rebel against formal constraints, we must begin with an examination of the tropes for the sonnet that are part of the history of that genre. Only then can we determine the particular uses a woman poet can make of the liberating fetters of the sonnet form. The power of Millay's sonnets, and their usefulness for the study of the relations between gender and genre in twentieth-century poetry, derives from the readiness with which, while working within formal boundaries, they challenge the figurations for which the sonnet has been traditionally a receptive home. Through her revisions of those tropes and related devices—particularly as found in sonnets of Wordsworth and Keats— Millay's allusive sonnets, I will contend, reclaim that genre as her plot of ground, not chiefly by planting it with "woman's" themes or using it as mouthpiece for the woman's voice (though she does both these things), but by rethinking the form's historical capacity for silencing her voice.

It is this kind of reflectiveness about what it means to work within traditional forms that another recent essay would seem to deny to Millay. In a study of the Elizabethan sonnets of Millay and Elinor Wylie, Judith Farr argues that Millay's particular temperaments, attitudes, and skills sometimes led her to "marshall against the lively but serene mathematics of contained forms like the sonnet, quatrain, or couplet a battery of disheveled impulses expressed in terms calculated to shock. . . . Millay's best work exhibits a tutored sensibility that enabled her to compose effectively within literary traditions she respected. The Petrarchan conventions to which she submitted in *Fatal Interview* served her well, moreover, disciplining her imagination yet encouraging the emotional scope her poetry instinctively sought."[4] One may readily take Farr's point that all of Millay's efforts in the Elizabethan mode are not equally successful. More questionable is the assumption here that the poet Millay is a creature of raw emotion or instinct who, when she is good, submits to a form that will tame that rawness, and when she is bad, invades the decorous parlors of poetic form like a spoiled child with her mad manners. The language of power in this passage from Farr's essay is also tellingly confused: the process whereby conventions to which the poet "submits" may then in turn submit to or "serve" her is a complicated one that needs to be explained and argued in specific instances. To assume, as Farr would appear to do, that in choosing "contained forms" Millay either bombards them with mischievous, whimsical "impulses" (are these the same as the "emotional scope her poetry instinctively sought"?) or submissively "composes" within them lest impulse get the better of her, is to imply that Millay worked unwittingly at the mercy of these opposed moods. But the question of whether writing in an established lyric genre is an act of taking command or of being commanded is one upon which Millay's sonnets reflect.

It is, moreover, a reflection to which Millay found the sonnet is supremely suited, in part because it is a subject explored in the English Romantic sonnets Millay knew well. One of the dubious things about Stanbrough's and Farr's accounts of why Millay found the sonnet suited to her poetic needs is that they so strikingly resemble Wordsworth's claim that he turned to the sonnet to find relief from "too much liberty." The sonnet is such a difficult form that from its inception in English it took as one of its topics the paradoxical release and scope to be derived from its intricate formal requirements. Stanbrough's remark that through the sonnet Millay "imaginatively reenacts her constant struggle against boundaries" is best scrutinized by setting it beside Wordsworth's "Nuns Fret Not at Their Convent's Narrow Room."

Although it is well known, we will need to look at the poem in some detail.

> Nuns fret not at their convent's narrow room;
> And hermits are contented with their cells;
> And students with their pensive citadels;
> Maids at the wheel, the weaver at his loom,
> Sit blithe and happy; bees that soar for bloom,
> High as the highest Peak of Furness-Fells,
> Will murmur by the hour in foxglove bells:
> In truth the prison, unto which we doom
> Ourselves, no prison is: and hence for me,
> In sundry moods, 'twas pastime to be bound
> Within the Sonnet's scanty plot of ground;
> Pleased if some Souls (for such there needs must be)

> Who have felt the weight of too much liberty,
> Should find brief solace there, as I have found.[5]

Through a series of analogies Wordsworth builds his argument that the sonnet is chosen less as a vehicle for expression than as a rest cure from the expansiveness of other expressive tasks. The poet turns to the sonnet for release from what he calls "the weight of too much liberty," bolstering his claims for the contentment this brief form can yield by adducing the figures of the nun, hermit, student, spinning maids, and weavers—all willingly enclosed in cells of work or thought. Yet it is precisely because he does not have the limited vocational contentment these figures enjoy that he requires the "brief solace" of a binding poetic form analogous in its "scanty plot" to their productive enclosures. They inhabit these containments willingly as the natural space for their labors, while the poet rather seeks such containment as a cure for a temporarily unsatisfying wildness. The nun is content in her "convent's narrow room" not because there she finds relief from too much liberty, the hermit, male counterpart of the nun, is hardly to be read as a libertine curing himself through isolation and self-imprisonment. In this sense the sonnet's analogies are rather startlingly inexact. When sought as cure for a dangerous freedom, the narrow room of poetic convention seems only faintly comparable to the nun's convent.

There is something deceptive, then, in Wordsworth's catalog of contented prisoners who help him to defend his free generic choice of the sonnet's prison house. This deception is hinted at in the shift to the culminating example of the soaring bees who willingly enclose themselves in "foxglove bells." The shift from individual human workers to generalized, plural creatures of nature, it might be argued, deftly clinches the proof by finding the principle of chosen enclosure in the tiniest phenomena and at the farthest geographical margins. In this sense we might suppose that in lines 5–7 the sonnet soars beyond the neatly allocated, gendered world of the opening lines. Yet this turn to the bees also hints at a felt inadequacy in the poem's preceding examples. The bees' erotic labor of entering and fertilizing flowers is out of tune with the opening catalog of closeted celibates and plyers of cottage industries, each sex performing its own labor by itself. The murmuring bees are more like the poet Wordsworth than like any of these pensive workers. Both bees and poet can choose enclosure because they are privileged to be creatures of "sundry moods." Promiscuous, musical, and free, the bees enjoy a specifically male power of voice that is beautifully muted and sustained by the delights of enclosure.

Unlike the paired figures of nun and hermit, maids and weaver, the bees would seem to have no corresponding female; but we might locate their partners in the foxglove bells they fertilize and in which they "murmur." If the flowers play the female in this natural coupling, it becomes clearer that the attribution of musical powers to the "foxglove bells" is somewhat deceptive, as they are so called in reference to their bell-like shape, while they are made musical only by the bees murmuring penetration of them.[6] The culminating example of the bees frets against the others. The mismatch between the free-ranging bees and the preceding figures of happy enclosure allows us to detect the gendered associations of the sonnet form. If the sonnet is historically associated with a liberating, because voluntary, constriction, such solace is implicitly the privilege of the sex that may choose as well to be free.

If we take "Nuns Fret Not at Their Convent's Narrow Room" as exemplifying a masculine poetics of the sonnet in the Romantic period, we find a divided allegiance in the claims that the poet frees himself by binding himself. The poet seeks through the writing of the sonnet the self-enclosed sense of vocation of the nun or hermit, but by cataloging these cloistered votaries to exemplify the poetic solace the sonnet can afford, he refuses to admit that this is a solace necessitated by a burdensome freedom they are not privileged to suffer. The image of the bees upsets the sonnet's opening symmetries, its series of pairings suggesting that male and female alike find solace in enclosure. It thereby prompts us to be skeptical about whether both sexes can be equally oppressed by "the weight of too much liberty" and can turn with the same relief to the sonnet's "scanty plot of ground." Confined by their sex in a scanty plot—small room to travel and small room to change the narrative of their lives, already plotted for them as the sex that stays enclosed at home—women poets, even the "new woman" of modernism that Millay was taken to typify, cannot enjoy quite this brand of Wordsworthian solace in putting on the corset of strict lyric form.

The question of whether the sonnet's delights of enclosure are unavailable to women becomes more vexed when we remember that the excess of liberty which the sonnet was to cure was, in Wordsworth's case, the freedom to write epic. In the course of writing *The Prelude*, Wordsworth learned that he needed literary strictures to counterbalance the weighty responsibility of the epic's relatively unlimited options. The sonnet's poetics of refuge serves the post-Miltonic epic poet as ballast to his vauntings, or, to cite another Wordsworthian trope of sonnet as enclosed space, as "little cells, oratories, or sepulchral recesses" in the "gothic church" to which he compared his projected great epic, *The Recluse*.[7] This figuration of the sonnet as a deliberately constricting antechamber to the grand edifice of bardic achievement arguably excludes the woman poet from the structure entirely. For her it is not "pastime to be bound" in the sonnet's restricted scope as respite from the effort of epic soaring. No one seriously expects her to undertake the epic, national or personal; her sonnets are not taken to be preparatory gestures for or lyric retreats from the longer, loftier genres. The entire notion of the Virgilian career from the simple, parochial modes like pastoral and georgic to the grand, public scope of epic implies a male bard at work refining the language of his race. The woman may be his muse, but she can never follow him up the graded ladder of poetic modes. The woman poet is not blessed with his mobility, a mobility which can become a burdensome independence sending the male poet to the comforting fold of the patterns of brief lyric forms. Thus her choice of the sonnet cannot mean the same thing as his.

If it is true, as Sandra Gilbert and Susan Gubar suggest, that "verse genres have been even more thoroughly male than fictional ones," it is so in part because verse genres are traditionally more subject to hierarchical ranking than fictional ones.[8] Only by acknowledging the woman writer's exclusion from this hierarchy of verse genres can we begin to understand what a woman poet may signify when she chooses to write sonnets. But first we must look more closely at what the male poet's choice entails.

For Wordsworth, the place of the sonnet in the hierarchy of poetic genres is clearly marked in the career of Milton. By modeling his sonnets on Milton's, Wordsworth attempts to reinforce the status of his sonnets as overtures to epic promise or breathers from epic responsibilities. He praised in particular Milton's tendency to loosen the binds of the form by working against the traditional units within the sonnet. In Milton's best sonnets, Wordsworth notes, "the sense does not close with the rhyme, at the eighth line, but overflows into the second portion of the metre. Now it has struck me, that this is not done merely to gratify the ear of variety and freedom of sound, but also to aid in giving that pervading sense of intense Unity in which the excellence of the Sonnet has always seemed to me mainly to consist."[9] Wordsworth admires the way Milton's sonnets do not submit to the Italian octet-sestet division, but rather fret at the barriers of rhyme, so that, in John Hollander's phrase, "the rhymes do not force logical and rhetorical units."[10] Enjambment serves to deemphasize the traditional units established by the rhyme scheme and thus gives the sonnet the feel of a fluid, rounded period. Milton loosens the sonnet's regimentation so that within this constricting form he may approximate the freedom of blank verse—the freedom, that is, that he would enjoy most thoroughly in the epic for which his sonnets are a training ground. "Nuns Fret Not" provides a good example of how Wordsworth takes Miltonic freedoms with the sonnet. By permitting the octet to push its way into the ninth line and thus delay the turn of the sonnet by a half-line (to cite just one characteristically Miltonic touch), Wordsworth empowers this single technical choice to engage his work with the tradition of Miltonic writing—not just with Milton's sonnets, but with the epic ambitions in which the sonnets find an important but decidedly secondary place.

The question that then arises is whether a woman poet whose sonnets displayed comparable virtues of flexibility, variety, and freedom could accrue to herself the Miltonic ambitions with which Wordsworth can associate himself in his sonnets. If the woman poet is exiled so sternly from this tradition that she is not privileged to charge the prosodic nuances of a

traditional lyric genre with the force of male literary history, the very resources by which poetic form can mean at all are thus curtailed for her.

Edna St. Vincent Millay found herself in what was perhaps a unique
position in the history of women writing poetry; she was called upon to
uphold the tradition of binding lyric forms against the onslaught of what
her supporters saw as a dangerously shapeless modernism. In 1917 the
prodigious schoolgirl who wrote "Renascence" represented "an alternative to
the 'new' poetry . . . whose work could serve as a rallying point for the
rejection of free verse, imagism, and Prufrockian ennui."[11] At the same time
Millay was identified with the bohemian literary life of Greenwich Village,
seen as a kind of poetic flapper who, as Elizabeth Atkins put it in 1936,
"represents our time to itself."[12] It was, in short, an interesting time for a
woman to be writing sonnets. The issues of poetic and sexual freedom were
being explicitly linked; why should free-spirited Millay stick to the sonnet
when other women poets were experimenting with free verse? It would be
easy to suspect the poet of merely posturing at promiscuity, aping a man's
freedom in order to earn the respite of poetic formalism on a man's ground.
But for her the sonnet's formal patterns and its brevity both come to figure
the price of freedom rather than a welcome retreat from it.

To the degree that Millay identifies the working of the sonnet with the
poetics of the bohemian life, she rejects the Wordsworthian figuration of the
sonnet as controlled respite from freedom. The self-fulfilling prophecies of
the sonnet's tight formalities—the set of interlocking rules and obligations
any sonnet sets itself early on and its "metrical contract," in Hollander's
terms, not to waver from it—Millay found useful as a trope for a poetics of
burning one's candle at both ends, of using one's life up completely. The
sonnet can embody metrically, sonorously, and syntactically a kind of perfectly efficient hedonism, culminating in a closure with no residue. The
sestet of "Thou famished grave, I will not fill thee yet" from *Huntsman, What
Quarry?* defiantly tells Death how lives and poems are to be ended:

> I cannot starve thee out: I am thy prey
> And thou shalt have me; but I dare defend
> That I can stave thee off; and I dare say,
> What with the life I lead, the force I spend,
> I'll be but bones and jewels on that day,
> And leave thee hungry even in the end.

The poet "staves off" death by the achieved design of her stanzas. Here
the sonnet's closure—completing its metrical and rhyming requirements,
leaving nothing formally unsatisfied, filling its staves—mimes the way the
poet vows to use up her force completely and leave nothing behind. Millay
allows her life to end with no residue of unlived days, as the completed

sonnet, ending "in the end," permits no residue of unpaired rhymes, unbalanced argument, or dangling syntax. Not a matter of wanton wastefulness but of almost methodical, tasking exhaustiveness, the bohemian project is thus aptly figured in the seemingly opposite, straitlacing, vow-keeping, binding contract any sonnet must be. Recalling Farr's charge that Millay "marshall[s] against the lively but serene mathematics of contained forms like the sonnet, quatrain, or couplet a battery of dissheveled impulses," we might rather say that the self-fulfilling equations of poetic forms provide the formula whereby Millay makes sure that those impulses play themselves out to the full.

All this insistence on the scrupulous hard work of being liberated suggests the occupational hazards this job has for women. For them, the weight of too much liberty too often can be translated into a demanding lover's "weight upon my breast" ("I, being born a woman and distressed" from *The Harp-Weaver*). Free love itself can be a prison. Dazzled by the sight of her lover, the speaker of "When I too long have looked upon your face" (*Second April*) compares her condition, when she "turn[s] away reluctant" from his "light," to a very scanty plot of ground indeed:

> Then is my daily life a narrow room
> In which a little while, uncertainly,
> Surrounded by impenetrable gloom,
> Among familiar things grown strange to me
> Making my way, I pause, and feel, and hark,
> Till I become accustomed to the dark.

The new woman may fret a great deal in her freedom's "narrow room," it seems; and we may take Millay's soft but audible allusion to the opening line of "Nuns Fret Not" as a reflection on the different kinds of narrowness to which their own freedom may condemn men and women. The enclosing solace of the Wordsworthian sonnet becomes here an almost tomblike, if chosen, claustrophobia, a prison into which the woman dooms herself when she turns away, a "silly, dazzled thing deprived of sight," from the overpowering brilliance of her lover's face.

In Millay's posthumous sonnet on the sonnet, the form appears not as a small plot of ground or a chosen cloister, but as an erotic prison:

> I will put Chaos into fourteen lines
> And keep him there; and let him thence escape
> If he be lucky; let him twist, and ape
> Flood, fire; and demon—his adroit designs
> Will strain to nothing in the strict confines
> Of this sweet Order, where, in pious rape,
> I hold his essence and amorphous shape,
> Till he with Order mingles and combines.

Past are the hours, the years, of our duress,
His arrogance, our awful servitude:
I have him. He is nothing more or less
Than something simple not yet understood:
I shall not even force him to confess;
Or answer. I will only make him good. [13]

When Millay claims that her sonnets "put Chaos into fourteen lines," she does more than simply repeat the inherited fiction of the sonnet as brief solace or momentary stay against profusion. The stakes seem higher than in Wordsworth's poem, the task put upon poetic form more demanding; this sonnet figures poetic form as a cage for a wild creature. Millay may have in mind Donne's dictum that "Grief brought to numbers cannot be so fierce, / For he tames it, that fetters it in verse" ("The Triple Fool"). But the fourteen lines of this sonnet's cage are not rigid iron bars or fetters but tethers whose strength derives from their flexibility. In refusing to make Chaos "confess," Millay refuses to use the machinery of rhyme and meter to force her stubborn, resistant subject into saying something against his will, perhaps with a glance at Ben Jonson's "A Fit of Rhyme against Rhyme," where rhyme is figured as a torture device to extort false words from the poem: "Rime the rack of finest wits / That expresseth but by fits / True conceit." She will not use the sonnet form to urge a confession or reply, to reveal the "something simple" that his complicated "designs" conceal. The simple goodness—virtuosity, well-craftedness—of the poem is sufficient, will "answer" or be adequate to the job of capturing Chaos. That alone will yield the solution, that is the way to make the prisoner speak up—to reform him, not punish him or make him squeal. This is a mildly coercive inquisition, a "pious rape." The curt, determined vows that close the sonnet leave us with a sense that this poetic mastery over an old rival takes its sweetest revenge from its substitution of an inescapable gentleness for the rival's former cruelty and "arrogance."

This late poem gathers up a recurring image in Millay's sonnets of eros as prison. In the fifth poem of the sequence *Fatal Interview,* the speaker counts herself the most abject of prisoners of love since "my chains throughout their iron length / Make such a golden clank upon my ear," and she would not escape even if she had the strength to do so. By sonnet XVIII in the sequence, the speaker questions her voluntary incarceration more closely: "Shall I be prisoner till my pulses stop / To hateful Love and drag his noisy chain?" Chaos is like a fugitive, faithless lover captured at last, his amorphousness like that of the unapproachable man of whom the woman says "I chase your colored phantom on the air. . . . Once more I clasp,—and there is nothing there" ("Once more into my arid days like dew" from *Second April*). "I will Put Chaos into Fourteen Lines" explicitly equates sexual and poetic dominance in its insistence on the control and compression required of the woman poet who seizes upon traditional forms in order to free herself from the forces that would deny her the power to order poetic forms—forces that include traditional male accounts of the need for poetic order.

Like "Nuns Fret Not," Millay's "I Will Put Chaos" ends in such a way as to suggest that the controlling process it describes has been enacted in the sonnet as we read it. Wordsworth's closing hope that in the sonnet the liberty-weary "Should find brief solace there, as I have found" fulfills the promise it expresses, as it refers to the solace afforded by this very sonnet as well as by the poet's habitual writing of them. In the same way, Millay's final promise—"I will only make him good"—points to her goal in all her sonnets as well as to the technical excellence of this one she has just finished. A pun gives this closure a double force. Millay makes the sonnet aesthetically good by tempering the behavior of the unruly subject in its artful cage, making him "good" in the sense of training him to be well-mannered, obedient, and orderly. In Millay's figure, the woman poet binds "Chaos"— a kind of male anti-muse, perhaps the divisive forces of sexuality, or whatever the force may be that tears poems apart rather than inspires them—with the "strict confines" of her ordering art.[14] The entire sonnet is almost an allegory of Judith Farr's somewhat paradoxical formula that the "conventions to which [Millay] submitted . . . served her well."

"I Will Put Chaos into Fourteen Lines" presents the struggle of the syntactic unit to find its completion, and to fit into the metrical and rhyming requirements of the sonnet (here, particularly of the octet), as an erotic tussling. The octet of "I Will Put Chaos" entertains the fiction that the single long sentence that comprises it is allowed free rein to flow from line to line, but is gently curbed (by the poet or by Order itself) at each line ending by the bars of rhyme and meter. The sestet, written in short sentences, largely end-stopped, looks back with precarious assurance on the struggle of the octet. The sonnet's trope for its own procedures is a peculiar one: the poet who dooms her subject into the prison of form acts almost like a pander supervising the mating of Chaos and Order. The twisting of the sentence from line to line illustrates Chaos' snaky attempts to wriggle out of the poem's snare, but the "adroit designs" the poem attributes to Chaos are, of course, the poet's designs by whose grace the caged creature may be as lively and various and protean as he wants. Only the sonnet's strict order of meter, rhyme, and syntax allows us to register the twists taken by the long sentence (lines 3–8) describing Chaos ineffectual attempts to escape.[15] Millay here makes enjambment positively sexy.

Perhaps this is merely to say that Millay makes good use of the resources of the sonnet, combining Miltonic or Romantic use of heavy enjambment with a strict Petrarchan division between octet and sestet. But, as we shall see, in the context of Millay's allusive polemic against the tradition of sexual myths for the sonnet, it is to say rather more. Again the figurative status of poetic closure is at issue. For Wordsworth, when in a sonnet "the sense does not close with the rhyme," the result desired is a "pervading sense of Unity."

The way in which that unity is achieved is made invisible in favor of the satisfying fullness of the closure. In Milton's sonnets Wordsworth admires not the unfolding spell of the "sense variously drawn out" in run-on lines, but the achieved plenitude of the completed experience. Once the "brief solace" is found, the poem is over, and the poet can go on to other things, to wander and soar at liberty. For Millay, such run-over lines in the orderly sonnet figure rather the difficult wrestling of the poet to achieve unity, a wrestling that is inseparable from a rallying of opposed sexual forces. Wordsworth's sonnet ends with a sigh of satisfaction, the remedy having done the trick ("as I have found"), Millay's with the challenge still ahead, a vow the poet makes to herself ("I will only make him good"). She focuses on the syntactic drama itself, rather than the feeling of satisfaction after the curtain is rung down. The tug of line against syntax figures the poet's constant struggle with "Chaos," not the assurance of Miltonic authority, or the comforting sense of respite and accomplishment Wordsworth claims to derive from the sweet order of sonnet constraints. Intricate play with enjambment is a way Millay demonstrates and monitors that she is in charge of the words, not in some "awful servitude" to them. [16] It is a game she knows she is playing, and knows which rules she has invented and which she has inherited. The critical view of Millay that judges her as in need of poetic form to control her emotional impulses merely repeats Millay's own strategic presentation of herself as such, a self-presentation that itself is in need of interpretation and cannot be taken as a straightforward outline of her poetics.

A sonnet from *Second April*, Millay's third volume (1921) brings together the two main figurations for the sonnet which we have been examining. Here a small plot of ground becomes an imprisoning site of too much liberty:

> Not with libations, but with shouts and laughter
> We drenched the altars of love's sacred grove,
> Shaking to earth green fruits, impatient after
> The launching of the coloured moths of Love.
> Love's proper myrtle and his mother's zone
> We bound about our irreligious brows,
> And fettered him with garlands of our own,
> And spread a banquet in his frugal house.
> Not yet the god has spoken; but I fear
> Though we should break out bodies in his flame,
> And pour our blood upon his altar, here
> Henceforward is a grove without a name,
> A pasture to the shaggy goats of Pan,
> Whence flee forever a woman and a man. [17]

Again we see the high price exacted by the bohemian life: the sonnet, and presumably the affair it commemorates, ends with the sickening sense of loss and satiety that follows from banqueting on unripe fruits. No sacrifice to love can make the grove suitable for proper worship again; such overeager illicit lovers can never thereafter become spouses, dutifully bound in marriage. This may be an illicit and transient affair, but as we expect from Shakespearean sonnets, the transient is transformed into something permanent, and the agent of this permanence is the poem itself; Millay's final vision of the goatish couple fleeing "forever" borrows from this expectation while giving it a bohemian twist. But instead of two lovers frozen in the instant before a kiss, as on Keats's urn, this overheated pair is caught in a gesture of self-exile from a hot pastoral they have sullied with their excesses.

As a character in Millay's all-male verse drama *Conversation at Midnight* (1937) argues, with a glance sidelong at Shakespeare's Sonnet 94,

> it seems
> Even to my nostrils that the lilies are beginning to smell;
> And that the time has come to deck our amorous themes
> With the honester stenches.

With its bracing candor about modern love, "Not with Libations" lets fresh air into the sonnet, but that air is already tainted with the stench of overindulgence. We might find it a sufficiently revisionary move on Millay's part simply to give the female half of the couple room to admit that she too knows desire and has a sexual will (Millay gives us simply "a woman and a man," no longer poet and disdainful mistress, burning lover and dark lady), and Millay's sonnets often testify that women, too, know the lust that the Renaissance sonnet traditionally allowed only men to feel. But it would be too simple to say that through its act of bestowing on the woman desires as impatient as the man's the poem bestows on the woman poet the capacity to write sonnets as weighted as a man's. The woman's desire cannot resonate in the room of the sonnet with the same force as his desire; it is a room that has been designed to amplify his tones and to silence hers.[18] To bring these issues to the fore, Millay treats the sonnet as an echo chamber, where we can listen to the voices this improperly proper sonnet has appropriated and revised.

"Not with Libations, but with Shouts and Laughter" is burdened with the weight of too much literature.[19] The poem addresses "Nuns Fret Not at Their Convent's Narrow Room" in its marking for erotic indulgence the scanty plot of ground Wordsworth identifies with serene retreat. The narrow room of conventional passion is too restrictive for these lovers, who turn their erotic bonds into a prison in which they doom themselves. Despite the Wordsworthian figures and the Shakespearean design, however, this poem's grove is drenched with Keats, from incidental glances at the hymn to Pan in *Endymion*, the "Ode to Psyche," and the sonnet "On Solitude," to more importantly polemical allusions to Keats's sonnet on the sonnet.

Typically, the Keatsian echoes resound in a coarser tone in Millay's "Not with Libations." The lovers crowning themselves with "love's proper myrtle" have plucked some foliage from the "many that are come to pay their vows / With leaves about their brows" (*Endymion*, 1.291–92) in the hymn to Pan, but Millay's lovers consign their grove to "the shaggy goats of Pan," not to an uplifted, Keatsian deity who is "the leaven / That spreading in this dull and clotted earth, / Gives it a touch ethereal" (1.296–98).[20] The music that drifts over from the "Ode to Psyche" becomes likewise sensualized. The closing prophecy in "Not with Libations" that "Henceforward is a grove without a name" alludes audibly enough to the vow in the ode to dress Psyche's sanctuary "With buds, and bells, and stars without a name" ("Ode to Psyche," 61). Like the speaker of the ode, Millay's lovers consecrate themselves as their own priests to a form of love which does not have its proper cult in poetry, and like him they adapt the available religious emblems to serve their new god and build him an altar that is erected more in the mind than in any special spot. Keats's ode closes with an invitation to "let the warm Love in," while Millay's sonnet ends with the exile of the warm lovers who, once they have celebrated their inventive rites, must abandon the spot. "Not with Libations" closes on a note from Keats's early sonnet beginning "O Solitude! if I must with thee dwell." Locating solitude on a natural prospect or "'mongst boughs pavilioned," the sonnet ends with the anticipation, addressing Solitude, that "it sure must be / Almost the highest bliss of human-kind, / When to thy haunts two kindred spirits flee" ("O Solitude, if I must with thee dwell," 12–14). Whereas Keats's kindred spirits are left fleeing into the grove of solitude, to engage in "sweet converse of an innocent mind" (10), Millay's lovers "flee forever" from the carnal pasture they have desanctified. Keats's gentle sensualism of anticipation becomes in Millay the disheartening aftermath of consummation.

The most resounding echo in Millay's "Not with Libations" is to Keats's sonnet on the sonnet, "If by Dull Rhymes Our English Must Be Chained." As in "Nuns Fret Not," in Keats's self-reflexive sonnet the poet effects the cure his poem complains of:

> If by dull rhymes our English must be chained,
> And, like Andromeda, the Sonnet sweet
> Fettered, in spite of pained loveliness,
> Let us find out, if we must be constrained,
> Sandals more interwoven and complete
> To fit the naked foot of Poesy:
> Let us inspect the lyre, and weigh the stress
> Of every chord, and see what may be gained
> By ear industrious and attention meet;
> Misers of sound and syllable, no less
> Than Midas of his coinage, let us be
> Jealous of dead leaves in the bay wreath crown;

So, if we may not let the Muse be free,
She will be bound with garlands of her own.

Like the "Ode to Psyche" and "Not with Libations," this sonnet adapts and loosens the instruments of tribute to a deity who is ultimately the muse. In contrast to the trope of the sonnet as a binding place—a scanty plot, writer's colony for one—the sonnet here is explicitly figured as a bound woman, the muse as Andromeda, with the poet as Perseus to the rescue. But rather than free the damsel in distress, this hero simply makes her chains less chafing. It is the fettering, the rules and rhymes and restrictions, that make the sonnet "sweet," for she is sweetest not when she is free but when she is "sweet / Fettered."[21] The intricacies of the sonnet form guarantee that in some measure the poet "must be constrained" in writing it; the poet's task is to make that multiple manacling—of poet to set pattern, of each line handcuffed to its rhyming partner—less constricting, less strictly ornamental and thereby more graceful.[22] The "dull rhymes" of the English sonnet as Keats inherited it are "more interwoven" in this poem's muted, complex rhyme scheme, a double liberation in that it led Keats to develop the pattern of his ode stanzas.[23]

Poetic form itself is the sea-monster that has chained Andromeda to the rock of dull rhyme and stony, unyielding traditions. The poet does not release her, but reweaves her chains, turning them into honoring garlands. The poetic tradition he works in itself has tightened the strands from which Keats is to release her by binding her with new ones, with the assurance that then "She will be bound with garlands of her own." The trick is to make Andromeda her own sea-monster, to craft a chain for her so cleverly natural that she can believe she has woven it herself as an adornment. In this sonnet Keats has woven a very powerful myth of poetic convention as a prison into which poetry willingly dooms itself, and part of its power derives from the identification of a constricting form with a willingly bound woman.

What are we to make of the echoes from Keats's sonnet of gentle shackling that resound in Millay's sonnet of unbridled eros? What in particular are echoes from a man's sonnet about the sonnet as bound woman doing in a woman's sonnet about the (perhaps enslaving) price of throwing off the conventional shackles of love between men and women? Keats promises Andromeda that she will be "bound with garlands of her own," while Millay's improper modern lovers, celebrating Love in their own reckless way, "fettered him with garlands of our own."[24] They impose their own shackles on Love, whereas Keats works to impose no shackles on the sonnet from outside poetry herself. Millay's lovers reject the miserly care marking Keats's project for the sonnet. In their profligacy they "spread a banquet in [Love's] frugal house"; they reinterpret the traditional cestus and myrtle of restrained love as celebratory garlands, binding their brows as a mark of erotic victory with the cinctures designed to bind the waist as a mark of purity in love.

In both sonnets, then, the iconography of celebratory, erotic, and poetic garlanding is playfully unraveled and rewoven into a new pattern. Millay's "grove without a name" should perhaps be named the grove of the Romantic poetics of the sonnet, a lightly constraining enclosure which Millay turns into a bower of irreverent excess. Just as traditionally the woman poet is denied the kind of freedom that may drive the male poet into the retreat of the sonnet's boundaries, so neither can she be given the responsibility of a poetic Perseus to free the muse from her formal strictures, since she is supposed herself to be the muse. Even if a poet wishes to bind her with "garlands of her own" they will be the garlands he has experimentally determined are proper to her, garlands of his own after all. Millay does not take up Keats's call to reshuffle the sonnet's pattern of rhyming, knowing that no rearrangement can make the form more "natural." Poetic forms and genres are not natural but ideological. Andromeda's unfelt, self-willed fetters can figure a perfect marriage (of man and woman, form and subject) or a perfectly crippling ideology. Looking at Keats through the lens of Millay, we can begin to see Andromeda as torn between having to stand for a poetic form herself or for a free spirit that the form holds chained. For a woman writing poetry in the years between the wars, the brittleness of oaths and the shaky fiction of new sexual freedom for women made the sonnet an apt form in which to scrutinize the inherited stances of men toward women and poets toward their muses. By identifying the sonnet's scanty plot of ground with an erotic grove of excess, turning the chastity belt of poetic form into a token of sexual indulgence, Millay invades the sanctuary of male poetic control with her unsettling formalism in the service of freedom, a freedom that can, as the lovers learn in "Not with Libations," turn into another kind of entrapment.

In "Not with Libations," as in "I Will Put Chaos into Fourteen Lines," Millay addresses the Romantic myths of the sonnet as liberating prison and pleasing fetters, the figurations governing Wordsworth's "Nuns Fret Not" and Keats's "If by Dull Rhymes." Her sonnets reshape those myths with the revisionary force of a woman poet who, however rearguard in the phalanx of modernism, recognizes that she has inherited a genre laden with figurations exclusive to a male poetic authority, and who knows that her adaptations of that genre must engage those very myths and figurations that would bar her from the ranks of legitimate practitioners of the sonnet. While more work on Millay along these lines is not likely to result in the elevation of her to the status of a major twentieth-century poet, it should lead to a more searching understanding of why we judge her to be minor, and to our estimate in general of poets in the modernist period who continued to write in traditional forms. Current feminist work on Millay suggests that in her use of poetic forms "the wish for freedom is always qualified by the sense of restriction": such an estimate, I believe, even when intended as evidence of

Millay's virtuosity, echoes older dismissals of Millay on the grounds that she moodily concedes to poetic forms or, crippled by emotional turmoil, desperately leans on them, because it tends to see the poet as an unwitting victim of these two desires rather than as working consciously in light of the fact that the tradition itself is constantly troping on just this very debate. I have only suggested how a few of Millay's most effective sonnets engage in and reflect upon the struggle between poet and form as to which shall be master. Such engagement is a sign not only that Millay has mastered these inherited forms, but also that she has taken into account the full implications for the woman poet of the figure of poetic "mastery."

Notes

1. For example, there is no work on Millay in the new collection edited by Diane Wood Middlebrook and Marilyn Yalom, *Coming to Light: American Women Poets in the Twentieth Century* (Ann Arbor: Univ. of Michigan Press, 1985).

2. Jean Gould, *The Poet and Her Book: A Biography of Edna St. Vincent Millay* (New York: Dodd, Mead, 1969), p. 42.

3. Jane Stanbrough, "Edna St. Vincent Millay and the Language of Vulnerability," in Sandra Gilbert and Susan Gubar, eds., *Shakespeare's Sisters: Feminist Essays on Women Poets* (Bloomington: Indiana Univ. Press, 1979), p. 198.

4. Judith Farr, "Elinor Wylie, Edna St. Vincent Millay, and the Elizabethan Sonnet Tradition," in Maynard Mack and George deForest Lord, eds., *Poetic Traditions of the English Renaissance* (New Haven: Yale Univ. Press, 1982), p. 297.

In this context, Farr's mention of Millay's "Petrarchan conventions" should invite some reflection. We cannot speak of a woman's sonnet as we do of a Shakespearean or Petrarchan or Wordsworthean sonnet; and yet the difficulty women writers may have in writing sonnets that respond to their poetic needs is at least nominally suggested in the very fact that we label sonnets after the achievements of the great male practitioners of the form. We commonly speak of one poet writing in the sonnet form named for another: we say that Keats or Frost writes Miltonic sonnets, or that Robinson or Rossetti writes Petrarchan sonnets. Such formulations may raise complicated questions of how American poets adopt English modes, or how modern poets adapt Romantic or Renaissance forms. But we are faced with all those issues and then a vexing number of others when we speak of Christina Rossetti writing Petrarchan sonnets or Edna St. Vincent Millay writing Shakespearean sonnets. The unthinking ease with which we label the generic choices of female poets after the poetic patterns established by male poets may suggest that we are not sufficiently accustomed to thinking of lyric genres in terms of gender. Such labels blind us to the possibility that purely formal criteria for lyric genres such as the sonnet may mask other gender-related criteria. But the genre, too, makes choices. A woman poet, like any poet, will choose to write sonnets for a range of varied reasons, but some of those reasons will necessarily spring from the fact that the tradition of sonnet writing is the work of men.

5. *The Poetical Works of William Wordsworth*. E. de Selincourt and Helen Darbishire, eds. (Oxford: Oxford Univ. Press. 1946), III, I.

6. If the sonnet form is thus loosely figured in the foxglove bells, the form itself is a readily available, female space, open to the male's visitation whenever he chooses to stop soaring for a while. As we shall see, Keats too compares the sonnet to a woman, the bound Andromeda. Andromeda, immobile, fettered emblem of the sonnet, is in no position to write

one. The woman poet is thus not merely confined to a scanty plot of ground, but she is one herself; poetic form is figured as a receptive female space. If she is herself a sonnet, how can she be expected to write one?

7. From *The Recluse*, cited in *The Oxford Anthology of English Literature*, ed. Harold Bloom and Lionel Trilling (New York: Oxford Univ. Press, 1973), p. 143.

8. Sandra Gilbert and Susan Gubar, *The Madwoman in the Attic: The Woman Writer and the Nineteenth-Century Literary Imagination* (New Haven: Yale Univ. Press, 1979), p. 68. See Lawrence Lipking, *The Life of the Poet: Beginning and Ending Poetic Careers* (Chicago: Univ. of Chicago Press, 1981), pp. 77–79, for a discussion of the model of the Virgilian career. For Lipking, Keats's sonnet "On First Looking into Chapman's Homer" passes muster as an initiation poem heralding a poet's bursting into full ambition, but Lipking does not consider what it might mean for redefinitions of that genre that a sonnet takes on this power of declaring poetic vocation.

9. *The Letters of William and Dorothy Wordsworth: The Later Years*, ed. Ernest de Selincourt (Oxford: Oxford Univ. Press, 1939), II, 653. Wordsworth's estimate of the Miltonic sonnet is perpetuated and canonized in the "Sonnet" article by Lawrence J. Zillman in the *Princeton Encyclopedia of Poetry and Poetics*: "It remained for Milton . . . to give a greater unity to the form by frequently permitting octave to run into sestet," enl. ed., ed. Alex Preminger (Princeton: Princeton Univ. Press, 1974), p. 783.

10. John Hollander, *Vision and Resonance: Two Senses of Poetic Form* (New York: Oxford Univ. Press, 1975), p. 199. For extended discussions of the resources of enjambment, see in the same volume, " 'Sense Variously Drawn Out': On English Enjambment," pp. 91–116, and the somewhat dissenting view in Justus George Lawler, *Celestial Pantomime: Poetic Structures of Transcendence* (New Haven: Yale Univ. Press, 1979), pp. 73–103. In his insistence that "the uses to which [enjambments] are put are as divergent as any verbal acts" in "The Metrical Frame" (p. 146), Hollander is more concerned than is Lawler with how formal and generic frames shape the effects and functions of run-on lines in poetry. Countering what he calls Hollander's "even-handed relativism," Lawler finds "one of the most salient and one of the most recurrent uses" of enjambment to be for "that situation in which, after repeated frustration, the human subject suddenly experiences the overcoming of limitations and an expansion into something beyond those limits," pp. 73–74. Many of Lawler's examples come from poems describing moments of sexual release or consummation (pp. 74–85). Lawler's desire to see "endstopped lines equated with imprisonment and delimitation, and enjambment equated with transcendence and union" (p. 90) almost reverses my sense of Millay's use of the device in the sonnets I discuss: more important, I would stress, following Hollander, that enjambment has significance in any poem as a "function of role of that device in the total poetic style" (*Vision and Resonance*, p. 110), including the matrix of allusions and the expectations established by genre.

11. Elizabeth P. Perlmutter. "A Doll's Heart: The Girl in the Poetry of Edna St. Vincent Millay and Louise Bogan." *Twentieth Century Literature*, 23 (1977), 158. See also Donald Barlow Stauffer, *A Short History of American Poetry* (New York: Dutton, 1974), p. 234.

12. Cited in Hyatt Waggoner, *American Poets from the Puritans to the Present* (Boston: Houghton, 1968), p. 464.

13. Edna St. Vincent Millay, *Mine the Harvest* (New York: Harper, 1954), p. 130.

14. Norman A. Brittin, *Edna St. Vincent Millay*, revised ed. (Boston: Twayne, 1982), p. 115, claims that the figure of Chaos in this poem is "based on the folk-motif of the shape-changer."

15. For example, it is the poet who guarantees that "ape," the verb suggesting the imitative beastliness of Chaos, although it does not bring the sentence to a close, will lock into the sonnet's rhyming grid and find its echoes in "pious rape" and finally in "shape," the force that undoes its action.

16. Millay's interest in the shifting misalliance between the unit of the poetic line and the completion of grammatical clauses and sentences is evidenced in the way she occasionally

repeats a clause that fills or closes a line early in a sonnet with a recurrence of it where it is made to straddle two lines. We find this device in one of her best-known sonnets, where the opening line, "Euclid alone has looked on beauty bare" is relineated in lines 11–12 as "Euclid alone / Has looked on beauty bare." In an early sonnet she puts in the same line a phrase standing complete in the line and almost the same phrase enjambed across two lines: "I should not cry aloud—I could not cry / Aloud, or wring my hands . . ." ("If I should learn, in some quite casual way" from *Renascence*.)

17.   *Collected Sonnets of Edna St. Vincent Millay* (New York: Harper, 1941) p. 14. All citations to Millay's sonnets are from this edition, unless otherwise noted.

18.   "Not with Libations" seems to have been part of the series of sonnets Millay exchanged with poet Arthur Davison Ficke. Ficke sent his *Sonnet of a Portrait Painter* (1914) to Millay "early in their correspondence," according to Gould, *The Poet and Her Book*, p. 205. The exchange of sonnets between them took place mostly in 1918; his half of the dialogue is collected in the sequence "Beauty in Exile." Certainly part of Millay's goal is to reclaim the sonnet sequence for the voice of the woman. But such a project invites more hazards than I have time to focus on here. See Dorothy Mermin, "The Female Poet and the Embarrassed Reader: Elizabeth Barrett Browning's *Sonnets from the Portuguese*," *ELH*, 248 (1918), 351–67, esp. p. 352: "Traditionally in English love poetry the man loves and speaks, the woman is devoted and silent. . . . In so far as the [female] speaker presents herself as the beloved, however, she transfers the verbal self-assertion and many of the attributes which in poems traditionally belong to the subject of desire, to desire's normally silent and mysterious object. The result is a devaluation of the erotic object that casts the whole amorous and poetical enterprise in doubt."

19.   Information about Millay's literary influences remains sketchy. For admission to Vassar Millay sent a "list of authors with whom she was 'very well acquainted,' " among them "Shakespeare, Tennyson, Milton, and Wordsworth," according to Brittin, *Edna St. Vincent Millay*, p. 4. Gould, *The Poet and Her Book*, pp. 260–62, reports that Millay drafted a "lengthy academic" preface for her 1941 *Collected Sonnets*, "involving the mechanics and history of the sonnet form, in the course of which she pointed to John Milton's glaring faults when he took liberties with the form." When at the urging of Arthur Davison Ficke she wrote instead a more simple autobiographical introduction, she omitted "parts of the preface in which she said that it was his [Ficke's] sonnets and Meredith's that had been the origin of her own use of the sonnet."

Several of the sonnets into which the characters' conversations array themselves in Millay's *Conversation at Midnight* include explicit allusions to the major sonnet traditions with which Millay's relation is most vexed. In the midst of a discussion about love, two characters share a sonnet to bicker about the attribution of one of the most famous lines in any sonnet:

> "It's true, the lilies are beginning to fester a bit,"
> Ricardo said: "who wrote that awful line?"
> "Why . . . it was Andrew Marvell, wasn't it?"
> Said Merton doubtfully. "Your guess is as good as mine,"
> Threw in Pygmalion . . . (p. 53)

During a political discussion, a monologue in sonnet form by the party's conservative host begins on a Wordsworthean note:

> "Not that the world is so much with us," Merton
> Remarked, "but such a world! It seems to me
> It's getting noisier every day; I'm certain
> 'Tis more uncivil . . ."(p. 64)

20.   All quotations from Keats are from *John Keats: The Complete Poems*, 2nd ed., John Barnard, ed. (Harmondsworth: Penguin, 1976).

21.   The "sweet" works both ways, and this Miltonic enjambment at the end of the second line, balancing "sweet" between the two words that surround it, links Keats with Milton, among other predecessors from whose grip he claims to release the sonnet, but that link reinforces our sense that Keats is not really at liberty to release her at all. She is too tightly bound in the garlands of tradition.

22.   See Hollander, *Vision and Resonance*, p. 119.

23.   See Barnard, *John Keats: The Complete Poems*, p. 645. In this innovative rhyme scheme, no rhyming pair of lines has less than two intervening lines until we reach the final quatrain, a pattern of delay in rhyming which approximates to the ear the muted music of a blank-verse paragraph. This effect is reinforced by the sonnet's single rounded period, gracing the tight form with the unity and freedom Wordsworth sought in the Miltonic model.

24.   That the resounding, solid last line of Keats's sonnet finds its corresponding echo not at the end of Millay's sonnet but at its midpoint may suggest that Millay is exploring what happens when you take up where Keats left off. For another Millay sonnet that takes up where a Keats poem leaves off, see "Sonnet in Dialectic" from *Mine the Harvest*, which begins "And is indeed truth beauty?" It often seems that when Millay alludes in her sonnets to sonnets by others, she recalls not simply the phrases or lines, but where those echoed lines fit in the architecture of the source sonnet and in her own, and designedly locates them in a different part of the structure. Thus the perhaps too openly derivative image of

> Thus in the winter stands the lonely tree,
> Nor knows what birds have vanished one by one,
> Yet knows its boughs more silent than before,

in "What Lips My Lips Have Kissed" from *The Harp-Weaver* recalls "those boughs which shake against the cold, / Bare, ruined choirs, where late the sweet birds sang" of Shakespeare's Sonnet 73. But the metaphor that opens Shakespeare's sonnet is switched to open the sestet in Millay's sonnet. Sonnet 36 from Millay's sequence "Epitaph for the Race of Man" from *Wine from These Grapes* begins, "His heatless room the watcher of the stars / Nightly inhabits when the night is clear," an allusion to the "watcher of the skies" that initiates the sestet of Keats's "On First Looking into Chapman's Homer." Likewise the first line of "Nuns Fret Not" is echoed in the opening line of the sestet of "When I too long have looked upon your face."

The Unwarranted Discourse:
Sentimental Community, Modernist Women,
and the Case of Millay

Suzanne Clark

"It is a dangerous lot, that of the charming, romantic public poet, especially if it falls to a woman." Louise Bogan, "Edna Millay (1939)"

Women writers in the age of modernism discovered a cruel paradox: the more successfully they wrote, both to appeal to a feminized community of readers and to help readers feel part of the literary community, the less they could be considered serious writers. The more clearly they appealed to the shared feelings of a popular community, the more they risked being labeled "sentimental," or merely popular. In the years of the great modernists— Eliot, Pound, Stevens, H. D., Williams—the project of poetry was to turn away from a mass culture, to establish a distance between literature and all other forms of writing. But, as Sandra Gilbert suggests,[1] women writers may have had a different task than men writers in the early twentieth century, involving not alienation from history but the building of agreement, not the tragic vision but the dialogue of human exchange. Furthermore, as Sherry O'Donnell taught me to see, women have long made poetry part of their community-building practice.[2] Embedded in the processes of middle-class history, women's writing has looked different. In the first decades of this century, what was recognizably women's writing was not at all like the new work of writers like Eliot or Stevens. But it was a difference that had no warrant in the project of modernism. This was not a matter of specific cases. Modernist poetics excluded female poets at the level of theory.

Feminist critics today write in a moment of critical history which seems to value difference and marginality and even feminist criticism itself, but our efforts may have some troublesome affinities with the problems of women writers in the heyday of modernist poetry—writers like H. D., Louise Bogan, and even Marianne Moore, as well as the

From *Genre* 20 (Summer 1987): 133–52. Copyright © 1987 The University of Oklahoma. Reprinted by permission. Excerpt from John Crowe Ransom's essay "The Poet as Woman" first printed in *Southern Review* 2 (Spring, 1937): 784. Used by permission of Helen Ransom Foreman, literary executor.

woman Harriet Monroe hailed as the Sappho of our times, Edna St. Vincent Millay. We should not accept without careful distinction modernist claims about the connection of revolution and the new word, the revolution of language. At a moment when the culture produces the separation of disciplines and the commodification of value, alienation is not novel. Then, as Baudrillard wants to assert: "He is truly a revolutionary who speaks of the world as non-separated."[3]

Modernism offers its own forms of repression: where will we draw the boundaries of literariness, the definitions of "interesting" texts? Sentimentality has no warrant in the literary history of modernism; whatever is called sentimental has been excluded from the serious, the literary, the tough, the interesting. And the sentimental in the annals of twentieth century criticism turns out to have an uncanny relationship to writing by women. The seemingly ahistorical critical term "sentimental" represses its historicity, its rejection of a literary history dominated by women. In the following examination of women's situation in literary modernism, I will suggest that we must face the question of the sentimental and its relationship to the history of writing by women. What is at issue, I will argue, in the question of the sentimental is the relationship of literary daughter to literary mother—the very possibility of a female tradition.

I

In the twentieth century, the horror of the "sentimental" helps define the good male poet much as the prostitute once defined the good woman. When a female literary history arises out of the generations of women writers, it appears as a reviled past: the anxiety of influence appears as the threat of the Mother (nature, love, tongue, muse), powerful in several guises. If the strong male poet may be said to rewrite his literary fathers in a Bloomian act of "misprision," what of the poet's literary mothers? He—and the disguised she—rejects the female literary ancestors altogether, making literary history the legends of warring kings, not a genealogy. Like the principle of the sentimental, the mother is constructed as powerful and dominant, but only in the very gesture of repudiation required for males to define themselves as "different." A woman poet is a contradiction in this history. So, perhaps, is a woman critic. A woman poet is *created by* this history as a poet-within-history, powerful, and so not really literary. Women's power is separated from poetry, domesticated.[4]

Maturity for modernist critics like John Crowe Ransom as for Freud involved a separation from the sentimental (m)Other. Therefore when Ransom evaluated the work of Edna St. Vincent Millay, he found her immature, all too womanly, "fixed in her famous attitudes." The story of the male mind which he rehearses in an essay on Millay seems to him so obvious he needs no argument. It has for him become a matter of biology, not culture or history.

Ransom writes:

> The minds of man and woman grow apart, and how shall we express their differentiation? In this way, I think: man, at best, is an intellectualized woman. Or, man distinguishes himself from woman by intellect, but it should be well feminized. He knows he should not abandon sensibility and tenderness, though perhaps he has generally done so, but now that he is so far removed from the world of the simple senses, he does not like to impeach his own integrity and leave his business in order to recover it; going back, as he is often directed, to first objects, the true and tried, like the moon, or the grass, or the dead girl. He would much prefer if it is possible to find poetry in his study, or even in his office, and not have to sit under the syringa bush. Sensibility and tenderness might qualify the general content of his mind, if he but knew the technique, however "mental" or self-constructed some of that content looks. But his problem does not arise for a woman. Less pliant, safer, as a biological organism, she remains fixed in her famous attitudes, and is indifferent to intellectuality. I mean, of course, comparatively indifferent; more so than a man. Miss Millay is rarely and barely very intellectual, and I think everybody knows it. (784)

At the same time that Ransom would seem to deny that a woman could be anything more than "indifferent to intellectuality," he maintains that a man at his best is "an intellectualized woman." The woman, precisely, is indifferent, incapable of entering into the play of differences. Ransom's interests in the feminine seem the reverse of the post-modernist view. In fact, however, they have disturbing resemblances to the interests of Derrida, for example, or Lyotard. To the extent that Postmodernism takes up the modernist move, it defines "difference" as what is interesting. In order to qualify for the avant-garde, the woman must be defined as something new, marginal, other, subversive—different. The woman must not be moralizing and sentimental.

My research on the sentimental has grown out of this historical situation governing our reading as well as our writing. The sentimental, we can probably all agree, is what I call an "unwarranted discourse." Recent work on the sentimental novel, notably Tompkins' *Sensational Designs*, has argued strongly for the literary importance of the genre. Nevertheless, to call writing "sentimental" is still to criticize it severely—whether the writing is rhetorical or literary, novel or poetry. But the sentimental is a tradition, a set of conventions and writing practices, and not just a failure to do something else. The very word "sentimental" came into being in eighteenth-century England, together with the sentimental novel, as a term of approval. It is connected to the pathetic appeal—the appeal to emotions, especially pity, as a means of persuasion.

In his *Philosophy of Rhetoric*, first published in 1776, George Campbell endorses the sentimental at the same time that he recognizes its connection to ideology, to "the moral powers of the mind." According to Campbell, the sentimental "occupies, so to speak, the middle place between the pathetic and that which is addressed to the imagination, and partakes of both, adding to the warmth of the former the grace and attractions of the latter." Campbell, like Hugh Blair, assumes the importance of appeals to passion. The pathetic works best, he says, "by some secret, sudden, and inexplicable association, awakening all the tenderest emotions of the heart . . . it will not permit the hearers even a moment's leisure for making the comparison, but as it were by some magical spell, hurries them, ere they are aware, into love, pity, grief, terror." Campbell was the dominant rhetorical text for much of the nineteenth century in America. It was not so bad to be sentimental then. What has happened to the once-positive connotation of the word? Campbell joined two things together that were firmly separated by modernism: he considered poetics to be a "particular mode" of rhetoric, and he considered both reason and passion to be legitimate parts of persuasion. A quick glance at the evening news will confirm our guess that the sentimental has not vanished—that it has pride of place, indeed, in journalism—a persuasive appeal in a genre supposed to be without persuasion. But when we apply the word "sentimental" to a piece of writing, we usually mean something pejorative. In his introduction to A Lover's Discourse, Roland Barthes writes: "Discredited by modern opinion, love's sentimentality must be assumed by the amorous subject as a powerful transgression which leaves him alone and exposed: by a reversal of values, then, it is this sentimentality which today constitutes love's obscenity." Episodes of love, like eruptions of the imaginary, appear in the modern, rational conversation, the discourse of our times, as something to be gotten over, grown out of, unwarranted. As Foucault has pointed out, it is sex, not love, which has been connected to freedom, subversion, and critical discourses in our time (5). The appeal to feeling has become increasingly suspect, more distant from the rational.

Paradoxically, in an age of elite poetry such as modernism, the poet who writes within conventions shared by bourgeois culture practices a version of difference. Marginality then is a version of the obscurity-in-plain-view women know so well. For women have long been writing in a well-populated solitude, "warranted," as Barthes says, "by no one." And modernist women poets were read with an eye to the gap between popular culture and serious writing. Tompkins has pointed this out in her work on Stowe. The sentimental tradition of women writers is connected to women's power—but also collides with modernist expectations. Ann Douglas, arguing for the "feminization" of American culture, associated this sentimental with the hegemony of consumer culture. But recently critics including Radway, Modleski, and Rabine have taught us to look again at the possibilities of popular fiction by women, arguing in various ways that the love story has been read too narrowly.[5] The Lover's Discourse suggests a stronger adversity: if sentiment is the modern "obscene," has it not suffered the oppression of censorship and disapproval once arrayed against sexual obscenity?

In spite of their dramatic presence at the birth of modernism, the women writers of the moment did not establish an authoritative place for women in modernist literature. There were many women, from Sara Teasdale to Gertrude Stein to Kay Boyle, appearing in modernist magazines and anthologies, and women were powerful editors too: Harriet Monroe of *Poetry*, Margaret Anderson and Jane Heap of *The Little Review*, H. D. of *The Egoist*, Marianne Moore of *The Dial*. Yet a list of names resists our collecting and abstracting: the case of Sara Teasdale seems quite unlike that of Gertrude Stein; Edna St. Vincent Millay and Marianne Moore seem to have little in common even if we wish to say both practice versions of subversion—or compliance. No sense of a women's tradition emerges. The powerful old domestic tradition is denied.

The fact is that for many woman writers in the twenties, poets and novelists alike, the woman's tradition was all too coherent. Kay Boyle, whose stories are filled with female heroines, refuses to this day to identify herself as a woman writer and rejects feminist criticism. Like Millay, she early established a reputation for independence of spirit. Boyle has characterized herself as "a dangerous 'radical' disguised as a perfect lady" (Spanier Illustration 32). She seems, that is, to want to keep her credentials as a revolutionary modernist—but she also seems to believe that revolution has a problematic relationship to the community of women.[6]

Louise Bogan, writing both as poet and critic, marked her love poetry with the bitter loss of authority, of the very warrant for her subject: woman, love, the lyric. Adopting modernist attitudes, she wrote critically of the sentimental past: "Women, it is true, contributed in large measure to the general leveling, dilution, and sentimentalization of verse, as well as of prose, during the nineteenth century" (*Achievement* 20). At the same time she argued that "the wave of poetic intensity which wavers and fades out and often completely fails in poetry written by men, on the feminine side moves on unbroken" (*Achievement* 19). The scorn of Bogan's critical modernism seems more harshly directed against her own work (and the volume of what she accepted is slender) than against the poetry she reviewed as critic for *The New Yorker* for so many years.

Perhaps this reflexivity itself, this self-wounding, has to do with the "feminine" in her work. She understood that the woman's place as imaginary object of the lyric (stopped, still) became terrible, "dreadful," Medusa-like, if fixed as the mirror image of the self. Her poetry rejected this imaginary. Bogan seemed at once to cite the rejected tradition and to inscribe the feminine into language as estrangement. On the cover of *The Blue Estuaries*, Roethke approves her "scorn" of what he calls the usual lyric "caterwauling," and Adrienne Rich praises her for committing a "female sensibility" to language. Bogan both constitutes and distances an ideology that is female, situating herself within the contradiction of asserting a lover's discourse which is at the same time a forsaken language. By refusing the "caterwaul," she also accedes to male standards, male codes, male criticism. Like Marianne Moore, Bogan was severe with her own work, pruning mercilessly, and perhaps giving the critical spirit so large a scope that she curtailed her own productivity, unbalancing the relationship between the critical and the assertive. Edna St. Vincent Millay, too middle-class, too "public," may have served her as an emblem of what could go wrong.

When a woman poet like Edna St. Vincent Millay defied the laws of modesty, obscurity, and constraint to reach out for her woman readers, she earned the contempt of critics. It's risky for a writer to appeal to a community of readers that identifies her with the feminine. How in the world, we might ask, could it possibly be a daring political gesture to write "O world, I cannot hold thee close enough"? But the popular appeal was precisely what was risky. Millay had grown so hugely popular by the late 1940's that her kitchen was featured in *Ladies Home Journal* ("Polished as a sonnet . . . Light as a lyric . . . Must be the kitchen for EDNA ST. VINCENT MILLAY." Only late in the article, at the back of the magazine, did they admit that her husband was really the cook of the household.) I want to argue that the risk of shame is especially daunting when the female readership is middle-class, bourgeois, and sentimental, and when the values affirmed have to do with love and motherhood. That feminine community, however populous, is non-literary and non-authoritative by definition. Therefore what Millay risked by writing poetry of inclusion rather than of exclusion—risked and perhaps lost—was poetry itself.

In certain ways too much the daughters of that bourgeois patriarchy which generated their mythologies, the women poets who wrote and were read in the first decades of the twentieth century, were perhaps also too much the mothers of ourselves as readers. Like our mothers they served to give us the texts for the first rush of poetic feeling ("O world, I cannot hold thee close enough."), the heat of romantic rebelliousness ("I've burned my candle at both ends"), the encounter with "poetic" language ("Little faces looking up / Holding wonder like a cup"), and even the first idea of poem as "image" ("Whirl up, sea— / Whirl your pointed pines"). Women quickly became textbook poets, schools texts, and they are still there, in the books for school children from elementary through high school: Millay, Wylie, Teasdale, H. D., Moore. The critical history of these women poets, then, has been shaped by the sentimental reader—by indulgent admirers who simply endorse motherhood, country, and Edna St. Vincent Millay, but also by ambitious critics who want to be mature and interesting, who feel they have to cast off their youthful memories of poetry in order to grow up.

In the literary world defined by modernism, however, the writer who wrote for women, whose audience included "the ladies," opened herself to the most terrible critical scorn. Morton D. Zabel characterized the awfulness of what he called "Popular Support" for the arts in a "Comment" for *Poetry* in 1930. Subtitled "Cattle in the Garden," Zabel's piece makes the connection between bad taste and writing for the ladies. An example of "Popular Support" are items from the Herald-Tribune Books, where "week after week, poetry is plucked from every bush that grows by the effusive Miss Taggard, that energetic specialist in Immortality" whose "style (and incidentally her critical standards) derive largely from Queen Marie's testimonials for Pond's Facial Creams" (269). But far worse is the General Federation of Womens' Clubs' fifth annual Poetry week. Zabel quotes from Mrs. Anita Browne, Founder-Organizer: "To the rhythmic beat of humming presses that puncture the air with their poetic metre as each revolution imprints a page of this Poetry Week Magazine, it seems a happy singing, as though the presses sense the harmonies within the printed program of the Poetry Week activities. . . . The marvel of the printing press! The pillar of education; the historian of all time; the etcher of the poet . . . the Monarch: the printed Word! So these pages proclaim the fifth annual celebration of Poetry Week, in which the whole nation joins" (274). There is a terrible innocence on the part of Browne about the great distance between her aims—"happy singing," "harmonies," a poetry "in which the whole nation joins"—and the ambitions of modernist criticism for toughness and excellence. But Zabel knows, and he drives the point home: "But while Mrs. Browne and her loyal cohorts celebrate their victories, certain of us by nature more sardonic than these will probably pause to wonder . . . where meanwhile Poetry was keeping herself . . . from the uproar and ribaldry while the cattle stampeded the flowers, fruit, and vines of her no-longer sacred-and-unprofaned gardens" (276). In fact, the scorn heaped on the ladies and their sentimental taste has been so very thick one wonders what it has been at work to create. Clearly, much literature in our century has been written with the idea of refusal, of offense, of violating the readers' expectations. We have grown used to the stories of the heroic author—D. H. Lawrence, for example—who offends the public (the women guarding public morality) with his exposés of love and adultery, his ever-more-graphic representation of sexuality. Refusals like those of Eliot or Williams or Stevens are less obviously gendered. Nevertheless, their rejection of the rhetorical and poetic conventions that might help readers gain access to their work is a rejection of the mass audience and a refusal to meet readerly expectations. The teachers and the cultivated ladies who made it their practice to translate the canon of great literature for children and for the unlettered—the community-building women—were disenfranchised by the practices of modernism, which required a more academic priesthood.

This context helps us to understand the antagonistic critical reception given Edna St. Vincent Millay as she grew in popularity during the '30's and '40's. John Crowe Ransom criticized Millay for her sensibility: "Miss Millay is rarely and barely very intellectual, and I think everybody knows it" (784). Allen Tate said "Miss Millay's success with stock symbolism is precariously won; I have said that she is not an intellect but a sensibility: if she were capable of a profound analysis of her imagery, she might not use it" (335–36). And Cleanth Brooks simply picked up Ransom's theme to conclude that Millay was "immature." She failed to be a major poet because she lacked irony: "Miss Millay has not grown up" (2).

In the age of Eliot, defined by the failure of relationship and the anti-heroics of the poetic loner, Millay was writing most of all about love, and her sentimental subject was only the beginning of her crime: more than that, she was writing in a way that is easily understood, that invites the reader in, that makes community with the reader and tries to heal alienation. Millay was of course flagrantly engaged during the twenties in the Bohemian leftish lifestyle of Greenwich village, with its tenets of free love and support for the working masses. But her radical lifestyle never put off her readers the way a radical poetics might have. Millay's poetic style is founded on commonality: in this it is classic rather than modern. She may shock her audience, but she does not separate herself from them. The accessibility of her work seems from the beginning of her career more important to her readers than her Bohemian attitudes. In Millay, we see that the gestures of social revolt don't always sever ties. She can write "My candle burns at both ends" and take a flippant attitude about her lovers, but the fact that she does it in sonnet form kept her credentials as a member of the American middle-class consensus in order. The epithet "bourgeois" or "middle-class" in the mouth of a modernist critic was meant to be as devastating as the charge of sentimentality. But some continuity with the middle class was for Millay as for many other women writers a prerequisite for maintaining a woman's tradition and for creating a community with women readers.

II

In the following pages, I want to look at a couple of pieces by Millay to see how she negotiates the contradictory demands of a modernist art and the appeal to a powerful community of readers. As we talk about the larger impact of modernism and its elevation of intellect over sensibility, let us not forget Millay's popular and sweeping success as a "poetess." Her sentimental readers were in the majority, and they recognized her immediately. I found an early piece on Millay in a 1922 volume called *Flames of Faith*, written by William Stidger, a New York evangelist also known as "Wild Bill" Stidger. He is responding to Millay's sentimental rhetoric, which he reads as an expression of feeling: "Whose heart will not be won by these lines," he asks by way of introduction to Millay's little poem, "Tavern" (48). A poem about a tavern may not seem a likely topic for the sentimental reader, but this poem is about a form of congeniality that recalls the poet's mother. The tradition may go all the way back to matrilineal Celtic materials; in any event it takes advantage of the fairy tale tradition which identifies "grey eyes" with the "old people." It goes like this:

> I'll keep a little tavern
>   Below the high hill's crest,
> Wherein all grey-eyed people
>   May set them down and rest.
>
> There shall be plates a-plenty,
>   And mugs to melt the chill
> Of all the grey-eyed people
>   Who happen up the hill.
>
> There sound will sleep the traveller,
>   And dream his journey's end,
> But I will rouse at midnight
>   The falling fire to tend.
>
> Aye, 'tis a curious fancy—
>   But all the good I know
> Was taught me out of two grey eyes
>   A long time ago. (35)

Stidger goes on to say, after quoting as well from "God's World" ("O World, I cannot hold thee close enough!") and "Renascence" ("The soul can split the sky in two, / And let the face of God shine through!") that "her first message was one of a great, groping sense of suffering. So men and women sing who have lost some loved one" (49).

The loss, one might argue, is a loss of female community itself, although the community of suffering and of loss is not simply female. It is the loss of a hearth which is tended. By Millay's time, the codes of pathetic appeals, together with the literary inheritance from sentimental narratives which had been associated with female writing, had been more or less firmly rejected by literary modernists. Millay's "Tavern" is about a love, but the beloved of the "grey eyes" is more motherly than romantic, and the speaker's response to loss is to found a hospitable retreat, not to withdraw from sociability.

What we have in Millay is in part at least a writing which unites rhetoric and poetics, appeals to conventional ideas, and appeals to feeling. Speaking from a place of authority which is female, Millay refuses the separation of the subject from social convention. Her work is at once personal and conventional. It's easy enough to call it sentimental. Modernism has given us an ideal of an impersonal, serious art, a poetics severely separated from rhetoric. This modernist poetics is indeed at odds with Millay's poetic practices, as with any text which fails to sufficiently separate itself from the personal or from the drama of its performance. Modernism assumes an estrangement between the poem and the reader—difference, not familiarity. Exile, not community.

The marginal subject has difficulty participating in the modernist revolution of poetic language. As we see with Millay, the marginal speaker must do something familiar. Difference is different if you're in danger of never being listened to in the first place. Millay's poetry may be read rhetorically, as an argument that she is to be considered a real poet. Paradoxically, the very fact that this persuasive appeal is going on keeps the poetry from being read as poetry, as a modernist text. Because she is accessible to readers, she is "marginal" only in a special sense, though it is a sense that she cared about very much. Millay is only as marginal as all the readers of *Vanity Fair* and *Ladies Home Journal*, and all the high school students who have put her poems to memory, and the former students who can recite them still, generations later. Because this powerful community, influenced by women as readers (and teachers), is invisible to literary criticism, it does indeed inflict on Millay a literary marginality. To this day she seems not quite interesting, not really subversive.

In spite of the reputation for rebellious marginality she acquired by her penchant for dramatic gesture, then, Millay wrote poetry which appears to do the opposite of demonstrating female difference. Far from subverting the masculine tradition by using poetic conventions in new ways, in the very age of "make it new," Millay was writing sonnets. She subverts male modernism by appropriating conventional male poetics from a more classic past, speaking a colonized discourse.

Does Millay's rhetoric betray feminine discourse, then? More popular and more widely read to this day than Pound or Williams, Millay disappears into the crowd. She writes within conventions so much a part of the dominant culture that she is easily assimilated by it. Millay's poetry celebrates the failure of independence even in its defiance, seeming to advocate a return to the domain of the natural, the simple, the pastoral order—to the myth which joins Christian sacrifice to nature in the figure of the mother. Thus Millay uses the rhetoric of sentiment on behalf of aspirations admittedly bourgeois, to a kind of power women were already used to claiming in the early years of this century—a power over human feelings and community which, in fact, modernist male writers rejected as they rejected all rhetorical and political ambitions for poetry. Readers could recognize immediately that she speaks as a poet in favor of interests long supported by the middle class—interests of importance to women because they had been established through the whole of the nineteenth century by female writers as the best means for women to exercise power, as Tompkins' work on *Uncle Tom's Cabin* demonstrates. The alienation which was modernism was bound to reject Millay, as it rejected in a larger sense the claims of women and sentimentalism to power and value.

Millay confronts the modernist tradition over the influential poetry of

Charles Baudelaire, whose *Flowers of Evil* she helped to translate. If we look at how Millay reads Baudelaire, a regular pattern of choices emerges which I think can be called sentimental, and which may also be characteristic of writing which is very concerned with audience identification. The fact that she understood herself as a woman intellectual rather than as an "intellectualized woman" may have shaped her translation, for she is very much concerned with creating communal understanding rather than an aesthetic object. We can usefully contrast her translation with a recent one by Richard Howard which is very different in effect, a bit closer to the literal, and more distant in form.

Here is the original poem:

> Sous les ifs noirs qui les abritent
> Les hiboux se tiennent rangés,
> Ainsi que des dieux étrangers,
> Dardant leur oeil rouge. Ils meditent.
>
> Sans remuer ils se tiendront
> Jusqu'à l'heure melancolique
> Ou, poussant le soleil oblique,
> Les ténèbres s'etabliront.
>
> Leur attitude au sage enseigne
> Qu'il faut en ce monde qu'il craigne
> Le tumulte et le mouvement;
>
> L'homme ivre d'une ombre qui passe
> Porte toujours le châtiment
> D'avoir voulu changer de place.
>
> (140)

Richard Howard's translation:

> Under black yews that protect them
>   the owls perch in a row
> like alien gods whose red eyes
>   glitter. They meditate.
>
> Petrified, they will perch there till
>   the melancholy hour
> when the slanting sun is ousted,
>   and darkness settles down.
>
> From their posture, the wise
> Learn to shun, in this world at least,
>   motion and commotion;

> Impassioned by passing shadows,
>   man will always be scourged
> for trying to change his place.
>
>   (70)

Edna St. Vincent Millay's translation:

> The owls that roost in the black yew
> Along one limb in solemn state,
> And with a red eye look you
>   through,
> Are eastern gods; they meditate.
>
> No feather stirs on them, not one,
> Until that melancholy hour
> When night, supplanting the weak
>   sun,
> Resumes her interrupted power.
>
> Their attitude instructs the wise
> To shun all action, all surprise.
> Suppose there passed a lovely face,—
>
> Who even longs to follow it,
> Must feel for ever the disgrace
> Of having all but moved a bit.
>
>   (35)

There are two central contrasts between the Millay translation and the Howard translation to which I would like to call attention.

First, Millay's work demonstrates a very different relationship to form. She maintains the eight-syllable lines and the rhyme scheme, as if an attention to that structural convention would also come closer to translating the voice of Baudelaire's poem. That is, she keeps the connection to traditional forms rather than emphasize the modernity of Baudelaire's poem. Howard abandons the rhyme and interposes six-syllable lines—brief enough to threaten making the poem more slight than it is.

But the second contrast is still more startling. While Howard makes a translation that is fairly close to the literal, Millay introduces vocabulary which might be called "stock symbolism"—several words which by their combined effect, I would argue, move the poem out of the category of symbolist poetry and make it romantic—or "sentimental," if you will. Her use of the "you" in the third line sets up a speaker of the poem who has a casual, personal relationship to the reader—the opposite of the distanced, impersonal speaker of the symbolist poem, the "I" who is an "other." She over-specifies: the strange, foreign or alien gods become "eastern." Again it is, perhaps, a move to make the reader more comfortable, the kind of specifying a story-teller might invent, and it makes the poem seem to be about some familiar romantic themes. She adds a personification of night in the second stanza, surely a humanizing touch Baudelaire would not have considered. Finally, and most strikingly, she changes Baudelaire's "ombre" or shadow to "a lovely face," so that it is no longer the mysterious, multiple, undecideable reference to the object of man's passions, but specifically a reference to a love affair with a woman.

Owls, then, in Millay's version, tend to remind us of the opposition of love and reason, as of male and female. In Baudelaire's poem, the owl as text or word seems to generate something else which is mysterious, non-verbal, intoxicating, absent—the very lack pursued by desire. The female is entirely repressed. What Millay does is to re-insert the female into the text. This makes the absence or lack seem conventional, familiar. Instead of writing a new word or rupturing the language, she makes Baudelaire seem part of a known history. There are relations, connections. We all share the same story. The motive is communal, the opposite of a making strange, or defamiliarization. The poem becomes more rhetorical, less poetic. Baudelaire's poem marks difference; Millay's rewriting works against alienation. This working toward the remembrance of love and loss is, in fact, likely to be one of the very qualities that seem negative about writing we call sentimental. Baudelaire is practicing another kind of poetics, decidedly not personal, undermining convention. No maternal connections appear in the poem. Baudelaire's poem mystifies and depersonalizes the repression of the feminine.

How are we to judge Millay's translation? A contradictory response by the reader may be characteristic of the legacy of modernism. We will not recognize as legitimate or serious either the pathetic appeal to feelings, love stories, or the conventionality of images drawn from the rhetorical stockpile. Yet the magic of authority, of the mastery over literary forms, depends upon being recognized as some kind of conventional speaker, within the context of a discourse. Marginal writers have trouble with authority in their writing. Millay, marginal as a woman poet in the age of modernism, writes her own authorship into her poems as the speaker of a community-making creation, daughter of a motherly tradition. It is a stance of contradiction, including her in the readership of women as it excludes her from the critics. The very gesture of hospitality, inviting the reader to join her, inscribes the female in Millay's text, and marks her poetry as unacceptable for male modernist critics. And as literary readers we are forced to reject the female or the literary.

Millay lets us see our readerly dilemma. We can be cold and lonesome critics, or we can join in the circle where "There will be plates plenty / And mugs to melt the chill." Tough choice. Instead, I suggest, we should reopen the question of the sentimental.

III

French feminist critics, including, importantly, Julia Kristeva, have made connections between the work of the avant-garde and the question of the feminine. Though the differences between Kristeva and feminists like Cixous and Irigaray are significant, they reflect a similar hope of joining feminism and the avant-garde in a literary practice which would rupture the phallocentricity of language from within the discourse of the Western tradition. The historical reading it might receive, however, makes a difference in the kind of rupture and renewal which may be effected by women's writing. In the twenties, the question of whether to "make it new" by writing in free verse and abandoning traditional forms did not simply involve women writers in a debate about new and old *forms*. The choice of form, convention, and style had consequences that were ideological and that propelled women writers into professional impasses at all levels of their work. The impasse which remains for us to confront now has to do with the separation of literary considerations from the devaluing of women's history. Thus Earl Rovit, writing in 1980, is not helpful even though he aims to call attention to "Our Lady-Poets of the Twenties." He seems, in fact, to blame feminist criticism for their neglect: "Current evaluation has condescended egregiously to these women, grossly overrating them by sentimental standards which patronize or upbraiding them for their failures to incarnate the feministic consciousness that today's militants require as the sole token of female integrity" (72).

The phenomenon addressed by Showalter in her review article "Critical Cross-Dressing" is very "interesting" to us as women. After years of being marginal, we find marginality in style; after the pain of difference we hear difference itself valorized. Liminal, split, founded on the personal as political and so on contradiction, the female subject is because of these one-time shameful flaws now the very model of subjectivity. Feminist criticism has become the very model of criticism—for many male critics—offering, as Showalter says, "the mixture of theoretical sophistication with the sort of effective political engagement they have been calling for in their own critical spheres." But Showalter raises important questions: "Is male feminism a form of critical cross-dressing, a fashion risk of the 1980's that is both radical chic and power play? Or is it the result of a genuine shift in critical, cultural, and sexual paradigms? . . . What is the sudden cultural appeal of serious female impersonation?" What has warranted this feminist discourse, and does the warrant include the female subject? Teresa de Lauretis has asked us to remember that the story of female subjectivity is a history of contradiction; that what we mean by woman must be referred to cultural codes which mark the private body, specifying sexual identity in the flesh, as part of the public, feminine self. The marked and contradictory female subject enters history as an ongoing experience which is political. What De Lauretis would have us remember is the female experience of power.[7]

If a "fantasy of power" is the repressed content of women's writing, then we ought perhaps to look at a critical response like Ransom's for its corresponding denials. Freud limits the wishes of women to erotic longings. Ransom allows us "sensibility." Women should be interested only in feelings or love, not the intellect. But, as Barthes says, "love falls outside of *interesting* time; no historical, polemical meaning can be given to it; it is in this that it is obscene." The figures which make up the lover's discourse are not connected by plot. "Interesting" or historical time defines the love story from outside, so that the lover's discourse is made up of figures which must be recuperated by the master narrative. These figures of love—these lyric moments—appear then as episodes of the imaginary, something to be gotten over, grown out of. These figures of love in Barthes have some qualities of the Lacanian "imaginary," articulated by the master codes of history, a symbolic order, but they partake as well of the Kristevan semiotic, that motility which is before meaning. Sensibility inhabits the figure.

Jane Gallop has already looked at some of the difficulties presented by the differences between the Kristevan "semiotic" and the Lacanian "Imaginary," as well as by our dismissive stance toward the imaginary: "The symbolic is politically healthy; the imaginary is regressive. . . . Since the imaginary embodies, fleshes out the skeletal symbolic, it is possible to see the Lacanian devaluation of the imaginary as related to a hatred of the flesh, of woman and of pleasure" (*Seduction* 149). This devaluation of the imaginary in the name of history is also a refusal to recognize the historicity of the feminine, of love, of the psyche, of the sentimental. It is a refusal to recognize that these very categories are not timeless but the creations of the time-bound. Barthes, like Ransom, inhabits modernity, and so to him the master narrative of historical time appears as the relentless renewal of intellectual novelty. A modern woman poet could not be a woman poet without reaching for a tradition that would violate the unconventionality of modernism and seem politically regressive.

> I am not resigned to the shutting away of loving hearts in the hard ground.
> So it is, and so it will be, for so it has been, time out of mind:
> Into the darkness they go, the wise and the lovely. Crowned
> With lilies and with laurel they go; but I am not resigned.
> "Dirge Without Music," Edna St. Vincent Millay

Notes

1. In "Soldier's Heart," Gilbert argues that during the First World War, life on the home front came to seem fulfilling for women, who found themselves taking on responsibilities in the world and working together successfully. The men, at the same time, came to see the very home they were fighting for as alien and demanding their sacrifice.

2. In her study of "genteel codes" in the writing of women, O'Donnell shows how the poetry associated with clubs like the National League of American Pen Women and regional

poetry societies has "designs on the world," and interrelations with the codes of female domesticity. Thus, she argues, a collection like the North Dakota "Prairie Wings," disdained by literary critics, is not marginal, but rather part of what the women involved perceived as a powerful gesture in the project of civilizing society.

3.   The alienation, separation, and irony which then come to seem the mark of a writer's maturity replicate the social processes of reification. Alienation, as Baudrillard argues in *The Mirror of Production* is the imaginary of the subject of history. Taking woman as the "other" of a binary code in order to revolt against "her," modernism collapsed the multiplicity of women's writing as it reduced popular culture and nonliterary works to a single, rejected past. Obviously, mass culture did not subsume everything that was not modern, and yet it came to seem that way.

4.   The fact is that literary modernism in America has constituted itself in opposition to a non-literariness which fatally engulfs the writing woman. Modernism pretended to reject ideology by rejecting the ideology in women's writing—the sentimental, the bourgeois imaginary. Alienation meant maturity. The story of desire for our times is Oedipal—the subject gets over his imaginary attachments in order to take his place in culture as a man. The modernist move, like psychoanalysis, psychologizes and internalizes a separate, once external, historically constituted feminine domain—the domestic. Nancy Armstrong gives us an account of this domestic region, of how the logic of literary institutions came to interact with the logic of sexuality in nineteenth-century history. Modernists made the struggle to outgrow a sentimental literary past homologous with the struggle to grow up.

5.   It might be accurate to say as well that the readers of the romance have been read too narrowly. Janice Radway interviewed women who were reading popular romances and found that they were not uncritical consumers of whatever conventionality the culture inflicted on them—that, indeed, their reading was prompted by a desire to escape from the demands of daily life, and a dissatisfaction with routine. Modleski, in *Loving with a Vengeance*, argues that mass art / high art polarizations are not helpful to our inquiries about women's writing—that the gaps and difficulties in texts like gothic novels, romances, or in soap operas, are very revealing about the conflicts in culture. In her anthology of *Studies in Entertainment*, Modleski and others pursue the critical analysis of mass and popular culture. Leslie Rabine writes about the romance tradition from Tristan to the Harlequins, including works by both men and women. Her critical history shows the interaction of text and cultural, gendered context.

6.   Boyle's work also falls away from a relationship to modernism in a development which parallels that of Millay. Although the early Boyle is quite experimental with literary form, she wrote novels during World War Two which meant to address a broad public, and which were therefore called by Edmund Wilson "propaganda." Millay wrote *Make Bright the Arrows* at the beginning of the war and fell to the very hell of critical rejection for her patriotic poetics.

7.   De Lauretis writes about the danger of theory to any consideration of woman as opposed to the heterogeneity of women: the risk "of elaborating a historical-materialist theory of culture which must deny the materiality and the historicity of the subject itself, or rather the *subjects* of culture. For it is not just the "speaking subject" of Kristeva's narrowly linguistic, or language-determined perspective that is at issue, but subjects who speak and listen, write and read, make and watch films, work and play, and so forth; who are, in short, concurrently and often contradictorily engaged in a plurality of heterogeneous experiences, practices and discourses, where subjectivity and gender are constructed, anchored, or reproduced" (171–72).

Works Cited

Armstrong, Nancy. *Desire and Domestic Fiction: A Political History of the Novel*. New York: Oxford UP, 1986.

Barthes, Roland. *A Lover's Discourse*. Trans. Richard Howard. New York: Hill and Wang, 1978.

Baudelaire, Charles. *Flowers of Evil*. Trans. George Dillon and Edna St. Vincent Millay. Preface Edna St. Vincent Millay. New York: Harper & Brothers, 1936.

———. *Les Fleurs du Mal*. Trans. Richard Howard. Boston: David R. Godine, 1983.

———. *Oeuvres Completes*. Ed. Y. G. Le Dantec. Paris: Bibliotheque de La Pleiade, 1954.

Baudrillard, Jean. *The Mirror of Production*. Introd., trans. Mark Poster. St. Louis: Telos Press, 1975.

Blair, Hugh. *Lectures on Rhetoric and Belles Lettres*. To Which Are Added Copious Questions and Notes by Abraham Mills. University and College School Edition. Philadelphia: Porter and Coates, n.d.

Bogan, Louise. *Achievement in American Poetry*. Chicago: Henry Regnery Company, 1951.

———. "Edna Millay (1939)." *A Poet's Alphabet: Reflections on the Literary Art and Vocation*. Ed. Robert Phelps and Ruth Limmer. New York: McGraw-Hill, 1970.

———. *The Blue Estuaries: Poems 1923–1968*. New York: Ecco Press, 1977.

Brooks, Cleanth. "Edna Millay's Maturity." *Southwest Review* 20 (January, 1935): 1–5.

Campbell, George. *The Philosophy of Rhetoric*. New Edition. London: William Tegg and Company, 1850.

Cixous, Helene. *La Jeune née*. Paris: Union Generale d'Editions, 1973.

De Lauretis, Teresa. *Alice Doesn't: Feminism, Semiotics, Cinema*. Bloomington: Indiana UP, 1984.

Douglas, Ann. *The Feminization of American Culture*. New York: Avon, 1977.

Foucault, Michel. *The History of Sexuality. Volume I: An Introduction*. Trans. Robert Hurley. New York: Random House, 1978.

Gallop, Jane. *The Daughter's Seduction: Feminism and Psychoanalysis*. Ithaca: Cornell UP, 1982.

Gilbert, Sandra. "Soldier's Heart: Literary Men, Literary Women, and the Great War." *Signs* 8.3 (1983): 422–450.

Irigaray, Luce. *Speculum de l'autre femme*. Paris: Editions de minuit, 1974.

———. *Ce Sexe qui n'en est pas un*. Paris: Editions de minuit, 1977.

Kristeva, Julia. "La femme, ce n'est jamais ça." *New French Feminisms*. E. Elaine Marks and Isabelle de Courtivron. New York: Schocken, 1981.

———. *Desire in Language: A Semiotic Approach to Literature and Art*. Ed. Leon S. Roudiez. Trans. Alice Jardine, Thomas A. Gora, and Leon S. Roudiez. Oxford: Blackwell / New York: Columbia UP, 1980.

———. *The Kristeva Reader*. Ed. Toril Moi. New York: Columbia UP. 1986.

Millay, Edna St. Vincent. *Collected Poems*. Ed. Norma Millay. New York: Harper & Row, 1956.

Modleski, Tanya. *Loving with a Vengeance: Mass-Produced Fantasies for Women*. New York and London: Methuen, 1982.

———, ed. *Studies in Entertainment: Critical Approaches to Mass Culture*. Bloomington and Indianapolis: Indiana UP, 1986.

Moi, Toril. *Sexual / Textual Politics: Feminist Literary Theory*. London: Methuen, 1985.

Monroe, Harriet. "Comment: Edna St. Vincent Millay." *Poetry* 24 (August, 1924): 260–266.

O'Donnell, Sheryl. "Letters from Nice Girls: Genteel Codes in Women's Writings." Proceedings of the Group for Interdisciplinary Theory and Praxis, "Getting beyond the Frame." University of North Dakota, 1983.

Rabine, Leslie W. *Reading the Romantic Heroine: Text, History, Ideology.* Ann Arbor: U of Michigan P, 1985.

Radway, Janice. *Reading the Romance: Women, Patriarchy, and Popular Culture.* Chapel Hill: North Carolina UP, 1984.

Ransom, John Crowe. "The Poet as Woman." *Southern Review* 2 (Spring, 1937): 784.

Rovit, Earl. "Our Lady-Poets of the Twenties." *Southern Review* 16 (Winter, 1980): 65–85.

Showalter, Elaine. "Critical Cross-Dressing: Male Feminists and the Woman of the Year." *Raritan* (Fall, 1983): 130–49.

Spanier, Sandra Whipple. *Kay Boyle: Artist and Activist.* Carbondale and Edwardsville: Southern Illinois UP, 1986.

Stidger, William L. *Flames of Faith.* New York: The Abingdon Press, 1922.

Taber, Gladys. "Poet's Kitchen." *Ladies Home Journal* 66 (February 1949):56-57; 183, 185.

Tate, Allen. "Miss Millay's Sonnets: A Review of *Fatal Interview.*" *New Republic* (May 6, 1931): 335.

Tompkins, Jane. *Sensational Designs: The Cultural Work of American Fiction, 1790–1860.* New York: Oxford UP, 1985.

Zabel, Morton D. "Comment: Cattle in the Garden." *Poetry* 38.5 (August, 1931): 268–276.

Millay and Modernism

Gilbert Allen

In *A History of Modern Poetry*, David Perkins makes a useful distinction between High Modernism and Popular Modernism. A rebellion against the versified pieties of the genteel tradition, Popular Modernism valued directness, accessibility, novelty in subject matter, and an openness to formal experimentation. For all of their stylistic and substantive differences, Edwin Arlington Robinson, Robert Frost, Carl Sandburg, Vachel Lindsay, Edgar Lee Masters, Amy Lowell, the early H.D., and the early Ezra Pound can be seen within the broad outlines of this movement. Established by 1912 and vital throughout the 1920s, Popular Modernism created an "atmosphere of bold and confident revolution"[1] that would help to sustain poets for the rest of the century.

High Modernism developed within this atmosphere. The two modernisms were not entirely discrete—Pound, for example, crossed over with the publication of *Hugh Selwyn Mauberley*—but High Modernism established a radically different relationship between writer and reader. Accessibility was sacrificed for a "more packed, dense, polysemous"[2] discourse, full of irony, rapid-fire allusions, multiple personae, and radical disjunctions. Its essential paradox was that to "make it new" (in Pound's phrase, borrowed from Confucius) one had to raid the distant past and scatter the booty throughout one's own poem.

T. S. Eliot's *The Waste Land*, published in 1922, soon became the essential High Modernist text. In the two decades that followed, High Modernism became the new orthodoxy. Its emphasis upon indirection and verbal ingenuity helped to create a new literary criticism, centered in the academy, that stressed explication and tended to find the most value in those works that were most in need of its services. One measure of High Modernism's success in reshaping the literary landscape is that today, over a half-century later, the term *modernism* is virtually synonymous with Perkins's *High Modernism* in literary studies. In contrast, much of Popular Modernism seems nearly as old-fashioned as the genteel tradition against which it defined itself.

In the work of Edna St. Vincent Millay, Perkins sees little innovation.

This essay was written specifically for this volume and is published here for the first time.

266

He asserts that she was "essentially traditionalist, but at the time [was] usually numbered among the 'new' poets"[3]—that is to say, among the Popular Modernists. Such an assessment needs qualification. Some of Millay's early work, especially in *A Few Figs from Thistles* (1920), seems firmly within the "new poetry" of the time. The urban landscapes of poems such as "Recuerdo" and "Macdougal Street," as well as the irreverent sensuality of "First Fig," "Thursday," and "To the Not Impossible Him," seem sufficient to place Millay within the technically conservative wing of Popular Modernism. And her play *Aria da Capo*, with its stylized antiwar ironies, shows that she was not entirely indifferent to formal experimentation.

But in the mind of the general reading public, which still existed for poetry in the 1920s, Millay soon became identified with her most conventionally "literary" poems—her sonnets. The best of them used familiar prosody and poetic diction to give a graceful dignity to emotions that had rarely found their way into print during the nineteenth century. "What lips my lips have kissed," for example, may be Petrarchan in form and imagery: a heart's "quiet pain,"[4] a cry at midnight. The poet's self-portrait as a bare tree in winter, forsaken by birds, may owe more than a little to Shakespeare's sonnet 73. But the overall effect of Millay's poem in the 1920s would have been contemporary rather than archaic for two reasons: the frankly sexual references from a woman's perspective and the mention of the "ghosts" of the Great War. These "unremembered lads" could have appeared in a sonnet by Wilfred Owen, whose posthumous reputation was just beginning to be established when Millay's sonnet appeared in *The Harp-Weaver* in 1923. And Millay's poetry is reminiscent of Owen's in one other important respect: the reader senses that only a vitally important theme could break through the high Romantic eloquence that both poets mastered in their juvenilia and never entirely abandoned.

Like many popular writers before and after her—Lord Byron, Alfred Lord Tennyson, F. Scott Fitzgerald, and John Updike come immediately to mind—Millay managed to satisfy her audience's demand for the unexpected and for the familiar simultaneously. Millay's sonnets seemed both new *and* eloquent, rather than either genteel or antipoetic. But Millay was more than her sonnets. If we look at her *Collected Poems*, not just at the work most responsible for making her a literary celebrity, we see many different, often contradictory Millays. There is, first of all, the wide-eyed naif of *Renascence*— a persona that appears less frequently in the later poems but does not vanish, as these lines from her 1928 volume attest:

> Oh, Bobolink, 'tis you!
> Over the buffeted orchard in the summer draught,
> Chuckling and singing, charging the rainy cloud,
> A little bird gone daft. . . .
>
> (*CP*, 211)

Then there is the irreverent Greenwich Village siren:

> After all, my erstwhile dear,
> My no longer cherished,
> Need we say it was not love,
> Just because it perished?
>
> (CP, 75)

And the tight-lipped disciple of A. E. Housman:

> And why should I be cold, my lad,
> And why should you repine,
> Because I love a dark head
> That never will be mine?
>
> (CP, 173)

And the sharp-eyed observer of the natural world:"How strange a thing is death, bringing to his knees, bringing to his antlers / The buck in the snow"(CP, 228). And even the sonnets are less uniform than we might at first suspect. The neo-Shakespearean mode predominates, but there are also the Frost-like "Sonnets from an Ungrafted Tree" and those of "Epitaph for the Race of Man" that were inspired by the cosmic broodings of her friend Robinson Jeffers.

Of course, there are variations among the works of every poet, but those in Millay's *Collected Poems* are disquieting to many readers accustomed to the evolution of a "signature" style that we see in the careers of William Butler Yeats, Pound, Eliot, Marianne Moore, and Wallace Stevens. From the perspective of the 1990s, High Modernism is a vigorously postFreudian literary movement that accepts not only the notion of a fragmented world but also the notion of a fragmented self. The collage of disparate allusions and multiple voices in the works of Pound, Eliot, and Moore is a formal expression of this philosophy of the mind. One of the internal contradictions of High Modernism, however, is that while it encourages fragmentation within poems it also encourages a consistent aesthetic stance toward that fragmentation as the poet moves from one poem to another. For the serious artist, stylistic evolution is permissible; stylistic uncertainty is not.

When judged according to these standards, Millay will never measure up. Her style does not evolve so much as vacillate. Like Theodore Roethke, early on in her career she developed a number of different, seemingly contradictory approaches to experience, and she is loath to abandon any of them. She returns to each one at will, as her mood or her chosen subject seems to strike her. The common element in her work is emotional rather than stylistic: what Norman A. Brittin has called "the electric personality supercharged with sensitivity that has been described by so many who knew [her]."[5]

About the only technique that never seems to have tempted her is High Modernism. Its disdainful irony elicted some irony of Millay's own in "It is the fashion now to wave aside," a sonnet from her posthumous volume, *Mine the Harvest*. Millay sees the new fashion as self-important, dismissive of any who dare question its cardinal rule: "Straightforwardness is wrong, evasion right" (*CP*, 725). Millay's alliteration in the poem's next line underscores her contempt for the obligatory French snippets in the tradition of T. S. Eliot's poetry of difficulty: "It is correct, *de rigueur*, to deride." She finishes her diatribe by invoking a real Frenchman, Voltaire. Despite his hypochondria, his archaic nightcap, and his "antique stuffiness," his clarity can still dispel the "fumy wits" of these modern pretenders. Their verse has mere "versatility" rather than genuine substance.

And so Millay decided to cultivate her own garden at Steepletop, struggling to satisfy both her traditional sense of eloquence and the demands of her many subjects: love, mortality, war, social injustice, human folly, and the natural world's beautiful indifference to human wishes.

As American poetry became increasingly dominated by the High Modernist aesthetic, her work seemed increasingly quaint and irrelevant. In the 1940s, when Millay became virtually a recluse at her farm in Austerlitz[6], the irony must have seemed overwhelming to her: such readers as poetry could still claim were flocking toward the writers who seemed most indifferent to being *readable* at all. Millay might have been able to dispel those fumy wits in one of her own sonnets, but when the smoke had cleared, Ezra Pound had won the Bollingen Prize, and T. S. Eliot had won the Nobel Prize for literature.

It had not always been so. In 1922 she had been narrowly edged out for the Pulitzer Prize not by T. S. Eliot but by Edwin Arlington Robinson. She had better luck the following year: *The Harp-Weaver* became the first volume written by a woman to receive the prize. In 1924, at the height of Millay's fame, Harriet Monroe called her the greatest female poet since Sappho—greater than Emily Bronte, Elizabeth Barrett Browning, Christina Rossetti, even Emily Dickinson.[7] Until Monroe's death in 1936, the founder and editor of *Poetry* never stopped praising Millay. But by 1931, even Monroe—one of the oldest and most reluctant "modernizers" of twentieth-century verse—was beginning to qualify that praise: "The trouble with Miss Millay's later work is that she has gradually accepted narrower horizons, has set sail into the restless waters of a smaller sea."[8] In the context of a review of *Fatal Interview*, Millay's sonnet sequence that chronicles her love affair with the young poet George Dillon, Monroe's criticism makes some sense. But it is a dubious general appraisal of the work published between 1923 and 1931. And, in the years to follow, "Epitaph for the Race of Man" may not have been her best poetry, and *The Murder of Lidice* may have been her worst, but neither effort can be faulted for having, in Monroe's words, "accepted narrower horizons." Millay's reputation would have eroded in the thirties and forties in any case, but her attempts to voice her social consciousness in her poems hastened that deterioration and made it more severe. Her early popularity made her a tempting target for critics eager to display their intellectual rigor. In "The Poet As Woman," John Crowe Ransom extended to Millay the same respect that Samuel Johnson had extended to women preachers more than 150 years before. The remarkable thing was not that she did it so badly but that she could do it at all: "Very well. Miss Millay is one of the best of the poets who are 'popular,' and loved by Circles and Leagues of young ladies; perhaps as good a combination as we can ever expect of the 'literary' poet and the poet who is loyal to the 'human interest' of the common reader."[9] Soon after Millay's death in 1950, John Ciardi depicted her as a literary fossil, important only for the personal memories imprinted upon her poems by her former readers:

> [Millay's poetry] swaggered with us like our first self-conscious cigarettes, an endless, very fine portrait of ourselves being very wise.
> It seems impossible now that we could have been so moved by such lines. Or is it simply that we can never again be so moved by anything? Whatever the truth of it, we were moved, we were filled, we were taken.
> Then somehow it was all over.[10]

It might have been over, but not because the overall quality of Millay's work had deteriorated. Lyric poets are apt to have more ups and downs than writers who work in large units of narration or meditation, and Millay was certainly no exception to this rule. The best of Millay's later poems, however, are deficient only in surprises: they seem technically equal to her earlier work and usually superior in terms of emotional depth. As Perkins has put it, "the evolution of her own poetry affected her reputation much less than the evolution of poetry at large."[11]

Almost from the day of the publication of *The Waste Land*—"the great catastrophe," as William Carlos Williams called it—American poets, while acknowledging the power of the High Modernist aesthetic, have busied themselves looking for alternatives to it. Since 1960, when the New Criticism began to wane in favor of more reader-oriented theories of interpretation, many literary critics have joined the search. For both contemporary poets and readers, the example of Millay would seem to have special relevance. In 1969 Richard Howard, for example, compared his fellow poets to the chastened King Midas, who decided to renounce the golden touch of artifice: ". . . what seems to me especially proper to these poets in the myth is the last development, the longing to *lose* the gift of order, despoiling the self of all that had been, merely, *propriety*. These then are the children of Midas, who address themselves to the current, to the flux, to the process of experience rather than to its precepts."[12] Millay did not renounce her golden touch, but her stylistic uncertainty, coupled with her willingness to write upon topics of social relevance, shows her uneasiness about it.

To decide upon Millay's place in twentieth-century literature, readers must first decide upon their own relationship to the modernist myth. Millay's work obviously rests upon assumptions that are different from those of High Modernism; but difference does not necessarily imply inferiority, and inferiority does not necessarily imply lack of value. Vacillation in style, for example, may be from the High Modernist perspective a symptom of imaginative weakness; but it can also point toward an openness to experience that is praiseworthy in its own right. And the power of irony may be no greater than the power of an eloquent directness:

> Down, down, down into the darkness of the grave
> Gently they go, the beautiful, the tender, the kind;
> Quietly they go, the intelligent, the witty, the brave.
> I know. But I do not approve. And I am not resigned.
>
> (*CP*, 241)

In these lines from "Dirge Without Music," some postmodernist readers will see a lack of intellectual sophistication. But many others will see a kind of courage.[13]

Notes

1. David Perkins, *A History of Modern Poetry: From the 1890s to the High Modernist Mode* (Cambridge, Massachusetts: Belknap Press of Harvard University Press, 1976), 300.

2. Ibid., 450.

3. Ibid., 369.

4. Edna St. Vincent Millay, *Collected Poems* (New York: Harper & Row, 1956), 602; hereafter cited in the text.

5. Norman A. Brittin, *Edna St. Vincent Millay*, rev. ed. (Boston: Twayne Publishers, 1982), 34.

6. See Edmund Wilson, "Edna St. Vincent Millay: A Memoir," *Nation*, 19 April 1952, especially 380–82.

7. Harriet Monroe, "Edna St. Vincent Millay," *Poetry* 24 (August 1924): 260–66.

8. Harriet Monroe, "Advance or Retreat?" *Poetry* 38 (July 1931): 218–19.

9. John Crowe Ransom, *The World's Body* (Baton Rouge: Louisiana State University Press, 1968), 76. Although in his 1968 "Postscript" Ransom felt compelled to apologize for some intemperate remarks that he had made about T. S. Eliot in the 1930s, evidently he felt that his remarks about Millay could stand without qualification.

10. John Ciardi, "Edna St. Vincent Millay: A Figure of Passionate Living," *Saturday Review of Literature*, 11 November 1950, 9.

11. Perkins, *History*, 374.

12. Richard Howard, *Alone with America: Essays on the Art of Poetry in the United States Since 1950*, enlarged edition (New York: Atheneum, 1980), xiii.

13.   For two different revaluations of Millay's work, see Suzanne Clark's "The Unwarranted Discourse: Sentimental Community, Modernist Women, and the Case of Millay," *Genre* 20 (Summer 1987), especially 147, and Ellen Bryant Voigt's "Poetry and Gender," *Kenyon Review* n.s. 9, no.3 (Summer 1987), especially 138.

Out of Reach of the Baby, the Artist, and Society: Millay's Fiction and Feminism

JOANNE VEATCH PULLEY

During her 1921–1922 European trip Edna St. Vincent Millay travelled extensively. Rumors circulated through Greenwich Village that she was having a series of love affairs, the most serious of which was with a French violinist. Millay told Esther Root and Doris Stevens of the affair, and according to Floyd Dell the rumors were confirmed by Gladys Brown Ficke.[1] The young violinist's family disapproved of his marrying Millay. When she became pregnant, she went to England and had an abortion without telling the father, about whom little is known, of her ordeal.[2] Norman Brittin suggests in his book on Millay that the pain of this love affair is reflected in the two poems "The Cameo" and "To a Musician."

"Out of Reach of the Baby," written shortly after the probable date of this experience, is, however, more autobiographical in detail than the two poems. This story, published under the pseudonym of Nancy Boyd, reads like a frivolous anecdote about a baby that is overprotected by its parents. This anecdote is pursued even to the extent that all adults in the house must give up their intellectual and artistic pursuits in order that the baby should never encounter an object, word or idea with which it is unfamiliar. In the end the older siblings either give up their art and die or they rebel and flee to less restrictive environs.

This story, however, is anything but frivolous. At one level the story reads as a political allegory. The house is the United States, and everything connected with the house fits neatly into the allegory. Carefully worked into less than eight pages of prose is a sincere argument for female autonomy of mind and body. Knowing that Millay had just undergone an abortion, and that abortions were not morally or legally acceptable alternatives in conservative America in 1922, a reader might understand this story as a justification for abortion told slant. As Emily Dickinson said, "Tell all the Truth but tell it slant—" and Millay well knew what she meant by that: "Tell your story so that only careful readers can cipher your meaning."[3] This second, deeper subtext reveals how powerless Millay felt over her own body. Perhaps because of her feeling of vulnerability, she chose to shield her own

This essay was written specifically for this volume and is published here for the first time.

voice by using a male narrator, Fyodor. Control of one's body is important to any woman; for a woman suffering from anorexia it is even more significant. By having an abortion and starving herself Millay is asserting control. She is acknowledging her appetites and she is restricting herself to prove she has the willpower to control her own body.

After the abortion Millay is no longer threatened with cumbersome motherhood and probably felt she was "Out of Reach of the Baby." With the specter of motherhood behind her she reflects about what could have happened to her as a woman and a poet if she had had a child. Millay says through Fyodor that she "was just as sorry as anybody when the baby swallowed the buttonhook and nearly died."[4] If the buttonhook is compared to the modern symbol of illegal abortion, the coat hanger, the narrator can be suddenly seen as a woman who almost had an abortion but changed her mind. She seems to plead with her audience that she has feelings and that she is sorry to have almost taken another life. The consequences, though, seem terrible now. Obviously, Millay is distancing herself by assuming a male identity in the story. The narrator says that having the baby is a "disgusting spectacle." "A large family of grown men and women all going about with their shoes unbuttoned; it does seem as though there might be a compromise."[5] This family becomes symbolic of a society that is unable to compromise. As a woman artist the narrator has had to put her art aside to raise the child. Society will not compromise and let her be both a mother and a writer. After watching her "siblings"—other women artists—lose the right to practice their arts she says in desperation that "they [the parents] have put [her] pen and ink and typewriter on the top shelf" where she cannot use them.[6] This, she bemoans, "is a handicap," but it does not stop her for she continues to write with a burnt match stub.[7] Her books have been taken away and put on the top shelf out of the reach of the baby and still she is prolific and pours out her passion in literature.

The trouble with society was started by Father, the patrimonial, Orwellian Big Brother who oppresses women. "Father is crazy about the baby," meaning he is perfectly satisfied with the way society operates now.[8] He sees no need for change because to him "weakness and helplessness [are] virtues."[9] The narrator is irate that women should be expected to be meek and mindless. The rest of the passage begins to demonstrate that women are not in control of their bodies. Father says that anyone who would hurt a baby will be put on the top shelf away from the rest of the family / society. This "top-shelf" attitude could be alluding to antiabortion laws that one day could lead to pregnant women being jailed for doing harm to their bodies. This image is reinforced by general chatter about how easy it is "to kill a baby" and how "the house" is also part of "the chapel." Taken literally this text makes little sense, but interpreted by female readers it hints that abortion is simple, though the church opposes it everywhere. Millay paints a picture of women's bodies as temples of the Lord, as patriarchal society keeps insisting. Women are not to achieve autonomy but should be satisfied to be vessels of society. It often has been preached that the woman's place is in the home. The narrator is reminded of this by her matriarchal heritage in the form of the Mother who pleads "gently and brightly, in the manner of one soliciting recruits in a holy cause."[10] Her mother, agreeing that the baby is dumb, suggests that it should be humored and that the narrator should limit her speech and thoughts so the baby will not feel its stupidity. The baby becomes representative of future generations of society. At this point it is no doubt Millay herself who declares "it's a pity someone doesn't drop a brick on his head."[11] She refuses to put motherhood before her artistic needs. Traditional women are aghast and mother cries out "For shame!"[12]

While the narrator is dealing with Mother, Father is struggling "to make the world safe for stupidity."[13] Millay is alluding to World War I rhetoric about "Making the world safe for democracy," and she is making the political statement that it is not all right to accept that idealistic philosophy. She observes that it appears Mother is giving in completely so that the father's dreams are about to come true. Millay is grimly saying that as men gain more power in an already patriarchal society, the society is declining. The power issue is reintroduced subtly by Mother, who represents all women. She is shown to be less than inventive because she accepts traditional limits of art without tolerating innovation. Mother follows the rules set down by the patriarchal Father. As an accomplished pianist Millay reflects this by saying, "She is so artistic that if you strike 'd' and 'c' together on the piano, it sets her teeth on edge."[14] At one level Mother will not tolerate a "D and C," or dilation and curettage. This surgical procedure, which is used to treat several disorders of the uterus, is performed as an elective abortion.[15] This is also a sly way of saying that society literally cannot accept the new art of this era, the Jazz Age, which does not resolve itself but leaves a disquieting impression. Artists during the twenties were trying very hard to upset society and get people to take an active role in the world around them.

Through the haze of societal blindness women artists are still rebelling quietly and keeping their artistic desires alive. Ms. Nancy Boyd says through the artists in this family that in the larger sense all artists must keep trying to get what is kept from them: freedom of expression. In the story there are ladders painted in bright camouflage to blend in with the decor. These ladders serve to help the artists get the supplies they want from the top shelf. The struggle goes on but is hidden. Those who manage to leave the family for the sake of their art survive, and those who surrender their artistic desires perish.

The mole-like baby is finally described as having weak eyes, a weak tummy and a loud scream. Motherhood is no fun because the baby is unforgivably ugly and obnoxious. Worst of all, the baby / bourgeois society is intellectually limited. It is old enough to walk but it is afraid and will only crawl. It can repeat words it hears: "mamma," "horsie," "capitalist," "communism," "art," though it seems not to understand their meanings.[16] Millay indicts modern society: it has reached a maturity which should allow it to walk, but it can only crawl. Society crawls because it fears all changes; the masses are not progressive enough to think. The Mother does not deny that the baby is pathetically limited; she just accepts it and slows down to the baby's crawling pace. Boyd is saying that women seem to understand that society is dysfunctional but generally prefer to go along for the good of family and society. They sublimate their own thoughts and feelings to further their husbands' and sons' ambitions. It is accepted that, as the saying goes, "behind every good man is a woman." Millay is infuriated that masses of women accept this role as second-class citizens. The mother in this story has no say in what goes on in her husband's house, just as women until the 1920s had no political vote or voice.

Millay takes this theme to its ultimate conclusion by interweaving the fates of several artists among her characters. Isadora wants to be a dancer but her dancing would rattle the floor and upset the baby. She is not allowed to practice, so she has to give it up. As a result she ends up teaching calisthenics at a girls' school. Because patriarchy asks her to, she abandons her art and just goes through the motions without experiencing the joy of artistic expression. This is an artist's Hell. Sara wants to be an actress and rebels when she is forbidden to speak. She has gone to Hollywood and is living the good life as a smashing success. Enrico would have been a singer but has given up his art and died of a broken heart. Pablo has left and is painting to his heart's content. He invites all artists to join him. The narrator is deciding that she probably will meet him to resume her writing. As for the remaining artists, the narrator says that "it is not so much that we remain as that we haven't gone yet."[17] True artists, regardless of their sex, will have to rebel against an unreasonable and uncompromising society in order to practice their art. This is especially true of women artists. When it comes to deciding between motherhood and artistic expression, Millay makes it clear that since society cannot compromise the only choice is art.

Typically, there are many layers to Millay's story. "Out of the Reach of the Baby" is more than an argument for female artistic autonomy. This story is an allegory dealing with American artists in self-imposed exile during the 1920s because of repression of artistic expression. The big house has forty-eight rooms with east and west exposures looking out onto oceans. Obviously the forty-eight rooms represent the forty-eight states (Hawaii and Alaska at that time had not yet entered the Union) bordered on east and west by the Atlantic and Pacific oceans. The house is further described as being unacceptable to "some people [perhaps meaning the world at large] because it wasn't built by the Egyptians, or the Romans, or the women of Tahiti; we built it ourselves, and nobody has quite forgiven us."[18] The narrator describes the visitors that used to come to the house in a tone full of blase American pride. She says "there was always a queen or two dropping in to tea."[19] The reason for American popularity, she suggests, is because "father is fairly well-to-do, and always gave everyone a wonderful time."[20] She attributes America's success not to a classical heritage but to its wealth as a nation. Europe and the Orient, two areas of the world in which Millay traveled extensively, both have long histories marked by Roman and Greek influences—influences that long preceded and thus did not impact on the comparatively young American nation.

If the reader has not caught on to this allegory, Millay says "Father is a politician."[21] Father is in fact more than just a politician—he is the president of the United States! Now the real political commentary begins. Millay may be making a recommendation for Marxism. The masculine narrator Fyodor is told by his father that "a house divided against itself cannot stand."[22] His reply is "Let it fall. It's time we had a new house."[23] This house is a wealthy nation built on capitalism; to him, it would be an improvement to get out of the war and build a new society.

This may seem like an outlandish interpretation; however, one must consider the narrator's name—Fyodor. The allegory describes many artists by their first names, including a slightly socialist narrator. In life—as in Millay's allegory—Fyodor Dostoyevsky led a life of deprivation and censorship. When he was caught by Czarist authorities with a press that was going to be used to print forbidden documents he was tormented first with the threat of execution and finally served four years' hard labor in Siberia. After prison he was allowed to write, but in 1863 again faced censorship when government officials misunderstood what he had written.[24] Fyodor Dostoyevsky is a recognizable symbol of censorship in Russia. Millay uses his name to draw attention to the possibility that the same sort of censorship is happening in the United States. James Joyce's novel *Ulysses* (1922) was first published in installments in the *Little Review* in 1918-1920. In the early 1920s, isolated passages were labelled as obscene, corrupting, or lascivious. Trials were held in both America and Britain, and eventually, copies were confiscated and burned. In 1915 D. H. Lawrence's *The Rainbow* was suppressed. The year 1915 brought the prosecution and suppression of D. H. Lawrence's *The Rainbow* under the Obscene Publications Act of 1857. Lawrence believed that the National Purity League may have instigated the prosecution. Some early reviewers had objected to what they perceived to be obscene passages or anti-British imperialism sentiments in the novel. Such adjectives as disgraceful and disgusting were applied to the book. The case was heard in open court and soon over 1,000 copies of the novel were destroyed by the authorities. In frustrated outrage during the Rainbow Trails, Lawrence gave a name to his pain, condemning his persecutors and prosecutors as "the censor morons." This typifies the sort of societal disapproval that writers faced. Millay wanted to alert readers to the broad spectrum of artistic censorship in America. She did this by alluding to famous contemporary artists of all kinds—painters, writers, dancers, singers, actresses, and musicians—who had been publicly prevented from practicing their art. Some were such innovators that had they been thwarted, their field of art would have suffered a grave loss. Fyodor [Dostoyevsky] as the narrator must write with a burnt match stub because everything has been put on the top shelf out of his reach. Next is Fritz [Kreisler], in reality a world-famous violinist whose skill in the context of the story is declining because he is forbidden to play his instrument because it might upset the baby. Isadora [Duncan] is the legendary dancer who in the story asks to be allowed to dance a new dance "where you don't lift your feet from the floor."[25] She broke with tradition to become one of America's forerunners of modern dance. In her time she was both loved and hated by American audiences. In "Out of the Reach of the Baby" father does not believe that her kind of dance is "really dancing," and eventually she is persuaded to give it up to become a calisthenics instructor. Sara [Bernhardt] has gone into the movies and is known as "The Divine Sarah" to her fans. It is said of her in this story that "She never opened her mouth but a little chill went up and down your spine, and you wanted to laugh and cry and kiss her shoes."[26] Fyodor tells readers confidentially that Sara was not allowed to speak above a whisper in the house, so she has left to become a film goddess. Enrico [Caruso] was not permitted to sing for the same reason Sara was not allowed to talk. He did not escape from the family legacy and "died . . . obscure, untended, and heart-broken."[27] Worse yet Fyodor says that his life need not have been so hopeless "if only he'd been brought up in a different family."[28] The allegory takes place in America but the artists are really international players. Enrico Caruso, for example, was Italian, Sarah Bernhardt was French, and Pablo Picasso was Spanish. Because of its essentially international context, this story in the larger sense alludes to censorship throughout the world; but it especially condemns it in the United States. America is supposed to be the land of opportunity where new ideas and styles are free to flourish. Millay emphasizes the American "melting pot" image in the beginning of the story by stressing the architectural nonconformity of the great house with forty-eight rooms.

"The Door," another Nancy Boyd story, deals not with censorship but with the public perceptions of legendary artists such as Isadora Duncan and Sarah Bernhardt. These figures received acclaim for their artistic gifts, and their personal lives were just as fascinating to fans as their performances. Ms. Bernhardt was a child star in the theatre. Her sassy personality enthralled audiences, enabling her to play the part of Napoleon's son in L'Aiglon and make the play one of the "greatest financial successes ever achieved in Paris."[29] In 1915 she had her right leg amputated due to acute suffering from an injury in 1905, but she continued to perform, even going to the front in World War I. Such beauty and heroism created a mythical image that surrounded her and helped create the illusion of the artist as a mythic personality.

Perhaps audiences throughout history have had the impression that artists of all varieties lead lives of incredible adventure and extraordinary happenings. During the twenties American artists began to capitalize on this to build or enhance their reputations. Writers, painters, musicians and others flocked to Europe to live or study or vacation. Eager fans greedily devoured sensational stories offered to them by newspaper columnists and the artists themselves. Even Ernest Hemingway maneuvered to enhance his status as a hero, to the point that he became a legend. With Hemingway (as with many of his contemporaries) it is hard to extricate the man from the myth because his real life was as exciting as the fictitious rumors circulated about him. Indeed the wartime had influenced immensely the personal lives of many artists. In the afterglow of the Roaring Twenties they assumed personas of epic stature. One example that stands out is Isadora Duncan. She discarded the traditional props of ballet and danced barefoot wearing Greek draperies. Her new style of dance included movements imitating nature, such as swaying like windblown trees and arm motions suggestive of ocean waves. It was Duncan also who first danced to masterworks by Franz Liszt, Johann Sebastian Bach and Ludwig van Beethoven. Her magnetic personality enabled her to break from tradition and woo audiences. She died as bizarrely and extraordinarily as she lived: she was strangled when her scarf caught in the wheel of a car in Nice, France. From beginning to end she fascinated the masses, who were at this time beginning to assume that Artists in general were an eccentric and special lot.

Millay describes the frustrations and benefits of being an artist in "The Door." This Nancy Boyd story describes the relationship that develops between Cynthia Bainbridge, a writer, and Peter Holloway, a painter. Both have come to a seaside resort in search of peace and quiet so they can write and paint. Neither artist, however, is able to create, distracted as they are by others at the resort who are fascinated by them because they are artists. Cynthia is hounded by women who continually ask her to luncheon or tennis. One particular woman is described in cold terms as someone who once spent two weeks in London and has assumed a British accent. She wants to pick wildflowers for Cynthia and talk with her about "art and understanding and her soul."[30] Millay is telling the public that one cannot try to be an artist or be artistic. One is either an artist or one is not; there is no in-between. Cynthia does not like the intruding woman. What she finds even more disturbing is the phone ringing incessantly in the room next door. Upon inquiry she discovers that the adjoining room houses Peter, who hates the phone too and leaves the hotel to paint all day.

Peter finds the telephone rudely interrupting and takes his boat out sailing to escape the pestering vacationers. He cannot paint because curious people keep asking him to paint their children or pets. Basically society in general is trying to dictate what it is he should be painting and this interference stunts his artistic expression. When Peter and Cynthia finally meet and commiserate over their similar experiences, they decide that they need to find a way to make society reject them and leave them alone to pursue their art. As Peter puts it: "What are we going to do about those people at the hotel? Things can't go on like this. We can't work. We can't even play, unless we get off on an island out of reach."[31] After bemoaning their untarnished reputations they decide that the quickest way to accomplish a public scandal would be to unbar the door that separates their adjoining rooms. If they leave the door open, they think that they might get thrown out of the hotel or, at the very least that people will avoid them for their scandalous behavior. What finally happens is that news circulates among the guests that they are having a love affair. As suspected lovers these artists become increasingly fascinating to everyone around them. Now more than before they are pestered and annoyed by intruding outsiders from society.

The narrator philosophizes about why Cynthia and Peter are not ostracized. Her commentary boils down to the fact that they are "a painter and a novelist—these [are] no common folk. One [has] always heard that such people did disreputable things . . . If they had not been so celebrated, and therefore so mysterious and so desirable, things might have been different."[32] Because they have become such a curiosity for the guests they are constantly observed. Both Cynthia and Peter become tired and desperate to escape their surroundings. They fall in love, consummate the affair, and run away together "to one of those God-forsaken islands."[33] Of the entire incident the narrator says she does not know "whether or not, before their departure, they had the good taste to drop in upon some languid justice of the peace and secure unto their radiant union his perfectly unimportant blessing, [she] cannot tell you."[34] Here Millay is speaking out for free love. She goes on to tell readers: "Cynthia wears no thin circlet of gold or platinum on the third finger of her left hand—but then she wouldn't anyway. She does not go by the name of Mrs. Peter Holloway—but then she wouldn't anyway. These advanced thinkers are the devil and all to keep track of."[35] This is the feminist Millay here explaining that as a woman artist on the leading edge of social culture she sees no reason why any woman needs to marry. If a woman chooses to get married there is no reason for her to assume her husband's name. She should retain her own name and cling to her autonomy.

Beyond the delightful tale of adventurous romance that this story seems at first glance, it shows the underlying stress that Millay felt as an artist and therefore a nonconformist in American society during her lifetime. "The Door" reveals the anxiety she suffered at not being understood and not fitting into the scheme of the world around her. Part of the problem as she sees it, is that she has artistic sensibilities which dispose her to view life differently from the nonartist. The other part of the problem is that her audience expects her to be different and entertaining. In the person of Cynthia one sees a young woman writer who feels both different from her peers and who is expected by them to be different. In no way is she comfortable when she is interacting with the public. She finds solace and understanding in Peter, who is another artist. Peter feels the same pressures Cynthia does, so they decide to escape the rest of the world by going off together and being Artists.

In other stories like "The Sentimental Solon" and "The Dark Horse" the woman artist may have a love affair with a nonartist, but she always finds she must leave him in order to be true to her art. In Millay's personal life this was also true. During college she felt misunderstood and different from her classmates. Often she would break curfew to roam about after dark, finding comfort in nature and solitude. After graduation she moved to the artistic haven of Greenwich Village to surround herself with other artists. She had numerous love affairs with fellow writers and artists. When she finally married Eugen Boissevain he moved her out to the country and took care of all the household duties, freeing her for her writing. Eventually they bought Ragged Island in Maine where they spent the summers in isolation.

Deep feelings of societal isolation are conveyed most clearly in "Tea for the Muse," a story collected in *Distressing Dialogues*. It is a satiric account of a tea given for a male poet, Mr. Cecil Payne, by a woman who wants to be thought of as a patron of the arts. The story is told through the conversations of the guests, who represent average middle to upper-middle income men and women. The hostess Mrs. Lang-Jennings is very silly. She allows the party to break down immediately after she introduces the poet to begin the reading. One woman has brought along her fifteen-year-old daughter's poems for him to read and hopefully find impressive. Another woman tells him she buys his books in order to support the arts, but confesses that she does not read them because she does not like poetry. Someone else tells the poet that she loved his latest volume of verse, *Beer and Skittles*, never giving him the opportunity to inform her that his book's correct title is *Cakes and Ale*.

In this conversation Millay conveys the impression that the poet and his work are unimportant. Society values him, indeed is fascinated by him, because he is a poet—an Artist. Nowhere in the story does the poet get to say a single word! People talk at him and about him but not with him. The party breaks up without the poet getting to read, though he has by the end sought refuge under the divan. The poet's hiding out under the sofa is autobiographical. In a distressed letter to Witter Bynner after their broken engagement, Millay writes that "[she is] now going under the divan and have a fit."[36] When everyone has left the Artist crawls out of his hiding place and exits crying, which is what Millay must have felt like doing at times. Readers are made to laugh at this and to know also the discomfort society has inflicted upon the perfectly innocent Artist.

Millay shows how ridiculous American society is in this microcosmic gathering at the tea party. All of the guests are described, in varying degrees, unfavorably. She seems to dislike most intensely those people who do not understand culture and art but who have posed as being artistic. Miss Lenox, for example, is described satirically as someone who spent two weeks in Japan and now feels she should forever kneel on a cushion. Though no different from her friends, she tries to seem artistic and eccentric by assuming one Japanese custom. Mrs. Sailer tells the poet encouragingly that she loves poetry and that they "are all very poetical in [her] family."[37] Her problem is that she does not care at all for poetry unless she can get attention by saying she is "poetical." Another girl, supposedly perfectly beautiful, talks to her "skinny and microscopic black god" that rides around in her muff.[38] She does not talk to the poet and her late arrival sets in motion the degeneration of the party. Others are described as having "a saccharine baritone" (the hostess) or as smelling sweet (Mr. Dallas).[39] There is nothing substantial or meaningful about these people. Mrs. Loomis, who has a dog named Mister Einstein, reminds one of Eliot's ladies coming and going, "talking of Michelangelo."[40] Millay takes a parting shot at her unappreciative audience by saying the "guests ooze out severally, chattering and lying."[41] This is not a complimentary picture of society, but it is a view of how the Artist sees and relates to the public.

In "Art and How to Fake It," Millay communicates unambiguously how she feels about people who pretend to be artistic in order to make themselves seem glamorous. Subtitled "Advice to the Art-Lorn," this letter is addressed to Miss Boyd and signed "ARTISTIC." The funny thing is that this correspondent is not in the least artistic, which is why she needs help from Millay. "It has been the dream of my life to be a literary and artistic center," she says, "but somehow people do not flock as I had hoped they would do."[42] This pathetic woman has rented an apartment in Greenwich Village and furnished it with "a black floor, orange curtains, a ukulele made of a cigar-box, a leaky gas-jet, a back-number of a Russian newspaper," etc.[43] Since it is decorated in artistic Greenwich style she does not understand why artists do not come to her haunt. She does not understand and could not ever understand that artists will not want to be around her because she is not an artist. It is her great desire to be artistic that drives away Artists. Miss Boyd does not try to explain this. She just tells her to crush out her cigarettes on the floor as a way to solve her decorating oversight. Millay seems to be telling the woman that her apartment is a mockery of all that is artistic, so she should finish profaning art by trashing it.

Another letter written to Miss Boyd in "Art and How to Fake It" is from a young man who has been sent to study art because he is unable to apply himself to any profession. He says that because he was different from his childhood friends and acted in a spoiled and eccentric manner his parents and he feel that he must be artistic. He finds, however, that he "can neither write, paint, model, sing, dance, play a musical instrument, design costumes, nor act, nor [is he] a sympathetic listener."[44] Millay has perfectly described someone who has no artistic talents or even a desire for artistic expression. Yet this person represents ranks of the generally nonartistic public, who nevertheless believe they have sufficient artistic feeling to be critical of real artists. Her suggestion for him is to remember this: "When all else fails, two courses remain open to a man: he can always give lectures on the drama, or edit anthologies of verse; for neither of these is either talent or training necessary."[45] Rather viciously Millay manages to insult not only her audience, but her critics as well. It is no surprise that she signed her pseudonym to this story. She does not even try to disguise the deep animosity she feels toward people who say they are artistic but who have no feeling for art.

Just as pointedly "Look Me Up" reiterates Millay's feelings of persecution by society. Narrated in the first person, this Nancy Boyd story does not specifically explain that she is an artist pursued by fans. She explains that she is "neither rich nor beautiful."[46] Everybody is chasing her around the world "simply [because she] made the mistake of starting to run."[47] She wants to get away from the crowd, where people live together in the suburbs and form clubs in order that they do not have to be alone. It is her belief that "They imagine that the volume of fatigue and avoirdupois of doom becomes in this way divided by the number of the club's membership."[48] She seems to be saying that the silly people have not figured out that all individuals must bear the full weight of their existence alone for they cannot share the burden.

Millay does not want to be a part of this. She states, "I fear no catastrophe save that of the companionship of tiresome people."[49] This explains why she spent enough money on travel to have bought a house in suburbia. She prefers nature to urban life and wants to go into the country to seek solitude. When she says "I refuse to be one of the group," she means that she will go to any lengths to escape that doom.[50] In this story, as in her life, Millay feels different from the general crowd and wants to keep to herself. The crowd does not understand her, but is attracted to her because she is different. She is different because she is an Artist. To Millay this is as fundamental as being right handed or having red hair. Being an artist is part of her nature and it makes her nervous to be so carefully scrutinized by the public. That is why she must flee the public in the story, and why it follows her.

Her pursuers are society. In the story society is described as a male enemy: "He was invariably inimical to my ideals, my aspirations, my opinions, even my welfare. He publicly disparaged my work, my mental capacities, my moral stamina, my habits, and my figure."[51] As long as Millay knew this about the relationship she could cope with it. The problem now is that he has sent her a note inviting her to luncheon. As the relationship takes on a less hateful perspective it becomes more menacing to her. If she is no longer despised by society she fears she will become a part of it. Instead she runs away to hide in a cave covered over with poison ivy. Millay does not want to have to relate in a noncombative way to society and this story is a study in wish fulfillment for her.

In "Madame a Tort!" Millay fantasizes about what would happen to the artist, to herself, if she became an integral part of society. The story is about a sculptress who goes to have her hair cut and is taken prisoner by the beauty parlor. Society's keepers give her a body makeover and after they have finished their work she finds that she is beautiful. Everyone admires her and positive social things happen, so that she ultimately gives up her art to be a slave to beauty. The clay, she figures, would ruin her hands and manicure. She spends so much time keeping her looks up that she does not have time to sculpt. This is a satire, of course, but it does explore an artistic nightmare—having to give up art in order to conform to society's demands for women to have conventionally beautiful bodies.

This story of an artist giving up art for society is countered by "The Implacable Aphrodite," the story of a woman who leaves the pressures of American societal constraints behind by moving to Europe. Like "The Door" this is the story of the relationship that develops between two artists. Miss White is a sculptress and Mr. Black is a violinist. As their names suggest they are as different as day and night. Mr. Black loves Miss White only for her beauty, though he goes to great lengths to explain that he appreciates her artistic abilities. Miss White is not romantically interested in Mr. Black but would value a sincere friendship based on their mutual appreciation of each other's art. In a confidential tone she tells Mr. Black that he is "the only man in [her] acquaintance, unmarried or married, who does not importune [her] with undesirable attentions."[52] He quickly responds in an understanding tone that it is only because other men do not understand that she must have her freedom of expression. He says, "It is your beauty which attracts them, your extraordinary grace, your voice, so thrillingly quiet, your ravishing gestures. They don't see you as I do."[53] But of course that is the way he sees her as well. He is no different from the suitors that flock to her doorstep proposing matrimony. In an aside from the narrator one sees another diverging vision of what sort of person Miss White really is. The aside reads, "She is cruelly slicing a lemon, by means of a small dagger with which a Castilian nun has slain three matadors."[54] This is a picture of Miss White as something less than refined, perhaps even a little atavistic. Yet at this same moment that Mr. Black sees her slicing the lemon for their tea he thinks "that she looks gentle and domestic."[55] He sees nothing of her natural fire and energy and instead places her within the circle of his dream as he would like her to be. When she tells him she is moving to Europe to escape the growing crowd of admirers who are hampering her work, Mr. Black panics and asks her to marry him. She turns him down in icy tones and he strikes back by insulting her art. He cries out at her, "All you think about is those damn little putty figures!"[56] She is frankly shocked and asks him to leave, contending she must have her freedom to work. In a patronizing tone he alienates Miss White forever by declaring that he does not care how much she works. After all "A man's wife ought to have some little thing to take up her time."[57] To a woman and to an artist this is the ultimate insult. This episode is set up within the frame of the story to be representative of the many times this has happened in just this way. Millay too felt this way. She was patronized by her audience, her publishers, her critics, and her lovers. She went to Europe to escape this sort of reception of herself and her poetry. In Europe she was a foreigner and people expected her to act differently. She aroused no serious speculation by her desire to be alone and write. Many American writers were hiding out in Europe during the twenties, so she was almost conforming to an artistic norm by living abroad.

Notes

1. Norman A. Brittin, *Edna St. Vincent Millay*, rev. ed. (Boston: Twayne Publishers, 1982), 139.

2. Brittin, 15.

3. Emily Dickinson, Poem no. 1129. *The Norton Anthology of Modern Poetry*, eds. Richard Ellmann and Robert O'Clair. (New York: W. W. Norton & Co., 1968), 41.

4. Nancy Boyd, "Out of Reach of the Baby," in *Distressing Dialogues* (New York: Harper & Brothers, 1924), 125.

5. Boyd, *Distressing Dialogues*, 125.

6. Boyd, *Distressing Dialogues*, 132.

7. Boyd, *Distressing Dialogues*, 132.

8. Boyd, *Distressing Dialogues*, 125.

9. Boyd, *Distressing Dialogues*, 125.

10. Boyd, *Distressing Dialogues*, 130.

11. Boyd, *Distressing Dialogues*, 130.

12. Boyd, *Distressing Dialogues*, 130.

13. Boyd, *Distressing Dialogues*, 128.

14. Boyd, *Distressing Dialogues*, 128.

15. The American Medical Association, *Home Medical Encyclopedia*, Charles B. Clayman, M.D., medical editor. (New York: Random House, 1989), vol. 1, 332.

16. Boyd, *Distressing Dialogues*, 129.

17. Boyd, *Distressing Dialogues*, 132.

18. Boyd, *Distressing Dialogues*, 126.

19. Boyd, *Distressing Dialogues*, 127.

20. Boyd, *Distressing Dialogues*, 127.

21. Boyd, *Distressing Dialogues*, 128.

22. Boyd, *Distressing Dialogues*, 127.

23. Boyd, *Distressing Dialogues*, 128.

24. Avrahm Yarmolinsky, "Fyodor Mikhailovich Dostoevski," in *Collier's Encyclopedia* (New York: Macmillan Educational Co., 1990), vol. 8, 354–58.

25. Boyd, *Distressing Dialogues*, 131.

26. Boyd, *Distressing Dialogues*, 131.

27. Boyd, *Distressing Dialogues*, 131.

28. Boyd, *Distressing Dialogues*, 131.

29. Joanna Richardson, "Sarah Bernhardt," in *Collier's Encyclopedia* (New York: Macmillan Educational Co., 1990), vol. 4, 92–93.

30. Edna St. Vincent Millay, "The Door," *Ainslee's*, vol. 43, no. 6 (May 1919): 131.

31. Millay, "The Door," 136.

32. Millay, "The Door," 138.

33. Millay, "The Door," 141.

34. Millay, "The Door," 141.

35. Millay, "The Door," 141.

36. *Letters of Edna St. Vincent Millay*, 146.

37. Nancy Boyd, "Tea For the Muse," *Distressing Dialogues* (New York: Harper & Brothers, 1924), 204.

38. Boyd, *Distressing Dialogues*, 205.

39. Boyd, *Distressing Dialogues*, 203.

40. T. S. Eliot, "The Love Song of J. Alfred Prufrock," *The Waste Land and other Poems* (New York: Harcourt Brace Jovanovich, 1988), 3.

41. Boyd, *Distressing Dialogues*, 211.

42. Nancy Boyd, "Art and How to Fake It," *Distressing Dialogues* (New York: Harper & Brothers, 1924), 97.

43. Boyd, *Distressing Dialogues*, 97.

44. Boyd, *Distressing Dialogues*, 104.

45. Boyd, *Distressing Dialogues*, 104.

46. Nancy Boyd, "Look Me Up," *Distressing Dialogues* (New York: Harper & Brothers, 1924), 137.

47. Boyd, *Distressing Dialogues*, 138.

48. Boyd, *Distressing Dialogues*, 138.

49. Boyd, *Distressing Dialogues*, 138.

50. Boyd, *Distressing Dialogues*, 139.

51. Boyd, *Distressing Dialogues*, 142.

52. Nancy Boyd, "The Door," *Ainslee's*, vol. 43, no. 6 (July 1919): 45.

53. Boyd, "The Door," 45.

54. Boyd, "The Door," 50.

55. Boyd, "The Door," 50.

56. Boyd, "The Door," 52.

57. Boyd, "The Door," 52.

Millay and the English Renaissance Lyric

Robert Wiltenburg

Edmund Wilson observes of Edna St. Vincent Millay that she had a "power of enhancing and ennobling life" by "charging" things "with her own intense feeling."[1] This willed intensity characterizes not only the effect of her personality on those who knew her, but also the nature of the poet's task as she undertook it: to see, to feel, and to speak for others less perceptive, less eloquent, less courageous, less exposed to the full range of life's pleasures and pains. One sees this motive in the touchstone poem "Renascence," in which she traces the progress of a heroic sensibility from innocence through experience into a deepening anguish, despair, and premature burial in preparation for a miraculous rebirth of insight and of joy. Yet despite its climactic affirmations ("O God, I cried, no dark disguise / Can e'er hereafter hide from me / Thy radiant identity!" [12]),[2] the poem's final note is not of triumph but of a wary determination that the ever-stretching and pushing "heart" and the soaring "soul" shall resist the constriction ("East and West will pinch the heart") and flattening ("the sky / Will cave in" [13]) that always threaten.

Her fundamental attitude toward experience and toward poetry has been variously described as romantic or neoromantic, and in assessing her many moods, purposes, and effects one is sometimes reminded of the wistfulness of John Keats, or the sibylline gravity of Alfred Lord Tennyson—and, of course, there is throughout a sense of the neoWordsworthian project memorably patronized by John Crowe Ransom as the "objective record of a natural woman's mind."[3]

But there are also ways in which to see Millay's work in the context of English Renaissance lyrics—a body of poetry that she knew intimately from early in her life; upon which she drew, early and late, for inspiration and example, both trivial and substantial; and to which her response was, from the beginning, continuous and continuously complicated.

The affinities run deep. First is the habitual framing of experience in terms of passionately perceived oppositions and alternations. Millay shares Hamlet's (and the Renaissance's) divided sense of humanity's potential exaltation and degradation, the "godlike" and the "dusty" uneasily commingled in a single personality, and commits herself to the candid, thorough represen-

This essay was written specifically for this volume and is published here for the first time.

tation of these divergent imperatives: thus the burying and soaring, the expanding and contracting, the loving and losing that run all through the poems.

Second, and no less important, is the primacy of voice and ear in her poetry. She is still, as most Renaissance poets were, an "aural" poet—a mesmerizing reader of her own poetry—with, as recordings show, a free-wheeling notion of the poetic text as script for performance: the fullest sense of a poem's rhythm, tone, and emphasis become available only in the act of speaking and hearing that the words and lines on the page more or less reliably—but not determinatively—provoke. As Wilson says, at her best she is "mistress of deeply moving rhythms, of a music which makes up for the ear what her page seems to lack for the eye."[4]

Third, she shares the Renaissance sense of discovering or being presented with an entire preexistent culture for her study, appropriation, endorsement, or rejection. This outlook owes something to her social status: the provincial talent from Camden, Maine, who assumes, through intent reading and writing, citizenship in a wider world of literature. It is an imagined posses-sion progressively and triumphantly affirmed in her many successes: Vassar, New York, Paris, the Pulitzer Prize, and the continuing chorus of critical, and then popular, recognition that continues into the thirties. Still more significant is her situation as a woman taking upon herself the welcome burden of the English poetic tradition. She studied (and memorized) earlier poetry all her life.[5] As Renaissance poets stood in complex awe, debt, affinity, and rivalry to their Greek and Roman predecessors (our guides, insisted Ben Jonson, not our commanders) so Millay stands to the male poets who preceded her. And she faces again the questions that had confronted them: How to define herself both with them and against them? How to appropriate what is still useful to her, and to separate what is not? What does she see that they have not seen? What can she say that they have not said?[6]

Perhaps most important of all is the help she found in Renaissance poetry for dealing with her most characteristic subjects: love, loss, change, loneliness, death. The many incidental reminiscences of William Shake-speare, John Donne, Andrew Marvell, the cavaliers, with here and there touches of Sir Philip Sidney, Ben Jonson, George Herbert, or John Milton seem to involve little more than the pleasures of familiarity for both Millay and her readers. But she is also indebted to them for technical hints and tricks, particularly the means of assuming, maintaining, and shifting an argumentative stance within a lyric. Beyond matters of craft she finds what was most useful to a woman of her generation determined to write freely about love: a thesaurus of attitudes to love as experienced by the active lover rather than passive beloved. What had been in English Renaissance poetry a cumulative exploration, covering two or three generations, of the many moods and facets of love, is for her a single complex stance immediately and simultaneously available for appropriation and revision.

Millay is most often and most self-consciously indebted to the Renaissance in her sonnets and sonnet sequences. She has, of course, several models available for the sonnet and draws freely on them: on the Romantics; on Milton, for example, for the voice attempted in the poems on public affairs.[7] But her relation to the Renaissance poetry of love is most deliberately apparent in *Fatal Interview*, the sonnet sequence, or rather, sonnet cycle, that appeared in 1931. She had throughout the twenties experimented with various voices in love, particularly that of the female libertine, and had achieved some Donne-like effects—the obscene playfulness of "Love, though for this you riddle me with darts"; the mocking poise of the abandoned and abandoning lover in "Oh, think not I am faithful to a vow!" or "I shall forget you presently, my dear"; or the elegiac wistfulness—more Catullus and Keats than Donne—of "And you as well must die, beloved dust."

But in *Fatal Interview* Millay attempts to do more than strike shocking, amusing, or pathetic poses. She aims to present a cyclic and therefore full account of a failed love affair, its narrative, and its many moods: excitement, uncertainty, possession, joy, remorse (anticipated and unanticipated), anger, anxiety, dispossession, and resignation. It was much praised when it first appeared; it is much less so now.[8] Its title is drawn from one of Donne's elegies, though its inspiration (as was Donne's in this case), is largely Shakespearean. In fifty-two sonnets it presents an entire "year" of love, yet it is a year that begins and ends in winter, loneliness, and need. It reminds one of Ben Jonson's remark that much of life consists in "making a little winter love in a dark corner."

Despite the excellence of individual sonnets, the sequence as a whole is uneven. Behind this judgment is the supposed weakness of the "plot." There is a strong opening (Sonnets I–XI) describing the moods and desires surrounding the approach of love and a still stronger ending (XXXIV–LII) on its loss and aftermath. In the middle, however, the love itself proves, despite some heroic assertions and mythological comparisons, strangely empty and unsatisfying. Millay is, after all, a more persuasive poet of desire and loss than of fulfillment. The strength of the best poems lies—setting aside for the moment the technical finesse of her imitation of the Petrarchan mode—in the dignity, the emotional range, and the moral courage of the woman who turns her gaze unflinchingly on her own needs and remorselessly exposes and clarifies them, however painful the exercise, however little the consolation attained.

Not that this process need always be grim. A charming pair of sonnets (IX and X) reveals her mixed desires at the start of the affair: both the surprisingly fierce need to possess the beloved (IX), and, at the same time, to come to him as a child bringing "Love in the open hand, no thing but that" (X). But then, mixed motives and effects are at the heart of this sequence. As in Shakespeare's sonnets, love and desire define themselves most vividly, most helplessly, in the presence of the things that threaten and finally overwhelm them: "Doubt . . . Time's ally, / Kinsman to Death, and leman of Despair" (XXXIV). Once these factors come into play, no Shakespearean redemptions ("But if the while I think on thee, dear friend, / All losses are restored and sorrows end" [Sonnet 30]) are on offer. For Millay, "Love is not all" and though she thinks she would not "sell" or "trade" it for "peace" or "food," she is not quite sure (XXX). She knows more certainly how to handle its loss. In the latter third of the sequence she turns, despite the breaking of her own heart (L), to attaining a generous, stoic resignation and forbearance:

> As the more injured party . . .
> The hour's amenities are all to me—
> The choice of weapons; and I gravely choose
> To let the weapons tarnish where they lie.
> (XL)

Thus a sequence that begins by bravely flourishing its associations with the Petrarchan tradition, with all past lovers, ends in a voice and on a note unmistakably her own.

More consistently successful as a connected sequence is *Sonnets from an Ungrafted Tree*. Unlike *Fatal Interview*, this is not deliberately literary or self-consciously reminiscent of the antique. Rather it undertakes a meditation on an emergent occasion worthy of Donne. Here is close, quiet observation of a moment, and of its intertwining of memories and desires with commonplace objects and actions, all told in a numbed voice, just sufficiently articulate for its purpose. The sequence observes and reports upon a grief experienced and incompletely mastered. This grief is not for the dying man—a wife, estranged from her husband, returns to nurse him briefly in his final illness—but for the love that never was between them, for the bleak, unbridgeable disjunction that was their marriage. It implies, in its quiet way, the high domestic tragedy of an action that did not happen. The first eight sonnets (of seventeen) establish the situation and her frame of mind. The sequence begins in medias res: "So she came back into his house again / And watched beside his bed until he died, / Loving him not at all" (46).[9] But this "middle" is already the end of the story. Again the scene is rainy winter, the woman going to the shed for firewood, observing "Where once her red geraniums had stood, / Where still their rotted stalks were to be seen," recollecting the blighted hopes she had once planted. Summer and a "small bird with iridescent wings" (47) have faded to an uncertain, scarcely credible memory. "Too impatient for a careful search" (48), she takes whatever wood comes to hand, even "knotty chunks that will not burn," though her passionate blowing forces the fire to kindle (49). She hears, and instinctively hides from, the grocer's man; she unwraps the parcels he has brought and cleans the floor: "Treacherously dear / and simple was the dull, familiar task" (51). She momentarily stills the "ever-clamorous care" by cleaning and polishing, "making mean and ugly objects fair" (52). She avoids conversation with solicitous neighbors and "her quiet ear" becomes painfully sensitive to every noise (53).

With Sonnets IX-X the reader moves into her mind, her memories of how her husband as a boy had "come into her life when anybody / Would have been welcome, so in need was she" (54); of their first acquaintance; of a moonstruck lake on an August night investing him with a "pleasant mystery," making "her body sluggish with desire" though he was "not her spirit's mate" (55). Sonnets XI–XIII continue her memories of their life together, gradually merging into the present moment. An apron lost from a clothesline in a winter storm, recovered in spring, only forces her to face "the whole year to be lived through once more" (56). Memory of their intimacies reminds her of her longing for "the magic World" from which he kept (and keeps) her (57). She remembers the "wan dream that was her waking day"—a dream of an unwilled journey, a motionless fleeing, a silent, empty scream.

The last four sonnets return to his impending death. The reader sees the loneliness and fear in which she keeps a "kettle boiling all night long, for company" (59). She imagines him as a stopped clock. Accustomed to this "death-in-life," she is repelled by the "hideous industry" that will surround his death. And finally, "Gazing upon him now, severe and dead," she

> sees a man she never saw before—
> The man who eats his victuals at her side,
> Small, and absurd, and hers: for once, not hers, unclassified.
>
> (62)

The sense of a final mystery retrospectively enshrouding their relationship is entirely appropriate: she has now lost what she never had; she is left only with her experience for her pains—and the reader's mute, unusable compassion.

What does this sequence owe to the Renaissance lyric? Very little directly, but very much in its characteristic spirit and address. In the midst of pain, as Edgar says at the end of *King Lear*, it is necessary to "Speak what we feel, not what we ought to say." That note is first sounded in Renaissance poetry. Hearing it again led Millay's early admirers to feel that hers was a spirit similar, in its way, to Shakespeare and Donne and all the rest, one sharing their sense that past forms must be tested against, and, if necessary, yield to, the imperative of her (and our) actual experience, that the world's book remains open, to be not only read but written in.

Whatever her "unevenness," Millay's response to the Renaissance lyricists, unlike that of such cool "objectivists" and high modernists as T. S. Eliot, remains perhaps truer to their original sense of the shifting interrelation between passion and form, libertinism and mutuality. She too is, in Shakespeare's phrase, "all in war with Time," (Sonnet 15) with a changeful world and a changeful self, on behalf of a love she finds continuing reason both to trust and to mistrust. Yet nothing is sacrificed to system, nothing folded into some hypothesized eternity. Rather she asks of love, in her time, and in her voice, the same questions they had asked. She is not—or not entirely—to blame, if the answers love provides are less than fully satisfying.

Notes

1. Edmund Wilson, *The Shores of Light* (New York: Farrar, Straus and Young, 1952), 745.

2. Citations of Millay's poetry, other than the sonnets, are taken from *Collected Poems*, ed. Norma Millay (New York: Harper & Row, 1956), with page references included in the text.

3. John Crowe Ransom, *The World's Body* (Baton Rouge: Louisiana State University Press, 1968), 104. This view of Millay's accomplishment is also reflected—albeit from a very different angle—in some recent feminist criticism; see, for example, Jane Stanbrough, "Edna St. Vincent Millay and the Language of Vulnerability," in *Shakespeare's Sisters: Feminist Essays on Woman Poets*, eds. Sandra M. Gilbert and Susan Gubar (Bloomington: Indiana University Press, 1979), 183–99.

4. Wilson, 242.

5. Elizabeth Barnett, in the most recent edition of the *Collected Sonnets* (New York: Harper & Row, 1988), prints, for example, a note reporting Millay's enthusiastic reading, memorization, and rereading of Wordsworth xiii–xiv).

6. Instructive in this regard is Debra Fried's analysis of Millay's response to the Romantic sonnet, "Andromeda Unbound: Gender and Genre in Millay's Sonnets," *Twentieth Century Literature* 32 (Spring 1986), 1–22.

7. They seem unsuccessful in that they do not, as Milton's "heroic" sonnets do, seem parts of a body of implied conviction, but rather mere scattered protests.

8. Typical is Judith Farr's recent account of it as representing "diligently embroidered" (301) and "well-mimed acts of homage" (301–2) to Elizabethan originals, less rewarding, with its "glitter" and "solicited effect" (303) than the more deeply realized emulations of, for example, Elinor Wylie. "Elinor Wylie, Edna St. Vincent Millay, and the Elizabethan Sonnet Tradition," in *Poetic Traditions of the English Renaissance*, eds. Maynard Mack and George deForest Lord (New Haven: Yale University Press, 1982), 287–305.

9. Sonnets are cited from *Collected Sonnets of Edna St. Vincent Millay* (New York: Harper & Row, 1988), with page references included in the text.

Female Female Impersonator:
Millay and the Theatre of Personality

SANDRA M. GILBERT

"It is a dangerous lot, that of the charming, romantic public poet, especially if it falls to a woman."

—Louise Bogan

". . . family, I discover that I have nothing to give readings in, I *must* have long dresses, trailing ones. The short ones won't do."

—Edna St. Vincent Millay

"In the late Forties Marianne Moore walked into a milliner's shop and asked to be fitted as Washington Crossing the Delaware."

—Bonnie Costello

In October 1917, at New York's Neighborhood Playhouse, the Wisconsin Players performed a new one-act work by the poet Wallace Stevens. Set in a curiously surrealistic seventeenth century, *Bowl, Cat and Broomstick* is a facetious piece of literary criticism in which the three oddly named title characters, exploring the idea that "there is a special power in the poetry of a beauty," meditate on the portrait of a French poetess called Claire Dupray.[1] Significantly, however, the play goes on to deconstruct both the image and the imagination of the hapless Claire. In doing so, Stevens's minidrama simultaneously underscores the surprising fetishization of the woman poet in a twentieth century of which the work's fictive seventeenth century is a bizarre reflection, emphasizes the aesthetic dissonance that marked the careers of male and female poets in the period, and indicates the intensity of the irony with which contemporary male litterateurs confronted these new developments. Perhaps more important, the play's action points to a situation that twentieth-century women poets both exploited and resisted in their struggle to transform themselves from art objects to artists.

This essay was written specifically for this volume and is published here for the first time. However, some portions of this essay have appeared in Sandra M. Gilbert, "Marianne Moore as Female Female Impersonator," in Joseph Paris: ed. *Marianne Moore: The Art of a Modernist* (Ann Arbor: UMI Research Press, 1990). William Carlos Williams reprinted by permission of New Directions Publishing Corporation.

When *Bowl, Cat and Broomstick* begins, Bowl, an ascetic aesthete, is translating Claire Dupray's verses for his admiring disciple Cat, but with the entrance of Broomstick, a "hard-looking" skeptic, the three turn their attention to the picture of the writer that decorates the frontispiece of her book and begin to speculate on Claire's age, as well as on the relationship between her age, her sex, her beauty, and her art. "She cannot be more than twenty-two," declares Bowl, adding that that "is an age . . . when a girl like Claire Dupray, becomes a poetess." "Say poet—poet. I hate poetess," remonstrates Cat, but Broomstick sardonically observes that "poetess is just the word at twenty-two!" (25) Further analysis of Claire Dupray's work seems to prove the justice of his claim, for the verse of this beauty sounds as extravagantly sentimental as any produced by the "lady writers with three names" whom most modernists deplored.[2] "This emotional waste," Broomstick notes, "is all thirty years old at the least. . . . What I hold against Claire Dupray, above everything else, is just that she is not herself in her day" (32). Finally, the play proves his judgment correct. When the three friends read the preface to Claire's collection, they discover (to the mortification of Bowl and Cat) that Claire Madeleine Colombier Dupray is really fifty-three years old—and "Damn all portraits of poets and poetesses," cries Cat in chagrin (34).

On the surface, of course, the stylish intellectual farce these characters enact is intended to instruct audiences in the distinction between appearance and reality even as, through the monitory figure of Broomstick, it advances a self-consciously twentieth-century aesthetic: poets should "make it new" and even old Broom(sticks) should sweep the world clean of the past's trashy sentimentality.[3] But why does the fastidious *philosophe* of "Sunday Morning" dramatize his allegory of art in terms of male critical gullibility and female poetic pretentiousness? A line spoken by Bowl, as he struggles to balance erotic admiration with aesthetic evaluation, suggests a clue: "It is a new thing that the eyes of a poetess should bring us to this"(27). For although Broomstick ironically responds that "We are not living in the seventeenth century for nothing," the creator of this bemused trio of (miss) readers would certainly have noticed that in just the year when he was composing his playlet "a new thing" was happening on the New York literary scene: Bowls and Cats all over town were talking, as Wallace Stevens would have it, about "the poetry of a beauty" that was thought by all to have a very "special power."

Edna St. Vincent Millay—whose name, interestingly enough, rhymes with that of Claire Dupray—had actually begun a meteoric career as poetess in 1912, when she was twenty years old and her long poem, "Renascence," won a prize in a contest sponsored by the *Lyric Year*. Taking the literary world by storm, the talented ingenue from Camden, Maine, was immediately taken up by a series of wealthy benefactors, who arranged for her to attend Vassar College on scholarship, and who joined in fêting her at parties in New York.[4] This astonishing debut was quickly followed by further triumphs about which Stevens would certainly have known, for throughout her college years Millay continued publishing poetry and, already Vassar's best-known undergraduate, she garnered even more attention for her acting.[5]

That this youthful poet was as physically lovely as *Bowl, Cat and Broomstick*'s Claire Dupray can only have contributed to her success. In the spring of 1913, the photographer Arnold Genthe posed her against a background of magnolia blossoms for a portrait that later made its way into the Museum of the City of New York, and that might well have served as the frontispiece on which Stevens's harried critics brood. But that Millay was as productive as she was attractive may have contributed even more than her notoriety to the ambivalence she must have aroused in some male contemporaries. It seems relevant here that her first collection, *Renascence and Other Poems*, appeared in the fall of 1917, shortly before Stevens's play was performed and six years before the author of *Harmonium* had published his own first volume. And it seems equally relevant that the works in *Renascence and Other Poems* could be either praised or blamed for their use of poetic strategies that were all "thirty years old at least."[6]

Millay continued to forge a brilliant public career throughout the twenties and thirties. In 1920 her bravura *A Few Figs from Thistles* was published to such acclaim that she became, in one critic's words, "the It-girl of the hour, the Miss America of 1920."[7] In 1922 she produced a highly traditional poem called *The Ballad of the Harp-Weaver*, for which she became (in 1923, the year when Stevens's *Harmonium* appeared) the first woman to receive the Pulitzer Prize in poetry. In 1924, she undertook a series of lucrative reading tours and in the thirties she began to broadcast her poems over the radio. By 1936 few readers would have questioned Elizabeth Atkins's assertion that—rather than being at least thirty years out of date, like Claire Dupray— Edna St. Vincent Millay "represents our time to itself."

Besides representing "the incarnation of our *Zeitgeist*,"[8] however, Edna Millay might be said to have stood for another phenomenon: the rise of a group of women poets whose fame was as theatrical as it was literary. Where even the most notable precursors of these women—Elizabeth Barrett Browning, Emily Dickinson, Christina Rossetti—had achieved their reputations despite (or, indeed, in some cases because of) lives of radical seclusion, such early twentieth-century poets as Amy Lowell, Edna Millay, Elinor Wylie, and Edith Sitwell ascended lecture platforms as exuberantly as they gave readings in private salons. Costuming themselves to reflect the self-definitions their poems recorded (Lowell in "high-collared dresses sprinkled with beads" that made her look like "Holbein's Henry VIII," Millay in floating chiffon, Wylie in heavy silver "armor," Sitwell in quasi-Elizabethan robes), they made literal the dream of the "poetess" as dramatic public personality that had captivated the nineteenth-century imagination in Madame de Staël's *Corinne*.[9]

Not surprisingly, many men of letters decided that, as F. R. Leavis quipped about Sitwell, such female aesthetic careers belonged "to the history of publicity rather than of poetry," and quite a few longed, with the skeptical ferocity of Stevens's Broomstick, to sweep away their debased, publicity-seeking women rivals.[10] Raging against Lowell's famous transformation of Imagism to "Amygism," Ezra Pound labeled the cigar-smoking New Englander a "hippopoetess," while Thomas Wolfe, in *The Web and the Rock*, produced a savage portrait of Elinor Wylie as a babyishly narcissistic ice queen.[11] More generally, T. S. Eliot, in an early draft of *The Waste Land*, sketched a composite portrait of a modern "poetess," a woman named Fresca whose lineaments limned all the faults—critical acclaim, sexual depravity, a derivative style—with which he and his contemporaries associated the Amy Lowells and Elinor Wylies, the Edna Millays and Claire Duprays. With Stevens's Broomstick, Eliot appears to have felt that serious (male) readers ought to sweep art clean of the commercially compelling "emotional waste" excreted by such popular artists before men of letters themselves were swept away.[12]

As literary history records, of course, male modernist poets were emphatically not swept away by the witches' brooms they may have associated with some of their female contemporaries. On the contrary, though in her own day Millay functioned as a kind of American Poetess Laureate, it was her achievement, along with the accomplishments of the women around her, which was rapidly dismissed by the canonizing judgment of time. That these "poetesses" have been eliminated from critical consideration is dramatically revealed by their absence from most major anthologies as well as from most of the supposedly serious studies of twentieth-century poetry which have appeared in recent decades. William Pritchard's *Lives of the Modern Poets* (1980), for instance, contains not one reference to Millay, Wylie, Lowell or Louise Bogan, nor does Jerome Mazzaro's *Modern American Poetry: Essays in Criticism* (1970). As for M. L. Rosenthal's influential *The Modern Poets: A Critical Introduction* (1960), this book offers a single allusion to Millay, a reference which illuminates the omissions that mark subsequent studies: in a discussion of Elizabeth Bishop, the author remarks that "In her poems about Negroes and the poor Miss Bishop can be sentimental; these and her love poetry have just the consistency of a typical Millay poem." Ten years after the death of the writer who had once seemed to "represent our time to itself," her name had become a code word for bad art.[13]

To be sure, there were at least a few women poets whom the taste-making theorists of modernism did not so rapidly consign to oblivion. Most strikingly, Marianne Moore was widely treated as an icon of the new, a kind of anti-Poetess Laureate whose work avoided the emotional excesses to which female flesh was generally thought to be heir. In fact, Wallace Stevens, the playwright who in 1917 had vented his spleen on Claire Dupray, magisterially opined that Moore was "A Poet That Matters" in the title of his book review of her *Selected Poems* that he published in *Life and Letters Today* in

1935, and William Carlos Williams, too, continually celebrated her achievements. In addition, T. S. Eliot and Ezra Pound were among a number of other crucial figures who found her work compelling.[14]

Can there have been two canons formed by twentieth-century women who wrote verse—the canon of work produced by "poetesses" and the canon of art created by anti-"poetesses"? Must contemporary female poets choose between radically opposed literary matrilineages, one which is poetically "incorrect" from the modernist perspective, and one which is aesthetically respectable? If Millay stands for a female poetic tradition that descends from "bad" (blatantly sentimental) nineteenth-century poetasters, does Moore stand for a female poetic tradition that descends from such a "good" (intellectually vigorous) nineteenth-century artist as Emily Dickinson? Though this may at first seem to be the case, there are a number of surprising similarities between the representative figures of Millay and Moore, similarities that reveal yet again the problematic situation of the woman poet in the twentieth century even while they dramatize the strategies through which both writers translated the "handicap" of "femininity" into an aesthetic advantage.[15]

To begin with "femininity": both Millay and Moore were quickly fetishized as women poets. As early as 1923, in just the years when Millay had become the "It-girl" of popular American verse, T. S. Eliot was implicitly defining Moore as the "It-girl" of the avant-garde intelligentsia, pointedly celebrating her not for the absence but for the presence of "femininity" in her *oeuvre*. And that this appropriately "modern" artist looked as "feminine" as Genthe's tenderly girlish Millay was continually emphasized by Williams, who liked to remember the "two cords, cables rather, of red hair coiled around her rather small cranium," and by the many other admiring observers who became as obsessed with her tricorn hat and cape as Millay's fans had been with her trailing gowns.[16]

Interestingly, too, as Moore's reputation among intellectuals began to decline during the fifties and sixties, even positive analyses of her work increasingly emphasized its stereotypically "feminine" qualities. M. L. Rosenthal spoke of her "precious and recherché impressions"; Roy Harvey Pearce noted her "polite and lady-like presence."[17] Nevertheless, in just these years Marianne Moore had become exactly the kind of public "incarnation of our *Zeitgeist*"—in the words of Elizabeth Atkins—that Millay was earlier. According to one observer, when Moore read at the Boston Arts Festival in 1958, "a crowd of something like five thousand persons" was waiting to applaud her.[18] In her tricorn hat and "great cape," she had become an icon of eccentric but distinctively female art. Perhaps it was inevitable, therefore, that—like Millay—she would be entirely excluded from Pritchard's *Lives of the Modern Poets*.

But Millay and Moore had more in common than feminizing publicity. In particular, though both may have thought of the poetic imagination as gender-free, both were ultimately brought to engender it; in fact, whether or not they felt as "naturally" feminine as their admirers and detractors thought they were, both deliberately adopted the mask of "the feminine" as an equivocally empowering one, a stance that allowed both to work from the positions of fetishized femininity in which critics had placed them, using the newly public roles of twentieth-century "poetess" laureate or anti "poetess" laureate as "free" (precisely because "female") spaces from which they could question many of the conventions of their culture.

In doing this, both were employing a characteristic female strategy defined in the forties by Karen Horney. In a study of this analyst's "social psychology of women," Marcia Westkott explains that the woman whom Horney classifies as an "onlooker" simultaneously participates in and detachedly analyzes the drama of her own life. "Critically observing herself and others," writes Westkott, "may be the way that a woman is looking at herself being looked at. She becomes the omniscient observer of her own sexualization, the voyeur of the voyeurs of her . . . body." As such, she complies with male demands for stereotypical "femininity" even while she rebels against them, "her superiority logged in stinging . . . observation and judgment."[19] Similarly, the French theorist Luce Irigaray has spoken of the "masquerade" of femininity, drawing on an important essay—"Womanliness as a Masquerade"—published by the psychoanalyst Joan Rivière in 1929. While Irigaray sees such impersonation, or masquerade, as a consequence of the fact that in patriarchal culture women are inevitably "exiled from themselves," Horney is correct in suggesting that for women like Millay and Moore such a self-exile, such an ironic estrangement, was in some sense deliberate.[20]

To be sure, as their reputations suggest, Millay and Moore masqueraded as—that is, they simultaneously impersonated and analyzed—very different sorts of "feminine" personalities. A comment by the poet-critic Elder Olson implies the degree of consciousness with which both adopted public characters that also infused and facilitated their verse: "Marianne Moore was very much the spinster schoolteacher. And Edna Millay was the medieval princess, fatigued by too many chivalric romances."[21] Thus Millay, as most readers noticed, generally presented herself as a prototypical *femme fatale*; Moore, as many observed, depicted herself as a paradigmatic "old maid." But the self-consciousness with which they responded to, and reinforced, their own female reification is evident not only in their verse but also in their most casual sketches of themselves.

In 1920, for instance, Millay-as-"onlooker" scribbled what she described as "a lewd portrait of myself" for Edmund Wilson:

E. St. V. M.

Hair which she still devoutly trusts is red . . .
A large mouth,
Lascivious,

Asceticized by blasphemies.
A long throat,
Which will someday
Be strangled . . .
A small body,
Unexclamatory,
But which,
Were it the fashion to wear no clothes,
Would be as well-dressed
As any.[22]

Decades later, Moore produced a similarly high-spirited self-analysis, though one that suggested a very different female image. For where Millay had depicted herself as seductive, Moore, gazing at a photograph of herself, transformed her physiognomy into a comically spinsterish menagerie: "I'm good natured but hideous as an old hop toad. I look like a scarecrow. . . . I look permanently alarmed, like a frog. I *aspire* to be neat, I try to do my hair with a lot of thought to avoid those explosive sunbursts, but when one hairpin goes in, another seems to come out. . . . My physiognomy isn't classic at all, it's like a banana-nosed monkey. (She stops for a second thought.) Well, I do seem at least to be awake, don't I?"[23]

Dissimilar as these self-portraits are, they suggest what was for early twentieth-century women poets an increasingly inescapable link between female anatomy and literary destiny, between the perceived body of the "feminine" poet and the body of her work. And although such a link had been in the first place at least partly forged by both positive and negative male reactions to female aspirations, it ultimately made the achievements of these writers especially vulnerable to attacks by modernist male theorists, for whom "good" poetry involved what Eliot called an "escape from personality." In fact, the critical struggles associated with the emergence of poetic modernism were consistently sexualized: "bad" verse was stereotypically "feminine" (i.e., formally conservative, sentimental, lacking in aesthetic or intellectual ambition), while "good" poetry was stereotypically masculine (i.e., formally innovative, "hard," abstract, ambitious). Or, as William Carlos Williams once put it:

And what is good poetry made of
And what is good poetry made of
Of rats and snails and puppy-dog's tails
And that is what good poetry is made of

And what is bad poetry made of
And what is bad poetry made of
Of sugar and spice and everything nice
That is what bad poetry is made of[24]

Thus, as the modernist aesthetic was gradually institutionalized during the first half of the century, the accomplishments of Millay and Moore as representative figures came to seem increasingly marginal, so much so that younger women who might have turned to them as heartening examples were often surprisingly ambivalent toward these important precursors. Traditional "poetesses" like Millay had been defined as offensively emotional and anachronistic; ostensible innovators like Moore were seen as "precious" and "recherché." The canon reflected in Pritchard's *Lives*—Thomas Hardy, William Butler Yeats, Edwin Arlington Robinson, Robert Frost, Pound, Eliot, Stevens, Hart Crane, Williams—had become *the* canon of the respectably modern. To focus on Millay as a paradigmatic "female female impersonator" in order to reread her work against the background of surprisingly similar writings by her apparent aesthetic opposite Marianne Moore—and to continue to bear in mind these writers' paradoxical but courageous deployment of the feminine masquerade as a response to the feminization-as-trivialization with which contemporary literary culture greeted them—is to discover that both worked in a poetic tradition whose deliberate dramatization of "womanliness" was in a number of significant ways to shape the achievements of such midcentury artists as Sylvia Plath, Anne Sexton, Adrienne Rich, and Elizabeth Bishop.

That Edna St. Vincent Millay was fatigued by "chivalric romance" even while she acted the part of a femme fatale was plain from the first, notably in some of the scornful jingles called *A Few Figs from Thistles*. These early verses, which made the poet notorious, function as wittily feminine manifestoes of the New Woman's new determination to be free. Celebrating sexual liberation, they reveal this self-assertively sexy and consciously feminist young female author's determination to revel in "modern" woman's unprecedented erotic autonomy—

> And if I love you Wednesday,
> Well, what is that to you?
> I do not love you Thursday—
> So much is true.[25]

To be sure, from a severely modernist perspective such works might not be considered serious poems, yet in their impudent way they begin to make claims about the early twentieth-century's battle of the sexes that are directly related to those made by, say, T. S. Eliot's "Cousin Nancy" or even by his "Love Song of J. Alfred Prufrock." But if Eliot masked himself as a balding young gentleman poised "on the doorstep of the Absolute" in order to question changes in what had earlier appeared to be the "unalterable law" of male superiority, Millay posed as an apparently conventional *femme fatale*— at once a cheerful flapper and a weary princess—in order to propose further changes in what had hitherto been "the unalterable law" of romance that governed women's lives. Indeed, though in such works as the sonnet cycle

Fatal Interview she does frankly write the poetry of passion with which her name has been consistently identified, even these verses implicitly question the conventions of Eros, for they tend to emphasize the ways in which the female speaker who acquiesces in romance is rendered vulnerable, the ways in which love (and the male lover) wound, scar, drown woman.[26] But perhaps more important, a number of other texts in Millay's *Collected Poems* radically undercut the aesthetic of heterosexual love, denying or deriding the emotional imperatives that would leave women drowned in desire.

Specifically, from *A Few Figs from Thistles* onward, Millay costumes herself as a *femme fatale* in order to recreate conventional love scenes as interviews which would be fatal to male rather than female lovers. Seducing her paramours with glittering rhymes and stylishly crafted sonnets, she betrays them in closing stanzas and final couplets that mock and shock. For example, such sonnets as "I, being born a woman and distressed," and "Oh, oh, you will be sorry for that word!" note the needs of the flesh with amused detachment but redefine romance as a comic game so that the female vulnerability which the writer stresses in her more serious works becomes merely a temporary problem. Though the speaker of "I, being born a woman and distressed" admits that desire may leave her "undone, possessed," she warns her lover that "I find this frenzy insufficient reason / For conversation when we meet again" (601). And though the protagonist of "Oh, oh, you will be sorry for that word!" responds to her lover's insulting remark "What a big book for such a little head!" by appearing to acquiesce in his patronizing misogyny—"You will not catch me reading any more"—her lighthearted remarks end with a threat:

> And some day when you knock and push the door,
> Some sane day, not too bright and not too stormy,
> I shall be gone, and you may whistle for me.
>
> (591)

Elsewhere, however, the flippancy of these stanzas is translated into a rhetoric of greater *hauteur*. "Women have loved before as I love now," from *Fatal Interview*, revises "chivalric romance" to cast its speaker as a Guinevere or Isolde whose autonomous consciousness is the controlled center, not the uncontrollable calamity, of romantic idyll; while "Well, I have lost you; and I lost you fairly," from the same sequence, characterizes the speaker as a female Good Soldier, tough and generous. Finally, "I too beneath your moon, almighty Sex" reviews and reappraises a post-Havelock Ellis, post-Freud love life with calm, if sardonic, self-scrutiny.

Throughout all these antiromantic poems about romance, Millay deliberately impersonates a *femme fatale* whose adventures are energized by, and issue in, proud independence. A late poem supposedly spoken by Sappho summarizes this twentieth-century poet's attitude, for, repudiating the old legend that the

Greek poet had died for love of the ferryman Phaon, Millay's Sappho declares in unapologetic tones that "I die, that the sweet tongue of bound Aeolia never from her throat be torn," adding "Phaon, I shall not die for you again. / There are few poets. And my own child tells me there are other men" (452).

But the feminist identification with women implicit in this poem about Millay's ancient precursor surfaces even more clearly in her verses about women than it does in her deconstructions of the ideology of romance. Most notably, her analysis of the courage of women and the authority of female experience is offered in her finest sonnet-sequence, "Sonnets from an Ungrafted Tree." This beautifully poised early narrative, set on a bleak New England farm, explores the privations of a failed marriage from the point of view of a disillusioned wife who left her husband but, hearing that he is ill, "came back into his house again / And watched beside his bed until he died, / Loving him not at all." And Millay here celebrates womanly "endurance," documenting her argument with domestic details which become resonant symbols of both the daily drudgery against which her protagonist's spirit must contend and the determination to survive through which this woman transforms housewifery into heroism.

Sawdust and laundry, jellyjars and kettles—these are the paraphernalia of the world that encloses the New England wife, but in "An Ungrafted Tree" such apparently trivial things become, as William Carlos Williams would have them, intractable ideas. Besides dramatizing the tedium of this woman's life, however, Millay explores the origins of wifely bitterness, recounting how youthful eroticism had forced the young woman into a bad marriage. Significantly, indeed, it is only when the husband dies that he becomes a figure of tragic dignity and, indeed, an icon of new life for his widow. The concluding sonnet of "An Ungrafted Tree" examines the inscrutability of death in a manner reminiscent of such great modernist meditations as Rainer Maria Rilke's poem "Corpse-Washing" or D. H. Lawrence's short story "Odour of Chrysanthemums": "Gazing upon him, now, severe and dead," the New England wife is

> . . . as one who enters, sly, and proud,
> To where her husband speaks before a crowd,
> And sees a man she never saw before—
> The man who eats his victuals at her side,
> Small, and absurd, and hers: for once, not hers, unclassified.
>
> (622)

But where Rilke emphasizes the corpse-washers' recognition of the dead man's authority and the widow in Lawrence's story feels "fear and shame" at the otherness of her dead husband, Millay's protagonist feels joy that this new stranger is "not hers, unclassified" and, by implication, exultation that she is no longer his and classified. This once troublesome lover has become an empowering figure for the woman who gazes on his body precisely because now he is *not*, he is "no man."

But of course, despite her celebrations of female survival, Millay could not deceive herself about the history in whose context both she herself as insouciant *femme fatale* and her New England woman as durable widow achieved their moments of triumph. Even her comparatively early and lighthearted *Aria da Capo*, for instance, has an undercurrent of bleakness. A Pirandello-like comedy of manners, this work—Millay's most popular drama and the one that she herself regarded as her best—offers the romantic frivolity of a stylized Pierrot and Columbine as a counterpoint to the pastoral calamity that overtakes two shepherds, Corydon and Thyrsis, when—forced by Cothurnus, the "Masque of Tragedy," to act out a miniature two-man war—they kill each other. Written at the end of World War I, the play offers a fatigued commentary on the foolishness of male battles, with Columbine complaining "what a mess / This set is in! . . . [Cothurnus] might at least have left the scene / The way he found it."[27] At the same time, the merry harlequinade which is rapidly resumed by the Commedia dell'Arte lovers could be taken as a pacifist critique of the civilian tendency to want to return to the oblivious superficiality of life as usual. But the drama's title—*Aria da Capo*—with its emphasis on the Freudian repetition compulsion that marks cycles of militarism, along with Columbine's bemused detachment ("How curious to strangle him like that, / With colored paper ribbons" [43]), suggests that Millay feels exactly the feminist scorn for the problems of Cothurnus's minions that Virginia Woolf was to express a decade and a half later in *Three Guineas*.

As Millay grew older, such masculine destructiveness came to seem even more oppressive to her. In the mid-1920s she was passionately involved in attempts to save Nicola Sacco and Bartolomeo Vanzetti from execution; in the thirties, she was horrified by the Spanish Civil War and by the encroaching shadows of fascism in Europe; in the forties, she dedicated her talent to propagandizing for the Allied cause during World War II. Thus, the strangely empowering image of the dead man with which "Sonnets from an Ungrafted Tree" concludes was gradually supplanted by a more frightening figure of death as a lover and of a lover as deadly, a figure that the poem "Wine from These Grapes" specifically politicizes.

"Wine from These Grapes" is clearly informed by Millay's rage at the case of Sacco and Vanzetti. Its central image draws upon Julia Ward Howe's famous "We are trampling out the vintage where the grapes of wrath are stored." But its conclusion is far more sinister than anything promised by "The Battle Hymn of the Republic." Beginning "Wine from these grapes I shall be treading surely / Morning and noon and night until I die," the poem moves to a curiously morbid climax:

> Death, fumbling to uncover
> My body in his bed,

> Shall know
> There has been one
> Before him.
>
> (234)

Rewriting the last sonnet of "An Ungrafted Tree" so that the gazing woman herself becomes no more than a dead creature, these lines unnervingly imply that, before it is chilled by the embrace of death, the body of the speaker will already have been contaminated by another love—"one / Before him"— whose clasp is even more horrifying.

Who is this lover more terrible than death? The poet does not specify, but the context in which she sets "Wine from These Grapes" implies that he is one among "Those Without Pity," the "Cruel of heart" who have formed and deformed history. Not surprisingly, then, from the mid-twenties on Millay alternates between hostile imaginings of the death of this deadly lover and diatribes against his ubiquitous powers, diatribes which become increasingly fierce as the poet is forced to recognize the helplessness of her revenge fantasies. The sardonically titled sonnet-sequence "Epitaph for the Race of Man" predicts a general apocalypse, a time when "Man and his engines [will] be no longer here." A curse-poem in the same volume, "Apostrophe to Man," subtitled "(on reflecting that the world is ready to go to war again)," even more frankly articulates the message implicit in the sonnet-sequence: "Detestable race, continue to expunge yourself, die out" (302).

But such fantastic curses were, of course, merely fantasies, as a series of yet more helplessly angry poems note. Perhaps the most striking of them, the late "An Ancient Gesture" questions the epic posturings of one of history's primordial heroes and, by setting them against the gestural primacy of an epic heroine, suggests that the only redemption of a male-dominated culture might come from the suffering—and the survival—of women like the protagonist of "An Ungrafted Tree."

> I thought, as I wiped my eyes on the corner of my apron:
> Penelope did this too. . . .
> This is an ancient gesture, authentic, antique,
> In the very best tradition, classic, Greek;
> Ulysses did this too.
> But only as a gesture,—a gesture which implied
> To the assembled throng that he was much too moved to speak.
> He learned it from Penelope . . .
> Penelope, who really cried.
>
> (501)

Yet even as this verse subverts the political glamour of the itinerant Ulysses, its ultimate irony is precisely Penelope's stationary helplessness as well as the helplessness of the poem's speaker, the uncontrollably sincere weeping of both women. In fact, the darkening of Millay's political vision in this period suggests that the once impudent *femme fatale* has had to accept the fatalities of a society in which, just as the woman cannot say to the man, "expunge yourself, die out," she cannot declare, either, that someday "I shall be gone and you may whistle for me." At the same time, however, the notably feminine images through which Millay has consistently chosen to dramatize her ideas should remind us of a constant throughout all her verse: her self-presentation as distinctively "female." If Penelope is known by her tear-stained apron, so Millay's earlier women characters are marked by the "long dresses, trailing ones" in which the poet herself gave readings—emblems of a stylized role adopted as much out of aesthetic and moral commitment as out of emotional necessity.

Indeed, it is arguable that even some of the verse genres in which this artist chose to work functioned metaphorically just as her costumes functioned literally: to dramatize the artifice and to question the arbitrariness of "feminine" (poetic) identity. Her love sonnets, for example, allowed her to enact an erotic role reversal comparable to the one Christina Rossetti defined in her prefatory note to "Monna Innominata," letting her show what might have happened had "such a lady [as Beatrice or Laura] spoken for herself."[28] But because Millay, unlike Rossetti, was working in this form at a time when it seemed (to quote Stevens again) "thirty years old at the least" to male modernist contemporaries, the genre itself became a kind of archaic costume in which this rebellious poet almost parodically attired herself so as to call attention to the antiquated garb of "femininity." Whether the corset of form in which she encased her ideas was Shakespearean or Petrarchan, the very process of rhyming and measuring that the composition of any sonnet entails would in effect let her become, in Marcia Westkott's words, the "voyeur of the voyeurs" of the "body" of her work.

At the same time, though, the mastery with which Millay deployed the sonnet form (with even Allen Tate conceding that her "best sonnets would adorn any of the great English sequences") made it just as crucially a garment in which she could in the octave seduce (male) readers and then in the sestet or concluding couplet betray them.[29] Her posthumously published "I will put Chaos into fourteen lines" is in fact a kind of manifesto for this essentially vengeful project:

> I will put Chaos into fourteen lines
> And keep him there; and let him thence escape
> If he be lucky; let him twist, and ape
> Flood, fire, and demon—his adroit designs
> Will strain to nothing in the strict confines
> Of this sweet Order, where, in pious rape,
> I hold his essence and amorphous shape,
> Till he with Order mingles and combines. . . .

I shall not even force him to confess;
Or answer. I will only make him good.

(728)

As Debra Fried points out in a fine essay on "Gender and Genre in Millay's Sonnets," "A pun gives this [poem's] closure double force. Millay makes the sonnet aesthetically good by tempering the behavior of the unruly subject in its artful cage. [Thus] the woman poet binds 'Chaos'—a kind of male anti-muse . . . with the 'strict confines' of her ordering art."[30] To occupy a "female" position, this strategy implies, allows a perception of the artifice of sex roles even while it also permits a celebration of the real values—nurturance, endurance—that the artificial role of "woman" paradoxically makes possible.

Millay's posthumous *Mine the Harvest* includes a poem that significantly links the "It-girl" of the antimodernists with the unlikely contemporary who was the "It-girl" of the intellectuals. "The Strawberry Shrub" offers a close analysis of a plant that is "quaint as quinces" and "duller / Than history." Interestingly, moreover, the poem praises this emblematic shrub for just the apparently "ladylike" virtues of "modesty" and "humility" that the self-effacing and ironically "spinsterish" Moore celebrated throughout her career: "You must bruise it a bit: it does not exude; it yields" (455).

It is not unlikely that Millay had been reading Moore when she wrote these lines, but the question of direct influence is not directly relevant. For as the precise observations of, say, "Sonnets from an Ungrafted Tree" suggest, the poet who wrote "The Strawberry Shrub" had long been interested in what Adrienne Rich has called "that detail outside ourselves that brings us to ourselves."[31] What she might well have intuited in the work of her apparent aesthetic opposite was a similar sense that such details, humble and "duller / Than history," incarnate the durability and the deliberately ironic differentness of that quality which has been labeled "the feminine."

Readers have, of course, long noted the ways in which Marianne Moore's observations of the natural world tended to emphasize the paradoxical strength of supposed weakness. Perhaps most famously, the late "His Shield" meditates on the mythical salamander, who triumphs by being willing, like Millay's strawberry bush, to "yield." Beyond the will to self-aggrandizement that constructs history, this creature understands "the power of relin-quishing / what one would keep; that is freedom."[32] It is a freedom, however, that Moore at least as a subtext associates with a female alienation from—or, to put the case more strongly, a female refusal to be complicitous in—history. And it is a freedom that this poet learned to imagine through her self-creation as a "spinster" outsider, that is, through a process of "female female impersonation" which paralleled (though it differed from) Millay's.

Even in some of Moore's first published poems the beginning of this process can be seen. For just as Millay's early *Figs* often seem designed to taunt male suitors by flaunting her charms as a *femme fatale* who is indifferent to their wiles, so Moore's early verses frequently seem meant to daunt male readers by forcing them to attend to the acerbic lessons taught by a "spinster schoolteacher" who is as apt to scold as to reward little boys for what they regard as their chief achievements. Such poems as "To Statecraft Embalmed" and "To Military Progress," for instance, are as fierce as Millay's angriest polemics in their chastisings of masculinist swagger. "To Statecraft Embalmed" begins with pure contempt—"There is nothing to be said for you" (35)—and "To Military Progress" excoriates the implicitly masculinist "mind / like a millstone" whose grindings inspire "black minute-men / to revive again, / war / / at little cost" (82).

Such overt misandry was associated with a commitment to feminism that was also analogous to Millay's. In her extraordinary "Marriage" Moore produced a critique of a central patriarchal institution that was comparable to the bitter analysis embedded in Millay's "Sonnets from an Ungrafted Tree." Besides elaborating the feminism embodied in Moore's early epigrammatic verses, however, "Marriage" demonstrates this poet's continuing construction of a female mask that both complemented and contradicted Millay's. For this complex meditation, which the poet herself called "an anthology" of quotations, is also a crucial statement of alienation spoken by a "spinsterish" outsider. Indeed, it is more specifically through its noncommittal alienation than through its committed feminism that this text reveals the direction which Moore's pose as "spinster schoolteacher" would take her.

To be even more specific: "Marriage" is clearly spoken by someone to whom what Adrienne Rich has called "compulsory heterosexuality" has simply never seemed either compulsory or compelling.[33] Indeed, this poem is a soliloquy that stands entirely outside sexuality to look at its erotic and romantic conventions from, as it were, an extraterrestrial perspective—or, perhaps more accurately, from the point of view of an entirely self-sufficient, apparently asexual creature, a genius of an amoeba, say. With scrupulously objective phrasing, the first lines of the poem establish this perspective, notably through the reiteration of the neutral pronoun "one":

> This institution,
> perhaps one should say enterprise
> out of respect for which
> one says one need not change one's mind
> about a thing one has believed in,
> requiring public promises
> of one's intention
> to fulfil a private obligation:
> I wonder what Adam and Eve
> think of it by this time.
>
> (62)

Such stereotypically "spinsterish" alienation must also have reinforced Moore's feminist inclination to deconstruct patriarchal history from the perspective of a nonparticipant in other crucial institutions even while it allowed her to reconstruct a history of her own—a natural history. Thus, coming at the very questions which concerned Millay—the relations between the sexes, the course of events that constituted Western culture—from a radically different position, the author of "Marriage" eventually expressed a notably similar point of view on such issues.

That perspective is perhaps best articulated in one of Moore's finest meditations on history—"Virginia Britannia," a poem that reviews the history of "England's Old / Dominion" to note simultaneously the absurdity and the evil of colonial voraciousness. Declares Moore in one of her most forceful political statements,

> . . . Like strangler figs choking
> a banyan, not an explorer, no imperialist,
> not one of us, in taking what we
> pleased—in colonizing as the
> saying is—has been a synonym for mercy.
>
> (110)

Expanding on this point in *"Too Much,"* the first section of "The Jerboa," she turns—as Millay did in her "Epitaph for the Race of Man"—to the Roman and Egyptian origins of Western civilization to consider, with detached contempt, the lives of "those with, everywhere, / / power over the poor" (12). Against the extravagant nature of the art produced by the hierarchies of culture, Moore sets the economical art of antihierarchical nature. The second section of "The Jerboa," entitled *"Abundance,"* continues the celebration, begun late in the first section, of the jerboa, "a small desert rat, / and not famous, that / lives without water" but "has happiness," explaining that "one would not be he / who has nothing but plenty" (13).

But if one reads Moore's natural history with care, it becomes plain that the animals through which she critiques culture are often female, like females, or associated with females. In "He 'Digesteth Harde Yron,' " for instance, the ostrich "watches his chicks with / a maternal concentration" (99). Similarly, her paper nautilus, who believes "love / is the only fortress / strong enough to trust to" (122), represents the endurance of the female as surely as does the patience of the woman portrayed in Millay's "Sonnets from an Ungrafted Tree." For, refusing to comply with the exigencies of romance, coolly distanced from "Marriage," this poet was liberated to imagine civilizing alternatives to "civilization." Playfully dressed as "Washington Crossing the Delaware"—wearing a skirt and a cloak and a tricorn hat—and thereby signalling her "old maid's" freedom from conventional femininity, Moore was casting herself as the leader of a new kind of war for independence. As president of an apparently whimsical but really fantastically serious state, she would lead her creatures across the Delaware into a different history. Her New World would be the old order of birds, beasts and flowers, of marginalized women and enslaved peoples, resanctified.

What are the implications of the "female female impersonation" that Millay and Moore so frequently deployed as both defense and offense—defense against trivialization, offense against masculinism? For one thing, through attention to the theater of the personal in which both these artists recreated themselves as public speakers readers can learn a great deal about the specifically female tradition out of which much contemporary poetry by women has arisen. It is a tradition in which, as Marcia Westkott remarks in her incisive commentary on Horney, woman's "alienation is informed not only by her visualized presence, her being taken as a fetish by others, and therefore by herself" but also "by her marginality."[34]

Such alienation means that, to quote Westkott again, the woman—in this case, the woman poet—"is the outsider who can see through the pretensions of the powerful" and construct aesthetic modes which seek to deflate those pretensions. Particularly in recent decades, such "seeing-through" has issued in insights into both fetishization and marginalization: lately, in fact, a number of literary women—notably Plath and Sexton, along with such other poets as Rich and Levertov—have followed Millay's path of female self-dramatization, narrating confessional histories of the self which use the fetishized private life of the woman to comment on the public state of the world. Similarly, others—H.D., Elizabeth Bishop, May Swenson, Mary Oliver—have chosen Moore's road, constructing a more apparently self-effacing self through which to critique culture by examining objects and events from the margins of discourse.

What do these two modes of impersonation ultimately have in common? To return to the seventeenth century inhabited by Stevens's Claire Dupray is to find the answer. Staring at the vexed portrait of the poetess, Broomstick asks: "Does the voice of tragedy dwell in this mouth?" And Bowl answers: "I was not thinking of that. I was thinking merely of the expression it gives to the portrait. That expression is vitally biographical" (27). Stevens is plainly being ironic here but his characters are correct. Whether frankly scrutinizing lovers and animals or more "objectively" meditating on Penelope and "Virginia Brittania," both Millay and Moore worked out of a secret feminine assumption that the personal is the poetical, so that both, as avatars of that new being Claire Dupray, attempted a mode of female female impersonation that was "vitally biographical" even as it subverted biography by suggesting its artifice. "What is the essential nature of fully developed femininity? What is *das ewig Weibliche*?" asked Joan Rivière in 1929, when Edna St. Vincent Millay's public career was at its height. And she replied, speculatively, that the "conception of womanliness as a mask, behind which man suspects some hidden danger, throws a little light on the enigma."[35]

Certainly such a light seems to clarify the achievement of Millay, whose poetry derived a "special power" from the brilliance with which she created a portrait of the artist as that supreme fiction, "woman."

Notes

Epigraphs: "It is a dangerous lot": Louise Bogan, review of Millay, *Huntsman, What Quarry?*, in Bogan, *A Poet's Alphabet: Reflections on the Literary Art and Vocation*, ed. Robert Phelps and Ruth Limmer (New York: McGraw-Hill, 1970), 298; also cited in Gloria Bowles, *Louise Bogan's Aesthetic of Limitation* (Bloomington: Indiana University Press, 1987), 45; " . . . family": Edna St. Vincent Millay, Letter to Mrs. Cora B. Millay and Norma Millay, 22 Sept. 1917, *Letters of Edna St. Vincent Millay*, ed. Allan Ross Macdougall (New York: Harper, 1952), 76; "In the late Forties": Bonnie Costello, *Marianne Moore, Imaginary Possessions* (Cambridge: Harvard University Press, 1981), 246.

1. *Bowl, Cat and Broomstick*, in Wallace Stevens, *The Palm at the End of the Mind: Selected Poems and a Play*, ed. Holly Stevens (New York: Vintage, 1972), 28. All references will be to this edition and page numbers will be included in the text.

2. For a discussion of "female writers" with "three names," see Nathanael West, *Miss Lonelyhearts*, in *Miss Lonelyhearts and the Day of the Locust* (New York: New Directions, 1969), 13–14; for a more extensive discussion of this passage, see Sandra M. Gilbert and Susan Gubar, *No Man's Land: The Place of the Woman Writer in the Twentieth Century*, vol. 1, *The War of the Words* (New Haven: Yale University Press, 1988), 146.

3. That Stevens is preaching to himself as well as to his interlocutors is made plain by his assignment of a poem title he himself would later use—"Banal Sojourn"—to Claire's canon. See *Palm*, 30 and 45. For further discussion of this point, see A. Walton Litz, "Introduction to *Bowl, Cat and Broomstick*," *Quarterly Review of Literature* 16 (1969): 230–35.

4. "Yesterday I got a note from Sara Teasdale," Millay wrote her family with naive delight at one point, "inviting me to take tea with her. Whaddayaknowaboutthat! The news of my arrival has *sprud clean* from here to East 29th Street!" (Millay, *Letters*, 33–34.)

5. While she was at Vassar, Millay published poems in the *Forum, Current Opinion, The Smart Set, Reedy's Mirror, Poetry*, and the *Yale Review*; her most gratifying part was in a play of John Masefield's, about which the Laureate himself wrote her a fan letter.

6. Whether Millay's admirers decided, with Arthur Davison Ficke, that in "Renascence" she had had "a real vision, such as Coleridge might have seen" and, with Floyd Dell, that her poem was "comparable in its power and vision to 'The Hound of Heaven' " or whether, with Edward Davison, her detractors deplored the "girlish pretty-prettyness" of some of her lines, they were defining her as a literary anachronism just like Stevens's Claire Dupray. Ficke is quoted in Millay's *Letters*, 118; Dell and Davison are both quoted in Norman Brittin, *Edna St. Vincent Millay* (Boston: Twayne, rev. ed. 1982), 33.

7. Elizabeth Atkins, *Edna St. Vincent Millay and Her Times* (New York: Russell & Russell, 1964 rpt.; 1st pub. Univ. of Chicago Press, 1936), 70.

8. "Our time" and "our *Zeitgeist*": both in Atkins, vii.

9. On Lowell, see C. David Heymann, *American Aristocracy: The Lives and Times of James Russell, Amy, and Robert Lowell* (New York: Dodd, Mead, 1980), 228; on Wylie, see Judith Farr, *The Life and Art of Elinor Wylie* (Baton Rouge: Louisiana State University Press, 1983), 13.

10. Leavis is quoted in James D. Brophy, *Edith Sitwell: The Symbolist Order* (Carbondale: Southern Illinois University Press, 1968), xii.

11. Pound is quoted in Heymann, 198; for Wolfe, see *The Web and the Rock* (New York: Scribners, 1939), 482–83. Millay herself was fictionalized (though not with comparable

hostility) as Vera St. Vitus, in Robert McAlmon's *Post-adolescence* (Dijon: Darantiere, 1923) and as Rita in Edmund Wilson's *I Thought of Daisy* (New York: Farrar, Straus, 1953).

12. See *The Waste Land: A Facsimile and Transcript of the Original Drafts*, ed. Valerie Eliot (New York: Harcourt, 1971), especially 27.

13. M. L. Rosenthal, *The Modern Poets* (New York: Oxford, 1960), 254–55.

14. Indeed, in letters to friends Stevens confided that Moore's innovative art "is really a good deal more important than what Williams does" and that "She is one of the angels: her style is an angelic style" (*Letters of Wallace Stevens*, ed. Holly Stevens [New York: Knopf, 1966], 278; 290. For Williams, see, for example, *Selected Essays of William Carlos Williams* (New York: Random House, 1954), 121 and 292. See also Ezra Pound, "Marianne Moore and Mina Loy," in Charles Tomlinson, ed. *Marianne Moore: A Collection of Critical Essays* (Englewood Cliffs, N.J.: Prentice-Hall, 1969), 46, and T. S. Eliot, "Marianne Moore," in Tomlinson, 48.

15. Critics from John Crowe Ransom to Charles Molesworth have repeatedly defined Millay and Moore as virtually polar opposites. See Ransom, "The Poet as Woman," *The World's Body* (New York: Scribners, 1938), who argues that because of Millay's "famous attitudes" of sentimentality her work lacked "intellectual interest" whereas Moore could be praised for "a lesser deficiency of masculinity" (103, 98). Similarly, Molesworth, in *Marianne Moore: A Literary Life* (New York: Atheneum, 1990), claims that Millay "was a poet who might instructively serve as Moore's exact opposite," labeling her poetry "sentimental and rather wan" and emphasizing her public image as "the very essence of the free-living, free-loving poet" in contrast to Moore's privacy, wit, and dedication (138–39). For a comparable formulation, see Suzanne Clark, "The Unwarranted Discourse: Sentimental Community, Modernist Women, and the Case of Millay," *Genre* 20 (Summer 1987): 139.

16. Eliot, in Tomlinson, 51; Williams, in Tomlinson, 112.

17. Rosenthal, *The Modern Poets*, 142; Pearce, "Marianne Moore," in Tomlinson, 150; Pearce added that "Her yes! is muted, cautious, and somewhat finicking . . . but it is as authentic as Molly Bloom's" (157–58).

18. Henrietta Holland, "Marianne Moore's New York England," *Yankee* (November 1963): 106, cited in Laurence Stapleton, *Marianne Moore: The Poet's Advance* (Princeton: Princeton University Press, 1978), 196.

19. Marcia Westkott, *The Feminist Legacy of Karen Horney* (New Haven: Yale University Press, 1986), 190–91.

20. Luce Irigaray, *This Sex Which Is Not One*, trans. Catherine Porter with Carolyn Burke (1977; Ithaca: Cornell University Press, 1985), 132–34. Joan Rivière, "Womanliness as a Masquerade," in *Formations of Fantasy*, ed. Victor Burgin, James Donald and Cora Kaplan (London & New York: Methuen, 1986), 35–44; 1st. pub. *International Journal of Psychoanalysis*, 10 (1929): 303–13; for a fine discussion of Rivière's essay, see Stephen Heath, "Joan Rivière and the Masquerade," *Formations*, 45–61.

21. Quoted in Peter Brazeau, *Parts of the World: Wallace Stevens Remembered* (New York: Random House, 1983), 211.

22. Millay, *Letters*, 99–100.

23. Quoted in Costello, 15.

24. Williams, "The Great American Novel," in *Imaginations*, ed. Webster Schott (New York: New Directions, 1970), 169; for a more extensive discussion of this passage, see *The War of the Words*, 155.

25. *The Collected Poems of Edna St. Vincent Millay* (New York: Harper, 1956; 1975 paper), 455. All references hereafter will be to this edition, and page numbers will be included parenthetically in the text.

26. For an interesting formulation of this point, see Jane Stanbrough, "Edna St. Vincent Millay and the Language of Vulnerability," in Sandra M. Gilbert and Susan Gubar,

eds., *Shakespeare's Sisters: Feminist Essays on Women Poets* (Bloomington: Indiana University Press, 1979), 183–99.

27. Millay, *Three Plays* (New York: Harper, 1926), 42. Further references will be to this edition, and page numbers will be included parenthetically in the text. For Millay's view of *Aria da Capo*, see her letter to Cass Canfield, October 1947, *Letters*, 337: "I am very proud of *Aria da Capo*. I wish I had a dozen more, not like it, but just as good."

28. See Rossetti, prefatory note to "Monna Innominata," in *The Complete Poems of Christina Rossetti* (Baton Rouge: Louisiana State University Press, 1986), 86.

29. Allen Tate, "Miss Millay's Sonnets," *New Republic* 66 (6 May 1931): 336.

30. Debra Fried, "Andromeda Unbound: Gender and Genre in Millay's Sonnets," *Twentieth-Century Literature* 32, 1 (Spring 1986): 11. On Millay, Wylie, and the sonnet form, see also Judith Farr, "Elinor Wylie, Edna St. Vincent Millay, and the Elizabethan Sonnet Tradition," in *Poetic Traditions of the English Renaissance*, eds. Maynard Mack and George deForest Lord (New Haven: Yale University Press, 1982), 287–305.

31. Adrienne Rich, "Twenty-One Love Poems," XI, in *The Dream of a Common Language: Poems 1974–1977* (New York: W. W. Norton, 1978), 30.

32. *The Complete Poems of Marianne Moore* (New York: Macmillan/Viking, 1967), 144. Unless otherwise noted, all references will be to this edition, and page numbers will be included parenthetically in the text.

33. See Adrienne Rich, "Compulsory Heterosexuality and Lesbian Existence," in *Blood, Bread, and Poetry* (New York: W. W. Norton, 1986), 23–75.

34. Westkott, 103.

35. See Rivière, "Womanliness as a Masquerade," 43.

Interview De Luxe with Edna St Vincent Millay

Arthur Davison Ficke

Headnote—by William B. Thesing

In late 1912 Arthur Davison Ficke (with Witter Bynner) wrote from Iowa to Edna St. Vincent Millay and also to their friend Ferdinand Earle expressing their admiration for the poem "Renascence" which appeared in the fall of 1912 in *The Lyric Year*. However, they also queried as to whether the poem's real author were not a middle-aged male. Millay responded to the two gentlemen with a letter and a photograph of herself. Many letters were exchanged among these three individuals in future years. Apparently, Millay and Ficke first met in February 1918 in New York City. They became lifelong friends, despite his marriage to the talented artist Gladys Brown in the early 1920s. Ficke was born in 1883; he died in 1945.

Ficke was a poet and writer. He and Millay exchanged ideas and criticisms of each other's work. Most biographers agree that they had a brief but passionate affair before he sailed for France in 1918, in the midst of World War I hostilities. He is probably the subject of some of her early poems about the transience of romantic love, especially in her volume *Second April*.

Millay lived in small Greenwich Village apartments—one of which seems to be the apparent setting of the interview—between 1918–1921 and 1923–1925.

The interview is most likely fictional. It was probably written entirely by Ficke, with Millay's responses being fabricated by him. It is of literary importance to include this interview / impression of Millay, even though it is fictitious, because it is a playful portrait of Millay by a close friend and fellow poet. The piece is a creative and imaginative dramatic interplay (note the reference to the curtain early on) in which Ficke offers his impressions of a lively public personnage of the time. The answers to the interviewer's questions are never factual or realistic; they are general and often comic opinions—such as the "doughnut-hole theory" for the origin of poetry.

Reprinted by permission of Yale University Library and Mrs. Stanhope B. Ficke, literary executor. Research work on this project was supported by a grant from the University of South Carolina Research and Productive Scholarship Office.

Publishing this interview here for the first time will contribute to a lively, healthy, and sound debate about the work and reception of Millay. It is a piece from the past that is unique in its nature.

The interview is owned by Yale University's Beinecke Rare Book and Manuscript Library. It is part of the Arthur Davison Ficke Collection. The exact title is Interview De Luxe with Edna St Vincent Millay and the document is an original typescript of six numbered leaves (28cm.). There are manuscript corrections and additions by the author. The transcription offered here includes those corrections and additions without indicating original phrasings. No date is evident on the manuscript.

THE INTERVIEWER—Miss Millay, I believe?

THE MILLAY—Yes, I believe so; I am not quite awake yet. Won't you come in? Stand here. Face the wall. Don't turn around until I tell you to. (*Curtain falls for twelve minutes; then rises on an improved scene.*)

THE INTERVIEWER—And now that you have so kindly acceded, Miss Millay, to my request for an interview, and have ensconsed me so comfortably in this handsome overstuffed chair before your fire of birch logs and sandalwood and driftwood, and have poured out from your jade tea pot two cups of tea flavored with buds of the chrysolia plant,—now that your prolonged but delicate labors are over, and you so gracefully and curlingly relax upon the orange divan, and through the smoke of your cigarette look quizically and a little wearily at my extended length,—now may I ask you, Miss Millay, to tell me confidentially, for the benefit of our readers, how you came to be a poet?

THE MILLAY—I think you might have enough imagination to know without asking. Mightn't you? But nevertheless I will tell you; yes, I will quite truly tell you, just to irritate you, perhaps. You see, as a child I was very fond of doughnuts. Do you see? I used to eat doughnuts beside a pump in Camden. And there, in my beautiful Maine, with the sea always calling me in the distance, and the knipperwell-moss and the lady-cloth flowers hiding in the woods, and those smells of very old seaweed blowing in always from the bay,—there I ate my doughnuts; and always as I ate my doughnuts I was aware of a hurting lack, I was aware of a great hunger,—a something that was there yet not there. And one day, after a little shower of rain had fallen, I heard a bird singing in the silver silence; and at that moment, as I ate my doughnut, I became a poet, for at that moment I discovered that the poignant and heart-breaking charm of the doughnut is the hole in the middle of it. It was then that I knew that that-which-is-not is the most exquisite and desirable part of that-which-is; and I determined to have it for my own; and that is what we call being a poet. Do you see?

THE INTERVIEWER—Ah yes, Miss Millay, I quite see. But may I ask you,—how then would you define your idea of Beauty, Miss Millay?

THE MILLAY—My idea of Beauty? It is too simple; you will hardly believe it. Still, I'll tell you.—Hold a doughnut up to your eye, look through the hole toward the far distance, see whatever you most want to see. And there you have Beauty! Isn't it childish!

THE INTERVIEWER—May I ask, Miss Millay, if this is what is referred to in the Gospels as "having your cake and eating it too"?

THE MILLAY—How cleverly you understand me!

THE INTERVIEWER—And was it in Maine, Miss Millay—in that Maine which you describe so feelingly,—in those incomparably rustic and naeieve [sic.] surroundings,—was it there that you acquired this expression of irrevocable innocence that appears to be characteristic of your face? And also, if I may ask,—why are you so diminutive in size,—a diminutiveness that is hard to reconcile with the reported legends of your greatness? And could you explain to me, Miss Millay, how, in view of all this, you, with your soft bobbed hair bear so strong a resemblance to a darling child of five years of age? If you get me, Miss Millay.

THE MILLAY—I get you. Don't you see the reason? Look carefully; really look at me. You have hardly looked at me. Don't you see that I have sage-green eyes; hadn't you really noticed that; and doesn't that explain everything? People with sage-green eyes never grow up. Young man, you should be more observing. Also, you should draw correct conclusions from what you observe.

THE INTERVIEWER—I observe that you keep the manuscripts of your poems in the percolator. How really original of you! But how dangerous!

THE MILLAY—I was merely cleaning the percolator last night; it needed it. It needed it very badly. As to the manuscripts, they are things of no importance to me.

THE INTERVIEWER—Of no importance! How humble of you! How true.

THE MILLAY—My good sir, I assure you that I am not in the least humble. The only reason that my manuscripts are of no importance to me is because I know all my poems quite by heart, every one of them. Shall I recite them to you? You really won't mind a bit. I can do it quite beautifully; I have a beautiful voice. I really have. This is the way one of my poems begins.—

> Oh what availed her good intent,
>   Oh what, his carven line,
> When all their vows and virtue went
> Bloo-ie in record time. . . .

That is the way it begins. It's called "Sea-urchin." Don't you like it?

THE INTERVIEWER—I adore it. Is it a recent work? . . . But Miss Millay, when you have that curious knotted look in the corners of your eyes, I can never tell whether you are serious or not.

THE MILLAY—Never? Oh that is a long time.

THE INTERVIEWER—Don't you ever feel, Miss Millay, that nobody understands you?

THE MILLAY—Yes, thank heaven!

THE INTERVIEWER—Dear Miss Millay! . . . Do you know, dear Miss Millay,—when you lean your head back, and your long throat rises like a flower stem from the line of your fragile sloping shoulders, then I am reminded of Boticelli [sic], Miss Millay. Has anybody ever said that to you before?

THE MILLAY—Several bodies . . . Are you, Mr. Interviewer, perhaps one of those who believe in art for heart's sake? I should be sorry to hear that of you.

THE INTERVIEWER—I don't quite understand you, Miss Millay. But after all, it is I who must ask questions of you, not you of me. So now, if I may ask another question, and a very important one,—how does one actually go through the process of writing a beautiful poem? I am sure our readers would like to know the answer to that question; it would interest them deeply.

THE MILLAY—They probably know the answer quite well; but since you yourself apparently do not, I will be so nice as to tell you. First, have an idea, combined with an emotion; secondly, write it down in a sharply accurate and appropriate manner; and thirdly, be sure you do it in your own way, a way that is right for you but wrong for any other human being who has ever lived. That is all. That is quite all. You see, of course. Of course you see!

THE INTERVIEWER—Thank you so much, Miss Millay. Yes, of course you are right . . . And now, before I go, may I read you a list of the things I have been observing and noting down in my little memorandum-book while we have been talking? I should like to have you tell me quite frankly, won't you, if I have put down anything that you would prefer I did not mention to our readers,—any too-intimate detail, perhaps, which you would rather I left sacred from the world at large. This is my list.—First: that the sun pours beautifully through your wide south windows, and that the alley beyond them is an alleycats' paradise. Second: that, small though you are, young though you are, and though you fool one a bit at first sight, still you apparently have a figure of incomparable beauty. Third: that a hasty inspection of the unwashed plates, cups, saucers, pots, pans, and other useful objects piled there in the corner leads me to the conclusion that your favorite articles of diet are chicken-salad sandwiches, leberwurst, milk, apples, and honey. Fourth: that yours is the only appartment [sic.] in New York that is not stocked with hooch, and that you don't even own any cocktail glasses. Fifth: that you wear no jewels in the morning. Sixth: that you do much of your writing at a blue-lacquer Chinese writing desk, using either pen or pencil; and usually on paper. Seventh: that you very much admire either your own feet or the new green-and-silver mules you are wearing this morning. Eighth—

THE MILLAY—Seven things are enough: no more. You may tell anything about me you wish, to your readers—but not to me.

THE INTERVIEWER—As you prefer, Miss Millay; as you prefer. And now, I am infinitely grateful to you for your delicious tea and for the courteous consideration you have given my questions. Must we now, perhaps, consider the interview at an end?

THE MILLAY—Yes, I did when you came in. . . . A little more tea, you nice understanding man?

Supplementary Selections

◆

Will Brantley, "The Force of Flippancy: Edna Millay's Satiric Sketches of the Early 1920s." *Colby Quarterly* 27, no. 3 (September 1991): 132–147.

Norman A. Brittin, *Edna St. Vincent Millay*, revised edition, (Boston: Twayne), 1982.

Norman A. Brittin, "Edna St. Vincent Millay's 'Nancy Boyd' Stories," *Ball State University Forum* 10 (Spring 1969): 31–36.

Witter Bynner, "Edna St. Vincent Millay," *New Republic* 41 (10 December 1924): 14–15.

Anne Cheney, *Millay in Greenwich Village* (University: University of Alabama Press), 1975.

Suzanne Clark, "Jouissance and the Sentimental Daughter: Edna St. Vincent Millay," *North Dakota Quarterly* 54, no. 2 (Spring 1986): 85–108.

Lawrence H. Conrad, "Edna St. Vincent Millay," *Landmark* 15 (June 1933): 297–300.

Carolyn Daffron, *Edna St. Vincent Millay* (New York: Chelsea House), 1989.

Edward Davison, "Edna St. Vincent Millay," *English Journal* 16, no. 9 (November 1927): 671–82.

Jeannine Dobbs, "Edna St. Vincent Millay and the Tradition of Domestic Poetry," *Journal of Women's Studies in Literature* 1 (1979): 89–106.

Robert Erwin, "The Case of the Missing T-Shirt," in *The Great Language Panic and Other Essays in Cultural History* (Athens: University of Georgia Press), 1990, 117–29.

Judith Farr, "Elinor Wylie, Edna St. Vincent Millay, and the Elizabethan Sonnet Tradition," in *Poetic Traditions of the English Renaissance*, eds. Maynard Mack and George deForest Lord (New Haven: Yale University Press), 1982, 287–305.

Hildegarde Flanner, "Two Poets: Jeffers and Millay," *New Republic* 89 (27 January 1937): 379–82.

Janet Gassman, "Edna St. Vincent Millay: 'Nobody's Own,' " *Colby Library Quarterly* 9 (1971): 297–310.

Jean Gould, "Edna St. Vincent Millay: Saint of the Modern Sonnet," in *Faith of a (Woman) Writer*, edited by Alice Kessler-Harris and William McBrien (Westport, CT: Greenwood), 1988, Pp. 129–42.

Sara Henderson Hay, "The Pulitzer Prize Poets: 2. Edna St. Vincent Millay," *Voices* 65 (May 1932): 316–21.

Maureen Howard, "City of Words," in *Women, the Arts, and the 1920s in Paris and New York*, edited by Kenneth W. Wheeler, Virginia Lee Lussier, and Catharine R. Stimpson (New Brunswick: Transaction Books), 1982, 42–48.

Rolfe Humphries, "Edna St. Vincent Millay: 1892–1950," *Nation* 171 (30 December 1950): 704.

Phyllis M. Jones, "Amatory Sonnet Sequences and the Female Perspective of Elinor Wylie and Edna St. Vincent Millay," *Women's Studies: An Interdisciplinary Journal* 10, no. 1 (1983): 41–61.

Theodore Maynard, "America's Lyric Writers," in *Our Best Poets: English and American*. (New York: Henry Holt), 1922. 226–31.

Walter S. Minot, "Millay's 'Ungrafted Tree': The Problem of the Artist as Woman," *New England Quarterly* 48 (1975): 260–69.

Harriet Monroe, "Poets of Today: Edna St. Vincent Millay," in *Poets & Their Art* (New York: Macmillan), 1932, 63–71.

Judith Nierman, *Edna St. Vincent Millay: A Reference Guide* (Boston: G. K. Hall), 1977.

John J. Patton, "Satiric Fiction in Millay's *Distressing Dialogues*," *Modern Language Studies* 2, no. 2 (1972): 63–67.

John J. Patton, "An Unpublished Hardy Letter to Millay," *Colby Library Quarterly* Series 5 (June 1961): 284–85.

John Crowe Ransom, "The Poet as Woman," *Southern Review* 2 (Spring 1937): 783–806.

Arnold T. Schwab, "Jeffers and Millay: A Literary Friendship," *Robinson Jeffers Newsletter* 59 (September 1981): 18–33.

Donald Smalley, "Millay's 'Renascence' and Browning's 'Easter-Day' ", *Bulletin of the Maine Library Association* 3 (February 1942): 10–12.

Tamarack: Journal of the Edna St. Vincent Millay Society, Three issues: volume 1 (Spring 1981); volume 2 (Winter 1982–1983); volume 3 (Fall 1985–Winter 1986). Each issue contains approximately a dozen biographical and critical essays.

Cheryl Walker, *Masks Outrageous and Austere: Culture, Psyche, and Persona in Modern Women Poets*. Bloomington: Indiana University Press, 1991.

Index

♦

DATE			